Technology's Past

America's Industrial Revolution and the People Who Delivered the Goods

By

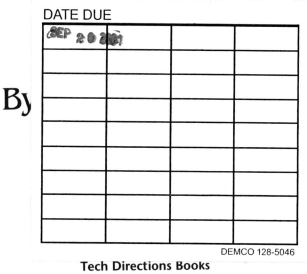

Tech Directions Books
Prakken Publications, Inc.

Dedication

This book is dedicated to Jan Matzeliger, a young nineteenth-century American inventor. Working with quiet confidence and strength of character, he left a technical legacy that remains an honorable model for everyone. He had faith in his ability, knew the difference between success and wealth, and never forgot his friends.

Contents

Special Section: Technology Overviews

Acknowledgments

No book writes itself. It comes into being only through the efforts of many people. The 53 listed here are among those who provided much-appreciated assistance.

The help came from six groups of people: editors, librarians, Smithsonian Institution researchers, company staff members, museum researchers, and other interested persons.

The editors at Prakken Publications have an uncanny ability to take a rough manuscript and convert it to a fluent flow of ideas. The insights provided by Paul Bamford, Alan Jones, and Susanne Peckham turned coarse words into smooth biographies.

When it was necessary to dig out some little-known fact, librarians were of immeasurable help. Among the most helpful were Emily Clark at the Chicago Historical Society, Carolyn Davis at Syracuse University, Marie-Helene Gold at Radcliffe College, and Jane Morley at the Hagley Research Library, Ruth Shoemaker at the Hall of History, and Ann Sindelar at the Western Reserve Historical Society.

Smithsonian researchers kept me from confusing folklore with fact. Portia James, Peggy Kidwell, Peter Liebhold, David Shayt, John White, and William Worthington helped keep me honest.

Some companies have printed histories of their organization. Many persons shared that information and answered detailed questions when they arose. They were Darlene J. Aiken at Eastman Kodak, T. P. Biederbeck at Caterpillar, Edward L. Crouse at ALCOA, and Barbara R. Donato at the Norton Co. Also, Coralie J. Fleming at Merganthaler Linotype, Ken Frausel at Brown & Sharpe, Harry Gann at McDonnell-Douglas, Robert F. Goerlich at Singer/Link, and David A. Hladik at Fruehauf.

Other company assistance came from D. J. Kaiser at Scovill/Yale, Greg Lennes at International Harvester, Donna S. Lipari at Xerox, Neal Lulofs at A. B. Dick, and J. A. McCaffrey at Westinghouse. Also, Chuck Merritt at OMC/Evinrude, Candice Pearce at Harrah's, Mary T. Roznowski at General Motors, and D. R. Starrett at L. S. Starrett. And finally, Les Stegh at John Deere, Bernice Steinberg at Otis, Karen Frindell Strom at A. O. Smith, and Rosalyn M. Zatezalo at Timken.

Particular help also came from museum researchers Sally Beddow at the MIT Museum, Larry Hendricks at the Branchville SC Railroad Museum, Cynthia Read-Miller at the Henry Ford Museum, Edgar A. Reeves at the African-American Museum in Cleveland, Pearl Robinson at the African-American Museum in Philadelphia, Tod Ruhstaller at the Haggin Museum, and Merrill Stickler at the Glenn Curtiss Museum.

Individuals with a personal interest in my subjects also provided useful information. Those people included Harold Bredin on Lillian Gilbreth, Judy Brown on George Washington, Henry A. Clark on the Thomas Flyer motor car, and C. Lyle Cummins, Jr., on his father, Clessie Cummins. Also, George W. Genero on Glenn Curtiss, John M. LeCato on the Best Friend locomotive, and Carter Litchfield on Oliver Evans.

The person who deserves the most acknowledgment is Howard Kahn, the editor at *School Shop* in 1980. He took a risky step when he agreed to print the unproven "Technology's Past" column, on which this book is based.

Dennis Karwatka
Morehead, Kentucky
August 1995

Preface

If you enjoy reading about inventors, engineers, and scientists from technology's past, this book is for you. It emphasizes the lives of several dozen Americans whose major technical accomplishments occurred during the Industrial Revolution and up through the beginning of World War II. The subjects are based on my "Technology's Past" column, which first appeared in 1980 in a monthly journal for teachers and students of industrial technology, then called *School Shop*. The name of the journal changed to *Tech Directions* in 1989.

As in all fields of human endeavor, the people from technology's past include both giants and less-well-known individuals. However, you will find no such distinction reflected in the treatment of featured people here—each person or invention highlighted receives three pages of attention in the book. I include at the end of each profile a list of references that will provide more information for those interested in exploring further. Note that I have listed these references in order of their helpfulness to my research, rather than following the usual alphabetical arrangement.

Profiles are arranged chronologically by the birth date of the technologist featured or in the case of three inanimate subjects—*The Best Friend* locomotive, the Thomas Flyer race car, and the earliest U.S. patents—by date of creation or most notable achievement. To assist readers who are particularly interested in certain areas of technology, subject designations are provided on the first page of each profile.

The book closes with a special section of technology overviews. These cover in greater breadth four areas of technology—computers, television, manned space flight, and robotics—that seem particularly interesting or relevant to our lives today. Several technologists who were previously profiled appear again in the technology overviews. Where this occurs, page references are given for the earlier coverage.

Illustrations accompany each profile. Although many people featured were in their twenties or thirties when they did their most significant work, the photographs and art often show them later in life, after they had become better known. Though the number is not consistent among the profiles, I tried to include as many photographs of featured inventions and devices as possible. Unfortunately, photos of some inventions do not exist—for example, no photos are available of Granville Woods's electric motors or Oliver Evans's steam engines. Also, some technologists worked with hardware that lent itself to images, while others didn't. For example, there are many museum displays of hardware associated with Alexander Graham Bell's telephone, but far fewer that show Lillian Gilbreth's work with factory efficiency.

With so much technical information included in this book, there are likely undiscovered errors. I take full responsibility for them and will correct any that come to my attention, in the next edition.

Finally, I hope that you will enjoy reading this book as much as I have enjoyed putting it together.

Dennis Karwatka
Morehead, Kentucky
August 1995

Benjamin Franklin

SOME people think of Benjamin Franklin, a printer by trade, as a diplomat sent to France to represent the American colonies during the Revolutionary War. He was chosen for that role because he commanded more respect in Europe than any other American. Franklin was also a brilliant scientific investigator—and we might even describe him as the world's first "electrician."

Using a step-by-step process unusual in experiments conducted in his day, Franklin proved that electricity was either positive or negative. Some of the very language associated with electricity started with him. Franklin was the first to describe electricity using words like *plus, minus, conductor, charge, battery, electric shock,* and *armature.* His writings on the subject were translated into French, German, and Italian.

Franklin earned the respect of Europeans as an excellent scientist, not as a successful printer or as one of America's best writers. The man who earned that reputation was not the aging, somewhat dumpy, stringy-haired fellow portrayed in paintings done almost 100 years after his death. Franklin the scientist was a vigorous athlete just entering his forties.

Franklin was born in Boston in 1706, the fifteenth of 17 children. His father was a soap and candle maker. The mostly self-taught Franklin had only two years of schooling, but he read every book he could find. His first job at age 12 was as a printer's apprentice to his older brother James, who started *The New England Courant.* (The newspaper is still published as *The Hartford Courant* in Hartford, Connecticut.)

After working for his brother, Franklin moved to Philadelphia, the largest city in colonial America. Between 1723 and 1729, he worked for various printers in Philadel-

National Portrait Gallery, Smithsonian Insititution

Born:
January 17, 1706, in Boston, Massachusetts

Died:
April 17, 1790, in Philadelphia, Pennsylvania

phia and in London, England, where he went to buy printing presses. He then opened a print shop in partnership with a friend and two years later was the sole owner.

He soon established *The Pennsylvania Gazette* newspaper. Because Franklin came from a poor family and had little formal education, his grammar was less elegant and more homey than that of most other writers. This made his work popular with ordinary people. His *Poor Richard's Almanack* was an immediate success when he introduced it in 1732. No other almanac has ever been so famous or so influential. Franklin typically sold 10,000 copies a year. A shortened form was translated into a dozen other languages.

Franklin personally handled all aspects of his print shop operation until he retired from the business in 1743. Then, for income to live on, Franklin kept a financial interest in the printing business and helped out occasionally. He received about 1,000 British pounds a year.

In 1746, Franklin happened to see some electrical experiments imperfectly conducted in Boston by a Dr. Spence. The mystery of electricity captivated Franklin, and experimentation became central to his life for the next 30 years. Perhaps his most dramatic and well-remembered experiment took place in 1752. It involved flying a kite from a Philadelphia field as a thunderstorm approached the city. With the help of his 15-year-old son William, Franklin tried to find out if lightning was fire or electricity. The kite Franklin used had a pointed wire on its top connected to the kite string. A metal key dangled from the kite string near Franklin's hand. As the thunderstorm approached, a light rain moistened the string and turned it into an electrical conductor. Lightning crackling in the distance sent a small amount of electricity through the air, to the pointed wire, and down the damp string. Franklin drew a spark from the key to his hand and proved that lightning was electricity. The experiment clearly showed that weak laboratory-produced electricity was directly related to powerful natural forces. Franklin was lucky he wasn't hurt that day. Lightning electrocuted the next two people who tried the same experiment.

Franklin's kite experiment led directly to the creation of the lightning rod. Franklin suggested placing pointed metal rods above the roofs of buildings, with wires leading to the ground. The rods discharged the clouds safely, protecting the buildings. By 1782, more than 400 were in use in Philadelphia alone. Many people called Franklin the man who caught and tamed lightning.

A replica of the Pennsylvania stove at the Henry Ford Museum, Dearborn, Michigan.

Franklin also improved home-heating techniques. Eighteenth-century New England colonists kept their bitterly cold winters at bay with inefficient fireplaces originally designed for milder European winters. People burned a great deal of wood to keep dwellings reasonably comfortable. Using today's cost of energy, the average house consumed around $3,000 to $4,000 worth of fuel per year.

Franklin introduced his Pennsylvania fireplace in 1742. It was a cast-iron stove and the first American product offering technical improvements that everyone could understand. Franklin knew he could extract more heat from a given amount of wood by increasing the length of time the flame and smoke remained inside the stove. He added a metal plate inside the firebox, extending from the bottom almost to the top. The

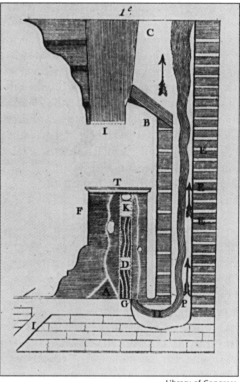

Library of Congress

Smoke exited the bottom rear of Franklin's stove.

smoke and fire had to go up and over the metal plate. Franklin closed off the original fireplace in his house and placed his stove against its sealed opening. Smoke came out at the rear of the stove near the bottom and left the house through a much smaller chimney. Franklin reported that his house was twice as warm as before, using only one fourth as much firewood.

Franklin's stoves proved so popular that he had agents in Boston, Newport, and New York. The governor of Pennsylvania offered a patent, but Franklin declined. He never held a patent for any of his inventions. Using the printed brochure as a guide, other people before long began to make and sell their own versions of Franklin's legally unprotected stove. All box-shaped stoves were soon known as Franklin stoves. Today's Franklin stove does not resemble the one Franklin invented, and no original examples are known to exist.

Franklin's abilities and interests were boundless. He helped establish the academy that eventually became the University of Pennsylvania. The public library he set up in 1731 was the first of its kind in the world. He was the first person to study the Gulf Stream in the Atlantic Ocean, and he organized the first hospital in America. Franklin also established the American Philosophical Society, America's first scientific society. His selection to the British Royal Society in 1756 and the French Academy of Sciences in 1772 reflected his fame as a leading eighteenth-century technologist.

In 1968, the International Swimming Hall of Fame in Fort Lauderdale, Florida, added Franklin's name to its honor roll as "America's first famous swimmer and coach." Franklin had regularly enjoyed swimming and invented wooden swim flippers for the hands. There was much more to Benjamin Franklin's life than some people might think!

References and Resources

Autobiography of Benjamin Franklin by Benjamin Franklin, The Century Co., 1901.

American Science and Invention by Mitchell Wilson, Bonanza, 1960.

Benjamin Franklin by Thomas Fleming, Harper and Row, 1972.

Ingenious Dr. Franklin by Nathan Goodman, University of Pennsylvania Press, 1931.

One Hundred Great Product Designs by Jay Doblin, Van Nostrand Reinhold Co., 1970.

Introduction to Technology by Alan Pierce and Dennis Karwatka, West Publishing Co., 1993.

International Swimming Hall of Fame Yearbook, Fort Lauderdale Florida, 1975.

Dictionary of American Biography, Charles Scribner's Sons Publishers, 1932; with supplemental updates.

National Cyclopedia of American Biography, James T. White & Co. Publishers, 1891; with supplemental updates.

McGraw-Hill Encyclopedia of Biography, McGraw-Hill Publishers, 1973.

Asimov's Biographical Encyclopedia of Science and Technology by Isaac Asimov, Doubleday and Co., 1964.

George Washington

Library of Congress

Born:
February 22,
1732, in
Westmoreland
County,
Virginia

Died:
December 14,
1799, in
Mount Vernon,
Virginia

THE first president of the United States did not always have a military or political career. His first profession was surveying and mapmaking. For several years during his teens, George Washington earned his living as a surveyor. He helped to lay out the city of Alexandria, Virginia, and was the official surveyor of Culpeper County when he was only 17 years old.

Washington was born into a financially comfortable farming family. His father had four children before his first wife died in 1729. He had six children with his second wife, Mary. She was Washington's mother. The family's livelihood rested on 5,000 acres of land that his shipwrecked British great-grandfather had obtained near Mount Vernon in 1656. The discovery of iron ore on the property often kept Washington's father away from home. He spent a considerable amount of time devel-

oping an iron works to exploit the resource. The younger Washington did not take part in the project because it was 30 miles away, and his father died when George was only 11 years old.

There are no accurate records of Washington's early education. He probably received instruction for seven years from his father and elder half-brother, Lawrence. Fourteen years older and educated in England, Lawrence was a strong influence on George. His father had intended to send him to school in England where he would have boarded with relatives living in the northeastern city of Washington. But Washington's plans for formal education ended with his father's untimely death. His mother requested that George, her eldest son, remain close to home.

A typically inquisitive and curious teenager, Washington wanted to leave Virginia and explore the new frontier over the Allegheny Mountains. He saw surveying as a way to visit the region. Washington often said that mathematics was his favorite subject, and he used his mathematical skills to teach himself geometry and trigonometry. Using his father's surveying instruments, the bright young man easily found work as an assistant with several local surveyors. He became quite good at his job, proving particularly adept at drafting, mapmaking, and designing tables of data. His first major project was one for Lord Fairfax, the largest land owner in Virginia. Fairfax was a cousin of Lawrence Washington's wife, and he owned most of the Shenandoah Valley. He asked James Genn, surveyor for Prince William County, to survey the western reaches of a 5-million-acre tract of land he owned. Genn invited Washington to accompany him. It was the young man's first real adventure, and he eagerly accepted the challenge.

After the rigors of the month-long expedition, Washington returned to lay out the city of Alexandria in 1749. Later that year, he received an appointment as official Culpeper County surveyor. His work paid well, and surveying was one of the few occupations in which a person received cash payment. Most other business involved payment in tobacco. Washington carefully saved his earnings and became self-supporting at 17. He even lent small amounts of money to relatives and friends. In 1750, he made many surveys for people moving into the Shenandoah Valley. When he came across a particularly good parcel of land that was for sale, he purchased it for himself. By the time he was 19, Washington owned 1,500 acres of land.

He was a tall blue-eyed young man with a radiant and charismatic personality that he retained throughout his life. His positive and upbeat outlook on life does not fit his image today. Perhaps too many people think of him as the serious-looking man appearing on one-dollar bills. The 1796 painting on which the dollar's image is based was by Gilbert Stuart, a temperamental artist who was once displeased by Washington's casual attitude toward his work. There is no convincing evidence, but it's been speculated that Stuart's opinion might have affected his portrayal of Washington. A more realistic young Washington appears in the painting at the bottom of this page. It shows him surveying a rugged mountainous region of Virginia.

Washington's surveying equipment included a portable box compass stored in the leather container near his feet in the painting below. The transit-like device was an alidade. It rotated over a circle graduated in degrees of angle. Angles could be sighted through the slits and read on the circle's scale. In the hands of a competent professional such as Washington, these seemingly crude instruments produced remarkably accurate results. Land boundaries of less than about 100 yards could be laid out as precisely as with sophisticated modern surveying equipment.

Surveying was an important part of early American education. Many local schools taught mathematics courses that included the word "surveying" in their course description. An 1827 Massachusetts state law specified, for example, that "every city, town, or district containing 500 fami-

Department of Civil Engineering Virginia Polytechnic Institute and State University

George Washington with a portable box compass at his feet and a tripod-mounted alidade used to measure angles.

lies . . . shall also be provided with a master . . . competent to instruct . . . geometry, surveying, and algebra."

In contrast to Washington's crude field equipment, his drafting instruments seem almost modern. His complete six-piece 1749 set is at his home in Mount Vernon. It has a divider, as well as compasses with pen and pencil attachments. The ruling pen included in the set has parallel blades similar to contemporary pens.

Washington traveled outside America only once in his life. His brother Lawrence became seriously ill and decided in November 1751 to sail to the warmer climate of the British West Indies. He asked George to accompany him. Two weeks after arriving, George contracted smallpox, which left him with a few facial scars for the rest of his life. His recovery, however, made him immune to a disease that took the lives of many men during the Revolutionary War. The brothers returned home, and the following summer Lawrence died of tuberculosis, leaving George a large portion of the 5,000-acre estate that became Mount Vernon.

Washington was an almost perfect choice for the first president. He was honest and trustworthy. A bigger-than-life war hero, Washington was polite and comfortable in any social setting. It was almost impossible to anger him and he was always fair minded. Although he had no close friends, he did have many acquaintances. The well-liked and well-respected Washington was not interested in a political career, and he accepted the presidency out of a sense of duty. Washington was even admired by those who did not like him. While he and Thomas Jefferson did not get along well, they respected each other. Jefferson even called Washington the best horseman of his age.

Washington refused a third term as president because he did not want to turn the office into a monarchy. He felt that he had fought to remove England's King George III, and he did not want to become his country's George I. Washington also wanted to spend his remaining days at Mount Vernon where he lived with several relatives. He loved his farm as much as Jefferson loved his Monticello. Washington's pride in agricultural efforts is exhibited in the wheat and scythe images carefully plastered on the ceiling of the dining room. He particularly enjoyed growing exotic trees and moving them around his property.

Washington and his wife, Martha, had no children. He died in 1799 and Martha died three years later.

References and Resources

The Unknown Washington by John Corbin, Books for Libraries Press, 1972.

The True George Washington by Paul Leicester Ford, Books for Libraries Press, 1971.

George Washington: The Making of an American Symbol by Barry Schwartz, Free Press, 1987.

"The Real George Washington" by Diane Ackerman, *Parade* Sunday newspaper supplement, 28 February 1988.

Surveying Instruments by Edmond Kiely, Columbia University Press, 1947.

Conversation with Dr. Gary Cox, Professor Emeritus of Geography, Morehead State University, Morehead, KY.

Dictionary of American Biography, Charles Scribner's Sons Publishers, 1932; with supplemental updates.

National Cyclopedia of American Biography, James T. White & Co. Publishers, 1891; with supplemental updates.

McGraw-Hill Encyclopedia of Biography, McGraw-Hill Publishers, 1973.

John Fitch

IN the rugged terrain of America 200 years ago, roads between cities were often muddy, badly rutted, and poorly maintained. Rivers truly functioned as the highways of the era. To expand the use of river travel, some people began to work on ways to incorporate steam engines into boats. John Fitch was the first person to operate a steamboat successfully. During 1790, his boat the *Thornton*, operated regularly on the Delaware River. He carried passengers between Burlington, New Jersey, and Philadelphia, a distance of about 20 miles. His boat traveled more than 2,000 total miles and carried about 1,000 passengers. Fitch's boat was in commercial use 17 years before Robert Fulton operated his *Clermont* on New York's Hudson River.

Fitch was the fifth of six children, and he started attending school at the age of four. Before he had completed primary education, his father put him to work on the family farm. He spent his free time reading as many books as he could find on mathematics, geography, and astronomy. Fitch had an unhappy childhood under a harsh father. He ran away to sea at 17, but he disliked the sailor's life. He then apprenticed himself to a clockmaker but broke his agreement, because his master had him doing farm work instead of learning a trade.

He had learned the basics of clock repair during his apprenticeship, though, and at 21 Fitch borrowed money to open his own clock shop. He did well enough to pay off his debts in two years but lost everything through a poor investment in a potash-manufacturing business. After a brief, quarrelsome marriage, in 1769 he left his family, business, and state.

Fitch eventually settled in New Jersey where he opened a shop to repair watches

Library of Congress

John Fitch with a model boat that features the stern-mounted paddles he used in his most successful steamboats.

Born:
January 21, 1743, in Hartford, Connecticut

Died:
July 2, 1798, in Bardstown, Kentucky

and make simple brass items. Over the course of seven years, he built a profitable brass and silversmith business. During the Revolutionary War, the British wrecked his shop, and he was refused a commission in the American Army. Because of his many troubles, the twentieth-century writer Isaac Asimov wrote of him, "It is hard to find a man so beset by misfortune as John Fitch." Fitch's difficult early years affected him greatly and made him distrust authority figures for the rest of his inventive and turbulent life.

Fitch became a tobacco merchant and bought land in Virginia. His youthful interest in mathematics and geography helped him to earn a surveyor's license. While in his thirties, Fitch made a living as a surveyor for the region between the Appalachian Mountains and the Mississippi River. During one trip into the wilderness, the

British captured him and held him captive in Canada for almost a year. He was released in a prisoner exchange. Fitch continued surveying until well after the Revolutionary War. He created a detailed "Map of the Northwest Parts of the United States of America." It was the only map at the time that was made, engraved, and printed by the same person, and it earned Fitch a reasonable profit.

Fitch's travels encouraged him to consider ways to construct a steam-powered boat to reach America's frontiers. Watt-type steam engines came to his attention in 1785, and he began to formulate detail designs. In an attempt to secure financial backing, Fitch unsuccessfully petitioned prominent people in Philadelphia, then the technological capital of America. His coarse, blunt manner put off potential investors. Fitch

gain the major financial support he sought.

Fitch finally persuaded 15 people to invest modest amounts in his venture. They put up a total of $300. That amount, coupled with what Fitch made through the sale of his map of the Northwest, gave him enough to start construction on his first full-sized boat. He took in a machinist as an assistant and advisor. German-born Henry Voigt and Fitch had similar personalities, and the two worked together to construct their own engine. The experimental boat they built surprised everyone who saw it. It was 45 feet long and weighed seven tons. Six paddles on each side dipped into the water and moved the craft forward. Arranged like those in a war canoe, the paddles obtained power from an endless chain.

The photograph at left shows a model of the boat on display at Philadelphia's Franklin Institute. Its paddles worked in sections: The front six (three on each side) stroked through the water at the same time. The back six stroked while the front six lifted from the water and returned to the beginning of their stroke. In the presence of members of the Constitutional Convention and other onlookers, Fitch successfully launched and operated the boat on August 22, 1787. The 18"-cylinder steam engine moved the boat at 4 mph, just barely fast enough to make it potentially profitable at hauling passengers and cargo. The audience witnessed a public demonstration of the world's first operational steamboat. Fitch had named it the *Perseverance*.

This model of Fitch's 1787 steamboat is on display at the Franklin Institute in Philadelphia.

also spoke with members of the U.S. Congress and even the ambassador from Spain. His idea involved the use of paddles on the sides or rear of a boat. He showed drawings and a model to the American Philosophical Society in Philadelphia, which included Benjamin Franklin among its members. Here, too, Fitch's abrasive personality grated against almost everyone. He only succeeded in alienating all the people he should have impressed. He even loudly accused one society member of wanting to steal his design. Fitch did not

Fitch made another boat for the Delaware River run and named it the *Thornton*, after a major investor, William Thornton. During an upstream test run against the wind, it easily outdistanced all challenging sailboats and oar boats. The *Thornton* entered regular service between Burlington and Philadelphia during the spring of 1790. Daily newspapers advertised its sailing schedule. Using stern-mounted paddles, it carried as many as 30 passengers at 8 mph with only minor mechanical problems that were all easily repaired. Unfortunately, the operation was not a financial success, and the service ended six months after it began.

Fitch then persuaded his financial backers to support him in building a larger steamboat. That operation did not make a profit either, and the public remained indifferent to steam navigation. Although they were less comfortable, people preferred the faster and less-expensive stage coaches. Fitch's financial failures and the destruction of a new boat in a storm shattered his hopes and dreams, though he made several more futile attempts to interest people in his steamboat. One design incorporated a screw propeller. Near the beginning of the Industrial Revolution, Fitch found himself struggling against people's resistance to technical innovation.

The lonely and dejected man headed to Bardstown, Kentucky. He had conducted surveying work in that region and owned some property there. In Bardstown, he took his own life with an overdose of medication.

Throughout his troubled life, Fitch built four operational steamboats and felt he had never received proper reward. He was right, and his pioneering contributions to steamboat design were recognized long after his death. The National Geographic Society has called him "one of the great American inventors."

References and Resources

Those Inventive Americans, National Geographic Society, 1971 (quote on p. 21).

The Smithsonian Book of Invention, Smithsonian Institution, 1978.

"The Improbable Success of John Fitch" by C. M. Harris, *American Heritage of Invention and Technology*, Winter 1989.

American Science and Invention by Mitchell Wilson, Bonanza Books, 1960.

Dictionary of American Biography, Charles Scribner's Sons Publishers, 1932; with supplemental updates.

National Cyclopedia of American Biography, James T. White & Co. Publishers, 1891; with supplemental updates.

McGraw-Hill Encyclopedia of Biography, McGraw-Hill Publishers, 1973.

Asimov's Biographical Encyclopedia of Science and Technology by Isaac Asimov, Doubleday & Co. Publishers, 1964.

Thomas Jefferson

National Portrait Gallery, Smithsonian Institution

Born:
April 13, 1743,
in
Charlottesville,
Virginia

Died:
July 4, 1826, in
Charlottesville,
Virginia

ONE outstanding early American technologist was a young man when Benjamin Franklin was an old man. He knew Franklin well and the two had many similar technical skills. He was a talented musician and brilliant writer. He was a great architect, leader, and inventor. He packed an astonishingly large number of accomplishments into his life. More than any other past American public figure, he epitomized a person with an inventive mind. Slim, sandy-haired, 6'2" tall, we know him as the third president of the United States, Thomas Jefferson.

Jefferson was born into a financially comfortable family on a farm called Shadwell, near Monticello, where he would later live. The house was not a great mansion but a simple, four-bedroom wooden structure. Jefferson's father worked part time as a surveyor and had several public service jobs, including a term in the state legislature. While teaching him to read and write,

Jefferson's father noticed his son's amazing ability to learn and retain information. Young Jefferson's education began at age 5 and he was fortunate in having many teachers during his formative years. They taught him such diverse subjects as French, surveying, government, science, and violin playing.

As Jefferson approached maturity, his mother agreed that he would greatly benefit from attending the College of William and Mary. Scientific thinking was replacing superstition in the late eighteenth century and Jefferson's education emphasized that answers to important questions came through study, reason, and logic. As he entered his twenties, he was among the best-educated and probably among the most intelligent people in colonial America.

As the oldest son of 11 children, Jefferson inherited the family estate at 14 when his father died. Four close friends took care of the property for Jefferson's mother and her eight children. Jefferson assumed that responsibility when he reached 21, and the well-tended 2,500 acres became the foundation of his livelihood. He enjoyed outdoor activities and was an excellent horseback rider who rode every day until almost the end of his life. Like others of his time, Jefferson hunted for food. In addition, though, he recorded the species, weight, size, and color of the animals he hunted. This kind of attention to detail stayed with him all his life.

Jefferson had a deep interest in science and technology, especially as they applied to agriculture. He greatly disliked the factory system of production that was being used in Great Britain. He considered the factories he had visited dismal places and felt that each family should be self-sufficient. He saw agriculture as the key to the self-sufficiency that was so important for a new country. He was always searching for some new plant or seed that might contribute to the country's prosperity. Among the foods he introduced to America were macaroni, almonds, vanilla, olives, and pistachio nuts.

Jefferson was an able draftsman who could quickly render an idea into visual form. His skilled farm workers constructed tools and equipment following Jefferson's designs and then used the products in practical experimentation. For example, processing hemp into rope on his farm required considerable physical effort to break and beat the crop. To overcome the problem, Jefferson developed an attachment for threshing machines that would break down the hemp plant. He also modified wool-processing machinery to minimize operator fatigue and invented a thresher that combined all parts onto a single frame. He was most proud of an improved plow that he designed on mathematical principles. It won an 1807 gold medal from the Agricultural Society of Paris. The plow had a new, lighter moldboard and plowed a deeper furrow with less effort. Pulled by two small horses, it tilled a furrow 9" wide by 6" deep. Although he had a complete set of tools, the incredibly busy Jefferson never found the time to fabricate his own devices.

Mechanical gadgets fascinated Jefferson and he remained "addicted" to them all his life. A few were adaptations of ones he saw on his trips, but many were of his own unique design. Among his original inventions, Jefferson created a rotating stand to hold his violin music, a combination walking stick and camp stool, and a folding ladder. He also invented a clock that told the time and day of the week, a pedometer for measuring distances, and a hand-held device with small wheels for generating secret messages. The military services used a similar one during World War II called Cipher Device M-94.

Jefferson corresponded with many people and always kept a copy of his letters. He wrote with a mechanical letter copier that used two quill-tipped pens. It was cumbersome to use, but much of his surviving correspondence consists of copies made by the device.

A competent architect, Jefferson designed his large 35-room home where an endless string of guests often visited. Employing more than 150, his farm was a community of people as well as machines. Besides threshers and other agricultural equipment, he had a nail-making machine, saw mill, textile mill, and one of Oliver Evans's automatic flour factories. Jefferson designed the Virginia state capitol. He also drew the architectural plans for the University of Virginia, and he supervised its construction down to the smallest detail. He even established the curriculum, selected the library books, and hired teachers.

Jefferson was a careful scientific observer and investigator. He unearthed an ancient native-American burial ground near his home. The methods he used in digging and recording preceded modern archaeological techniques by more than a century. When not otherwise occupied, he spent a great deal of time making notes or writing letters. One of the many scientists with whom he regularly corresponded was the British chemist Joseph Priestly, who discovered the existence of oxygen. Jefferson's interests in botany, geography, and prehistoric life led to his 18-year tenure as president of the

The U.S. Army developed a cipher machine based on a prototype Jefferson invented. Called the M-94, this one is on display at the Deutsches Museum in Munich, Germany.

American Philosophical Society. It was a major U.S. scientific organization founded by Benjamin Franklin. During Jefferson's lifetime, no other American-born person ever served as president of the society.

During his service as secretary of state

to George Washington, Jefferson was the nation's first patent administrator. The United States Constitution encouraged and protected the rights of inventors by establishing the framework of the patent system. Its Article I, Section 8, sets forth the intent to "promote the progress of science and useful arts, by securing for limited times to authors and inventors the exclusive right to their respective writings and discoveries." Nowhere else did the Constitution grant an exclusive right to a particular group. When the Patent Act became law in 1790, it provided for a board of three persons headed by the secretary of state. The board also included the secretary of war and attorney general. Jefferson did not initially approve of the granting of patents. He later changed his mind and said the law "has given a new spring to invention beyond my comprehensions." Nevertheless, he did not seek patents for his own inventions.

The even-tempered and scrupulously honest Jefferson was not a good speaker, but he was a clear and brilliant writer. Many call the Declaration of Independence his finest creation. A linguist who knew Latin, Greek, French, Spanish, and Italian, he started the first systematic collection of na-tive-American dialects. His own 6,400 book library formed the nucleus for the Library of Congress. After his wife of 10 years died, he raised their two daughters alone and never remarried. He died 50 years to the day after July 4, 1776.

President John Kennedy once said to a group of Nobel Prize winners: "I think this is the most extraordinary collection of human knowledge that has ever gathered at the White House, with the possible exception of when Thomas Jefferson dined alone."

References and Resources

Nuts and Bolts of the Past by David Freeman Hawke, Harper and Row, 1988.

The Smithsonian Book of Invention, Smithsonian Institution, 1978.

Young Thomas Jefferson by Francene Sabin, Troll Associates, 1986.

Constitution of the United States.

Dictionary of American Biography, Charles Scribner's Sons Publishers, 1932; with supplemental updates.

National Cyclopedia of American Biography, James T. White & Co. Publishers, 1891; with supplemental updates.

McGraw-Hill Encyclopedia of Biography, McGraw-Hill Publishers, 1973.

Oliver Evans

AT the beginning of the Industrial Revolution, early atmospheric steam engines were used only to pump water from coal mines. Their low power and big-as-a-house size made them unsuitable for factories or transportation. Oliver Evans invented the first practical steam engine to operate safely at pressures above 100 psi in 1804. His compact engine was as powerful as atmospheric steam engines 5 to 10 times larger.

Evans was born into a farming family, about halfway along a line of 12 children. He became a wagonmaker's apprentice at 14 and quickly learned the technical details of working with metal and wood. His mechanical ability surprised everyone, even Evans himself. He worked to increase his knowledge by spending considerable time reading books on mathematics and mechanics.

At age 22, he invented a device involved in wool production. To comb out tangles in raw wool, workers at the time used leather paddles with many iron wires sticking out from them. Evans built a machine to cut, bend, and install teeth into the paddles. A weak state patent law and dishonest competitors resulted in his making little profit from the invention.

American business was booming in the late 1700s when Evans opened a general store. Before seriously working on steam engines, he devoted attention to flour mills, the most important industry in Delaware. Evans noticed the vast amount of labor used for simple operations. The traditional mill had two or three floors, and its operation required the services of four strong men and a young person. Two men carried heavy sacks of wheat on their backs to the top floor and poured them into large containers. The wheat flowed down one or two floors, and

Smithsonian Institution Photo No. 33990-D

Born:
September 13, 1755, in Newport, Delaware

Died:
April 15, 1819, in New York, New York

into the space between two large circular stones. One stone rotating on top of a stationary stone ground the wheat into meal, a mixture of flour and chaff.

Two other men shoveled the meal into tubs and carried it to an upper level where the youngster raked it over the floor for drying and cooling. (The processed wheat became damp from its own released moisture and hot from friction between the stones.) After the wheat dried, the youngster shoveled the meal onto a ramp where it flowed to the ground floor. The chaff was sifted out and the flour stored in wooden barrels.

Over a five-year period, Evans built a sequence of machines, all geared to the same waterwheel. Wooden shafts and gears, and leather or canvas belts transferred power to the components. Although Evans used principles known since ancient times, they had never been combined in industry. His mill automatically moved wheat from one operation to another, eliminating much human effort. He reduced the labor force to two workers, one to empty wheat from the sacks, and the other to seal and move full barrels of flour. The Evans family mill first used this technique in 1787.

Wheat from wagons or ships entered the factory on an almost vertical, endless leather belt that had small buckets attached. This elevator hoisted 280 bushels per hour to the top floor. Broad strips of canvas moving over rollers transported the wheat to a storage bin. It flowed down to the mill stones and was ground into meal. It dropped into a 5"-diameter trough containing a

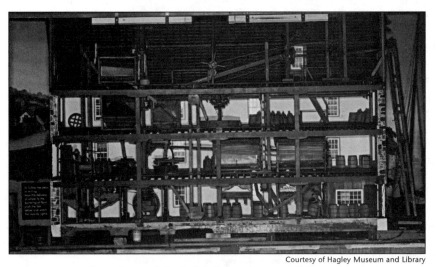

Courtesy of Hagley Museum and Library

A scale model of the first automated factory

long rotating screw, which moved the damp meal horizontally to another elevator. It went to the top floor again and was deposited in a 14'-diameter wooden tub. A rotating rake spread the meal evenly. It slowly dried and gathered at the center. Then, it automatically flowed down a ramp to the ground floor, where it was sifted and stored in barrels for shipping. Evans's method saved 20 pounds of flour per barrel by minimizing waste, it was three times faster than earlier methods, and it eliminated contamination with dirt from the mill floor.

Most millers showed little interest in Evans's mechanization because they were already making a profit. However, at $33, Evans soon sold his design to about 100 existing mills. Water wheels powered the first mills, but steam engines were installed in later ones. George Washington and Tho-

mas Jefferson used Evans's mill machinery on their farms. His flour mill represented the first successful automation of an entire production process.

Evans held patents from three states. After passage of the 1790 Patent Act, he received the third-ever U.S. patent. It was issued December 18, 1790, for "Manufacturing Flour and Meal." (See page 23.) In 1836, a fire destroyed all government copies of the patent and no one came forward with a personal copy of Evans's patent. It was never restored.

While working on parts for his flour factory, Evans often made toys for local children. He once gave them a very dangerous demonstration in his private blacksmith shop. Evans took a rejected gun barrel and partly filled it with water. Using his forge, he sealed both ends of the barrel, then threw it into a fire. The resulting explosion was almost as powerful as one caused by gunpowder. Evans had read about steam engines that used atmospheric pressure to push a piston inside a cylinder. The experiment convinced him that the piston should be pushed with steam.

Evans petitioned legislatures in Pennsylvania and Maryland to grant him exclusive rights for steam power in flour mills and steam carriages. Maryland granted rights to both applications and Pennsylvania agreed to the four-mill section of Evans's petition. Evans spent the rest of his life trying to convince a skeptical public of the importance of high-pressure steam engines for factories and transportation.

By 1802, Evans was self-sufficient and devoted all his time to building steam engines. He was the first person in America to devote himself to the specialty. Evans spent the large sum of $3,700 building his first experimental engine. Soon, steam powered his family's flour mill. Evans was far ahead of his time and many people could not understand his work. Because of financial strain and a certain amount of public ridicule, he was well past 40 before he became the first American manufacturer of steam engines.

Evans built more than 100 steam engines

for factories and river steamboats. His most powerful was made in 1817 for a water-plant pump. The engine had a 20" cylinder and a 60" stroke. It operated at a phenomenal 200 psi.

Evans received much-needed positive publicity in 1804. The city of Philadelphia gave him a $2,200 contract to build a steam-powered dredge. City residents had illegally used the Delaware River as a garbage dump, which created a health problem. Showing a certain wittiness, Evans named his 1805 15-ton road-worthy river dredge the *Orukter Amphibolos*, or "amphibious digger". An engine of about 5 hp powered the ponderous wooden contraption. Its single cylinder had a diameter of 5" and a stroke of 19". The drive system was a crude affair of ropes and belts, but it worked. Although it operated successfully for three years, no accurate drawing of the dredge exists.

Evans was the father of two daughters. Their husbands helped him operate his steam engine business. Unlike many early technologists, he wrote a great deal and published technical books. His most successful was *The Young Millwright and Miller's Guide*, published in 1795. It went into 15 editions, and some mill owners consulted it as late as the 1930s.

References and Resources

"Improvements in the Art of Manufacturing Grain into Flour or Meal" (an advertisement, circa 1791). Reprinted by Oliver Evans Press, Wallingford, Pennsylvania, 1990.

Engines of Change by Steven Lubar, Smithsonian Institution, 1986.

American Science and Invention by Mitchell Wilson, Bonanza Books, 1960.

The Smithsonian Book of Invention, Smithsonian Exposition Books, 1978.

Those Inventive Americans, National Geographic Society, 1971.

Machines that Built America by Roger Burlingame, New American Library, 1953.

Dictionary of American Biography, Charles Scribner's Sons Publishers, 1932, with supplemental updates.

National Cyclopedia of American Biography, James T. White & Co. Publishers, 1891, with supplemental updates.

McGraw-Hill Encyclopedia of Biography, McGraw-Hill Publishers, 1973.

Eli Whitney

Born:
December 8,
1765, in
Westborough,
Massachusetts

Died:
January 8,
1825, in
New Haven,
Connecticut

Smithsonian Institution Photo No. 649-G

AT the beginning of the Industrial Revolution, entrepreneurs used their technical skills to establish modern production facilities. Some also called on acting and marketing ability to sell an idea. Eli Whitney was such a person. He was an inventor, an opportunist, and an expert at public relations. He persuaded the government to grant him a musket contract in 1798 because he offered the possibility of producing interchangeable parts—a goal he never achieved.

Like most people in the eighteenth century, Whitney was born into a farming household. His father and mother both descended from successful agricultural families, and Whitney had a comfortable upbringing. Although he did not like farm work, it gave him the opportunity to work with simple machines. He seemed to have an almost instinctive understanding of mechanisms. Raised during the Revolution-

ary War, the teenaged Whitney worked at several jobs. He became a nail maker at 15 and was successful enough that he needed to hire an assistant. He switched to hat-pin making at the end of the war and was the major manufacturer in eastern Massachusetts.

Early on, Whitney showed no particular interest in school, but he changed his mind at 18 when he realized the value of an education. He worked his way through a preparatory school to gain admittance to college. He entered Yale College at the age of 23. His father helped him financially, but Whitney also worked at repairing laboratory equipment and instruments. He graduated in 1792 with a degree in law. The young man then traveled south, anticipating finding a law or teaching position. On the way to Savannah, Georgia, he met Catharine Greene, widow of General Nathanael Greene. She offered him a room in the mansion located on a plantation that her husband had received from the state of Georgia. Perhaps infatuated with the wealthy woman, Whitney accepted. He made himself useful by making and repairing items around the plantation.

Cotton was the family's main form of income. However, removing seeds by hand from ripe cotton was so tedious that one person could produce only one pound of cleaned cotton per day. Greene noticed how the tines of a comb passed through a person's hair and wondered if that process could be applied to removing cotton seeds. She discussed it with Whitney. Using his mechanical abilities, Whitney soon constructed a cotton gin based on the comb principle. After some experimentation, a machine he built in 1793 cleaned 50 pounds of cotton a day. Whitney established a partnership with Phineas Miller and returned to New Haven to work on the patent. The cotton gin was such a straightforward machine that a person seeing one could easily copy it. The new federal patent law was

This replica shows that Eli Whitney's cotton gin was a small and simple hand-cranked device.

quite weak, and so many infringing machines were built that Whitney exhausted himself and his money while fighting them in court. By 1798, he was almost penniless and his patent, important as it was to the economy of the South, was worthless to him. Whitney turned his back on the cotton gin forever.

About that time, the new United States government was looking for a manufacturer to provide 10,000 flintlock muskets in two years. The muskets got their name from a mechanism that locked a piece of flint in a small vise. Pulling the trigger caused the flint to strike a metal pan and create a spark. The spark ignited a small gunpowder trail that fired the main charge inside the gun barrel. Whitney had no background in making firearms, the most sophisticated product in the world. He had no factory, no raw materials, and no workers. Even well-established armories had never produced 5,000 muskets in one year. Whitney won the contract in June 1798 by offering the possibility of producing interchangeable parts. Interchangeability of parts appealed to the government because it would allow for easy manufacture and repair of the muskets.

Using money from 10 local investors, Whitney built a water-powered factory in New Haven. It did not have any particularly unique machinery, but Whitney hoped that a division of labor would improve production. Unlike his competitors, he did not have each worker make one musket from start to finish. He had his 50 workers making or assembling particular individual parts. Whitney broke the process into simple, easy-to-complete jobs. He was the first to use this method and had some problems getting it established. Although his contract eventually took 10 years to complete, Whitney completed a later one for 15,000 muskets in only two years. Stung by his experience with the cotton gin, Whitney never revealed the details of his factory. No descriptions or drawings were ever found.

The first delivery of 500 muskets to the U.S. government came in 1801. To assure government officials that production was going well, Whitney conducted a well-publicized demonstra-

The most difficult rifle part that Whitney had to make was the lock. It held a piece of flint in the small vise that created a spark to ignite gunpowder in the rifle barrel.

tion at the Capitol in January 1801. His audience included President John Adams, President-elect Thomas Jefferson, members of Congress, and other officials. In an attempt to show that he was making firearms with interchangeable parts, he fastened 10 different flintlock mechanisms to the same musket using only a screwdriver. The officials present were impressed and had no reason to believe the muskets had been specially prepared.

Whitney, however, had not disassembled the locks, mixed the parts, and then reassembled them. Jefferson said of the demonstration: "Mr. Whitney has invented molds and machines for making all the pieces of his locks so exactly equal, that take 100 locks to pieces and mingle their parts and the 100 locks may be put together as well by taking the first pieces which come to hand." In reality, no such demonstration had taken place.

The belief that Whitney had made interchangeable parts continued into this century. Then, in the 1960s, researchers noticed differences between written records and existing muskets. The physical evidence was unmistakable. Individual components had special identifying marks, something unnecessary for truly interchangeable parts. Also, Whitney muskets in collections such as those at the Smithsonian Institution do not have parts that interchange. It appears that Whitney purposely duped the government authorities.

In spite of that shortcoming, Whitney was still a technical pioneer. His division of labor was a landmark innovation. The government saved $25,000 a year after using it at two federal gun-making factories. Whitney also made the first milling machine worthy of the name. It was a tabletop device about the size of a bread box. Driven by a worm gear and screw thread, it had a multiple-edge cutting wheel and a movable work bed.

Whitney might have married Catharine Greene, if his partner Phineas Miller had not proposed to her first. Greene accepted Miller's offer. Whitney was 51 when he married Henrietta Edwards, a widow 20 years his junior. His unstable business life prevented him from marrying at an earlier age. His new wife brought her three children with her to the marriage, and Whitney finally had a normal domestic life.

Whitney suffered from an incurable abdominal ailment for many years. Before his death at 59, he made sure that his new family would control his factory. The Whitney Arms Co. remained a dominant manufacturer for 90 years, until the Winchester Repeating Arms Co. purchased it in 1888.

References and Resources

"Eli Whitney and the Development of American Technology" by Robert R. Macdonald, *Discovery*, Spring 1973.

"The Legend of Eli Whitney and Interchangeable Parts" by Robert S. Woodbury, *Technology and Culture*, Summer 1960.

Technology in America edited by Carroll Pursell, Jr., MIT Press, 1981.

Those Inventive Americans, National Geographic Society, 1971.

Dictionary of American Biography, Charles Scribner's Sons Publishers, 1932; with supplemental updates.

National Cyclopedia of American Biography, James T. White & Co. Publishers, 1891; with supplemental updates.

McGraw-Hill Encyclopedia of Biography, McGraw-Hill Publishers, 1973.

Asimov's Biographical Encyclopedia of Science and Technology by Isaac Asimov, Doubleday & Co. Publishers, 1964.

Samuel Slater

Library of Congress

Born:
June 9, 1768, in Belper, England

Died:
April 21, 1835, in Webster, Massachusetts

MANY years ago, people did not come together in groups to manufacture a product in a central location. Artisans completed individual items in their homes. A supervisor periodically picked up the finished products and took them to a central warehouse. The factory system made possible more efficient manufacturing in a single building. Materials went in and out of only one building, production schedules could be established, and expensive machinery shared. The first person to establish a successful spinning mill in America was Samuel Slater. His water-powered Rhode Island textile mill produced its first cotton thread in 1790.

Raised on a farm, the English-born Slater received an ordinary basic education. He showed an aptitude for mathematics and at 14 he was apprenticed to Jedediah Strutt, a family friend. Strutt made manufacturing machinery for British textile factories, and he was a partner of Richard Arkwright, the person most responsible for establishing efficient textile factories. When Slater's father unexpectedly died, Strutt assumed responsibility for raising the young man. Strutt felt that cotton manufacturing would always provide a satisfactory living, but he saw no great future in it. The opinion of this respected man had a significant effect on the young Slater. Partly influenced by advertisements from America that offered a bonus to textile workers, Slater decided to move to this country.

Factory production began in the 1760s in the textile mills of Great Britain. The Industrial Revolution changed Great Britain, the United States, and other countries from farming-based to industry-based economies. England wanted to maintain its dominance in the field of textile factories, so it passed laws that forbade English citizens to export machinery, data, or drawings of textile factories. Laws also forbade the emigration of textile workers. Many in the British government were still unhappy about so recently losing the Revolutionary War, and they did not want to encourage the emergence of a factory system in the U.S.

Slater decided to leave England in secret and prepared himself by obtaining knowledge of all aspects of textile factories. He had a photographic memory and could memorize machinery plans. He was also an excellent technologist and could recall the size of every major part in a given machine down to a fraction of an inch. On September 1, 1789, Slater arrived at the London dock disguised as a farmer. He took no documents or sketches since they could have incriminated him if discovered during mandatory searches before departure. He told no one of his plans. Not even his family knew until they received letters that

Slater served as an apprentice in this factory in Belper, England. Once owned by Jedediah Strutt, the factory has been remodeled into offices.

Slater mailed shortly before boarding the ship. He was 21.

The cold north Atlantic sailing brought Slater to New York City in 66 days. The practically penniless man heard of a recently completed mill in Pawtucket, Rhode Island, that was looking for a manager. Slater wrote to the owner, Moses Brown, to apply for the position by mail. He received an immediate reply offering him all factory profits if he could operate the machinery on hand. It was an incredible offer, and Slater accepted. When he arrived in Pawtucket, he found the machinery unacceptable because much of it was made of wood. Such machinery produced low-quality textile products. Most Americans preferred high-quality English textiles, and the factory would have produced unsalable goods. Slater convinced Brown to allow him to refit it with proper machinery.

Slater found himself handicapped by the lack of skilled machinists, tools, and metal parts available to him. Most machinists lacked skill in making sophisticated metal parts. The most commonly made items were simple products like scythes, shovels, anchors, and horseshoes. Slater worked for about a year, using details from English factories and adapting them to the U.S. environment. In December 1790, the factory produced its first cotton thread.

Slater's factory took raw cotton and first straightened the fibers in a carding machine. The machine had a series of rollers covered with short wire teeth and a funnel-like device at the end. It produced continuous loose lengths of straightened raw cotton. The carding machines were the ones that gave Slater the most problems.

Several lengths of layered, carded cotton formed a loose rope. Ropes were attached to spindles that spun the cotton to the required twist, firmness, and strength. Filled spindles were about the size of today's coffee cans.

Before factory thread was available, hand-operated early-American spinning wheels made thread by twisting together raw cotton or wool fibers. The quality of the handmade thread was variable and depended on the skill of the operator. More important, home-spun cotton was not suitable for the lengthwise threads on a weaving loom. The cotton threads were not strong enough, and linen thread was more commonly used. Slater's factory made consistently high-quality cotton thread and yarn, suitable for weaving on a home loom or knitting. It did not make finished cloth.

Water power from the Blackstone River operated Slater's three carding machines and two spinning frames with 48 spindles

One of Samuel Slater's original water-powered frames for spinning cotton thread is on display in Washington, D.C., at the Smithsonian Institution's National Museum of American History.

in each. Because of their power source, they were often called *water frames*. Within two years, the company was doing well enough that Slater and other investors opened a second factory. The mills worked so rapidly that they ran out of raw cotton and Slater had to shut down for a short time. The Smithsonian's National Museum of American History in Washington, D.C., has one of original spinning frames that Slater used on display.

Luckily, Eli Whitney's cotton gin came into general use about that time. Within one year, the annual amount of factory-ready raw cotton increased from five to eight million pounds. By 1810, 226 textile mills were operating in 12 states. Most produced yarn for hand looms used in homes. Once Americans knew that mills in this country could produce consistently high-quality textiles, they abandoned English goods. The U.S. textile market boomed. Others tried to imitate Slater's results, but he always stayed in the lead. His last factory had 8,000 spindles and was powered by a steam engine. He eventually opened additional factories in Massachusetts and New Hampshire. His younger brother joined him in 1805.

Slater did not invent or improve anything he brought to this country. He used the ideas of others, and the British still view him as somewhat mutinous. Nonetheless, he did establish the American factory system, and he is frequently called the founder of the U.S. cotton industry.

Slater's manufacturing steps were so simple that most early factory workers were children. His first factory was operated by nine children, aged 7 to 12. School attendance at the time was not compulsory and many parents preferred having their children engaged in a useful and money-making activity. Compared with the sweat shops that followed, early U.S. factories were relatively pleasant places to work. Slater even established a Sunday school for his young employees. The children met in Slater's home for basic instruction by ministers whom Slater personally paid.

Although his estimated worth was $500,000, Slater was frugal with his money. He was generous to religious charities and contributed to feeding the poor. Early on, he lived in an ordinary house and drove an ordinary carriage to set a good example for his nine children. He wanted them to be self-sufficient. His first wife died in 1812 and he remarried five years later. Slater's second wife convinced him to improve his standard of living.

References and Resources

A Dozen Captains of American Industry by Walter Wilson Jennings, Vantage Press, 1954.

The Samuel Slater Story (pamphlet), Old Slater Mill Association, Pawtucket, RI, 1948.

Machines That Built America by Roger Burlingame, Harcourt Brace World, 1953.

Dictionary of American Biography, Charles Scribner's Sons Publishers, 1932; with supplemental updates.

National Cyclopedia of American Biography, James T. White and Co. Publishers, 1891; with supplemental updates.

McGraw-Hill Encyclopedia of Biography, McGraw-Hill Publishers, 1973.

The First United States Patent

Issued:
July 31, 1790,
in
Philadelphia,
Pennsylvania

U.S. Patent Office

The first United States patent was issued to Samuel Hopkins in 1790.

"WHAT was the first patent issued in our country?" That seems like a straightforward question that should have a single answer. In fact, though, there was more than one "first" patent.

Before the establishment of the U.S. Patent Office, colony and state governments provided exclusive grants to individuals. These grants served as legal patents. The colony of Massachusetts issued the first grant in 1641 to Samuel Winslow for a more efficient way of producing salt for the fishing industry. The document contained just 134 crudely stated and spelled words, such as: "it shall not bee lawfull to any other pson to make salt after the same way during the said yeares." It contained few specific legal provisions and, like other documents of the period, it did not describe a process or piece of hardware in detail.

Pennsylvania issued the first patent in America, using similarly nonspecific language, in 1780 to Henry Guest. It gave Guest "the sole and exclusive right, for the term of five years, of manufacturing oil and blubber from the materials he has discovered." Guest had to post his own printed account of his new process. Note that neither the Winslow nor the Guest patent was issued by the federal government of the United States of America. Before the establishment of U.S. patents, six states had their own patent laws: Connecticut, Delaware, New Jersey, New York, Pennsylvania, and Virginia.

The U.S. Patent Act was signed on April 10, 1790. It was short and simple. Inventors could patent anything that was a "useful art, manufacture, engine, machine, or device, or any improvement therein not before known or used." Patterned after the British model, the U.S. system offered the inventor a 14-year monopoly. The Patent Act resulted from a provision in the 1787 Constitution. Under Article I, Section 8, Congress had to provide legal protection for authors and inventors through copyrights and patents. This was an unusual and unique concept—nowhere else does the Constitution provide such an exclusive right to a select group of persons. President George Washington referred to that provision when he presented his first message to both houses of Congress.

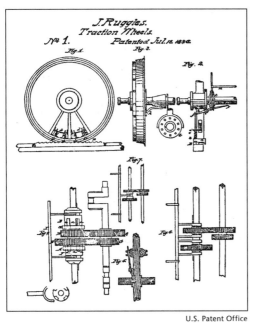

The first U.S. patent to carry "No. 1" was issued to John Ruggles, head of the Committee on Patents of the U.S. Senate.

The first United States patent was issued in July 1790 to Samuel Hopkins for "Making Pot and Pearl Ashes." Hopkins had developed an improved method of producing potash. America's first industrial chemical, potash was essential for making gunpowder and soap. It was also used in dying fabrics and baking. Potash came from the ashes of a large fire. The *ashes* were mixed with water and boiled in a large thick-walled *pot*—hence, the name *potash*. The boiled down, dark, thick mass that the process produced was a crude form of potash.

Hopkins paid a $4 or $5 application fee for his patent. President Washington signed his one-page patent in New York, the capital of the U.S. at that time. Attorney General Edmund Randolph co-signed the document. Its back carried an endorsement by Secretary of State Thomas Jefferson who was also the nation's first patent administrator. Jefferson reviewed all early patent applications. Randolph and Jefferson served as members of the first U. S. Patent Board, and their approval was required.

The Hopkins patent carried no number. No statement described it as the first of many millions to come. The patent board issued only three patents during its first year. Joseph Sampson received the second on August 6 for "Making Candles." The third, "Manufacturing Flour and Meal," went to Oliver Evans on December 18, and it held particular significance. This patent covered a series of four or five inventions used in Evans's flour mill. That mill represented the first successful automation of an entire production process.

Samuel Hopkins had been born in New York in 1765 and moved to Pittsford, Vermont, when he was 16. He lived there for the next 30 years but his 1790 patent clearly states that he was from Philadelphia. Vermont was not admitted to the United States until 1791, after the Patent Act became law. Some people have theorized that Hopkins took a temporary residence in Philadelphia to strengthen his application.

Hopkins's method required burning raw ashes in a furnace before dissolving them in water. The process increased potash yields enough that many commercial operators wanted to use it. The patent called for an initial payment of $50 and another $150 annual payment for five years for anyone using the process. Hopkins profited handsomely from his patent—as did the commercial potash producers who used his process. Thanks partly to the new procedure, the U.S.

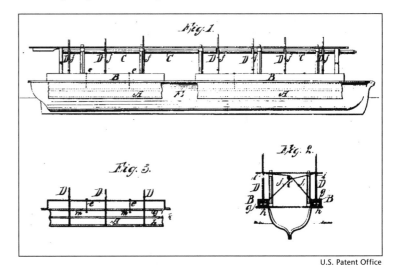

Abraham Lincoln was the only president to receive a patent. Issued in 1849, patent no. 6469 described a method for freeing a boat from a sandbar.

was the world's largest producer of potash until the 1860s.

The Quebec parliament also passed an ordinance to reward Hopkins for his discovery. Legal experts now view that ordinance as Canada's first patent. Hopkins took out two additional United States patents before his death in 1840.

The government stored the Hopkins patent and many others at temporary locations for several years after they were issued. One such storage area was Blodgett's Hotel at Eighth and E Streets in Washington, D.C.

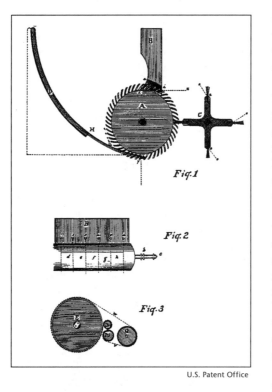

Patent materials for Eli Whitney's cotton gin were destroyed in an 1836 fire. This is part of the first page of the unnumbered restored patent.

U.S. Patent Office

Blodgett's was the only federal building that the British did not destroy during the War of 1812. British troops entered Washington on August 24, 1814. Patent Office Director William Thornton persuaded the officers that the patents were not threatening and that they had great historic significance. British officers agreed to spare the building. Unfortunately, the hotel accidentally burned to the ground in 1836. The fire destroyed 9,000 drawings, 7,000 patent models, and 230 books, in addition to patent applications and many patents already issued. The destroyed patents were restored only if a relative, friend, or other person came forward with a copy for duplication. Eli Whitney's 1794 cotton gin patent was restored in that manner. However, no original copy of Evans's flour mill patent was found, and it remains unrestored.

For many years, people assumed that flames had consumed the Hopkins patent in 1836. However, through a sequence of events that has not yet been revealed, the patent came into the possession of an avid Chicago collector of historical items, Charles Gunther. At his death in 1920, Gunther left the Hopkins patent and the rest of his collection to the Chicago Historical Society, which holds it today.

Just a few months before the 1836 fire, Congress passed a new patent law. Before then, the Patent Office had issued 9,957 unnumbered patents. The first to display the designation "No. 1" was issued on July 13, 1836, to John Ruggles of Thomaston, Maine. It was for "Traction Wheels," improved railroad wheels intended to keep a train from slipping as it climbed hills on snowy or icy rails. History does not record how well Ruggles's invention succeeded, but it does show that he headed the Committee on Patents of the U.S. Senate.

The only U.S. president to receive a patent was Abraham Lincoln. (See page 23.) At the age of 40, while a U.S. Congressional representative from Illinois, he received a patent for "Buoying Vessels Over Shoals." His technique involved forcing flotation under a boat that had struck a sand bar to allow it to float freely away. Like the vast majority of patents, Lincoln's was not a commercial success.

At the beginning of the 1990s, more than five million U.S. patents had been issued. This is particularly notable considering that in 1833, Patent Office Director William Thornton thought he should resign because he felt that "everything seems to have been done"!

References and Resources

Genesis of American Patent and Copyright Law by Bruce Bugbee, Public Affairs Press, 1967.

The Patent Office by Stacy Jones, Praeger Publishers, 1971.

"The First U.S. Patent" by Henry Paynter, in *American Heritage of Invention and Technology*, Fall 1990.

"Two Hundred Years of Patents and Copyrights" by Cathleen Schurr, in *American History Illustrated*, July/August 1990.

Famous First Facts by Joseph Nathan Kane, H. W. Wilson Co., 1981.

Photocopied material provided by the Chicago Historical Society and the American Precision Museum (Vermont).

Samuel Finley Breese Morse

Smithsonian Institution Photo No. 10-799

Samuel Morse during the last year of his life.

Born:
April 27, 1791,
in
Charlestown,
Massachusetts

Died:
April 2, 1872,
in New York,
New York

IT is not unusual for some people to start on a different career path before discovering technology. Even so, it seems unlikely that a talented painter should invent the first electrical communication device. It is even more unlikely that that person would be nearly 50 years old—most successful inventors start at half that age. The technologist referred to here, Samuel Finley Breese Morse, patented his telegraph in 1840.

Morse was born to a minister and his wife, both of whom appreciated the value of a proper education. Morse attended local schools and an academy for gifted youngsters. He received excellent instruction that prepared him well for studies at Yale University. There, Morse majored in art but also took classes in electricity, chemistry, and mathematics. Several of his teachers had the best technical minds in the country, but Morse never showed an interest in science or technology as a career. After graduation, his parents financed a trip to London that allowed him to study under the leading painters of the time.

The War of 1812, between America and England, broke out the year after his arrival, and Morse stayed overseas for four years. His travel was not hampered by the war, and he met many excellent artists. He returned to Boston in 1815, where he made his living as a portrait painter. The talented Morse once did a portrait of his friend Eli Whitney, which is now in the collection of Yale University's Art Gallery. New York City Hall and the New York Public Library also currently own and display his paintings. Morse helped found the National Academy of Design in 1826 and served as its president for 20 years.

A series of personal tragedies rained down on Morse during the 1820s. One of his children died while he was living in Charleston, South Carolina. Shortly after returning to New York, Morse's wife died, as did his father and mother. He left for Europe to seek inner peace and fresh ideas for his painting career. Morse spent most of the next three years in France and Italy. He met Louis Daguerre and was the first American to see a daguerreotype. He made plans to open a photographic studio on his return to the United States.

Morse sailed back in 1832. One of the other passengers on the voyage was Charles Thomas Jackson, a Boston physician. Jackson brought up the subject of electricity and its ability to travel almost instantaneously over any length of wire. The idea of applying this concept to the rapid transfer of information fascinated Morse, and he engaged Jackson in lengthy conversation. Later that evening, Morse started sketching a crude wood-framed telegraph. He used the little knowledge of electricity that he retained from his college days in this diversion during the crossing.

Immediately after landing in America, Morse sought work to support himself and three young children. He taught painting and sculpture at the newly opened New York University and functioned as the first professor of art in America. One of his students was Mathew Brady, the famous Civil War photographer. Morse also made and sold daguerreotypes, and he opened one of the first photographic portrait studios. He

worked on the telegraph in his spare time. He redoubled his inventive efforts in 1837 after he heard that Europeans were making great strides in telegraphy. In England, Charles Wheatstone was developing a method in which needles pointed to letters on a dial. About that time, Congress turned down Morse's bid to provide a painting for the Capitol rotunda. Taking this as a final failure to gain recognition as a great artist, he decided to concentrate his efforts on the telegraph.

Morse soon discovered that he lacked adequate knowledge of electricity. One of his early electromagnets did not work simply because he used uninsulated wire. Since the electromagnet was basic to the telegraph, Morse approached Joseph Henry, secretary of the Smithsonian Institution. Henry had invented the electromagnet, and he freely gave all the help he could. Morse spent seven years trying different designs while selling partnerships and a few paintings to pay the bills. At one time, his net worth had dropped to 37 cents.

The receiver Morse patented in 1840 did not resemble the standard telegraph receiver common a few years later. His original was a printing instrument. Morse used a small wooden frame to support a pendulum with a pencil on the end. One wooden crosspiece near the bottom had a roll of paper tape and a clockwork mechanism that pulled the paper under the pendulum. Another crosspiece had an electromagnet near the center of the iron pendulum. The transmitter was a key that closed an electrical switch, and it had some similarity to modern keys.

Morse's transmission code was a series of dots and dashes. Briefly closing the transmitter key caused the electromagnet to move the pendulum a very short distance. That motion produced a "dot." Closing the key longer made a "dash." As the paper moved under the pencil-tipped pendulum, the pencil drew an image resembling a small mountain peak for each dot and a small plateau for each dash. The pencil lines formed a distinct pattern for each letter that Morse had devised. In the first version of the Morse Code, for example, the letter "T" had two dashes and a dot. "P" had five dots. Morse's receiver was a cumbersome affair, but it worked. By 1845, trained telegraphers listened to the dot-dash pattern from an elec-

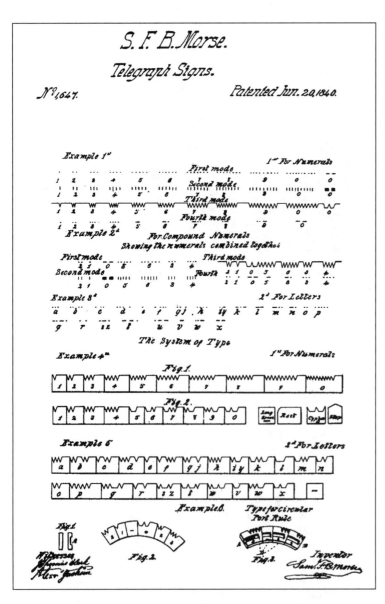

Morse's telegraph patent included his first attempt at a Morse code.

tromagnet in a sounding box and wrote messages directly.

Morse gave demonstrations of his new equipment in Newark, New York, and Philadelphia. He took it to Washington in 1842 to demonstrate for government leaders. From the beginning of his experiments, Morse never saw his telegraph as simply a convenient method of communication. He thought it would be used only for messages of the utmost importance and hoped the government would buy his patent rights. Members of Congress showed no interest in buying, but they did approve a $30,000 grant for installing a 41-mile trial telegraph line between Washington and Baltimore.

Morse accepted a suggestion to use a single wire strung on glass insulators mounted on trees and poles. Using the earth as a ground eliminated the necessity for a two-wire system. The young Ezra Cornell completed the installation work. He would soon make a fortune in the telegraph business and provide money to establish Cornell University. The telegraph's terminal points were the Supreme Court chambers in Washington and the Baltimore and Ohio Railroad depot on Pratt Street in Baltimore. On May 24, 1844, from Washington, Morse tapped out the message, "WHAT HATH GOD WROUGHT?" It took one minute to send the four words to a partner, Alfred Vail, in Baltimore. The message was chosen by Annie Ellsworth. She was the young daughter of Henry Ellsworth, U.S. Commissioner of Patents and a Yale classmate of Morse's. Although this was not the first message ever sent by telegraph, it was the first official intercity message. The telegraph became an immediate success.

With the exception of Florida, every state east of the Mississippi River had telegraph service just four years later. London went on line in 1866. Morse lived to see all those early major developments in telegraphy. American colleges, foreign governments, and professional societies showered him with awards. Morse's years of poverty had ended, and he spent his remaining days as a wealthy man on his 200-acre estate on the Hudson River. The photograph on page 25 is a silver print taken during the last year of his life.

References and Resources

Those Inventive Americans, National Geographic Society, 1971.

American Science and Invention by Mitchell Wilson, Bonanza Books, 1960.

"What Hath God Wrought?" by Maury Klein, in *American Heritage of Invention and Technology*, Spring 1993.

Dictionary of American Biography, Charles Scribner's Sons Publishers, 1932; with supplemental updates.

National Cyclopedia of American Biography, James T. White & Co. Publishers, 1891; with supplemental updates.

McGraw-Hill Encyclopedia of Biography, McGraw-Hill, 1973.

Asimov's Biographical Encyclopedia of Science and Technology, by Isaac Asimov, Doubleday & Co. Publishers, 1964.

Joseph Henry

Born:
December 17,
1797, in
Albany,
New York

Died:
May 13, 1878,
in Washington,
D.C.

Smithsonian Institution Photo No. 42836

IT would be difficult to name a piece of machinery that does not use a transformer or electric motor. These essential pieces of modern technology were developed by a quiet, unassuming American who always maintained a dignified bearing. Joseph Henry presented useful electromagnetism to the world in 1831 — but some say that the Smithsonian Institution was his greatest invention.

Henry came from a poor home. His father was a day laborer, and as a boy Henry went to live with his grandmother in a nearby county. He attended the local school and worked as a clerk in a local store. In his early teens, he returned to Albany to live with his recently widowed mother and became a jeweler's apprentice. Henry also started to pursue a career as a stage actor and even wrote two plays, but he changed his mind after reading a popularly written science book. Henry later said that the book

was not particularly well written or profound. It was merely the first one on a technical subject that he had come across.

Henry worked his way through a local college by teaching and serving as an administrative assistant. His work and knowledge were so highly regarded that the Albany Academy offered him a full-time teaching position in 1826. There, he began his investigations into the emerging field of electricity and its relationship to magnetism. He was the first American to experiment with electricity in any important way since Benjamin Franklin had done so, almost 80 years earlier.

Using homemade batteries, Henry tried various lengths and diameters of wire wrapped around a soft iron core to produce electromagnetism. The wire available was not insulated, so Henry began by using a single loose wrapping separated from the iron core with a layer of wax. The resulting magnet could pick up only a few ounces. Henry became the first to experiment with layers of wire, which required insulation. Insulated wire was not easy to come by in those pre-electricity days. Henry tore up a silk petticoat and spent much time engaged in the boring task of wrapping insulation around wires. He found that he could wind the wires in sections, allowing him to join them in different combinations. When he connected the sections in parallel with a battery, the magnet became quite strong. Even a weak battery could produce a great deal of magnetism in this way. In 1831, Henry made a 21-pound electromagnet that could lift 750 pounds. Later that year, using the current from a storage battery, he made a one-foot-high horseshoe-shaped electromagnet that lifted one ton of iron. People at the Penfield Iron Works in Crown

Point near Fort Ticonderoga heard of the powerful magnet. To help them separate iron from iron ore, they asked Henry to make two of the magnets. Shortly afterward, Crown Point was renamed Port Henry.

The next year Henry married, and he took a job at the College of New Jersey in Princeton. He conducted experiments on smaller electromagnets that could be used for fine control, and in 1835 he made the first electromagnetic relay. In effect, he had invented the telegraph nine years before Samuel Morse. He later freely gave advice to Morse, who was woefully ignorant of electrical principles. Henry never patented any of his inventions because he believed that technical discoveries should benefit everyone. Others—including Thomas Jefferson—shared his view.

In 1830, Henry had discovered and worked out the theoretical problems associated with induced electrical currents such as those connected with transformers. He worked at the Albany Academy then, and he had a heavy teaching load. Preoccupied with daily work, he put off publicizing his results. Michael Faraday discovered the same effect a few months later in England, and Faraday did publish his findings. Henry gracefully handled his disappointment over not being recognized as the discoverer. Faraday went on to create the electrical generator and was one of the foremost nineteenth-century British scientists. The unit of capacitance, the *farad*, is named in his honor. Like Henry, Faraday came from a poor family, had little schooling, and needed to go to work at an early age. The two met in 1835 when Henry visited England. Faraday proposed that the Royal Society of London, the world's most prestigious scientific organization, award Henry its coveted Copley Medal. Benjamin Franklin was the only other American so honored.

Henry continued investigating electricity and described the construction of an electric motor. He called the first one a "philosophical toy." It was a bar-shaped electromagnet positioned horizontally that rocked back and forth when the current reversed. From that humble beginning, Henry expanded the world's understanding of electric motors. Inexpensive electrical power was just becoming available and Henry's motor provided a method for con-

verting electrical energy to mechanical energy. The unit of magnetic inductance, the *henry*, is named in his honor. Professionally active and respected by everyone, Henry helped organize the American Association for the Advancement of Science. He was an original member of the National Academy of Sciences and served as its president for 10 years.

Henry left Princeton for Washington, D.C., because of an 1829 bequest made by James Smithson, a British citizen. Smithson was a wealthy philanthropist who had a strong interest in science. In his will, he left $515,000 "for the purpose of founding an institution at Washington to be called the Smithsonian Institution for the increase and diffusion of knowledge." Because of legal technicalities, the organization was not founded until 1846 when the board of directors asked Henry to become the first secretary and director of the Smithsonian Institution. Always pleasant, approachable, and highly respected, he served in that position for the rest of his life, over 30 years.

The fledgling organization searched for a purpose and a direction. Many people had ideas at the time, such as having the Smithsonian sponsor a school of steam engineering or an extensive lecture series. Henry resisted all these ideas and developed a unique goal. He considered it important to distribute technical and scientific information among all people working in technology. He proposed to assist people "in making original researches, to publish these in a series of volumes, and to give a copy to every first-class library on the face of the earth." The Smithsonian's board of directors approved Henry's plan, and the National Geographic Society called it his greatest invention. Henry, more than anyone else, helped with the invention of American science.

The Smithsonian's impact on American technology was enormous. Henry interviewed young up-and-coming scientists and recommended them for jobs. He kept track of who was doing what and put investigators in contact with each other. In his later years, Henry once met with the youthful Alexander Graham Bell, who was anxious to discuss his experiments. Despite having a severe cold, Henry listened patiently and offered encouragement. Bell later said that had Henry not been so understanding, "I should never have gone on with the telephone."

No American better served the technology of his time, and Henry's death was viewed as a great loss to the public. A memorial service was held for him in the Hall of the House of Representatives on January 16, 1879. It was attended by the president and his cabinet, both houses of Congress, members of the Supreme Court, and many other distinguished people. Few Americans have been so honored by their government.

References and Resources

Those Inventive Americans, National Geographic Society, 1971.

Famous American Men of Science by J. G. Crowther, Books for Libraries Press, 1969.

Joseph Henry: His Life and Work by Thomas Coulson, Princeton University Press, 1950.

Dictionary of American Biography, Charles Scribner's Sons Publishers, 1932; with supplemental updates.

National Cyclopedia of American Biography, James T. White & Co. Publishers, 1891; with supplemental updates.

McGraw-Hill Encyclopedia of Biography, McGraw-Hill, 1973.

Asimov's Biographical Encyclopedia of Science and Technology, by Isaac Asimov, Doubleday & Co. Publishers, 1964.

Charles Goodyear

Goodyear Tire and Rubber Co.

Born:
December 29, 1800, in New Haven, Connecticut

Died:
July 1, 1860, in New York, New York

THE person who operated the first retail hardware store in America also took out several patents. The patents were for such diverse items as buttons, a spring-lever faucet, an air pump, a pontoon boat, and a hay fork. However, this person would not be remembered for any of those inventions. Charles Goodyear also vulcanized rubber, which is the primary reason that we remember him. As a result of his invention, the world's largest rubber manufacturer chose his name for its corporate title in 1898, 38 years after his death.

The oldest of six children, Goodyear was the son of an inventor who manufactured a variety of agricultural items. He received an average public school education. He seldom played as a youngster, preferring to spend his free time reading. At 17, he went to Philadelphia to serve a four-year apprenticeship with a hardware importer. When he returned home, his father took him in as a partner, and their business flourished. Several years later, Goodyear returned to Philadelphia to open the nation's first hardware store. He sold items manufactured by his father and brother. Unfortunately, a nationwide financial crisis in 1830 caused severe financial losses for Goodyear and many other people. Goodyear spent three months in debtors' prison, as prescribed by law. This was the first of many such imprisonments. For the rest of his life, Goodyear was never out of financial difficulty.

During his early 30s, Goodyear purchased a life preserver from the Roxbury India Rubber Co. in New York. Formed in 1833, Roxbury was the first American rubber manufacturing company. Goodyear modified the life preserver's air valve and offered an improved version to the manager. The manager showed little interest, but he told Goodyear of the problems associated with taming raw rubber. During warm weather, rubber melted and gave off an unpleasant odor. During cold weather, it stiffened and cracked. Manufacturers used rubber only because no other equally effective waterproofing material existed.

Goodyear's conversation with the rubber company manager set him to thinking of ways to improve rubber. He was not a chemist and had no idea how to begin. With his kitchen serving as a laboratory, he started by using common items available in drug stores. His experiments often began with his kneading minced raw rubber with solvents such as turpentine or alcohol. Goodyear then mixed in lime, magnesia, lamp black, talcum, or sulfur on a marble slab with a rolling pin. His mixtures gave off foul odors that offended members of his family and caused his neighbors to complain. Goodyear used all his money to finance his experiments. To obtain more money, he sold his family's furniture and his children's school books. He fished nearby rivers and bays for food until neighbors offered milk and bread for the children. While he and his wife had 12 children, only 6 survived past childhood. Many of his associates considered him something of a madman. He primarily lived on loans from relatives and friends, as well as the money offered to him by small investors.

In January 1839, Goodyear was working with sulfur when an accident occurred. In his words, "The specimen, being carelessly brought in contact with a hot stove, charred like leather." He had accidentally dropped some raw rubber on the stove top. It had not melted and after removing it, he noticed that the material was no longer sticky. In spite of the cold weather, when he took the specimen outdoors, it remained firm and flexible. Goodyear had accidentally vulcanized rubber. Named for Vulcan, the mythological Roman god of fire and metalworking, *vulcanization* refers to treating raw rubber with chemicals.

Goodyear foolishly did not immediately take out a patent but relied instead on trying to keep his process secret. He knew that heat and sulfur played key roles in vulcanization, but he did not know the ideal degree of heat or length of exposure. He toasted marshmallow-sized pieces of rubber over an open fire. He steamed rubber bits over a tea kettle. He pressed rubber between hot rollers. In the end, he discovered that steam or hot air applied to a combination of thin raw rubber and sulfur for five hours at 270° F produced good results. Goodyear took out his basic rubber vulcanization patent in 1844.

In the meantime, British rubber pioneer Thomas Hancock had been working with raw rubber for 20 years. He joined forces with Charles Macintosh of Scotland and sandwiched rubber between layers of cloth to make a waterproof outer coat called a mackintosh. The uncured rubber worked satisfactorily in Great Britain's temperate climate. Hancock obtained a sample of Goodyear's rubber in 1843 and figured out the vulcanization process. Openly stealing Goodyear's idea, Hancock filed for a British patent. Goodyear had waited too long to patent his findings. He filed a legal suit against Hancock anyway—one he would ultimately lose. Offered a half share of the Hancock patent to drop the suit, Goodyear senselessly declined. It would have made him and his family wealthy.

The discovery of vulcanization was not immediately appreciated by the American public. Many were disappointed by earlier inventors who made similar claims only to find raincoats giving off bad odors in summer heat and boots cracking in winter cold. The public slowly realized that rubber had been tamed, and useful products became available. Rubber's first profitable use was in shirred fabric. Interwoven rubber and cotton threads produced a fashionable puckered effect in men's shirts. Manufacturing rights might have made Goodyear wealthy, but he was forced to set very low licensing rates. He had borrowed so much money in the past and been such a poor family provider that no one trusted him. Another problem was that Goodyear's process was so simple that many manufacturers could use it without paying royalties. Goodyear took 32 of them to the U.S. Supreme

Charles Goodyear is shown inspecting the first vulcanized piece of rubber in this fanciful painting. In actuality, Goodyear was not tall, was in poor health, and often conducted his experiments on crutches.

Goodyear Tire and Rubber Co.

Court, which further drained his limited finances. In a major case in 1852, he hired Secretary of State Daniel Webster as his lawyer against the India Rubber Co. Webster won, but he charged Goodyear $15,000 for his services. At the time, it was the largest amount ever paid to a lawyer for a single court case. The case made headlines, but piracy of Goodyear's discoveries continued.

Goodyear spent $30,000 for a display at the first world's fair, the 1851 Crystal Palace Exhibition in London. A similar display he presented in Paris cost $50,000. Goodyear paid for both with borrowed money in anticipation of large returns. Emperor Napoleon III was so impressed with the Paris display that he awarded Goodyear the Cross of the Legion of Honor. But the medal was delivered to Goodyear at his cell in Clichy prison, where he spent 16 days for nonpayment of a debt. Goodyear's wife had died during their time in Europe and he sold her jewelry to pay for boat passage home.

Goodyear often wore rubber hats, vests, shoes, and ties. He had business cards made of rubber and had his autobiography printed on rubber sheets. Never a healthy person, the slender and frail Goodyear suffered lifelong problems of acute indigestion and painful gout. In 1860, overcome with grief upon hearing that a favorite daughter was near death, he died in New York while traveling from Washington to her bedside. Goodyear left his family $200,000 in debt, but later royalties eventually gave his descendants a comfortable lifestyle.

References and Resources

Inventing: How the Masters Did It by Byron M. Vanderbilt, Moore Publishing, 1974.

Those Inventive Americans, National Geographic Society, 1971.

"Crazy about Rubber" by Robert Friedel, in *American Heritage of Invention and Technology*, Winter 1990.

Materials provided by Goodyear Tire and Rubber Co.

Dictionary of American Biography, Charles Scribner's Sons Publishers, 1932; with supplemental updates.

National Cyclopedia of American Biography, James T. White & Co. Publishers, 1891; with supplemental updates.

McGraw-Hill Encyclopedia of Biography, McGraw-Hill, 1973.

Asimov's Biographical Encyclopedia of Science and Technology, by Isaac Asimov, Doubleday & Co. Publishers, 1964.

John Deere

Born:
February 7,
1804,
in Rutland,
Vermont

Died:
May 17, 1886,
in Moline,
Illinois

Photo courtesy of Deere and Co.

ROUGH-SURFACED iron and wooden plows worked well in the sandy and coarse soils of eastern America. However, they were not well suited to the sticky, fertile soils of the Midwest. Many farmers experimented with different designs, and by 1813 inventors had filed at least 20 patents. Yet, only one early plow truly fits the description of "revolutionary": John Deere's 1837 polished-steel plow.

The fourth of five children, Deere received a typical rural childhood education in the schools of Vermont. He became a blacksmith's apprentice at 17 and spent four years in Middlebury learning his trade. Deere soon developed a reputation as a talented and careful worker. Some shovels he made lasted more than 50 years. His first blacksmith shop burned soon after he established it. Later, a second shop also burned down. His losses proved so great that Deere could not find enough work to

recover financially. Saw mill owner Leonard Andrus, a former Vermonter living in northern Illinois, sent back reports of a prosperous and growing area. Deere decided to move to Illinois in 1836.

With a tool kit and $73, Deere stopped in Grand Detour, a new town about 80 miles west of Chicago. The town's name came from the obstruction created by a large bend in the nearby Rock River. Andrus lived there, and his saw mill was down because of a broken metal part. Deere easily repaired the part. He then decided to settle in the town, and within two days had constructed a crude outdoor blacksmith shop. He built a small 18' x 24' half-story house and sent for his wife and five children the next year.

Deere quickly grew familiar with a problem that eastern farmers had not encountered. Midwestern soil was so rich that it stuck to the rough surfaces of wooden and iron plows. Farmers complained of plowing soil that felt like a mixture of tar, mud, and molasses. Every few steps, they had to stop and scrape soil from parts of the plow. This made field work slow and laborious.

To plow a furrow quickly and cleanly, the soil must peel away in a smooth curl. Other inventors had tried to improve the curl by reshaping the plow. Deere was the first to realize that neither iron nor wood would scour, or be self cleaning, in sticky soil. Iron had small cavities called blow holes and could not take a high polish. While visiting Andrus's saw mill in 1837, Deere noticed how a discarded circular steel saw blade shined where friction had polished it. He bought it to use in making a polished and carefully shaped plow. The 1/4"-thick saw blade was only 10" to 12" in diameter, too small for a standard plow. So Deere used the steel for the cutting edge at the bottom,

One of the first three plows made by John Deere in Grand Detour, Illinois. It is on display at the Smithsonian Institution.

maker grew rapidly. By 1846, the 10 employees in his 1,400-square-foot factory were manufacturing 1,000 plows per year. Deere's first plows were made from whatever steel he could find. In 1843, he ordered special rolled steel from Sheffield, England, because no American mill could meet his specifications.

or plowshare. He fastened the steel to an upper section of wrought iron. Quite unconventional in construction, the shape approximated a parallelogram curved in a concave fashion. Deere obviously gave a great deal of thought to its shape. He even used a wooden mallet to avoid denting the metal's surface. Deere said, "I cut the teeth off with a hand chisel . . . and shaped [the metal] as best I could with the hand hammer. After making the upright standard out of bar iron, I was ready for the wood parts . . . and finally succeeded in constructing a very rough plow." With its strong white-oak rails, the plow passed every test that local farmers could give it. The self-scouring action of the smooth steel kept the soil from sticking to this first steel plow. Deere's plows were called "singing plows" because they vibrated with a humming sound while in use.

One of his original three plows has been on display at the Smithsonian Institution since 1938. A curator once subjected the metal to a spark test. The results showed that the plowshare and landside (the flat part of the plow turned toward the unbroken land) were steel. The moldboard (the plate attached to the wooden parts) was wrought iron. From this humble beginning, Deere established a company that became the world's largest producer of agricultural equipment.

Deere's plows were originally a sideline and he made only two more in 1838. He sold them for $10 each. He made 10 in 1839 and 40 in 1840, each with a money-back guarantee. His fame as a plow

He used the initial batch of Sheffield steel to make 400 plows.

Deere stayed in Grand Detour until 1847. A new railroad was going to bypass the town and his growing business needed a dependable method of transportation. Deere moved to Moline, Illinois, to take advantage of the water power and transportation advantages of the Mississippi River. His first plant was 1,500 square feet in size and constructed in only a few weeks. Two years later, increased demand required Deere to build a 30' x 80' two-story building.

The smoothness of steel demanded by

Photo courtesy of Deere and Company

Deere's 1875 Gilpin Sulky was the first riding plow. He is shown at the left and a representation of his Moline factory is at the right.

Deere was one quality that set his plows apart from those of his competition. He contracted with the Jones and Quigg Steel Works in Pittsburgh, and during 1846 he took delivery of the first slab of high-carbon heat-treated plow steel made in America. Deere's annual production rate reached 10,000 plows just 10 years later. Although Deere manufactured increasingly larger numbers of plows, the product quality remained uniformly high. Field trials of more than 50 plows were held at the 1878 Paris Exposition. Deere's plow was declared superior to all others and received international recognition.

Deere was a family man who had eight children and strong ties to his community. His civic accomplishments included founding the local public library and contributing to local charities. Deere always dressed well. He worked as a bank president for a time and also served a term as mayor of Moline. He was, unfortunately, a poor recorder of his business and personal life. He kept no diary, wrote few letters, and documented many of his business dealings only on tiny scraps of paper. The picture of Deere on page 34 was made at a time when unsmiling expressions were common in formal portraits. Contrary to his gruff appearance here, he was a gentle and pleasant person who had an impeccable reputation.

As his company grew, Deere realized his shortcomings as a business person. Although he remained his company's president, in 1848 his activities began to center more on sales and transportation. Ten years later, he sold his interests jointly to a daughter and a son. After that, he still often went to the plant, and he remained an active participant in his company until his death in 1886.

References and Resources

The Story of John Deere by Darragh Aldrich, 1942 (privately printed).

American Science and Invention by Mitchell Wilson, Bonanza Books, 1960.

Pamphlets supplied by Deere and Co.

Dictionary of American Biography, Charles Scribner's Sons Publishers, 1932; with supplemental updates.

National Cyclopedia of American Biography, James T. White & Co. Publishers, 1891; with supplemental updates.

Norbert Rillieux

U.S. Department of Energy

Born:
March 17,
1806, in New
Orleans,
Louisiana

Died:
October 8,
1894, in Paris,
France

THE average American uses about 90 pounds of sugar per year. Most of this popular sweetner comes in the form of white granulated sugar used in food processed by factories. In the first half of the nineteenth century, however, the only sugar available to consumers was dark. It was also either lumpy or thick and syrupy like molasses. The considerable heat needed to remove water from cane or beet juice tended to caramelize the sugar. Heat produced the sugar's brown color and altered its taste. More important, the production process involved dangerous work because people hand poured the boiling juice. Norbert Rillieux made sugar production safer and less energy intensive with his invention in 1843 of the multiple-effect vacuum evaporator.

Rillieux was free born in New Orleans to a wealthy French engineer father who had invented a steam-powered cotton-baling process. His mother was a slave. Rillieux received good grades in primary school and showed an aptitude for mechanical subjects. With advanced educational opportunities limited for black Americans in the early 1800s, Rillieux's father sent him to study in Paris, France. He earned an engineering degree at L'Ecole Centrale. His academic performance was so superior that he became an instructor of applied mechanics after graduation. At the age of 24, Rillieux published well-regarded scientific papers on steam engines and the efficient use of steam energy. During this period, he developed the theory for his sealed evaporator.

The old way of refining sugar involved boiling cane juice in a series of open pots. Workers using long-handled ladles transferred the boiling juice from one kettle to another as the sugar concentrations increased. This was back-breaking and dangerous work. One hundred pounds of cane juice yielded only 11 or 12 pounds of sugar. Open-kettle evaporation was a slow process and produced lumpy brown sugar. It also proved inefficient because much of the sweetener evaporated away.

Rillieux knew that a liquid under a vacuum would boil at a temperature lower than 212° F. He tried this with a container of cane juice, placing the liquid inside a sealed copper kettle and lowering the container's pressure with a vacuum pump. By maintaining a small fire underneath the kettle, Rillieux kept the boiling temperature below the point at which caramelization occurred but still evaporated the unwanted water. The water vapor left the container through the vacuum pump. Others had tried the same technique with limited success, so Rillieux improved his system through an ingenious method. He enclosed condensing coils in the vacuum chamber and used the vapor from one chamber to evaporate the juice in another chamber kept at a lower pressure. Since the pressure in the second chamber was lower than that in the first, the liquid boiled at a lower temperature. Rillieux used the same heat over and over again—a brilliant idea. Rillieux's multistage evaporator greatly reduced the amount of heat energy required. His invention laid the foundation for all modern industrial evaporation operations that require fast and inexpensive processing of large quantities of liquids.

Because the equipment involved was complicated and the system unproven, Rillieux could not interest French machinery manufacturers. He returned to New Orleans in 1832 to try his luck at making a

prototype in the land of his birth. He first established himself as the chief engineer in a New Orleans sugar factory owned by Edmund Forstall. Partly relying on his father's reputation, he persuaded some sugar plantation owners to take a gamble on his new method of production. He had some early failures until he began using superior equipment made to his specifications by Merrick and Towne Co. of Philadelphia. One of his showpiece installations was a three-stage evaporator at Theodore Packwood's Myrtle Grove plantation near New Orleans. It was a complicated installation that took two years to become operational, but it functioned with complete success. In Rillieux's vacuum pan, the cane juice boiled at only 120° to 140° F and produced excellent white granulated sugar. Myrtle Grove sugar was the highest quality ever seen and cost only half as much to produce. After his experimental work on the plantations, Rillieux took out a patent in 1843 that he titled "Vacuum Pan." It was the first basic patent issued to a black American. The Rillieux System represented a complete change in procedure. A single worker, using safely positioned external valves, operated a completely enclosed device. Sugar producers in the United States, Cuba, and Mexico almost immediately adopted the evaporators, and Rillieux became quite prosperous.

Rillieux's evaporation system revolutionized the world's sugar industry, and it is used today in practically every factory that produces a liquid product. Examples of processes that use it include the making of soap, glue, soup, and condensed milk. Rillieux's evaporators also remove salt from sea water and recycle liquids on the space shuttles. Nonetheless, few people know of Rillieux—partly because his invention is not a consumer product. The National Geographic Society described him as "one of the most neglected of major American inventors."

As a youngster, Rillieux lived in a cultured and well-to-do atmosphere. He grew to be a proud and confident man. Later in life, he had a reputation for brutal frankness and often said exactly what was on his mind. His personality irritated many people in a region of the country where diplomacy was a way of life. Rillieux was financially inde-

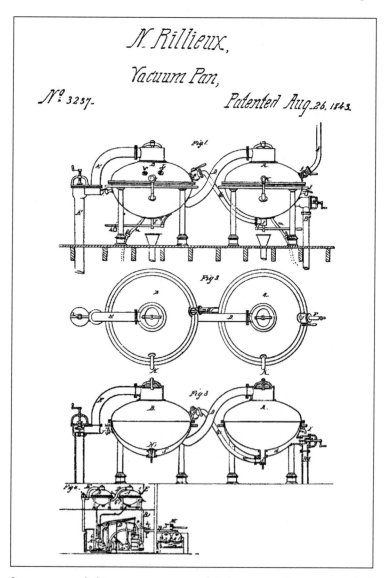

Sugar-cane juice was processed into sugar in two sealed evaporators. The one on the right used waste heat from the one on the left.

pendent and one of the most successful people in Louisiana in his day. Yet he was excluded from many social functions because of his fiery disposition and his color. With poor grace, he tolerated the situation until 1854. That year, free blacks in America were required to carry special identification. The indignity was more than this proud, intelligent, and outspoken man could tolerate. Rillieux left New Orleans for Paris and never returned.

He found a different sort of prejudice in France. Certain French technologists had misused his process and made it look ineffective. That hurt the good name he had developed in America. Rillieux turned his back on technology and took up archeology. He spent a great deal of time in his advanced years in the study and translation of Egyptian hieroglyphics. He continued some minor work on evaporating systems for sugar beets and took out his final patent at the age of 75. Just before his death, he said his biggest disappointment was France's refusal to credit him for the invention of multistage evaporation.

Rillieux kept no diary and wrote few letters. Little is known of his personal life but his tombstone suggests that he married a woman who was 21 years younger than he was. No known painting or photograph of Rillieux exists. However, he was described in his later years as an imposing figure with "a high forehead, luxuriant white hair, and a mustache and full beard trimmed in the French style."

A 1934 bronze plaque designed and made in Holland belatedly commemorates his work on behalf of every sugar-producing country in the world. Sponsored by the International Sugar Cane Technologists, it is now displayed at the Louisiana State Museum in New Orleans.

References and Resources

Black Pioneers of Science and Invention by Louis Haber, Harcourt Brace World, 1970.

Black American Inventors by R. C. Hayden, Addison-Wesley, 1972.

A Biographical History of Blacks in America Since 1528 by Edgar Toppin, David McKay, 1971.

Those Inventive Americans, National Geographic Society, 1971.

Engines of Our Ingenuity–Norbert Rillieux (No. 236) by John Lienhard, National Public Radio (program produced by University of Houston).

The Story of Sugar by C. D. Bardorf, Chemical Publishing Co., 1924.

The Thomas Flyer

Around-the-World Race, February to July 1908

National Automobile Museum, Reno, Nevada

This photograph shows the Thomas Flyer restored to its 1908 appearance.

WARNER Brothers Studios in Hollywood produced an entertaining tongue-in-cheek comedy in 1965 titled "The Great Race." Tony Curtis played the hero, The Great Leslie. Jack Lemmon was the villainous Professor Fate, who tried continually to outwit Leslie. Natalie Wood starred as reporter Maggie Dubois, who accompanied both Leslie and Fate at various times during the motion picture. Set in the early 1900s, the story centered on an around-the-world automobile race that started in New York City and ended in Paris. It was based on an actual event. The race took place in 1908, and an American car, the Thomas Flyer, won it.

In the days before radio and television, road races provided a popular means for advertising a motor car. The Stanley twins used this method with their steamer, as did Henry Ford with his Number 999 race car. Automobile manufacturers often approached newspapers to see if they might want to sponsor races. Through such a sequence of events the *New York Times* and Paris's *Le Matin* agreed to jointly sponsor the longest road race in history. The race attracted six entrants, including three from France: a 24 hp De Dion, a 30 hp Moto-Bloc, and a Sizaire-Naudin, the smallest vehicle in the race, with a 12 hp engine. A 40 hp Protos from Germany and a 24 hp Zust from Italy rounded out the European field. At 60 hp, the Thomas Flyer, with its chain drive, was the most powerful car in the race. It was the only one not specially modified for the race. The Thomas was a stock model selected just six days before the beginning of the race. Built by the E. R. Thomas Motor Co. in Buffalo, New York, the car sold for $4,500.

The race route went west toward the Pacific Ocean at a time when roads outside of cities were practically nonexistent. Fuel centers and repair facilities were miles apart. In addition, the motor cars of that day were not the smooth-running machines we know today. To take such a vehicle on a 22,000 mile trip around the world took courageous drivers and mechanics.

The cars lined up at Times Square on a bright but cold February 12. It was Abraham Lincoln's birthday, a holiday for many. The president of the Automobile Club of America started the race at 11:15 A.M. with a gold-plated pistol. For the next five months, readers of the *New York Times* eagerly followed the race in dispatches written by W. J. Henley and other reporters. Henley rode in the Thomas car with driver Montague Roberts, mechanic George Schuster, and assistant driver J. P. Birdener. Each wore a heavy coat and packed for a long cold journey.

The start was witnessed by 250,000 people who lined the first eight miles of the route. The cars headed north over snow-covered roads to Hudson for the first night. The excitement of the start caused some first-day difficulties. With the snow four feet deep along some parts of the road, both the De Dion and the Thomas became stuck. Local citizens had to push them out. The Zust missed a turn in Poughkeepsie and the driver refused to stop to ask directions until he was hopelessly off track. The Protos lost its way at Peekskill and had to take a rugged four-mile detour. Roads at that time were generally unmarked, and reliable maps were not available. The underpowered single-cylinder Sizaire-Naudin dropped out the second day.

The five racers turned west and drove across New York. They continued to northern Ohio and then along a route that roughly paralleled the current Interstate 80. The Moto-Bloc had engine problems in Cedar Rapids, Iowa, and left the race. The remaining four cars drove to San Francisco and then to Seattle.

The German Protos, which came in second, is on display at the Deutsches Museum in Munich.

The Thomas reached Seattle 11 days ahead of its nearest rival. It then went by ship to Valdez, Alaska, the next target city, arriving March 30. The crew found that the spring thaw made the roads impassable, and the Thomas returned to Seattle. In the meantime, the cars were redirected to travel by ship to Yokohama, Japan. The Thomas arrived in Yokohama on May 12 and started the 350-mile cross-country trip on May 18. The Japanese roads were very narrow, and the mountainous ascents were steep and hazardous. Groups of local citizens often had to haul the car. The Thomas took three days to reach the western port of Tsuruoka for shipment to Vladivostok, Russia.

All the competitors arrived in Vladivostok at about the same time and continued on toward Paris, 9,280 miles away. The Thomas crew reported a particularly difficult trip across Russia. The De Dion dropped out during the Russian leg. The Thomas engine held up remarkably well throughout the race, but the poor conditions of the Russian roads required an estimated 8,000 miles of driving in low gear. (As an example of conditions, more than 450 miles of the road consisted of railroad ties.) The Thomas was not designed for extended low-gear operation, and the crew had to replace transmission gears twice. It completed both transmission repairs out of doors in rural villages. During the entire 72 days crossing Russia, the crew had poor food and water. They slept only five nights in bed. Because of the uncertainty of supplies, they often carried two barrels of oil in addition to their normal 800-pound load. The drivers, mechanics, and reporters changed several times and Schuster, the mechanic, was the only original crew member left. He also acted as head driver after the car left American soil.

The cars were often close, and they passed each other at various times while racing through Russia. The Thomas crossed into Europe on July 9 with a commanding lead. It reached the outskirts of Paris on the evening of July 30. Throngs of well wishers were cheering the crew when a local police officer stopped Schuster. The Thomas had no lights. They had broken off earlier in the race and the officer would not allow the car to continue. A helpful man riding a lighted bicycle provided assistance. The crew put the bicycle between the two front seats and the Thomas finished the race at 8:00 P.M. in front of *Le Matin*'s newspaper office. The German Protos came in second, 26 days later. The Italian Zust was third, an additional 3 days farther back.

The longest road race in history was over!

The overall distance was approximately 22,000 miles, with 13,341 miles over land. The E. R. Thomas Motor Co. proudly advertised that after an engine check in Chicago near the beginning of the race, none of its engine valves were ground or replaced. Not one spark plug was changed and the Thomas never went inside a repair shop.

Sales of Thomas motor cars soared. However, the company went out of production in 1919. The Thomas Flyer was sold in 1912, and it deteriorated in storage until Harrah's Automobile Collection of Reno, Nevada, obtained it in 1964. With the help of 92-year-old George Schuster, Harrah's restored the car to simulate its appearance during the race. The Thomas Flyer's unveiling in the mid-1960s inspired a Hollywood producer to make a movie based on the great race won by an American driving an American car.

References and Resources

The New York Times, 13 February 1908; 1 March 1908; 5 July 1908; 31 July 1908; 16 August 1908.

Harrah's Automobile Collection, two undated news releases, circa 1965.

The Thomas Flyer (brochure), E. R. Thomas Motor Co., from Ford Motor Archives, Dearborn, MI.

Cyrus Hall McCormick

Chicago Historical Society

MANY people might identify the incandescent lamp, photography, or the automobile as the greatest invention of the nineteenth century. However, some experts in the history of technology give that distinction to the less-exciting reaper. Cyrus McCormick's successful 1831 reaper freed many people from working the soil, permitting them to get on with the Industrial Revolution.

McCormick was the forty-seventh person to file a patent for a reaper. He initially had no interest in being an inventor, but merely wanted to adapt his father's mower to cut wheat on the family farm. His first public demonstration took place in 1831, but McCormick didn't patent his reaper until 1834 and didn't seek a market until 1840.

As a youth, McCormick attended the rural elementary school near his home irregularly. He received much of his basic education from his parents. His father, Robert, was a successful farmer who owned 1,200 acres of land in the Shenandoah Valley. He also had two grist mills, two saw mills, a lime kiln, and a blacksmith shop. The elder McCormick was a constant tinkerer, and he invented a crude grain-reaping machine that he worked on over a 20-year period. The younger McCormick had similar mechanical interests and decided to work on the reaper after his father abandoned it.

Cutting wheat, or reaping, was a difficult and labor-intensive farming practice. Swinging long-handled scythes, lines of men cut the wheat at harvest time. Each man could cut only two or three acres per day. Women and children followed the men, tying the grain in sheaves for several days of drying. This was back-breaking, arm-wrenching work for everyone involved, and the process had not changed much since

Born:
February 15, 1809, in Rockbridge County, Virginia

Died:
May 13, 1884, in Chicago, Illinois

the time of the ancient Romans. To mechanize the operation, some inventors tried using a revolving reel of blades, much like that used in a reel-type lawn mower. Other designs used a sharpened rotating disk or mechanical scissors. Robert McCormick's reaper used revolving beaters to press stalks against stationary knives. Like earlier designs, it worked only under ideal conditions and proved ineffective on hillside fields and with wet crops.

Cyrus McCormick took over the project in May 1831 when he was 22. His biggest change was to develop a horizontal toothed sickle bar that moved back and forth to cut the grain. A large reel gently pressed the brittle wheat stalks against the sickle bar and a platform caught the severed stalks. The reaper rode on one broad wheel that powered both the cutter and reel through a

version of a reaper. But the financial depression known as the Panic of 1837 kept him from success. He had a 500-acre farm, received as a gift from his father, and it required time to manage properly. Nonetheless, McCormick licensed several manufacturers in New York, Virginia, and Ohio, and sold two reapers in 1840. He sold six or seven in 1842 and 29 in 1843. His reaper cost about $100, and he marketed it as the "Virginia Reaper."

series of gears. It was offset to allow the horses pulling the reaper to walk in the most recently cut row. McCormick tried it out in a neighbor's oat field the following July. Noisy, awkward, and ugly, it rattled across the field frightening horses as it successfully cut the grain. In just a few hours, McCormick's crude reaper did the daily work of three men. McCormick continued to make improvements and adjustments

The most successful of McCormick's competitors was a one-eyed ex-sailor, Obed Hussey. A gentle, quiet man, Hussey patented his machine just a few months before McCormick. Hussey's reaper was mostly a mower, but it did an adequate job. The rivalry between McCormick and Hussey generally took the form of reaping contests. Field conditions varied so much that neither man's reaper turned out to be the clear victor. Then, Hussey made a strategic marketing error. He settled in Baltimore and concentrated his efforts on farmers east of the Appalachian Mountains. McCormick, on the other hand, had recently visited what was then the western frontier: Ohio, Michigan, Illinois, Wisconsin, Indiana, and Missouri. He found prairies waiting for John Deere's plow and his reaper. Although he disliked farming, McCormick moved to Chicago in 1848. At the time, it was a small city of only 17,000 and the center of the agricultural market. The city had excellent road, rail, and water transportation. It attracted immigrants by the thousands.

This reaper was made in 1850 and is virtually identical to the one demonstrated at the 1851 Crystal Palace Exposition in London.

over the next two years. In 1833, his reaper cut all the grain on the family's farm and on several neighboring farms. He applied for and received a patent in 1834.

In competition with others, McCormick half-heartedly went on the road to sell his

McCormick struck a deal with two investors to open a factory near the north end of the Michigan Avenue bridge. His factory proved so successful that after just one year McCormick bought out his two partners. He asked his two brothers to operate the business. At this point, McCormick gave up inventing because he found he had a flair for selling his product. He developed several modern marketing techniques.

From his own farming experience, McCormick knew that farmers could pay for a reaper only after the harvest. Consequently, he asked for a down payment of just $35, with the balance due in December, and with further credit available. Each reaper had a written money-back guarantee, and customer complaints received prompt attention. McCormick and his brothers often visited wheat fields during the harvest season, flattering all there by their presence and helping to build product loyalty. McCormick advertised heavily in newspapers and with handbills. He knew that most farmers would make their own adjustments and repairs. To accommodate them, he printed an instruction manual—and he was the first manufacturer to do so. His sales grew from 700 in 1848 to 1,603 in 1850.

In 1851, the Great Chicago Fire destroyed McCormick's factory and almost everything else over the surrounding 2,000-acre area. McCormick had bought land on the southwest side of the city just four days before the fire, and he rebuilt on that site. Newspapers of the time described his new factory as the largest in the world. McCormick lent substantial amounts of his own money to help other businesses and families during the rebuilding of Chicago. The city's convention center, McCormick Place, is named in his honor.

Also in 1851, McCormick employees took a reaper to London for display at the Crystal Palace Exhibition, the first world's fair. *The Times* newspaper of London called it a "cross between a flying machine, a wheel barrow, and a chariot." During a competition working with wet grain, a Hussey machine soon clogged and stopped. A British machine could not even start cutting. But the Virginia Reaper smoothly cut at the rate of 20 acres per day. *The Times* then wrote that McCormick's reaper was worth more to England than the entire cost of the exposition. McCormick opened sales offices in Europe and saw total annual sales increase to over 5,000 by the outbreak of the Civil War.

Throughout his life, McCormick enjoyed tailor-made clothes, lavish floral displays, and travel. He was an honest and deeply

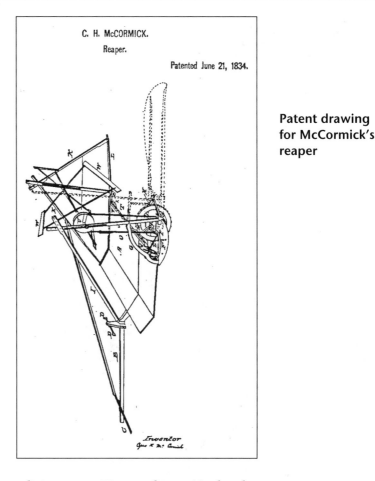

C. H. McCORMICK.
Reaper.

Patented June 21, 1834.

Inventor
Cyrus H. McCormick

Patent drawing for McCormick's reaper

religious man. He was almost 49 when he married. Eighteen years after his death, his company merged with others to become International Harvester.

References and Resources

Those Inventive Americans, National Geographic Society, 1971.

"The Great Reaper War" by Joseph Gies, in *American Heritage of Invention and Technology*, Winter 1990.

McCormick Reaper Centennial, International Harvester, 1931.

History of American Science and Invention by Mitchell Wilson, Bonanza Books, 1960.

Dictionary of American Biography, Charles Scribner's Sons Publishers, 1931; with supplemental updates.

National Cyclopedia of American Biography, James T. White & Co. Publishers, 1891; with supplemental updates.

McGraw-Hill Encyclopedia of Biography, McGraw-Hill Publishers, 1973.

Joseph Rogers Brown

Brown & Sharpe

Born:
January 26, 1810, in Warren, Rhode Island

Died:
July 23, 1876, on the Isle of Shoals, New Hampshire

Joseph Rogers Brown, inventor of the universal milling machine

MANY modern factories manufacture their products by shaping metal. They use machine tools to cut, bend, drill, mill, and grind. One American inventor stands out as the person most responsible for introducing modern milling machines and grinders for factory production: Joseph Rogers Brown. Brown was a man who could operate machine tools as well as a concert violinist could play a violin.

Brown's father operated a machine shop that specialized in clock and watchmaking. His father introduced him to the machinist's trade, which at that time attracted young people who wanted to work with modern technical equipment. Brown attended local public school and left home at 17 to work as a machinist at a textile mill. After a short term with a second manufacturer, he re-turned to help his father complete contracts to construct tower clocks in Pawtucket, Taunton, and New Bedford. Both men emphasized precision and quality work. Some of their clocks were still operating perfectly 100 years later.

Brown set up his own shop in Providence to manufacture small lathes and machinist's tools. His father soon joined him, and they formed the David Brown and Son Co. The two worked together for eight years until Brown's father retired. The company continued to make and repair clocks and watches and added precision instruments. The younger Brown's first significant invention was a linear dividing machine. It was the first automatic machine that accurately made precise rulers. A year later, Brown brought out a vernier caliper reading to 0.001". It was the first practical tool for exact measurement that had a price that the average machinist could afford. Brown introduced and mass produced the world's first practical vernier-scaled micrometer. He called it the Pocket Sheet Metal Gage, and the tool was an immediate success. Brown's measuring equipment was so popular that he had to expand his 14-person workforce. His Providence factory would soon grow to 141,000 square feet, more than three acres under roof, and 2,000 employees.

Lucian Sharpe was an apprentice who showed an aptitude for business. Always a person who encouraged others who had talent, Brown knew that ability was rare in a person who understood machines and processes. Brown took Sharpe in as a partner in 1853, and the company became the J. R. Brown & Sharpe Co.

The business began to slowly grow. Sharpe very ably took care of financial matters, leaving Brown to develop his inventions. The company's reputation grew to the extent that Willcox and Gibbs, a new company in Philadelphia, asked Brown & Sharpe to make the first 12 production models of their sewing machines. At the time, Brown & Sharpe was fairly well equipped. The company had two engine lathes, two hand lathes, a drill press, and two planers. It decided to take a gamble with the unproven sewing machine company. Instead of using item-by-item production, Brown & Sharpe adopted a production-line technique using equipment that was 4 to 10 times more costly. The risk paid off. The sewing machines they made for Willcox and Gibbs were of such high quality that they sold immediately. Willcox and Gibbs ordered 100 more. It was a huge order and proved that Brown & Sharpe's production decision was the correct one. The contract with Willcox and Gibbs led Brown & Sharpe into the machine tool industry. It gave the company the opportunity to test the tools it would market and kept it conscious of the real needs of manufacturers in precision, speed, and cost. Brown & Sharpe continued to make sewing machines for Willcox and Gibbs until the 1950s.

High production rates required the use of machine tools that simply did not exist. So Brown invented them. He invented the universal milling machine so he could quickly make any size of twist drill. He also used the four-speed 1,800-pound machine for spiral milling, gear cutting, and other work that previously required tedious hand operations. It took up only 55" x 44" of floor space. All adjustments were read on a dial that was accurate to 0.001". Brown invented a formed gear cutter to go with the mill. The cutter could be sharpened without changing its shape. Brown & Sharpe sold 10 universal milling machines in 1862 and 17 over the next three years. By 1870, 20 had been sold overseas in 12 different countries.

Brown also invented the universal grinding machine to grind needle bars for the sewing machines the company made. This was his greatest achievement, and it took 10 years of work to perfect. Use of the universal grinder permitted hardening items first and then accurately grinding them to size with little waste. According to Brown in his 1876 patent application, the universal grinder was "a machine on which

straight, tapering, curved, and irregular work, either inside or outside, can be ground with great accuracy." The 2,600-pound machine could handle 8"-diameter work up to 16" long. It had six speeds between 2,000 rpm and 3,400 rpm. Universal grinders are still in use throughout the world and differ little from Brown's original design. Brown conceived his inventions in such broad terms that they became important tools in all machine shop work. His machines won industrial awards at exhibitions in Paris (1867, 1878, and 1889) Vienna (1873), and

Brown & Sharpe

The first universal milling machine

at the United States Centennial in Philadelphia (1876).

Brown & Sharpe often communicated with company sales representatives by telegraph. It was not uncommon for a telegraph operator to occasionally misread a transmission. Like many companies, Brown & Sharpe used a non-secret code that would be difficult to misread even if a letter or two were dropped out. To save telegraph words, it was standard among many companies to

Brown & Sharpe

The No. 2 universal grinding machine

transmit the term ARMOUR to mean "By what line have you shipped?" AFFRAY meant "What is the price of?" Those codes were published in books such as Bloomer's *Commercial Cryptograph* and *A, B, C Telegraph Code*. Brown & Sharpe code-named their universal milling machine ABBOTT and their universal grinding machine MARIA. An "AFFRAY ABBOTT" message meant "What is the price of the universal milling machine?"

The dour facial expression in the portrait of Brown shown on page 46 is quite mis-

leading. In Brown's day, such expressions were common in portraits. In reality, Brown was a pleasant man. He loved machine shop work and could expertly operate any piece of equipment. His enthusiasm was contagious and people eagerly helped him in his experimental work. He kept nothing secret and never felt threatened by exceptionally bright employees. Brown's personality and intelligence encouraged many talented people to join his company. One of the more notable was Charles Norton who worked for him for 20 years. (See pages 112-114.) In 1900, Norton went on to establish the Norton Grinder Co. in Massachusetts.

Brown married twice and had one daughter. His unexpected death occurred while on a short vacation on the Isle of Shoals, just off New Hampshire's sea coast.

References and Resources

This Is Brown & Sharpe, a brochure from Brown & Sharpe Co., code 3M 11/78F.

Brown & Sharpe Precision Tools 1990 catalog.

Brown & Sharpe trade publications, collected at the archives of the Henry Ford Museum, Dearborn, MI.

Nuts and Bolts of the Past by David Freeman Hawke, Harper & Row, 1988.

Dictionary of American Biograhy, Charles Scribner's Sons Publishers, 1932; with supplemental updates.

National Cyclopedia of American Biography, James T. White & Co. Publishers, 1891; with supplemental updates.

Elisha Graves Otis

Courtesy of Otis Elevator Co.

Born: August 11, 1811, in Halifax, Vermont

Died: April 8, 1861, in Yonkers, New York

IF you ask a dozen people what they consider the safest method of transportation, few would pick the elevator. Yet the total distance traveled in 1979 by all the elevators in North America was 1.7 billion miles—with fewer than one fatality per 100 million miles. The elevator remains the safest form of public transportation, and it is five times safer than using stairs. The elevator has not always had such an excellent record. Early hoists relied exclusively on the strength of the lifting rope to raise a load safely. Failure of the rope could prove fatal. Elisha Graves Otis was the first person to create an elevator that would not fall if its hoisting rope broke. He called his 1852 invention the safety elevator or *safety hoister*. Some people feel that this invention made the construction of skyscrapers possible. Even representatives of the Smithsonian Institution have written that a strong argument can be made for regarding Otis as the skyscraper's inventor.

Otis was born on a Vermont farm, where he remained until the age of 19. He received a typical rural-school education before moving to Troy, New York, to seek his fortune. Over the next five years, he worked for several construction companies. Then for another three years, he hauled goods for a living. With the money he saved, he opened a small machine shop, then a grist mill, and finally a saw mill, where he produced lumber for making carriages. None of these businesses was particularly successful because chronic poor health often kept Otis from his work.

In 1845, Otis moved across the Hudson River to Albany and went to work as a master mechanic at a bed-manufacturing factory, O. Tingley and Co. He stayed there for three years before moving to another bed factory in Yonkers. The expanding Maize and Burns Co. hired Otis to organize and install its machinery. In particular, Maize and Burns wanted him to build a steam-powered hoist to lift heavy equipment to the upper floor. A steam engine turned a winding drum wrapped with rope tied to the lifting platform. Reversing the steam engine allowed for a controlled descent.

Early hoists used muscle power to raise and lower materials. James Watt's steam engine provided the first mechanical power for elevators. The steam engine was first used around 1800 to lift coal up mine shafts in England. Elevators came into common use for moving freight in American and English factories during the early 1800s. Hydraulically operated ones pushed from the bottom with a piston, usually using water in a cylinder. Although safer than pulling from the top with ropes, as is the design in today's hydraulic elevators, they were quite slow.

Otis had some early experience with inventing. While working in Albany, he constructed a turbine water wheel of his own design. He also invented improved brakes for rail-operated vehicles, an automatic wood-turning machine, a rotary oven for bakeries, and several other items. Building an elevator was not a difficult assignment for him, but Otis felt particularly concerned about safety. He wanted to design an elevator that would not fall if the lifting rope or

Otis demonstrates his safety elevator at the 1853 Crystal Palace Exposition.

chain broke. The key element in his first experimental safety elevator was a wagon spring at the top of the platform. The ends of the spring locked into ratchets on either side of the hoist's guide rails. With the lifting rope attached to the center of the spring, the weight of the platform exerted enough tension on the spring to pull its ends in and keep them from touching the two ratchets. If the rope broke, the spring's tension would be released and the ends would jam into the ratchets, securely locking the elevator in place. This method worked well at the factory, and Otis's patent was based on it.

In 1853, America sponsored the second

world's fair. It was officially known as the Exhibition of the Industry of All Nations, and more commonly called the New York Crystal Palace Exposition. At this exposition, Otis publicly demonstrated his invention in a most dramatic way. With a large audience on hand, he ascended approximately 20 feet on a platform loaded with boxes, barrels, and other freight. At the proper dramatic moment, an assistant cut the hoisting rope with an ax. The elevator spring's tension released immediately and engaged the rachets. The elevator held fast. The crowd applauded while Otis removed his silk top hat, bowed, and said, "All safe, ladies and gentlemen, all safe." He made many demonstrations, always before a large audience.

About that time, Maize and Burns went bankrupt and Otis considered going to California to search for gold. He might have done so, but he changed his mind after receiving an unexpected order for two safety elevators from a furniture manufacturer. Two of the manufacturer's employees had died when a hoisting rope broke on their elevator. The request encouraged Otis to open his own factory on September 20, 1853, and he established the entire elevator industry on that date. He used some of the space vacated by his bankrupt employer. However, there was little need for elevators as passenger-carrying devices because skyscrapers were not yet being constructed. The E. G. Otis Co. had only 10 employees and by 1856 had sold only 45 elevators. All of them were used for freight purposes.

Finally, in 1857, Otis installed the world's first passenger elevator in New York City. It was used in the five-story building of E. V. Haughwout and Co. at Broadway and Broome Streets. Haughwout dealt in French china and glassware. The elevator that Otis installed lifted seven passengers from the first floor to the fifth in about one minute. A little over a century later, two million elevators were in use throughout the world. Elevators allowed companies to add more usable space by erecting taller buildings,

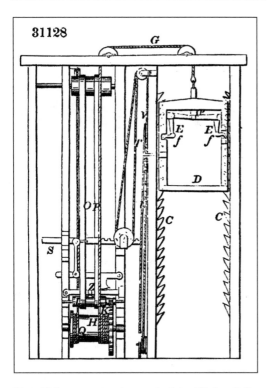

Detail from patent granted to Elisha Otis for elevator safety device. The patent also covered a drum counterweight.

first hotel elevator in 1866 in New York's St. James Hotel, and one of their elevators was the only non-French item allowed on the 1889 Eiffel Tower. Otis's sons built the inclined elevator between the first and second levels because no French manufacturer wanted that particularly difficult part of the job.

References and Resources

Tell Me about Elevators, Otis Elevator Co., 1974.

Elisha Graves Otis by Peter Thompson, Otis Elevator Co. (undated press release).

Smithsonian Book of Invention, Smithsonian Institution, 1978.

Dictionary of American Biography, Charles Scribner's Sons Publishers, 1932; with supplemental updates.

National Cyclopedia of American Biography, James T. White and Co. Publishers, 1891; with supplemental updates.

McGraw-Hill Encyclopedia of Biography, McGraw-Hill Publishers, 1973.

and cities began to expand toward the sky instead of just across the horizon.

Otis spent much of his time improving his basic invention. For a source of lifting power, he invented and patented the Otis Improved Double Oscillating Steam Engine with an attached winding drum. Its two connected and reversible oscillating cylinders were compactly designed, taking up a minimal 20 square feet of floor space. The independently controlled engine was part of a system, or package, that the company heavily advertised. Previously, most elevators operated from a belt connected to a rotating power shaft attached to the factory's main steam engine.

Orders for Otis's company increased, many for public buildings throughout the country, but Otis died before it became a complete success. With his great mental ability, he contributed immensely to the potential of the elevator business. He did not die a rich man, but he left a strong reputation and a large technical base that his sons built upon. His only children, Charles and Norton, expanded the company and together shared 53 patents for elevator design and safety devices. They installed the

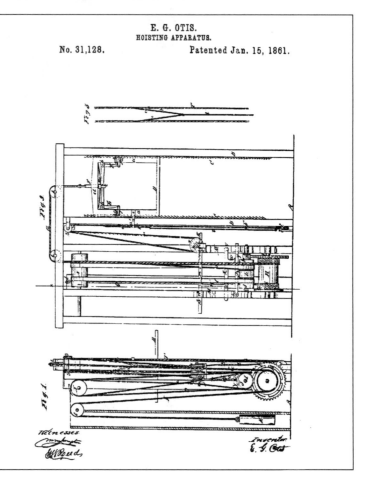

Full drawing from Otis's safety elevator patent

Christopher Latham Sholes

Smithsonian Institution Photo No. 38142

Born:
February 14, 1819, in Morresburg, Pennsylvania

Died:
February 17, 1890, in Milwaukee, Wisconsin

By the middle 1800s, several inventors had patented a number of different styles of typewriters. They called them "writing machines," and most were cumbersome and hard to use. One design required securely clamping a sheet of paper to a large roller. The user then positioned letters by hand on a circular metal frame over the paper and made impressions with a plunger. The typewriter was necessarily complex, and all early designs proved so complicated and tedious to use that potential purchasers showed no interest in them. In 1868, however, one design came to dominate typewriter construction with two unique ideas: The linkage mechanism resembled familiar piano keys, and the paper carriage moved one space after each letter was printed. The person who developed this first modern typewriter was Christopher Latham Sholes, a printer, newspaper editor, postmaster, and politician.

Sholes was born on a farm. At the age of 14, he left school to apprentice with a local newspaper, the *Danville Intelligencer*. His interest in inventing began during his apprenticeship. The young Sholes devised a method of addressing newspapers by printing subscriber names in the margin. After completing his four-year apprenticeship, Sholes moved with his family to Wisconsin. He spent the rest of his life there.

Within a year of moving to Wisconsin, Sholes became the editor of the territorial legislature's journal, the *Wisconsin Enquirer*. During his early working life, Sholes worked for five newspapers, usually as an editor. He also served for a while as postmaster of Kenosha. After Wisconsin became the thirtieth state, Sholes became active in politics, in addition to his work as postmaster and journalist. He was poorly suited to the role of politician, being soft spoken and suffering frail health. Still, he was elected to and honorably served two terms as senator and one in the state assembly.

Sholes's extremely busy life kept him from devoting much time to inventing until 1862. That year, President Abraham Lincoln appointed him to serve as Milwaukee's Harbor Customs Collector. The job was not time consuming, and it allowed Sholes to devote more energy to refining the typewriter. An article on writing machines by inventor Ely Beach in *Scientific American* encouraged him. After discussing the article, Sholes and two friends decided to try to invent an easier-to-use, more efficient typewriter.

Sholes worked on the typewriter with a machinist named Samuel Soule. Sholes and Soule had already patented a device for automatically numbering book pages. They created their invention in a small machine shop they rented on the second floor of a brass foundry. They shared space with a third inventor, Carlos Glidden, a lawyer and court reporter. With Sholes as their unofficial leader, the three inventors collaborated on a typewriter and received a joint patent in 1868. Their invention is regarded as the first modern typewriter. They also devised the four-row universal keyboard in use today. It is often called the QWERTY layout, after the first six letters in the upper row of letter keys. The patent model had only 11 keys and was not intended as a production unit.

Sholes and his partners had an excellent product, but they soon found there was no market for it. They offered their typewriter to bankers and authors but made few sales. Bankers disliked it because they felt that typewritten contracts could be too easily altered, rendering them illegal. Although Mark Twain purchased a typewriter, there were in general too few authors to provide a reasonable market. No one considered the massive business possibilities of the typewriter. The three inventors continued to work on improvements, especially on the keyboard arrangement. One early experiment involved a single row of 44 characters, with the letters in alphabetical order.

In the Sholes typewriter, each letter was at the end of a type bar that swung in an arc on its way to the paper. Sometimes the bars collided with each other and jammed— a problem particularly for fast typists. Sholes tried many arrangements. He decided to locate the most frequently used letter combinations as far apart as possible. This would tend to slow down a fast typist and minimize jamming the type bars. The result was the QWERTY, or universal, keyboard. Mark Twain described the QWERTY keyboard arrangement as a "curiosity-breeding little joker."

Improvements to the partners' 1871 model made it the first to look like the typewriters we know. This model had a four-row keyboard and a horizontal rubber roller to hold the paper. The typewriter was mounted on a table, and a lead weight hanging from the end pulled the roller between keystrokes. A push on a foot pedal returned the paper and moved it down one line.

Sholes's typewriter patent model is on public display at the National Museum of American History in Washington, D.C.

Sholes became the machine's champion and tried without success to sell the improved version. He gave many personal demonstrations to bankers and stock brokers. But the mild-mannered man was not well suited for the job, and he made only a few sales. An 1872 front-page article in *Scientific American* generated some customers but not enough to make a difference.

With little money coming from the invention, Soule and Glidden decided to sell their rights to Sholes. Sholes patented additional improvements, mortgaging his home to finance the work. He was the only one who had faith in his design, and he persisted in working on it as long as he could. Finally, in 1873, poor sales forced him to sell out to Philo Remington for $12,000. The Remington Arms Co. wanted a new product to manufacture after making guns for the Civil War. It had excellent manufacturing machinery and skilled machinists, who perfected Sholes's invention. Using a well-established sales force, Remington introduced the successful and expensive $125 Remington-Sholes typewriter in 1874.

After purchasing the patent rights, Remington hired Sholes and two of his sons as consultants. Advanced age and delicate health cut into Sholes's productivity with inventions. He took out his last patent application in 1889. It was for an even more improved keyboard. Sholes lived to the age of 71, but he was quite weak during his last nine years. He did much of his work propped up in bed. He devoted much of his time to the perfection of the typewriter and lived to see its use established throughout the world.

The QWERTY keyboard arrangement Sholes developed is not the most efficient, though it has remained standard since the nineteenth century. To date, the most serious attempt to improve it was launched by August Dvorak in the 1930s. With a grant from the Carnegie Foundation, Dvorak and his brother-in-law William Dealey conducted studies that showed that typing students learned more rapidly with the Dvorak simplified keyboard. They also noted a reduction in errors. Dvorak and Dealey received a patent for the keyboard in 1936. Like the QWERTY arrangement, it has four rows of keys. The characters "?,.PYFGCRL/" are in the first row of letters. The Dvorak arrangement has not gained much popularity and it appears on few keyboards today.

References and Resources

The Early Word Processors by Carrol H. Blanchard, Educators Project IV, Lake George, NY, 1981.

American Science and Invention by Mitchell Wilson, Bonanza Books, 1960.

Typewriting Behavior by August Dvorak and others, American Book Co., 1936.

Dvorak typewriter layout display, National Museum of American History, Washington, DC.

Dictionary of American Biography, Charles Scribner's Sons Publishers, 1932; with supplemental updates

National Cyclopedia of American Biography, James T. White & Co. Publishers, 1891; with supplemental updates.

Elias Howe

A young apprentice in a small Massachusetts machine shop overheard a conversation between his employer and a customer. The customer predicted that the invention of a sewing machine would earn its inventor a fortune. That was the first time Elias Howe had heard of the possibility of a sewing machine. He immediately began to think of ways to make one. A few years later, in 1846, he received a patent for the first successful sewing machine.

One of eight children, Howe was born into a farming family that also operated a grain mill and a saw mill. His school attendance was erratic—he generally attended only occasionally in the winter. Howe particularly enjoyed working with the machinery in his family's saw mill. Ambitious to learn more about machinery, he apprenticed himself in 1835 to a company in Lowell that made textile equipment. An economic downturn forced him to change employers several times until he wound up in Boston with Ari Davis, a maker of surveying instruments. Davis was a superb machinist with the best equipment. In this ideal setting, Howe learned modern techniques and he gained skill in the use of many metalworking machines. His salary was $9 per week.

After marrying, Howe spent his evening hours making drawings and considering prototype sewing machines. Having three children to feed, he kept in mind the conversation he had overheard a few years earlier. He saw the sewing machine as his path to riches.

Howe first thought that the needle had to pass completely through the fabric, as in hand sewing. To test his idea, he constructed a machine with a double-pointed needle that had an eye in the middle. It proved to be a failure. Howe then thought he might try a

H. Holt and Co. Publishers, 1912

Born:
July 9, 1819, in Spenser, Massachusetts

Died:
October 3, 1867, in Brooklyn, New York

lock stitch using a needle with an eye at the point and a shuttle that would pass through the loop of thread at the proper time. Howe got the idea from the textile looms he had helped build during his apprenticeship in Lowell.

The idea was a good one and serves as the basis for all modern sewing machines. However, Howe first had to design a system with a thread-loaded shuttle on one side of the fabric, and a thread-loaded needle on the other. The shuttle had to go through the loop of thread at just the right instant—timing and positioning were all important. Howe started to make the machine in 1844 and quit his job with Davis so that he could devote full time to the project. He received financial assistance from his father and a friend whom he talked into becoming a partner. Howe and his young family moved into the top floor of the friend's home, where he began perfecting his invention. He worked on the prototype machine over the winter, completing it in April 1845. It was one of the finest working models of any invention ever constructed on the first try.

Howe's machine sewed in a different manner from that of modern sewing machines. His needle moved horizontally instead of vertically. The cloth was suspended vertically and held in place by sharp pins on a sewing plate. The curved needle moved left and right. The machine was hand operated with a crank on a small flywheel. It was somewhat awkward to use, but worked effectively. Tailors showed no interest in buying it, so Howe tried to sell it to clothing factories. During a demonstration, Howe's machine surpassed the speed of five of the fastest hand sewers at Boston's Quincy Hall Clothing Manufacturing Co. Although sewing machines could make 250 stitches per minute, the owners declined to buy any.

Howe did not consider his machine for use in the home and only tried to sell to manufacturers. But potential industrial buyers showed little interest because they thought sewing machines would force many people out of work. Also, at $300 each, the cost seemed too high. Most clothing facto-

ries would have needed 40 machines to produce the volume of hand sewing they completed. Sewing machines were the most complex item manufactured in America before the Civil War, and manufacturers were somewhat afraid of them. After months of demonstrating his machine, Howe had not sold a single one.

Howe's brother Amasa took a machine to England and struck a deal with the manufacturer of umbrellas, luggage, and shoes. For $1,500, Will Thomas received the rights to use the sewing machine in his factory, which had 5,000 employees. Thomas would patent the machine in England for Howe. Howe was to receive royalties on any machines sold in that country. Thomas insisted that Howe move to London to perfect a leather-sewing machine. Howe was reluctant, but he needed the money and soon agreed. He moved his wife and children to England in 1847, traveling in steerage, the lowest class below deck.

The working arrangement with Thomas was not satisfactory. Paid $15 a week, Howe had to do menial chores unrelated to the operation of his sewing machines. He was being treated as an employee, not a partner. After a quarrel with Howe, the manufacturer fired him. Howe then borrowed money from a coach maker named Charles Inglis, to send his family home by ship. While rooming with Inglis, he continued to work on sewing machine improvements. Still finding no customers for his machine, in 1849 he sold a model for about $25 to buy a ticket to America. He was so poor that he worked his way across to pay for food. He arrived home just in time to hear his wife was gravely ill with tuberculosis. He had to borrow $10 from his father to travel to her deathbed.

During the two and a half years Howe had spent in England, manufacturers in the U.S. had begun to use sewing machines. Howe inspected every sewing machine he could find, and he saw that

Elias Howe's original 1846 sewing machine

Smithsonian Institution Photo No. 45525B

they all contained one or more features covered by his patent. Manufacturers had made and sold sewing machines designed exactly like Howe's without paying royalties. One even advertised that its model was an improved version of the original Howe machine. Howe was determined to fight those infringing on his patent not only to protect himself, but out of anger that his family had been needlessly deprived. Howe's father mortgaged his farm to finance the court battles. Howe relentlessly fought every infringer, including Isaac Singer, who would go on to organize the huge Singer Sewing Machine Co. After long and bitter legal battles, every court ruled in Howe's favor. His patent was declared as basic in 1854 and a judgment was granted to him for every machine that infringed on his patent. Singer paid him $15,000 outright plus $25 for each future machine. Other companies paid comparable amounts, and Howe became a very wealthy man. During the late 1850s, his royalties often exceeded $4,000 per week.

The sewing machine was the first product of the industrial revolution that eased the performance of household tasks. Singer saw that characteristic and capitalized on it in his advertising. Through 1866, more than 750,000 sewing machines were sold in America, with Howe's competitors selling most of them. The Howe Sewing Machine Co., established in 1853 by Howe's brother, went out of business about 20 years after Howe died.

References and Resources

Sincere's History of the Sewing Machine by William Ewers and H. W. Baylor, Sincere Press, 1970.

The Invention of the Sewing Machine by Grace Rogers Cooper, Smithsonian Institution Press, 1968.

Nuts and Bolts of the Past by David Freeman Hawke, Harper and Row, 1988.

Dictionary of American Biography, Charles Scribner's Sons Publishers, 1932; with supplemental updates.

National Cyclopedia of American Biography, James T. White and Co. Publishers, 1891; with supplemental updates.

McGraw-Hill Encyclopedia of Biography, McGraw-Hill Publishers, 1973.

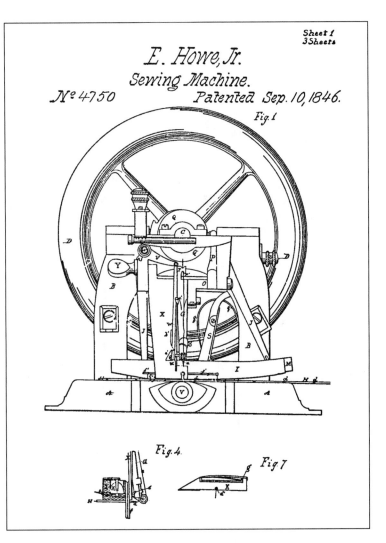

Howe's patent drawing shows the vertical wheel.

Cyrus West Field

Cyrus Field with a section of his transatlantic telegraph cable

Born:
November 30, 1819, in Stockbridge, Massachusetts

Died:
July 11, 1892, in New York, New York

To obtain European news during the mid 1800s, U.S. journalists frequently interviewed passengers leaving ships. Communication was so haphazard that freighters cruised from port to port searching for cargo. The situation greatly improved in 1866 when Cyrus Field established the first permanent transatlantic telegraph cable between Europe and North America. The project wasn't trouble free, and Field endured more than a decade of expensive cable-laying failures. Each of his 40 transatlantic crossings made him seasick.

Field was the youngest of seven sons. At the age of 15, unlike his older brothers, he decided not to attend college. (One of his brothers later became a chief justice on the U.S. Supreme Court.) Leaving home with only $8, Field found employment as an errand boy in New York City. Three years later, he went to work at a wholesale paper dealership. Field became a junior partner at 21 and almost single-handedly worked the organization out of bankruptcy. He amassed a personal wealth of $250,000. Yet long hours and six-day work weeks had left him exhausted and in frail health. He retired from the paper business at 33.

Then, Field met British engineer Frederick Gisborne, who was working on a telegraph line across the wild terrain of Canada's Newfoundland. By obtaining information from ships that first stopped at St. John's, Newfoundland, his company got news several days before the ships would arrive with it in Boston and New York. Discussions with Gisborne gave Field the idea of laying a connecting cable across the Atlantic Ocean. He also discussed possible telegraphic transmission problems with Samuel Morse. Morse assured Field that a signal could be transmitted over the 2,300-mile underwater distance. Field consulted a globe to verify that the shortest distance for the first transatlantic cable would require that it come ashore in Newfoundland. This would be an enormous undertaking, one on a scale unlike anything previously attempted. In modern times, a governmental body—rather than a single individual—would spearhead a comparable project.

At this point no U.S. company made underwater cable, so Field contacted a British manufacturer to design one. It started as a single conductor with seven strands of copper wire. The wire was insulated with three layers of a new type of rubber called *gutta-percha*. The insulation was rigid and strong, and for the next 70 years, nothing could match it for use in underwater cables. It came from the jungles of Malaya, and the name evolved from the Malaysian words for gum (*getah*) and tree (*percha*).

The insulated conductor in Field's cable was strengthened with spirally wrapped iron wires. In all, Field used 367,000 miles of iron wire. Hemp and tar sealed the entire cable. All the necessary 2,600 miles of cable was made ready in only six months. The photograph on page 58 shows the slender Field holding a piece of the cable alongside a globe, to symbolize the cable's ability to bind the world together.

The cable weighed 2,000 pounds per mile, and huge ships were needed to carry it. The U.S. and British governments offered support, each providing a ship with special cable-handling equipment and trained personnel. The U.S. Navy used its largest ship, the *Niagara*, and the Royal Navy used the *Agamemnon*, one of the last wooden-hulled ships in the British fleet. During the summer of 1857, each was loaded in Ireland with about 1,300 miles of cable. The plan was for the *Niagara* to begin laying cable and splice it to that on the *Agamemnon* halfway to Newfoundland. Complex machinery let out the garden-hose-sized cable as the ships sailed west at a slow 4 mph. Tension was carefully adjusted using sensitive brakes to support the enormous weight of the cable hanging thousands of feet to the ocean floor.

After only 335 miles, the brakes grabbed too firmly and the cable broke. It fell into the ocean, and could not be retrieved. Although the corporation lost $500,000, Field used his persuasive manner and impressive organizing skills to arrange four more attempts. The fourth succeeded temporarily. On August 16, 1858, Queen Victoria sent the first official transatlantic telegraph message to President James Buchanan. It consisted of a 90-word greeting.

Receivers at each end of the cable used unique signal amplifiers. Silk thread suspended a magnet inside a coil of fine copper wire. The thread had a mirror attached near its midpoint. Weak electrical telegraph signals arrived at the coil, causing the magnet to rotate slightly. The rotation made the

mirror move slowly one way or the other. Light reflected by the mirror would move to the left or right indicating Morse code dots and dashes. This sensitive galvanometer sometimes gave incorrect readings and required confirmation from the sender. The photograph below shows the setup used in Newfoundland. At a maximum transmission rate of four words per minute, transatlantic telegraphy was much slower than land telegraphy. Queen Victoria's message took more than 16 hours to send and verify.

About 400 messages were transmitted before the cable broke on September 1. An economic depression in 1860 and the Civil War that followed delayed further efforts. Yet Field had tremendous personal drive and never lost sight of his goal. The American and British governments realized that

This sensitive galvanometer was used in Newfoundland in 1858. It received a message from Queen Victoria to President James Buchanan.

the cable was more necessary than ever and supported Field in every way possible. Before the Civil War was over, Field had engaged the services of a huge British steamship.

At 692 feet in length, the *Great Eastern* had about five times more capacity than the next-largest ship. No ship larger was built for almost 50 years. The ship had been designed to transport 4,000 passengers to the

East Indies without having to refuel. Instead, the owners decided to operate it on the shorter, more competitive Atlantic Ocean routes. The *Great Eastern* never made a profit as a passenger vessel, but its great size proved ideal for carrying all the underwater cable necessary to span the ocean.

The crew of the *Great Eastern* started laying cable from Ireland in 1865. About 600 miles from completion, the cable broke and

The British steamship, *Great Eastern*

fell two and a half miles to the ocean floor. Weak grappling equipment could not lift the broken end of the new heavier cable. Yet, even this sixth failure did not deter Field. The next year he made another attempt and that one succeeded completely. The cable was permanently completed on July 27 between Valentia, Ireland, and Hearts Content, Newfoundland. The project was called the greatest engineering feat of the century up to that time.

This event was almost immediately followed by completion of a second cable. Field ordered the *Great Eastern* back out to sea the day after it landed. Using better grappling equipment, trained personnel recovered the broken end of the cable that had fallen in 1865 and spliced it to a new section. Within days, people were literally standing in line to send transatlantic messages at $5 to $10 per word.

Field received innumerable awards and other forms of recognition. He donated most of his monetary awards to the New York Metropolitan Museum of Art. Field went on to assist with cable laying in many other countries. He also helped with the elevated railroads in New York City and devoted much time to their completion. While in his seventies, Field discovered that most of his wealth was gone through mishandling by financial advisors whom he considered friends. A bright spot came in 1890 when he and his wife, Mary, celebrated their golden anniversary. They had seven children and numerous grandchildren.

References and Resources

History of the Atlantic Telegraph by Henry Field (a relative of Cyrus's), Books for Libraries Press, 1866.

Voice Across the Sea by Arthur C. Clarke, William Luscombe Publisher, 1958.

"The Cable Under the Sea" by James R. Chiles, in *American Heritage of Invention and Technology*, Fall 1987.

American Science and Invention by Mitchell Wilson, Bonanza Books, 1960.

Dictionary of American Biography, Charles Scribner's Sons Publishers, 1932; with supplemental updates.

National Cyclopedia of American Biography, James T. White and Co. Publishers, 1891; with supplemental updates.

McGraw-Hill Encyclopedia of Biography, McGraw-Hill Publishers, 1973.

Asimov's Biographical Encyclopedia of Science and Technology, by Isaac Asimov, Doubleday & Co. Publishers, 1964.

James Buchanan Eads

Smithsonian Institution Photo No. 80-5512

Born:
May 23, 1820,
in
Lawrenceburg,
Indiana

Died:
March 8, 1887,
in Nassau,
Bahamas

BRIDGES are among the most beautiful structures made by people. Two of America's best known are on either coast. The Brooklyn Bridge, spanning the East River in New York City, opened in 1883. The Golden Gate Bridge, crossing the entrance to San Francisco Bay, opened in 1937. Both are strong steel suspension bridges. In this type of construction, the roadway hangs, or is suspended, from two huge cables connected to the tops of towers. The middle section of the U.S. was the site of the first major bridge in the world that used steel construction, which spanned the Mississippi River at St. Louis. The bridge was designed in 1867 by James Buchanan Eads, a man who had no previous experience at building bridges.

Eads was born into a merchant family. His education ended at age 13 when his family moved to St. Louis. To help support his family, he sold apples on the street before finding work in a dry goods store. His employer had a fine library and allowed the young Eads to spend his spare time in it. After five years, Eads took work as a purser on a Mississippi River steamboat, which exposed him to the machinery and economics of river transportation. While steaming up and down the river between St. Louis and New Orleans, Eads designed a diving bell to help salvage sunken boats. He patented his invention and formed a salvage company. Successes followed losses, and after 12 years at an occupation requiring almost continual absences from home, he became independently wealthy. Eads gave up the business and went into semiretirement.

Eads's reputation as a mechanical innovator and as a person who understood the vagaries of the Mississippi River came to the attention of President Abraham Lincoln. With the onset of the Civil War just over

the horizon, Eads advised Lincoln on the use of western rivers for defense purposes. After the war began, the government awarded him a contract to build seven steam-powered and armor-plated river gunboats within 60 days. It seemed an impossible task in view of the chaotic industrial conditions that existed at the time. Within two weeks, though, Eads had 4,000 workers, scattered over the entire country, engaged in various details of construction. In another month, he launched the first 600-ton boat. The first ever armored warship, it was named the *St. Louis*. The other six gunboats followed in quick succession, and Eads ultimately constructed a total of 14.

In 1865, Congress authorized funding for the construction of a bridge over the Mississippi River. The project was viewed as impossible because of the shifting mud and sand on which the foundation might have to sit. No technical professional wanted to head the project. Because he was innovative, courageous, and willing, the St. Louis and Illinois Bridge Co. chose Eads as the project's chief engineer. He started the project having absolutely no bridge-building experience.

Eads spent much time and effort constructing the bridge's supports and approaches. Building them involved such unique equipment that only an inventive

planned for three arches with a roadway on top, and 50 feet of clearance under the center at the river's high water mark. The center arch's span was 520 feet, and those on either side were each 502 feet. Each span had two rows of four major ribs made of hollow steel tubes, each 18 inches in diameter, braced with metal ties. The steel's yield strength was specified as a minimum of 60,000 psi. Eads personally checked every shipment. Once he returned the same shipment three times when it failed to meet the strength specification.

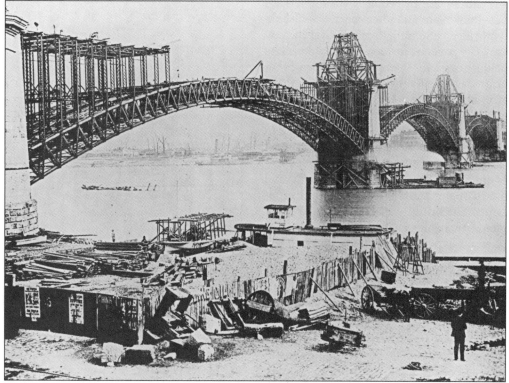

Construction of the Eads Bridge across the Mississippi River at St. Louis in 1872

Smithsonian Institution Photo

genius such as Eads could have supervised such a complex project. Among other things, he designed equipment that allowed workers to dig well below the high-water level. Air locks and other inventions patented by Eads permitted workers to locate solid rock on which to position supports. In some places, they had to go down 103 feet below the covering of sand and water.

Eads designed a cantilever bridge, rather than a suspension bridge. A cantilever is a self-supporting beam securely fastened to the ground at one end. Two cantilevers— one secured on either side of the river— meet in the middle to form a bridge. Eads

The bridge was built from both shores toward the river's middle, and workers connected the arches in September 1873. The strong steel bridge looked so delicate that the chief engineer for the Pennsylvania Central Railroad called it "entirely unsafe and impractical." Over two dozen civil engineers agreed. Other bridges of the time were made of stone, wood, or iron. All three are weaker than steel and consequently require more material in their construction, giving them the illusory appearance of greater strength. The ancient Romans built the first great stone bridges. In 1779, the first iron bridge was built to span the Severn River at

Coalbrookdale, England. It is designated a United Nations World Heritage Site.

In December 1873, workers fastened a temporary metal walkway to the nearly completed bridge. Thousands of people crossed the river during the cold and windy winter that followed. One of only a few major bridges named for its designer, the Eads Bridge is just a short distance upriver from the Gateway Arch. It was officially opened on July 4, 1874. It is a tribute to Eads's inventive genius that his bridge still carries traffic after more than 100 years of spanning the most powerful river in the United States.

The Mississippi River was always special to Eads. Within weeks of completing his bridge work, he made a formal proposal to Congress to open the clogged outlets where the river enters the Gulf of Mexico. The Mississippi River carries great quantities of silt and sand through four channels where it empties into the gulf. The passes were so choked that large ocean going ships could not get through to the port of New Orleans. Eads proposed a system of jetties, or walls, to force the river through a narrower channel. He reasoned that the increased current speed that this method produced would carry the sand and silt out to sea. Once again, Eads met opposition—this time from the U.S. Corps of Engineers. In a compromise, Congress allowed Eads to try his method on the small South Pass. His stone jetty worked exactly as predicted. By the time it was completed in 1879, the South Pass already had made its own 30-foot-deep channel.

Eads became internationally recognized and worked on water projects across the world. He planned improvements to harbors at Toronto, Canada, and Veracruz, Mexico. He also worked on harbors at Liverpool, England; Hong Kong; and many other cities. Among his numerous awards was the Albert Medal from the British Society for the Encouragement of Art, Manufacture, and Commerce. Eads was the first U.S. citizen so honored. Suffering from poor health, Eads spent his last months in the Bahamas.

References and Resources

Works of Man by Ronald Clark, Viking Press, 1985.

Big Bridge by Rupert Sargent Holland, Macrae-Smith Co., 1934.

Dictionary of American Biography, Charles Scribner's Sons Publishers, 1932; with supplemental updates.

National Cyclopedia of American Biography, James T. White and Co. Publishers, 1891; with supplemental updates.

McGraw-Hill Encyclopedia of Biography, McGraw-Hill Publishers, 1973.

Linus Yale, Jr.

Born:
April 4, 1821,
in Salisbury,
New York

Died:
December 25,
1868, in
New York,
New York

Scovill, Security Products Div.

PEOPLE today are very security conscious. They use mechanical locks to disable automobile steering wheels, magnetic locks to read codes on plastic cards, and electronically controlled push-button locks that can be reprogrammed in seconds. This security awareness is not new. Key-operated locks were used in Egypt as early as 2000 B.C. They used large wooden pins that fell into corresponding holes in a bolt, to lock large doors. A wooden key lifted the pins flush with the bolt to allow the door to open. This was an early example of a pin-type lock. Linus Yale, Sr., took that idea in 1844, and invented the modern pin-tumbler lock. For the first time in recorded history, the lock provided security for everyone. Pin-tumbler locks are still among the most secure key-operated locking devices.

Yale, Sr., made sophisticated bank locks from 1847 to 1857 in a small shop in Newport, New York. He hoped to expand his business and make pin-tumbler locks for the outside doors of stores. But he primarily adapted his lock for safes, vaults, and prisons. He claimed that it was "burglar and powder proof." It used a key that resembled a dented dowel rod. The lock did not sell well because its large size limited its range of applications. In addition, it was expensive. Yale's son Linus, Jr., was the one who greatly improved the pin-tumbler lock by making it smaller and adding a more practical rotating cylinder. His innovations opened the possibility of countless applications.

Being the son of a financially comfortable manufacturer, Linus Yale, Jr., received a good education in the local schools of his north-central New York community. He had keen mechanical abilities and often worked in his father's small factory after school. Though he was distantly related to Elihu Yale, for whom Yale College was named, the younger Yale chose not to attend college. He aimed to be a portrait painter instead. He was quite good at painting and, partly subsidized by his father, he operated a portrait studio for several years. Then, wanting to find a more reliable career, he asked to join his father in work at the factory.

The father-son team specialized in intricate and expensive bank locks. Their locks were individually hand made and sold for $100 to $500. The locks had model names to poetically suggest their strength, such as the Yale Infallible Bank Lock, the Yale Magic Bank Lock, and the Yale Double Treasury Bank Lock. Yale, Jr., received his first lock patent in 1851 for a pin-tumbler cylinder lock that closely resembled modern designs. Only after the pins lined up in a single row could a cylinder be turned to unlatch a door. In Yale Sr.'s design, the cylinder was more like a thick disk. Also, the pins were arranged around the outside as on a clock face. One pin was at 12:00, the second at 3:00, the third at 6:00, and the fourth at 9:00.

The younger Yale had mechanical insights that surpassed those of his father. He independently developed innovations such as the changeable key. The key was made in several parts that could be separated and reassembled to change the locking pattern. His locks were masterpieces of ingenious design and skillful construction, but the keys were invariably bulky and heavy. The thicker the door, the longer the key needed to reach the lock. Some weighed as much as a pound, and Yale, Sr., was always looking for ways to reduce the size of the key. He also developed the combination lock and time lock, which needed no keys at all.

Yale, Sr., died in 1857, and his two partners continued operating the business. For unknown reasons, Yale, Jr., did not get involved. He moved to Philadelphia and opened the L. Yale, Jr., Co. and continued to make high-security locks. His locks were clearly the best in the marketplace, and he wanted to provide lock security for average people.

In 1861, Yale patented the lock with which his name became widely identified. He developed a small pin-tumbler cylinder lock that could be adapted for many ordinary situations. In some ways, it resembled his father's 1844 invention, but it had the distinct advantage of using a small flat key. It was the first lock to use a key of thin metal. It measured 1-1/2" in length and weighed next to nothing. Henry R. Towne, a later partner of Yale's, once described its many potential applications. He said, "It is now made in such a variety of forms as to adapt it to almost every use, from a lady's jewelry case or tradesman's cash drawer to the heaviest house and store doors." The new lock provided greater security than was otherwise available. Since the locks could be mass produced, they sold at a reasonable price. Today, we commonly see such circular locks on cabinet doors and on some car trunks.

With the Civil War in progress during the early 1860s, Yale hesitated to bring out a new consumer product. However, he did move his factory from Philadelphia to

Shelburne Falls, Massachusetts. He continued to make bank locks and spent more time as a security consultant. But he also worked on his cylinder lock and added another patent for it in 1865. Yale began manufacturing the locks that year. Anticipating a high demand, he developed machinery to automate certain aspects of lock manufacture. One of his advertisements read: "Manufacturers of Linus Yale, Jr.'s patent new store door locks, drawer locks, mortise night latches, cupboard locks. Combines the four elements of a perfect lock: (1) elegance of pattern; (2) greater security from picking; (3) convenience of key being but 1/20th the size of ordinary door keys; (4) no key ever opening any lock but its own."

In spite of optimistic sales predictions, Yale was still not prepared for the explosive demand for his cylinder lock. His factory could not meet the orders. He looked for a larger facility and new capital with which to purchase manufacturing equipment. He established a partnership with Henry Towne to construct a new factory in Stamford, Connecticut. With its location right on the New York, New Haven, and Hartford Railroad line, 38 trains passed the factory daily

One of the first pin-tumbler cabinet locks made by Linus Yale, Jr. This lock is displayed at the Yale Lock Collection.

in each direction. Over 800 people were initially employed in the factory's eight buildings. Yale and Towne formalized their agreement on December 9, 1868. A little more than two weeks later, Yale unexpectedly died of a heart attack at the age of 47.

Yale, Jr.,—he always used the Jr., even after his father died—was a modest and unassuming man. He was well liked by his em-

This was one of the first pin-tumbler cabinet locks made by Linus Yale, Jr. The lock, patented in 1865, used a small flat key.

Scovill, Security Products Div.

ployees but little known outside his immediate circle of friends and family. His locks were only occasionally entered in industrial competitions and he belonged to few pro-fessional organizations. He married Catherine Brooks in 1844, and they had three children.

Yale received eight major lock patents during his lifetime, and his last was probably the most important. It was the mortise cylinder lock for wooden doors. The invention simplified the installation of a threaded cylinder, as well as its removal for rekeying. The mortise cylinder lock provided inexpensive and convenient security for the front and rear doors of most homes.

References and Resources

"Scoville Manufacturing Company Opens Door," *Locksmith Ledger*, March 1979.

The History of Locks, Yale Lock and Hardware Div., circa 1975.

Information from Yale trade journals stored at Ford Archives, Dearborn, MI.

Visit to Yale Lock Collection, Monroe, North Carolina.

Dictionary of American Biography, Charles Scribner's Sons Publishers, 1932; with supplemental updates.

National Cyclopedia of American Biography, James T. White and Co. Publishers, 1891; with supplemental updates.

The Best Friend of Charleston

Library of Congress

First test run on November 2, 1830, Charleston, South Carolina

Destroyed June 17, 1831, Charleston, South Carolina

IN the America of the early 1800s, much effort went to investigating efficient ways to transport goods and people. Canals were the preferred method for moving large quantities of materials, but their construction was expensive and time consuming. Trains pulled by steam locomotives presented an obvious possibility. Everyone looked to the British as the pioneers of this emerging transportation technology. The *Rocket*, a locomotive built by the father-and-son team of George and Robert Stephenson, won a competition in 1829 sponsored by the Liverpool and Manchester Railway Co. Its top speed was 30 mph, though speed had nothing to do with its name. A British engineering journal had said that passengers would be safer riding a rocket than a train. The Stephensons took up the challenge, built a locomotive, and named it the *Rocket*. Considered the world's first successful locomotive, it is now on public display in London's Science Museum.

The Delaware and Hudson Canal Co. sent Horatio Allen to England in 1828 to buy a locomotive for use in America. The company wanted the locomotive for use in processing coal deposits in northeastern Pennsylvania. Allen met with the Stephen-sons, but he chose to buy a locomotive and tender made in the city of Stourbridge. Its $2,914 price beat the Stephenson's $3,663. The *Stourbridge Lion* arrived in New York in May 1829. It is considered the first locomotive in America. The crude-looking seven-ton locomotive resembled a horizontal water tank with a smokestack. It rode on four large spoked wheels. It was tested and evaluated, but never placed in regular service. The *Stourbridge Lion* proved to be too heavy for the iron-clad wooden rails used in America. The locomotive's considerable weight tended to push the rails further apart.

At about the same time, Peter Cooper built a much lighter locomotive in Baltimore. Using materials on hand, he improvised the first American-built locomotive that could haul a payload. The *Tom Thumb* weighed only one ton and had a single-cylinder 1-1/2 hp engine. Its name came from its relatively small size. In August 1830, pulling passengers in stagecoach-like cars, it made a successful 26-mile trip in slightly over two hours. In one of the more colorful events of the era, the small locomotive ran a seven-mile race against a horse. Both pulled rail-mounted carriages loaded with passengers. Although the horse won after a belt slipped from the engine, the *Tom Thumb* helped prove the practicality of American-built locomotives.

Less well known is the first locomotive built in America for commercial service. The four-ton locomotive inaugurated scheduled rail operations in this country. *The Best Friend*, or *The Best Friend of Charleston*, was built in 1830 by the West Point Foundry in New York. The South Carolina Canal and

Railroad (SCC&RR) Co. paid $4,000 for the locomotive. The rail line was established to encourage farmers to ship their produce out of Charleston's seaport instead of Savannah's. Before the railroad's existence, growers could more easily float cotton to Savannah on riverboats than ship it by wagon train to Charleston.

The Best Friend was shipped disassembled in October 1830 and then reassembled in Charleston under the direction of Horatio Allen, who was by then the chief engineer for the SCC&RR. It made several experimental runs, then took its first excursion trip on Christmas Day. The old lithograph print on the previous page shows a representation of that journey with a cannon that was occasionally fired for dramatic effect. The local newspaper reported that the 6 hp locomotive pulled five open coaches and that the 141 passengers "flew on the wings of the wind . . . [with the smokestack] scattering sparks and flames on either side." *The Best Friend* burned rich pine wood for fuel. Large amounts of smoke, sparks, and smoldering debris left the smokestack. The smoke was bad enough, but the sparks caused clothing to catch fire. Passengers sometimes tried to address the problem by shielding themselves with umbrellas, but the umbrellas frequently caught fire and had to be rapidly discarded.

The SCC&RR used wooden rails with 2-1/2" x 1/2" iron strapping nailed to the top. The rails were five feet apart and spiked to 6" x 9" pine railroad ties. The line originally

Early American railroad tracks were made out of wood with wrought iron nailed to the top.

ran from Charleston to Hamburg using a 200-foot right of way. Many landowners literally gave their land and timber to the railroad. Of the $600,000 the project cost, only 2.3 percent went to land acquisition. Initially, one-way passenger tickets cost $6.75 and each trip took a full day, beginning at 6:00 A.M.

The Best Friend used a direct drive to the axle. Its two cylinders were inside the frame, with the drive machinery hidden beneath the engine. The idea was to place the reciprocating parts near the centerline to minimize side-to-side motion. Technical problems prevented extensive use of this design, and most later locomotives placed the steam cylinders outside the frame. The cylinders on those later locomotives were typically above the front wheels and power was delivered to the drive wheels instead of the axle. The photograph below shows a large-scale model of *The Best Friend* constructed about 1890.

Its vertical boiler allowed the locomotive to have a short wheelbase that could easily make sharp curves. The boiler was typical

Smithsonian Institution Photo No. 43054

Model of *The Best Friend*'s vertical boiler

of the period and probably developed 50 to 90 psi of pressure. It did not use a gauge—the direct reading tube gauge was not invented until 1849. Leakage through the safety valve maintained the proper pressure. The engine had two 6"-diameter cylinders with a 17" stroke. Its 54"-diameter iron drive wheels had wooden spokes. On a regular run, the locomotive typically pulled four 10-passenger cars at speeds of 16 to 21 mph.

Unfortunately, the engine had a short life. On June 17, 1831, it had stopped on a revolving platform in Charleston. The fireman, who apparently had little knowledge of steam engine technology, felt uneasy about the sound of the steam escaping from the safety valve. He tied the valve shut. The boiler exploded, killing the fireman and destroying *The Best Friend*. It was not rebuilt, but its salvageable parts were used to construct another locomotive, *The Phoenix*. (The new locomotive took its name from a mythical bird that rose from the ashes of another bird that was consumed by fire.)

Ezra Miller completed much of *The Best Friend's* engine design. A pioneer in boiler making, Miller's life also included successes as an inventor, financier, and agronomist. After developing a hereditary mental illness, Miller took his own life. Historians suspect that someone destroyed many of his papers to spare his family embarrassment. This misguided act resulted in the loss of a detailed history of *The Best Friend's* development.

The United States got a late start in railroading. However, just five years after *The Best Friend* made its initial trip, this country had 800 of the world's 1,600 miles of track. In fairness to other countries, though, the U.S. was the only major user of iron-clad wooden rails. While easy to construct, they didn't last long. The SCC&RR had only $700,000, and the iron-clad design allowed it to lay track rapidly and inexpensively. In spite of the reduced durability, the railroad company's approach is now considered the wisest of its options at the time.

References and Resources

American Locomotives by John H. White, Jr., Johns Hopkins Press, 1968.

Personal letter from John H. White, retired Senior Historian, Smithsonian Institution.

Personal letter from CPT John M. LeCato, by request of The Charleston Museum (24 Gadsden St., Charleston SC 29401).

Numerous materials from the Charleston County Museum.

Henry Timken

Born:
August 16,
1831, in
Bremen,
Germany

Died:
March 16,
1909, in
San Diego,
California

MOST inventors do their best work when they are in their twenties or thirties. Charles Martin Hall, for example, was just 22 when he developed an economical method for producing aluminum from bauxite. At 23, George Westinghouse invented the air brake that launched his company. Thomas Edison took out his phonograph patent at 30. On the other hand, some American inventors are late bloomers. One such individual was Henry Timken. He operated a carriage-building company for many years, and he also held 13 patents. His most important was for the tapered roller bearing, which he patented at age 67.

Timken was born into a farming family near Bremen in northwestern Germany. His mother died when he was four, and his father moved the family to a farm in central Missouri three years later. The region was on America's frontier, and other people of German heritage had already settled there. Timken attended the local elementary school and also did his share of farm chores. However, he made it no secret that he disliked farming, and he moved to St. Louis at age 16. There, he apprenticed himself to a wagon and carriage manufacturer.

Timken worked hard, saved his money, and opened his own small carriage company at age 24. That year, he married Fredericka Heinzelman, whose father was also a carriage maker. Timken formed a partnership with his father-in-law, and they opened a factory just across the Mississippi River in Illinois. The company succeeded and Timken kept at it until 1860, when he was struck by "gold fever." Newspaper articles and personal accounts of gold prospecting in Colorado sparked his youthful enthusiasm. Timken sold his share of the carriage company to his wife's father and headed to Pike's Peak.

Six months of prospecting convinced Timken that he was better at carriage building. He returned to St. Louis completely penniless. Lacking money to build up a new business, he decided to join the army. He enlisted in the local militia and received a promotion to captain after the Civil War broke out. Timken served with distinction in the 13th Regiment of the Missouri militia, until mustering out at war's end. He then obtained the necessary financing to build a small carriage plant. A fire destroyed his business a short time later, and he built another. From that point on, his success was almost continuous.

Timken possessed an aptitude for invention. He took out his most important early patent in 1877 for a leaf spring between a carriage's axle and its body. The Timken spring was an immediate success and gained acceptance throughout the world. When viewed from the front or rear, the two-piece Timken spring appeared to form the letter X. One leaf connected the right side of the axle with the left side of the carriage. The second leaf crossed behind the first and connected the left side of the axle with the right side of the carriage. The strong, durable spring provided a more comfortable ride. Demand for it grew so much that Timken's carriage company gradually became a spring-manufacturing plant. It made Timken wealthy, and he used part of his income to buy citrus groves in California. He also took time off to travel with his wife and five children.

Timken retired in 1887 and moved to a house he had built in San Diego. After completing college, two of his children showed interest in wagon and carriage making. So, bored with inactivity, Timken returned to St. Louis after an absence of seven years and opened up a new factory with himself as president. He worked in research and development, and left the day-to-day operations to sons Henry Jr. and William. Timken said the pinnacle of his career came in 1895 when he was elected president of the Carriage Builders National Association, the largest and oldest trade association in America. Yet, others might argue that his tapered roller bearing, patented three years later, represented the true pinnacle.

Three types of bearings supported the wheels of nineteenth-century wagons and carriages. The simplest were journal or sleeve bearings, which had existed for centuries. Ancient Romans used them on their chariots. Ball bearings are antifriction bearings that first appeared about 1860. Made of cast iron, the early ones easily split under stress when used in carriages, water turbines, and wind mills. Bicycle production in the 1880s contributed to the perfection of the steel ball bearing, which was used in bicycle wheel hubs. Another type of antifriction bearing, the ordinary straight roller bearing soon followed. Ball and roller bearings change sliding motion to rolling motion. The small amount of friction involved takes placed at a series of points on the ball or roller instead of on a large surface, as happens in a journal bearing.

All three types of bearings allowed wagon wheels to spin easily, and the two antifriction types helped distribute the load. But the bearings did little to reduce friction produced by thrust load, the binding effect created as a heavy carriage rounded a corner. During turning, weight pushes outward on a wheel as well as downward. The problem of thrust loads was not new, and Europeans had tried using tapered rollers instead of straight rollers in bearing design. However, their bearings could be used only in

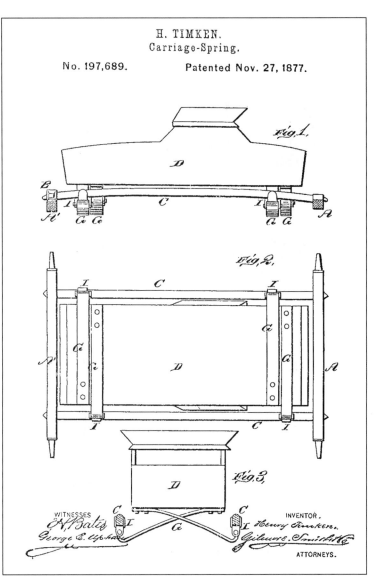

Drawing from Timken's X-shaped carriage spring patent

specific applications. Timken's design allowed tapered bearings to relieve friction regardless of the angle from which the load was applied.

Timken's sons hand made the first set of bearings in 1895. They mounted them on a wagon and loaded it up. Two small mules easily pulled the heavy wagon, but the driver was arrested for cruelty to animals. William Timken proved in court that his father's new bearing created no hardship on the mules. The dismissal of the charges created considerable publicity for the remarkable new bearing. Timken received a basic patent in 1898, as well as a subsequent related one.

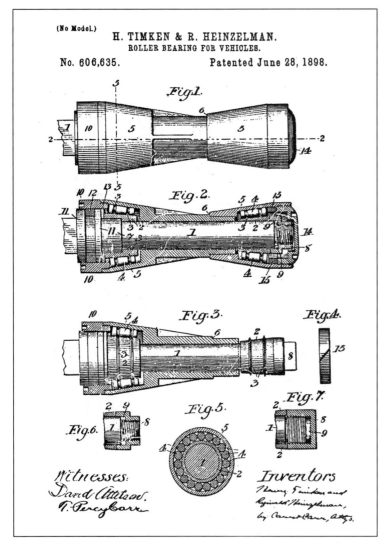

Drawing from Timken's tapered roller-bearing patent

They were his only patents not related exclusively to carriage construction.

Timken and his sons organized the Timken Roller Bearing Axle Co. in 1899. They originally intended to supply bearings only to wagon and carriage builders. However, the sons quickly saw the automobile as an emerging transportation force. When the demand for their bearings required a new factory in 1902, they chose Canton, Ohio, for its location. That city was about halfway between the steel mills of Pennsylvania, which provided their raw material, and the automobile assembly plants in Detroit. The Timkens were conservative and did not want to overextend themselves. The new factory had a modest 7,500 square feet of floor area and employed about 35 people. Its first major order was 25 sets of bearings for the Winton Car Co. in Cleveland.

Timken retired a second time in 1897. He moved to San Diego and left the business to his sons. As worldwide automobile production increased, so did the demand for Timken's tapered roller bearing. At his death just 12 years later, the company that he had started had grown tremendously. It provided jobs for more than 1,200 people and produced 850,000 sets of bearings in 1909.

References and Resources

History of the Timken Company, Timken Co., 1978.

"Small Wonder: The Magnificent Ball Bearing" by James R. Chiles, *American Heritage of Invention and Technology*, Summer 1985.

Dictionary of American Biography, Charles Scribner's Sons Publishers, 1932; with supplemental updates.

National Cyclopedia of American Biography, James T. White and Co. Publishers, 1891; with supplemental updates.

George Mortimer Pullman

TRY to imagine a long-distance train trip in the mid-1800s. Travelers sat on uncomfortable hard-backed bench seats bolted to a rough wooden floor. Poorly constructed rattling windows and engine noises made conversation or resting almost impossible. Lack of meals, poor heating, and inadequate sanitation facilities added to the difficulties. For those reasons, the 1865 introduction of George Pullman's well-built, comfortable sleeper cars drew immediate favorable response from the long-suffering public.

Pullman was born in western New York and received his early education in local schools. One of 10 children, he left school at 14 to work in a general store. He soon realized that such a career held no future for him, and he joined his oldest brother in the cabinetmaker's trade in the city of Albion. During the next seven years, he learned the details of cabinet construction that he later used in his Pullman sleeper cars. The Erie Canal was under construction in the area and Pullman occasionally worked at moving buildings away from the banks. The canal work led him to Chicago where he helped raise downtown buildings and streets as much as seven feet to eliminate flooding caused by poor drainage. His most dramatic project was raising the fashionable four-story Tremont Hotel without disturbing its occupants.

To visit his family, Pullman took uncomfortable train trips that he said persuaded him to build an improved sleeper car. He wasn't the first to consider such a project. In 1837, the Cumberland Valley Railroad of Baltimore was the first rail line to offer sleeping accommodations. Sleeper cars of the period typically had three wooden shelves attached to the walls. Because of the discomfort and lack of privacy this arrange-

National Portrait Gallery, Smithsonian Institution

George Pullman at 39

Born:
March 3, 1831,
in Brocton,
New York

Died:
October 19,
1897, in
Chicago,
Illinois

ment afforded, only men traveled at night. The 32-year-old Pullman wanted to design a new, quiet, and comfortable sleeper car for which travelers would pay a premium price.

Pullman combined his life savings with financial backing from a close boyhood friend, Benjamin Field, with whom he formed a partnership. Field held the rights to operate sleeper cars on two railroad lines, and he and Pullman organized their small company to remodel railroad cars. Pullman converted two ordinary 44-foot-long passenger cars into sleepers using hinged upper berths. When his conversions proved popular with passengers on the Chicago and Alton Railroad, he modified a third passenger car. Unfortunately, the railroads were reluctant to adopt Pullman's cars because they differed so greatly from existing sleeper cars. In 1859, the disappointed Pullman left for the Colorado gold fields.

While in Colorado, Pullman operated a

general store and sketched ideas for a railroad sleeper car in his spare time. Returning to Chicago in 1863 with some savings, Pullman and Field reestablished their partnership and targeted the manufacture of just one sleeper car. In a rented railroad repair shed, Pullman's small crew of hand-picked employees built the heaviest and most glamorous passenger car in America.

Named *The Pioneer*, it had a comfortable sleeping shelf near the ceiling that folded up for daytime travel. Hand-carved ornamental wood paneling concealed the hinged beds. Well-cushioned Victorian-style seats helped make the elaborate interior look more like an expensive hotel room than a railroad car. Plush red carpets covered the floor and many light-reflecting gilt-edged mirrors covered the walls. The 54'-long car took a year's time and $20,000 to construct—five times the cost of other sleepers. To accommodate the hinged beds, Pullman raised the roof of *The Pioneer* by two feet and extended its width by one foot. Those alterations made the car too tall for underpasses and too wide for railroad platforms. Pullman took a calculated risk, hoping that the car's interior size, comfort, and beauty

stations had to be altered to allow the oversized car to pass. That was *The Pioneer*'s first use on any railroad line. The car attracted national attention and five more like it went into service in 1866. Pullman soon established the Pullman Palace Car Co.

Overnight travel on a Pullman car cost an additional $2, but the public readily paid the difference. People seemed just as interested in the car's improved atmosphere as in its improved comfort. Pullman cars featured luxurious interiors and their glossy varnished exteriors were lavishly decorated with gold-leaf striping and scrollwork. Travelers in Pullman cars didn't put muddy boots on the fancy seats, they didn't use coarse language, and they dressed well. Sleeping berths were more private, which encouraged families to travel.

Pullman never sold his cars to the railroads. He leased them so that he could hire his own conductors, porters, and other service personnel. This allowed Pullman to maintain the highest standards of passenger comfort, which promoted future business. His cars were introduced into German railroads in 1872 and were the first sleepers used in regular service in England in 1874.

By 1875, he had 700 elegant cars in worldwide use and completely dominated the sleeping car industry. Pullman's real invention was railroad comfort.

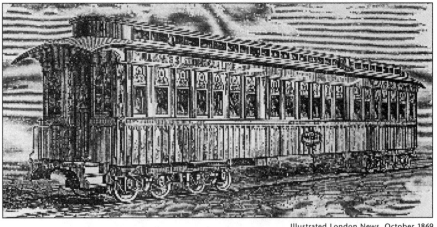

Illustrated London News, October 1869

The Pioneer, Pullman's first sleeper, was similar to this 1869 car, except that it rode on four-wheel trucks.

would persuade railroads to make the adjustments. None were eager to do it.

The death of President Abraham Lincoln forced the railroads to change their minds. Mary Todd Lincoln personally chose *The Pioneer* to carry her husband's body from Chicago to Springfield, Illinois. Every station platform and bridge between the two

He held a patent on the upper folding bed and another to convert seats into a lower bed. He also invented a hotel car, a parlor car, and a dining car. Among his more important inventions was the enclosed connector between railroad cars. Called a vestibule, it was Pullman's greatest contribution to passenger safety. The vestibule was a bellows-like device that connected the end of one car to the front of the next. Passengers moved between cars without having to go outside and risk falling off the train. Pullman incorporated his innovations in almost all the cars built by his 14,000 employees. They made over 2,000 railroad cars, costing as much as $100,000 each.

Pullman was a master at public relations. One of the first trains to make a transcontinental trip carried a Pullman car provided at no charge. Directors of the Union Pacific and Central Pacific Railroads used it in the course of inspecting the new line.

An immaculate and conservative dresser, Pullman had a round face that made him look young for his age. He grew a chin beard to give himself a more mature appearance and kept the beard throughout his adult life. He was polite, but he had no interest in idle chatter and was abrupt with people who wasted his time. He built the town of Pullman just south of Chicago in 1880 and was one of the last industrialists to operate a company town. Deeply disturbed by the depressing conditions of urban living, he viewed his town as a model of cleanliness, safety, and efficiency. It cost him more than $5 million to construct, including $1.2 million for the establishment of a vocational-technical high school. Pullman paid for the parks, roads, public buildings, and other major construction projects. Not all of the town's 12,000 residents agreed with his manufacturing techniques and financial reforms, however. Many believed that paid informers were constantly watching them. The community erupted into a violent labor strike in 1894 that ended only after much bloodshed. The town of Pullman merged with Chicago shortly before Pullman's death in 1897.

The interior of a Pullman sleeping car in 1869

Illustrated London News, October 1869

References and Resources

American Science and Invention by Mitchell Wilson, Bonanza Books, 1960.

The Story of the Pullman Car by Joseph Hubbard, Arno Press, 1972 (reprint of 1917 publication).

The Railroad Passenger Car by August Mencken, John Hopkins Press, 1957.

Pullman by Stanley Buder, Oxford University Press, 1967.

The Story of American Railroads by Stewart Holbrook, Crown Publishers, 1947.

Dictionary of American Biography, Charles Scribner's Sons Publishers, 1932; with supplemental updates.

National Cyclopedia of American Biography, James T. White and Co. Publishers, 1891; with supplemental updates.

McGraw-Hill Encyclopedia of Biography, McGraw-Hill Publishers, 1973.

William LeBaron Jenney

Born:
September 25, 1832, in Fairhaven, Massachusetts

Died:
June 15, 1907, in Los Angeles, California

Chicago Historical Society

THE word *skyscraper* was coined in 1884 to refer to a tall building with a metal supporting frame. The first one was built in Chicago following a disastrous 1871 fire that destroyed almost every building in the business district and left 90,000 people homeless. William LeBaron Jenney designed that first skyscraper, the 10-story Home Insurance Building that stood at LaSalle and Adams Streets for nearly 50 years.

The $200 million Chicago fire destroyed buildings on 2,000 acres and much of the city's wealth, but it did not destroy the city's economic base. Grain and livestock continued to arrive by ship, road, and rail. In an era before rapid long-distance communication was common, businesses had little choice but to rebuild in the same high-density downtown area. With financial institutions in disarray, they borrowed much of the necessary money from Cyrus McCor-

mick, designer and manufacturer of the McCormick reaper. Land values had increased so much over the years that the need for high-rise structures became obvious. Much of what burned down had been made of wood and brick. Many of the nation's architects and engineers moved to the city to involve themselves with new materials and methods of construction. It gave them the opportunity to test new ideas during the city's rebuilding.

Chicago had long before established its reputation as a city where new ideas in building technology flourished. During the 1840s, a form of wooden construction called *balloon frame*, or *Chicago construction*, developed. The new technique did not require skilled workers to make the intricate doweled connections used in post-and-beam construction. The greatest obstacle to construction in America had arisen from a shortage of skilled workers, and with the introduction of balloon-framing techniques, almost anyone could construct a building. Today we call the method *stud framing*, and it dominates residential construction.

Before skyscrapers, the only tall masonry structures built were monuments, not functional buildings. The walls of an all-masonry building have to support the entire weight of the structure. Large buildings require thick bases such as those found in European castles and cathedrals. Another example is the Washington Monument in Washington, D.C. At 555' tall, it towers over the Egyptian pyramids. It is the world's tallest all-masonry structure.

The construction technologists who settled in Chicago designed many innovative, fire-resistant skyscrapers. Their buildings featured separate metal frames that supported the entire weight of the building.

Downtown Chicago has relatively water-logged soil that requires reliable foundations. Resourceful architects designed an underground grillwork of iron rails that spread a building's weight over a large area. The graceful buildings they constructed had beautiful non-load-bearing curtain walls and many exterior windows to let in natural light. Safety elevators made by Elisha Graves Otis's company rapidly carried people to and from upper floors. Modern plumbing brought in fresh water and removed waste. Chicago became the center of modern architecture in the United States during the late 1800s and early 1900s.

Jenney is considered the originator of the delicate and airy design of skyscraper that became known by the designation "Chicago school of architecture." He received an outstanding education at Harvard University. Like many American architects, he took his advanced training in Europe, studying at the Ecole Central des Arts et Manufactures in Paris. He studied art and architecture, graduating with high honors in 1856. Ecole Centrale was the same school that educated Gustave Eiffel, who designed the internal frame for the Statue of Liberty in 1885. Eiffel also designed and built the wrought-iron Eiffel Tower in 1889. After Jenney returned to the United States, he designed railbeds and bridges for the Tehuantepec Railroad Co. of New Orleans. Jenney then returned to France to study architecture for an additional 18 months. When the Civil War broke out, Jenney received an officer's commission and was assigned to engineering duties with General Ulysses Grant. He took charge of roads, buildings, and bridges in Memphis, Tennessee, and he served as chief engineer of the 15th Army Corps until he left the military in 1866.

After working on a variety of projects in Pennsylvania, Jenney moved to Chicago in 1868. He opened an architectural office, and for his first contract he designed a large church. Soon, he developed a reputation for designing office buildings with attractive entrances, large hallways, and bright rooms. The Home Insurance Co. of New York commissioned him to construct a fire-resistant metal-framed office building in Chicago. As the most respected local architect, Jenney was the obvious choice for breaking new architectural ground.

Built in 1884, the Home Insurance Building was considered the first skyscraper, but not because it was tall enough to "scrape the sky." It was the first high-rise building to use an all-metal framework as its basic design principle. Previously, some French theater roofs had used iron trusses, and British mills occasionally used them in place of wooden columns for fire prevention purposes. Jenney did not invent the metal-framed building. It arose from an evolutionary process contributed to by many designers, but Jenney was there to see it all come together. He used vertical cast-iron columns to support horizontal I-beams, on which the floors rested. Jenney used wrought-iron beams up to the fifth floor, with Bessemer steel beams above that. The photograph shows a preserved remnant of an actual section from an upper building floor. The exterior walls used square columns (at front in photo below) and the interior walls used cylindrical columns (at rear in photo). The beams on each floor were bolted to each other and to the columns. (Future skyscrapers would use stronger rivets.) The metal skeleton made a rigid cage that provided the main load-bearing members of the building. The exterior walls were of brick, stone, and terra cotta, a brown-red unglazed

A preserved section of the Home Insurance Building, showing the wrought iron columns, steel I beam, and parts of the exterior wall

pottery. They provided little structural support.

Following the construction of the Home Insurance Building, Jenney found his services in constant demand. He designed at least 14 buildings, but his most significant contribution to architecture was education. His architectural firm produced many fine young architects who then struck out on their own, including Louis Sullivan and Daniel Burnham. Those he influenced and trained went on to build other skyscrapers in Chicago and New York. The well-respected Jenney organized several successful firms, wrote numerous technical articles, and wrote a book on architecture. He founded the Department of Architecture at the University of Michigan and taught there between 1876 and 1880. To honor Jenney for using its steel in constructing the Home Insurance Building, the Bessemer Steamship Co. named one of its ships after him in 1897. Jenney retired to Los Angeles in 1905 for health reasons, and he died two years later. The Home Insurance Building was torn down in 1931.

Chicago has maintained contact with its past by continuing to use three downtown nineteenth-century skyscrapers that are masterpieces of the Chicago school of architecture: the Sears Roebuck and Co. Building (by Jenney), the Reliance Building (by Burnham), and the Carson Pirie Scott and Co. Building (by Sullivan). The city also remains a leader in modern high-rise construction. It is home to three of the world's five tallest buildings, including the tallest—the Sears Tower at 1,454 feet.

References and Resources

"The Rise of the Skyscraper from the Ashes of Chicago" by Tom Peters, *American Heritage of Invention and Technology,* Fall 1987.

Dictionary of American Biography, Charles Scribner's Sons Publishers, 1932; with supplemental updates.

National Cyclopedia of American Biography, James T. White and Co. Publishers, 1891; with supplemental updates.

Laroy Sunderland Starrett

L.S. Starrett Co.

Born:
April 25, 1836,
in China,
Maine

Died:
April 23, 1922,
in
St. Petersburg,
Florida

MEASUREMENTS of shaft diameters and sheet-metal thickness often require the use of a micrometer. English astronomer William Gascoigne made the first one in 1640. Gascoigne wanted to measure the diameters of planets as he looked at them through a telescope. He put two thin wires near the eyepiece, one stationary and the other movable through use of a screw. From that humble beginning, the micrometer evolved into a highly accurate measuring tool for scientists, engineers, and technologists. One of the most accurate and easiest to use was manufactured by a man who enjoyed and was good at farming. He might have happily remained a farmer if memories of economic difficulties during his youth had not troubled him. Laroy Starrett went on to establish a business that made the most accurate measuring tools in nineteenth-century America.

Starrett was born on a farm in Maine, the sixth of 12 children. He worked long hours to help support his family. Like many other youngsters in his day, he went to school during the winter months and worked on the farm in the summer. He once wrote that his father was a natural mechanic and his mother possessed great ingenuity. Possibly because of those combined influences, Starrett developed an interest in farm mechanics. He spent many cold winter nights in a room above the stable trying to create new devices.

At one point, due to financial misfortunes, Starrett's father had to mortgage his farm. His mother worried about the possibility of losing the family's land. To help his parents, Starrett worked on a nearby farm at the age of 17. After six months, he moved to a farm in Massachusetts that offered higher wages, and he soon helped pay off the mortgage.

Starrett stayed at the Massachusetts farm for seven years. In 1861, he married and began renting 600 acres from a farmer in the area. He settled into a life of successfully farming wheat, beans, and potatoes. Starrett was always willing to try new methods as long as they sounded reasonable. One year, he proudly produced 60 bushels of wheat per acre—40 more than was normally considered a good yield.

At the age of 28, remembering the anguish of his parents when they had to mortgage their farm, Starrett decided to try another career. He had designed a meat chopper in his spare time and took out his first patent on it in 1865. He arranged with a manufacturer in Athol, Massachusetts, to make the chopper, while he concentrated on selling it in his home state. Starrett developed a close working relationship with the Athol Machine Co. and soon accepted a position there as plant superintendent.

Starrett continued to work on inventions in his spare time. One was an improved shoe-hook fastener that would have made him wealthy if he had developed the market. But viewing it as having secondary importance to precision tools, he sold his patent rights for a few hundred dollars.

During his years with Athol Machine Co., Starrett invented a washing machine, butter churn, and a number of tools for the building trades. He stayed there for about 10 years, until several misfortunes combined during one unhappy period. His wife died, leaving him with four small children. He lost his hearing and also lost his job because of a jealous rivalry.

Among the hand tools Starrett had patented while working for Athol Machine Tool was the combination square. He made patterns of it working at his kitchen table night after night. His final design used a grooved steel rule, graduated into small parts of an inch on both sides. A sliding head moved along the rule or could be removed entirely. Starrett had worked as a patternmaker and

Laroy Starrett's desk. The sign says: "L. S. Starrett's Desk; the first desk used by the founder of the company."

had been unhappy with clumsy fixed-blade squares. He realized the need for a more useful instrument. After losing his job at Athol Machine Co., Starrett established a small machine shop in 1877 to manufacture combination squares. In spite of their usefulness, he had trouble selling them because

there was little immediate demand. Some people worried that the tools would not remain square over their entire sliding range. But Starret had been aware of the potential problem, and he had built special machines to cut the groove. He also had machines made to accurately grind graduations into the rule. While the new combination square attracted only a small market initially, sales grew as the tool showed its ability to stand up to rigorous use. The Stanley Tool works of New Britain, Connecticut, bought 5,000 and sold them under its own name.

As his small company was growing during the 1880s, Starrett also improved steel rules, surface gauges, dividers, and other measuring tools. He moved to larger quarters in 1881 and set up sales offices in Europe. Starrett worked on improving the micrometers then in use. Many came from France, where the modern micrometer had originated. Starrett felt that the head was too large on existing designs, which prevented their use in tight places. The screw threads were not enclosed and thus could be damaged, and there was no locking device to hold a measurement. Starrett made changes accordingly and added what he called a "speeder." It took 40 revolutions to open or close one inch, so Starrett added a small end piece that speeded up measurement taking. His one-inch micrometer in a leather case sold for $6.50 in 1899.

Like other manufacturers of measuring tools, Starrett often added a vernier scale to improve an instrument's accuracy. The vernier scale is an adjacent scale of slightly different size devised in 1631 by Pierre Vernier, a French mathematician and engineer. A micrometer accurate to hundredths of an inch could have its accuracy improved to thousandths of an inch simply by adding a vernier scale.

Starrett made every tool he patented. He never sold his patent rights to another manufacturer. His company prospered, and in 1906 it employed about 1,000 people. It made an endless variety of squares, steel rules, steel tapes, levels, depth gauges, micrometers, calipers, and dividers. The tools were available with metric or inch graduations. A 12-inch combination square sold for about $2, and a 15 cm steel rule cost 65¢. Like many technologists, Starrett used the spelling "gage" instead of "gauge" in all his patents and correspondences.

The Athol Machine Co. brought a suit against Starrett during the 1880s. Starrett replied with a countersuit, which he won. About 20 years later, remembering that court action, Starrett bought out the Athol Machine Co. He eventually had the building torn down and a modern $50,000 factory built on the site. By 1917, the L. S. Starrett Co. had 2,100 tools in its catalog.

Starrett was a civic-minded and deeply religious man. He financed the 1917 construction of a $100,000 Young Men's Christian Association (YMCA) building on the site where he originally manufactured his combination square. He also paid for two large church buildings and a new pipe or-gan. A man whose spirit never grew old, Starrett celebrated his 85th birthday as a passenger in a spindly Wright Brothers'-type airplane. Starrett never remarried after his wife's death, and he died at his winter home in Florida.

References and Resources

The Starrett Story, L. S. Starrett Co., 1982.

A History of Astronomy by A. Pannekoek, Interscience Publishers, 1961.

Dictionary of American Biography, Charles Scribner's Sons Publishers, 1932; with suplemental updates.

National Cyclopedia of American Biography, James T. White and Co. Publishers, 1891; with supplemental updates.

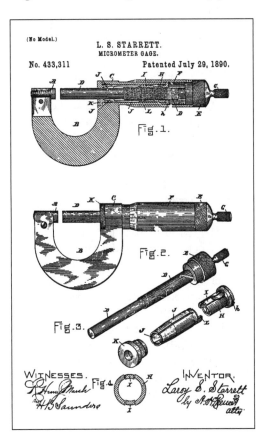

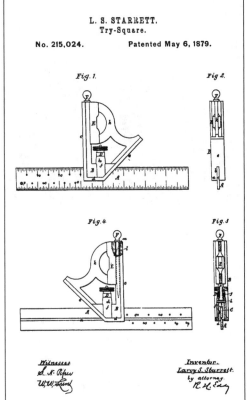

Starrett's micrometer patent included a special end to speed up measurements. His try square combination square had a sliding head to adapt to different situations.

John Wesley Hyatt

Smithsonian Institution; Photo No. 42731E

Born:
November 28,
1837, in
Starkey,
New York

Died:
May 10, 1920,
in Short Hills,
New Jersey

PLASTIC is easily the most diverse manufacturing material in the world. It can replace wood in furniture and glass in windows and eyeglasses. Plastic textiles replace natural fibers in clothing and steel in bicycle frames. Special high-strength plastic even replaces some metal parts inside experimental automobile engines. The first synthetic plastic to receive wide commercial use was made in 1869. That year, a printer who had no training in the field of chemistry, John Wesley Hyatt, discovered celluloid.

Hyatt received the same grade-school education as most other nineteenth-century Americans. His father was a blacksmith. Hyatt's family sent him to a seminary for a year to study for the ministry. He decided against a religious career, however, and traveled to Illinois at age 16 to work as a printer's apprentice. He was good at the trade and continued printing work for 10 years.

Hyatt had no formal technical training, but he found that he had natural mechanical and scientific ability. He read all that he could about the printing industry and its machines. He spent a great deal of time working on inventions, and he received his first patent at the age of 24, for a device that sharpened kitchen knives. It involved a new method for making solid emery wheels.

While working as a journeyman printer in Albany, Hyatt saw a reward advertised in the newspaper. The Phelan and Collender Co. of New York City offered $10,000 for an ivory substitute for billiard balls. Hyatt experimented at night and on weekends with compounds made from wood pulp. He produced several new materials, but none was good enough to collect the reward. However, Hyatt found that his new moldable wood fibers were satisfactory for use in checkers and dominoes. He and his two brothers established the Embossing Co. of Albany to produce the items for sale to the public. With his youngest brother operating the successful plant, Hyatt continued to search for the elusive plastic.

While working with his compounds of wood pulp, Hyatt noticed a thin skin left after some liquids had evaporated. Though he had little knowledge of chemistry, Hyatt decided to expand on what he had discovered earlier. Also, others before him had tackled the problem and Hyatt built on their results. It was a dangerous undertaking because he continued to experiment with nitrocellulose as a foundation for plastic. A hazardous and highly flammable material, nitrocellulose is chemically related to explosives. Working with his brother Isaiah, Hyatt achieved his goal by combining paper flock with shellac and a syrupy gel made of nitrocellulose and camphor under a very high pressure. In his short one-page 1869 patent, Hyatt wrote about pressures as high as "5 to 20 tons per square inch" necessary to produce a "solid collodion." He had produced a synthetic plastic that could be softened by heat and formed with a mold. At normal atmospheric conditions, it became a hard, solid material. The word plastic comes from the Greek word *plastikos*, which means "to form."

To make the collodion, a thick liquid that dried quickly, Hyatt started with cotton. He treated it with nitric and sulfuric acids, and then dissolved the pulpy mass with alcohol and ether. Other inventors had tried without success to make the collodion thicker. Hyatt discovered the trick of mixing in a solvent, such as camphor, while heating and pressurizing the material. It produced a hard and translucent solid that he named *celluloid*, for cellulose nitrate. As is often typical for successful inventors, others legally contested his discovery. Yet, the courts consistently sustained Hyatt's patent.

The new material could be formed and colored, and it easily replaced ivory for billiard balls. Hyatt collected the $10,000 reward offered by Phelan and Collender Co. He combined that money with more from investors to establish the Celluloid Manufacturing Co. with his brothers in 1872. Hyatt developed complicated industrial processing techniques and invented special machinery to manufacture the new plastic. For many years, the Hyatt brothers' Newark plant was the only manufacturer of raw celluloid in the United States. Unsure of the market for the new material, the brothers initially concentrated on sporting goods. Some of their early finished products were billiard balls, bowling balls, and golf-club heads.

Celluloid could be sawed, carved, molded, bent, stamped, and formed into many different shapes. Its invention brought about a minor revolution by providing an inexpensive synthetic substitute for costly natural materials such as ivory, amber, and tortoiseshell. Because it looked and felt like the substances it replaced, people found many decorative uses for it. While often used as a replacement material, celluloid was also used as a raw material for artistry and ornamentation. Manufacturers used it to make jewelry boxes, dice, hatpin ends,

letter openers, shoehorns, brush handles, toothpicks, nameplates, combs, baby rattles, shirt collars, and many other common items. George Eastman used it as a smooth flexible carrier for his photographic emulsions. Eastman had previously used glass plates or paper, but celluloid worked even better. In the twentieth century, the word celluloid has been more often used to refer to motion picture film than to plastic.

Celluloid was not a perfect replacement for natural materials. One major drawback was that it easily caught on fire, a particular concern for motion picture producers. They started to use nonflammable safety film, cellulose acetate, when it became widely available in the 1920s. When used in dental plates, celluloid never totally lost its camphor odor and taste. It also tended

UNITED STATES PATENT OFFICE.

JOHN W. HYATT, JR., OF ALBANY, NEW YORK, AND ISAIAH S. HYATT, OF ROCKFORD, ILLINOIS.

IMPROVED METHOD OF MAKING SOLID COLLODION.

Specification forming part of Letters Patent No. 91,341, dated June 15, 1869.

To all whom it may concern:

Be it known that we, JOHN W. HYATT, Jr., of the city of Albany, in the State of New York, and ISAIAH S. HYATT, of the city of Rockford, in the State of Illinois, have invented a new and useful Method of Making Solid Collodion, or compounds of pyroxyline; and we do hereby declare the following specification to be a true and exact description of the nature of our invention.

Our invention consists of a new and improved method of manufacturing solid collodion and its compounds; its essential feature being the employment of a very small quantity of ether or other appropriate solvent, and dissolving pyroxyline therewith, under a heavy pressure, so that a comparatively hard and solid product is obtained, with great economy of solvents and saving of time.

The following description will enable others skilled in the art to use our process:

We place soluble cotton, pyroxyline, or prepared cellulose into a strong cylinder or suitably-shaped mold. With the pyroxyline may be mixed ivory-dust, bone-dust, asbestus, flake-white, or any other desirable substance, according to the nature of the product required.

This compound is then pressed into a tolerably compact mass by means of a plunger in the cylinder, or by a movable part of the mold. The plunger, to said cylinder or part of the mold is then retracted to give room for the ether or other solvent. The proportion of solvent to the pyroxyline is as five to ten, seven to ten, or equal parts, by weight, according to the nature and proportions of the compound. When the pyroxyline is used alone, from one-half to three-fourths, by weight, of solvent will be sufficient; but when ivory-dust or other material is added, a somewhat greater proportion of solvent will be required, which can readily be determined by trial. After the plunger to the cylinder or part of the mold has been retracted, as aforesaid, the

solvent is poured or forced in through a hole, which is then closed, and the plunger or movable part of the mold is immediately forced against the contents with great power—a pressure of from five to twenty tons per square inch being required to produce the best results. The pressure must be applied quickly, so that the solvent will be forced into contact with every particle of the pyroxyline before the dissolving process has time to commence. This, however, may be varied according to the degree of activity of the solvent employed. The cylinder or mold must be made or packed to work so closely that none of the solvent can escape the pressure. Other mechanical means may be employed equivalent to the foregoing, and we do not confine ourselves to the precise apparatus described.

The product is then taken out of the cylinder or mold, and will be found to be hard and solid, of uniform quality throughout, and liable to only a very slight degree of shrinkage, because of the very small proportion of volatile elements which it contains.

After the solid compound thus formed is taken out of the cylinder or mold, and before it thoroughly seasons, we subject it, in the manufacture of many articles, to additional pressure in molds, whereby it is caused to conform perfectly with all the configurations of the mold.

Having thus described our invention, what we claim, and desire to secure by Letters Patent, is—

1. Dissolving pyroxyline under pressure, substantially as described.

2. Dissolving pyroxyline under pressure, when combined with ivory-dust or other material, substantially as described.

JOHN W. HYATT, JR.
ISAIAH S. HYATT.

Witnesses:
HENRY DEITZ,
C. M. HYATT.

Hyatt's invention of celluloid is covered in this one-page patent.

to soften upon contact with very hot water.

Hyatt was not content merely to manufacture plastic, and he involved himself in other technical pursuits. Partly in response to a water-treatment problem at his celluloid factory, he developed a water purification technique using synthetic filters that could be cleaned by back flushing. This technique proved especially popular with paper and woolen mills, as well as with municipal water-treatment plants. Hyatt established the Hyatt Pure Water Co. and sold many systems in America and Europe.

In designing machinery for his celluloid factory, Hyatt noticed many devices that would benefit from improved roller bearings. Using his wide-ranging technical abilities, he invented roller bearings for industrial machinery. This led to the establishment of the Hyatt Roller Bearing Co. in Harrison, New Jersey. Hyatt's fertile mind also developed a more efficient method for extracting juice from sugar cane. The resulting pressed cane was dry enough to use as fuel. In 1900, Hyatt invented an improved sewing machine for making industrial belts. One year later, he invented machinery for cold rolling steel and straightening shafts. He received over 250 patents, many for manufacturing commercial articles and novelties from celluloid.

The Society of Chemical Industry in London, England, awarded Hyatt the Perkin Medal in 1914. This was a distinguished honor, particularly for a nonchemist. Hyatt and his wife had two sons who followed careers in law and electrical engineering.

With the advancement of newer plastics, celluloid's market had shrunk drastically by the late 1940s. It has few modern applications, though its density makes it particularly well suited for ping pong balls. It is also still used for some eyeglass frames and piano key coverings. Cellophane, a plastic with a similar-sounding name, was invented almost 40 years later in Switzerland. Its only relationship to celluloid is that both are cellulose based.

References and Resouces

"The First Plastic" by Robert Friedel, *American Heritage of Invention and Technology*, Summer 1987.

Dictionary of American Biography, Charles Scribner's Sons Publishers, 1932; with supplemental updates.

National Cyclopedia of American Biography, James T. White and Co. Publishers, 1891; with supplemental updates.

Asimov's Biographical Encyclopedia of Science and Technology by Isaac Asimov, Doubleday and Co. Publishers, 1964.

Ellen Henrietta Swallow Richards

The MIT Museum

Born:
December 3, 1842, in Dunstable, Massachusetts

Died:
March 30, 1911, in Jamaica Plain, Massachusetts

THE first American woman to earn a technical degree was also the first woman accepted for membership in an engineering society. She was a founder of the profession of sanitary engineering and among the first women to formally work as a scientist. Technologist, scientist, author, and teacher, Ellen Richards improved domestic technology and had a profound impact on the way people lead their daily lives. She almost single-handedly created the field of home economics, then called domestic science, in 1897.

Richards was born Ellen Swallow in a small village in northeastern Massachusetts. Her parents were school teachers and occasional farmers who also owned a general store. Perhaps because she was an only child, Richards's parents made sure their daughter received as good an education as possible. They first educated her at home and then moved to a larger community so that she could attend high school. Following graduation, Richards became a teacher and searched for a college that admitted women. Her timing couldn't have been better, because Vassar College for women opened in Poughkeepsie, New York, in 1865. Vassar provided the first real movement toward full collegiate education for women.

Richards entered Vassar during 1868. Self-supporting and 25 years old, she found herself surrounded by other students who were wealthier and younger than she was. She worked her way through college by tutoring them in Latin and mathematics. One of her teachers was Maria Mitchell, a professor of astronomy and America's first important woman scientist. Mitchell's discovery of a comet in 1847, at the age of 28, catapulted her to international fame. She won a gold medal that the king of Denmark had promised to the discoverer. In 1848, she became the first female member of the American Academy of Arts and Sciences. Strongly influenced by Mitchell, Richards took practically every science course she could. She graduated with a Bachelor of Arts, the only degree offered by Vassar, in 1870.

Her teachers supported Richards's petition to the Massachusetts Institute of Technology (MIT) as the institute's first female entrant. MIT was almost as new as Vassar, having opened its doors in Cambridge, Massachusetts, in 1861. Admitting a woman was an unusual step at that time, and MIT made an unusual arrangement with Richards. It would allow her to attend classes but refused to let her pay tuition so that she would not officially be a student. Richards naturally agreed to the arrangement, and she received a Bachelor of Science degree in chemistry in 1873. She was the first woman to graduate from MIT and the first woman to receive a technical degree in America.

Richards stayed at MIT for two more years. She took additional classes in chemistry and also analyzed air, water, and sewage samples for the city of Boston. In addition, she analyzed the arsenic content of wallpaper and various food additives. Through this work, she helped establish the discipline of sanitary engineering and taught in the field. Because of her position at MIT, Richards had contact with wealthy members of Boston society. She persuaded them to contribute to the Women's Laboratory she was establishing. Richards used the lab, which was not officially connected to MIT, to teach basic science to young women

Title page from Richards's book, *The Science of Controllable Environment*

EUTHENICS

THE SCIENCE OF CONTROLLABLE ENVIRONMENT

A PLEA FOR BETTER LIVING CONDITIONS AS A FIRST STEP TOWARD HIGHER HUMAN EFFICIENCY

The national annual unnecessary loss of capitalized net earnings is about $1,000,000,000.
Report on National Vitality

By ELLEN H. RICHARDS
Author of Cost of Living Series, Art of Right Living, etc.

WHITCOMB & BARROWS
BOSTON, 1910

who wanted to teach school. Another of her projects was the Society to Encourage Studies at Home. It offered a series of courses intended to help homebound women obtain an education. Richards established the New England Kitchen to study the diets of working-class families. She demonstrated the preparation of less costly, more nutritious meals.

Not forgetting her own technical career, in 1875, Richards became the first woman scientist to serve on any state board of health. Her technical papers on mineral chemistry were of such high quality that the American Institute of Mining Engineers admitted her to membership in 1879. She was

also the first female member of any U.S. engineering organization.

Following continued recommendations from Richards, MIT decided in 1882 to admit women as regular students. Two years later, MIT opened the country's first sanitation laboratory and appointed Richards as its first female instructor. Her title was Instructor in Sanitary Chemistry, and she taught courses in the chemical study of public water supplies and waste-water treatment. From that time until her death, Richards regularly both taught courses and participated in research projects. Her many technical accomplishments and unwavering high regard for the technical ability of other women show Richards to be a great contributor to both scientific and social progress. A person with an eternally pleasant disposition, Richards once said, "Perhaps the fact that I am not a radical . . . is winning me stronger allies than anything else."

Her status as a "feminine first" in so many areas of technology gave Richards the opportunity to publicize her interest in efficiency within the home. The home was the workplace for many people, most of whom were women. Richards stressed the challenging nature of efficient housework and the opportunities to improve it through application of scientific principles. She first taught domestic science classes to vocationally oriented women students at Simmons College. Richards often used her own home as a personal laboratory. She eliminated her heavy dust-gathering rugs, used window plants to replace curtains, and designed easily prepared, nutritious meals. She was quick to use such new products as gas stoves, gas water heaters, vacuum cleaners, and ventilators. Richards campaigned to have domestic science taught in high school. She believed the home was the center of civilized society. Properly trained women could manage their homes better and leave time for other pursuits.

The efficient Rumford Kitchen demonstration at the 1893 World's Columbian Exposition in Chicago was one of Richards's accomplishments. Visitors bought nutritious, scientifically prepared lunches for 32¢. The Exposition was the greatest showpiece of technical achievements since the 1876 Centennial.

Throughout her professional life,

Richards continually worked to establish the field of domestic science. She gave demonstrations and raised money. She inspired her co-workers and organized the field's professional associations. When she found handbooks unavailable, she wrote several. She successfully worked to create a new profession for women.

In September 1897, Richards met with others at Lake Placid, New York, to discuss ways to encourage professionalism in the field. One of the 12 people present was Melvil Dewey, originator of the Dewey decimal system for classifying library books. Richards discussed bringing homes into the twentieth century by integrating them with the technical advances of the time. Annual meetings followed until the 1908 establishment of the American Home Economics Association. Richards was elected the association's first president. Within 20 years, young women and men were earning home economics degrees at most major universities in the United States, and readily finding jobs in the field.

During her first years at MIT, Richards met and married Robert Richards, a professor of mining engineering. She was one of very few nineteenth-century women who achieved professional recognition while being married. Following her death in 1911, the Ellen Richards Research Prize was established to promote scientific research by women. Its initial cash award of $1,000 almost equalled a year's salary. The best-known recipient was Polish-born Marie Sklodowska Curie. Curie, the first person to win two Nobel Prizes, received the Richards award in 1921.

References and Resources

Women Scientists in America by Margaret W. Rossiter, Johns Hopkins University Press, 1982.

"Ellen Swallow Richards: Technology and Women" by Ruth Schwartz Cowan, in *Technology in America: A History of Individuals and Ideas*, edited by Carroll W. Pursell, Jr., MIT Press, 1983.

American Women of Science by Edna Yost, J. B. Lippincott Co., 1955.

Dictionary of American Biography, Charles Scribner's Sons Publishers, 1932; with supplemental updates.

Elijah McCoy

Born:
March 27, 1843, in Colchester, Ontario, Canada

Died:
October 10, 1929, in Eloise, Michigan

"IT'S the real McCoy!" is a phrase that means high product quality. Although its origin is uncertain, it may have come from the work of Elijah McCoy. He invented an automatic lubrication system for locomotive steam engines and factory machinery.

McCoy's parents were slaves who escaped to Canada from Kentucky. They were quite poor and barely kept themselves alive with odd jobs during the winter months. McCoy was born in Canada, shortly before the family moved to Ypsilanti, Michigan. As a youth, his parents noticed that he enjoyed working on mechanical equipment. McCoy attended grammar school but probably did not graduate. Nonetheless, his parents saw the education of their children as the only way to success. They labored and sacrificed to send their 15-year-old son overseas for technical study.

Because of his Scottish-sounding family name, McCoy was encouraged to seek education in Scotland. Its capital, Edinburgh, was the center of a region that produced many great technologists during the industrial revolution. James Nasmyth, inventor of the steam-operated forge, was born there in 1839. William Rankine, who developed the degrees Rankine scale, an absolute temperature scale for degrees Fahrenheit, was also born in Edinburgh, in 1820. James Watt was born in nearby Glasgow. Like the New Orleans-born black technologist Norbert Rillieux, McCoy chose to go overseas to learn his trade in a more socially stable and accepting setting. He obtained an apprenticeship in mechanical engineering in Edinburgh.

Returning home several years later, he went to work for the Michigan Central Railroad at its headquarters in Ypsilanti. His duties included lubricating the steam engines and moving parts of locomotives. The pistons and wheel bearings generated so much heat from friction that they had to be periodically lubricated by hand. Each of two pistons had a small outside cup with a valve at its bottom. Before the engine left the station, McCoy placed a small amount of oil in the cylinder through the cup. Since most trains stopped every few miles, this was sufficient lubrication to last until the next stop. Locomotives typically used one pint of oil every 20 to 35 miles. In that pre-petroleum period, processed beef fat was the most commonly used cylinder oil. For wheel bearing lubrication, oil from sperm whales or lard from pigs was often used.

Every time a locomotive needed this routine lubrication, the entire train stopped, whether or not there were passengers and cargo. The stops were time consuming, and in 1867 the longest run between them was only 40 miles. Lubrication was a problem that hindered the expansion of the railroad system. In a similar situation, factory machinery also had to be periodically stopped for lubrication. The average loss of time accounted for as much as 25 percent of potential profits. McCoy asked himself why machines couldn't be modified to lubricate themselves.

In a small, crude machine shop at his home, McCoy experimented with automatic lubrication. He designed a lubricating cup that had its own oil supply. The cup supplied intermittent drops of oil, automatically lubricating moving parts. Following two years of after-hours effort, McCoy received his first patent for his lubricator in 1872. He wrote that it "provided for the continuous flow of oil on the gears and other moving parts of a machine in order to keep it lubricated properly and continuously and thereby do away with the necessity of shutting down the machine periodically." With McCoy's invention, rotating machinery no longer had to stop for frequent lubrication.

McCoy's invention was particularly well suited to lubricating the slow-moving piston in a steam engine that powered factory tools. A hollow stem extended from the bottom of the cup into the cylinder. A rod passed through the hollow stem and connected to a simple plug valve in the lubricating cup. The other end of the rod attached to the piston. When the cylinder reached the top of the stroke, the rod opened the plug valve, allowing oil to enter the cylinder. It was not a precise system because the steam pressure tended to hold back much of the oil, but it worked well enough. A year later, McCoy improved his invention by designing valves that allowed his lubricator to pass oil during the exhaust stroke, when the steam pressure was much lower.

McCoy then worked on a lubricator for the pistons inside a locomotive's steam engine. They operated with steam at about 100 psi pressure and 400° F. It was hard to provide controlled quantities of oil to the rapidly rotating hot engines, and parts often wore out. McCoy found a solution to the problem by using a combination of oil and graphite, a solid lubricant, and using steam pressure to help force oil into the cylinder.

His graphite lubricator greatly reduced wear and saved fuel. McCoy considered it his finest invention. His advertisements described it as: "The Perfect Graphite Lubricator for Locomotives." The Michigan Central Railroad relieved him of his maintenance duties and employed him as an instructor in the use of his new lubricators. The lubricators quickly found use on all long-distance western locomotives, Great Lakes steamers, and transatlantic ships.

For factory machines, McCoy replaced his 1872 cup with a more sophisticated one. Instead of providing a constant drip of oil, the new model regulated the time intervals between lubrications. His automatic lubricators were an instant success and machinery operators retrofitted them as soon as they could. For the next 25 years, McCoy continually made improvements to his original invention. Others patented their version of an automatic lubricator, but none could match the quality of McCoy's.

McCoy often assigned partial or total rights to others for his patents. That way,

McCoy's sophisticated lubricator used steam pressure to force oil to the internal parts of steam engines on locomotives.

he immediately received money to continue his evening experiments. He assigned his first patent totally to William and S. C. Hamlin. He kept his second patent for himself. But for his third and fourth, McCoy assigned half his rights to Sullivan Cutcheon and Edward Allen. After his invention came into general use, McCoy became a consultant for many large companies. He lectured, conducted seminars, and spent time on research in his machine shop.

McCoy received 57 patents, most related to lubrication. His patents covered lubrication with thin oil, heavy grease, and slippery solids, such as graphite. Around 1920, investors established the Elijah McCoy Manufacturing Co. in the Broadway Market Building in Detroit. The company's products were based on McCoy's patents, but since he had sold his patent rights, McCoy was not a major stockholder. An improved railroad air-brake lubricator that he developed for the company was his most significant invention during that period. Part of it supplied a mixture of oil and graphite to the cylinder in the air compressor near the steam engine. Another part provided dry graphite to the air cylinders at each wheel's brake. A short time after formation of the company, McCoy's wife died. McCoy's own health then began to deteriorate, and he died a few years later in a nursing home.

McCoy resided in Detroit after 1882. Until his health began to fail he lived a productive and active life. Even at 80, he walked erect and was proud that he could touch his toes without bending his knees. While he distinguished himself among his professional colleagues, he lived as an ordinary civic-minded citizen. McCoy preferred the company of his wife, family, and a few close friends. He spent much of his free time counseling black teenagers at a local youth center. McCoy tried to impress upon the young people that they could accomplish even more than he had if they got a proper education.

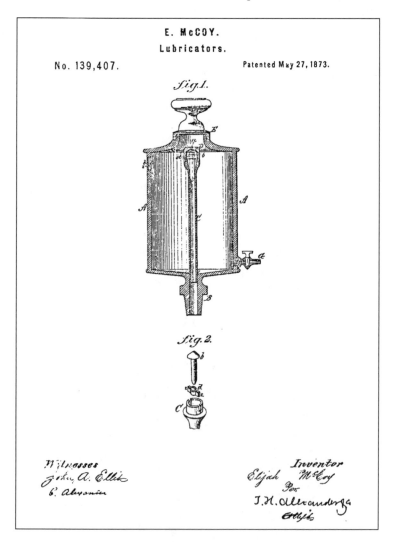

McCoy had several lubricator patents. This was among his early ones.

References and Resources

The Real McCoy: African-American Invention and Innovation by Portia P. James, Smithsonian Institution Press, 1989.

American Locomotives by John H. White, Jr., Johns Hopkins Press, 1968.

American Black Scientists and Inventors by Edward S. Jenkins and others, National Science Teachers Association, circa 1970.

Black Pioneers of Science and Invention by Louis Haber, Harcourt Brace World, 1970.

Dictionary of American Biography, Charles Scribner's Sons Publishers, 1932; with supplemental updates.

George Westinghouse

ONLY a few teenagers have ever received a patent. Even fewer people in their twenties establish a corporation based on a single invention. George Westinghouse did both. He patented a commercially unsuccessful rotary steam engine at the age of 19. But his railroad air brake was another matter. During a dramatic demonstration in 1869, his invention impressed many influential people. They helped the 23-year-old Westinghouse establish the Westinghouse Air Brake Co. with an initial capitalization of a half million dollars.

Westinghouse was one of nine children born into a large family in eastern New York. His father, a manufacturer of agricultural implements, introduced all his children to the technical aspects of production. At the age of 10, the younger Westinghouse worked in the machine shop each day after school. A generally disagreeable youngster, Westinghouse never showed interest in learning the use of tools. He was prone to temper tantrums and continually disrupted his school classroom. He disliked his studies and at the age of 16, asked his parents for permission to join the U.S. Navy. The earlier enlistment of two of his older brothers and Westinghouse's difficulties at school encouraged his parents to consent. Westinghouse subsequently served on several ships and attained the rank of Acting Third Assistant Engineer.

Westinghouse returned home in 1865. Family members immediately noticed the maturing effect that military service had had on him. He had learned self-discipline and developed a sense of responsibility. Those qualities served him well when he returned to work in his father's machine shop, taking on the rotary steam engine as his first project. Westinghouse got the idea

Westinghouse Electric Corp.

Born:
October 6, 1846, in Central Bridge, New York

Died:
March 12, 1914, in New York, New York

for the engine while serving on steam-powered ships. He received patent number 50,759 for the engine three weeks after his nineteenth birthday, but the engine proved impractical. This early experience did, however, lead him to work on steam turbines later in his life.

Westinghouse read that Europeans used compressed air to operate drills and hammers. He was particularly fascinated by the use of compressed air in constructing the Mount Cenis Tunnel through the Italian Alps. After witnessing the collision of two trains, Westinghouse wondered if he might also use compressed air to stop trains.

Before 1869, trains were usually no more than five cars long and they traveled no faster than 30 mph. The method used to stop them made the speed limitation necessary. Each car had its own brake operator. On hearing a whistle signal from the locomotive engineer, the brake operators on each car turned brake handles. The engineer did not directly control the brakes, and it usually took about a mile to stop a train. If there was an emergency on the tracks ahead, it was often impossible to stop in time to avoid a problem. Because of this difficulty, and the existence of poor signaling systems, trains

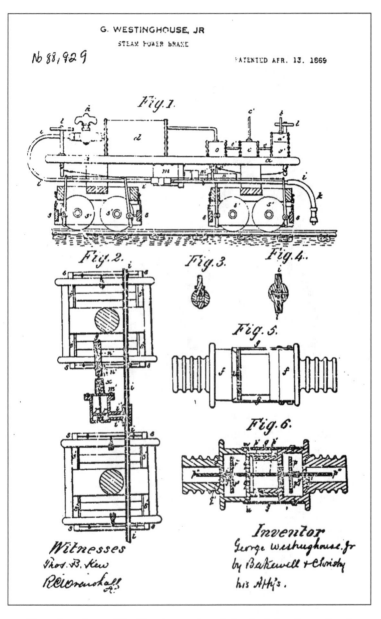

Drawing from Westinghouse's original air brake patent

sometimes collided. They also occasionally ran off the tracks and crashed because of washed out bridges or defective rails. The engineer might see these hazards far ahead but still not be able to stop in time. Because of poor brake design, railroad travel was not as safe as it might have been. By 1867, there

were more than 600 patents addressing the concern. Many inventors tried using steam pressure, but the steam condensed to water in brake lines and proved ineffective.

Westinghouse was the first to use air pressure. He invented and patented a brake that operated from compressed air at 60 psi. He designed a compressor installed near the engine that used steam power to develop air pressure. But Westinghouse found himself unable to interest others in this new idea. Financier Cornelius Vanderbilt turned the young man down for trying to "stop a train with wind." Nonetheless, Westinghouse arranged a test with the Panhandle Railroad in Pennsylvania. He installed air brakes on four passenger cars and brake controls in the locomotive, borrowing all the money he could to personally pay for the work. He scheduled a test to take place in April 1869 over 35 miles of open country between Pittsburgh and Steubenville, Ohio. Since brake operators would not ride on the train, he took special precautions to keep people from crossing the tracks.

Before the start of the test, the locomotive pulled out of Pittsburgh's Union Station with Westinghouse and several railroad officials riding in the last car. Soon, as the train emerged from the Grant Hill tunnel, the locomotive engineer saw a horse-drawn wagon on the tracks, with the horses rearing in the air. The engineer immediately applied Westinghouse's experimental air brakes. The rapid stop threw all the passengers onto the floor, and the train came to a halt just four feet from the wagon. The railroad officials were impressed. The scheduled testing went on later that day, but the officials had already made up their minds. Shortly after that, Westinghouse established the Westinghouse Air Brake Co. and had no difficulty locating $500,000 in capitalization money. At 23 years of age, he was the president of a company.

Westinghouse's original air brake patent was the first of his 103 patents for railroad brakes. Just five years later, more than 7,000 passenger cars were equipped with his air brake. With his fertile imagination and driving energy, Westinghouse also developed a railroad signaling system that kept trains moving safely and efficiently. Moving on to natural gas systems, he devised a meter to measure gas consumption. Westinghouse also invented a leakproof piping system and an automatic cutoff that turned off the gas if pressure dropped below 0.25 psi. In all, he held 361 patents.

After the air brake, Westinghouse's most important contribution was probably his introduction of alternating current (ac) to the public. Westinghouse knew that ac was easily changed in transformers and could be more efficiently sent over high-voltage transmission wires. His company developed ac equipment and steam turbines to power the alternators. He bought Nikola Tesla's ac motor patents and hired Tesla to work on development. Thomas Edison, on the other hand, advocated the use of direct current (dc) because it could easily be stored in batteries. All the generating equipment Edison sold was dc. Because of their difference of opinion, Edison and Westinghouse became professional rivals competing for the huge consumer electrical market. For his part, Westinghouse avoided bringing personalities into the argument. Following a competition that newspapers called "The Battle of the Currents," Westinghouse won a crucial victory over Edison. He received the contract to install three massive 5,000 horsepower ac alternators at Niagara Falls. The alternators went on line on November 16, 1896, to deliver power to Buffalo, New York, 22 miles away.

Westinghouse received many honors and was the first American awarded Germany's Grashoff Medal. He became wealthy at a fairly early age, but in most ways he lived modestly. He had no expensive hobbies and did little traveling. However, he did have a large home on the east side of Pittsburgh for his wife and only child, and he had a private railroad car. Westinghouse was a private person with no vices beyond a tendency to eat too much. He kept no diary, wrote few letters, and refused to let reporters interview him. Few photographs were taken of him. Near the end of his life, he wrote the inscription for his own tombstone, which acknowledged the importance of his military service: "George Westinghouse (1846-1914)—Acting Third Assistant Engineer, U.S. Navy (1864-1865)."

References and Resources

Inventing: How the Masters Did It by Byron Vanderbilt, Moore Publishing, 1974.

George Westinghouse (1846-1994), Westinghouse Electric Corp., 1946.

American Science and Invention by Mitchell Wilson, Bonanza Books, 1960.

Dictionary of American Biography, Charles Scribner's Sons Publishers, 1932; with supplemental updates.

National Cyclopedia of American Biography, James T. White and Co. Publishers, 1891; with supplemental updates.

McGraw-Hill Encyclopedia of Biography, McGraw-Hill Publishers, 1973.

Asimov's Biographical Encyclopedia of Science and Technology by Isaac Asimov, Doubleday and Co. Publishers, 1964.

Thomas Alva Edison

Born:
February 11,
1847, in Milan,
Ohio

Died:
October 18,
1931, in
Orange,
New Jersey

National Portrait Gallery, Smithsonian Institution

Thomas Edison at 23

THE words "Mary had a little lamb. . ." are far from technical. Nonetheless, they were the first intelligible sounds ever permanently recorded. Thomas Alva Edison said them loudly into the speaker of an experimental phonograph in 1877. Edison patented the phonograph—frequently described as his most novel and original invention—when he was a dark-haired and slender 30-year-old. It was his favorite invention and the 141st he patented out of a lifetime total of 1,093—the most ever granted by the U.S. Patent Office.

Called Al or Alva, Edison attended grade school for only a few weeks. His insatiable curiosity prompted him to ask many questions that his teachers could not answer. They were all happy when Edison's mother chose to teach him at home. At 14, Edison went to work for the Grand Trunk Railroad

as a newsboy and general vendor. The job introduced him to steam engines, machine shops, telegraph offices, and other aspects of technology. Long train stops gave him time to visit Detroit's public library. There, he read books on science and technology that were not available in his hometown. The young Edison was a speed reader who went through books almost as fast as he could turn their pages. His native intelligence, nurtured by his mother's instruction, and his interest in technology combined to place him on a remarkable path of discovery and invention.

In 1869, Edison applied for a job in New York City. While he waited for his interview, a ticker-tape machine used to report stock prices broke down in a nearby office. Edison repaired the machine, and he received a job offer on the spot. He accepted the job, and in his spare time continued to experiment with the ticker-tape machine. He invented a better one and offered it to the president of the Gold and Stock Telegraph Co. Hoping to receive $5,000 for it, but willing to settle for $3,000, Edison was speechless when the president offered him $40,000. He was only 23. He used the money to establish the first industrial research laboratory. The photo on this page shows Edison that year. His stated goal was to produce a new invention every 10 days, and he didn't fall far short. He averaged one invention every 24 days for the rest of his life. Edison's first large laboratory was in Menlo Park, New Jersey, and the public commonly called him "the Wizard of Menlo Park."

Edison is probably best known for his 1879 electric lamp. However, he did not invent the incandescent light bulb. Sir Joseph Swan of England had one operating with a carbon filament almost 20 years earlier. Still,

Edison made the lamp practical. One major problem was identifying an effective filament. Edison wanted one with a high melting point. It had to conduct electricity poorly, having a resistance value of about 100 ohms. The filament also had to be strong enough to cycle many times between room temperature and incandescent temperature. After three years of searching, Edison found that carbonized thread worked reasonably well. He used thread in his 1879 lamp, but he found that its fragile nature made it unsuitable for large-scale production. The first lamps he sold to the public used filaments made from carbonized bamboo fiber. They lasted an average of 600 hours, compared with 40 hours for carbonized cotton thread. Edison called the company that he established to manufacture his electric lamps the Edison General Electric Co.

Although Edison's laboratory typically employed upwards of 100 people, it was essentially a one-man operation. Edison's diversity, sense of detail, and powers of concentration seemed unequaled. Many of his inventions focused on electrical items, but he worked in other areas as well. For example, he received patents for a mimeograph duplicator, organic chemicals, iron production, and motion pictures, as well as the all-mechanical phonograph. Edison's imagination was boundless. By the time he reached his early thirties, he had already received half his lifetime total of patents.

Edison was an expert telegrapher, and he wanted to find a way to permanently record the dot-dash code. His first design used a sheet of waxed paper wrapped around a cylinder. A blunted needle connected to a telephone speaker rested on the paper. Edison rotated the cylinder while loudly making dots and dashes with a telegraph key. He then backed up the needle and tried to play back the sound through the telephone speaker. He couldn't tell a dot from a dash, but he noticed that the rapidly rotating cylinder produced a humming sound.

Edison's most trusted employee was John Kruesi, the man who made all of Edison's patent models. Edison asked Kruesi to make an experimental phonograph similar to the one in the photograph on this page. Edison wrapped the spiral-grooved brass cylinder with tin foil. A blunted needle attached to a speaker pressed against the tin foil. On December 3, 1877, Edison's squeaky voice shouted a nursery rhyme into the speaker as the cylinder was rotated by hand. Then, the blunted needle was returned to its starting point. As the cylinder was again rotated, the needle picked up peaks and valleys on the tin foil. A scratchy but intelligible sound came from the speaker. Edison was just as stunned as the others. He later said, "I was always afraid of things that worked the first time."

When the U.S. Patent Office made its usual search for an earlier patent, it found nothing that even remotely anticipated the phonograph. It was a completely new device. The phonograph was Edison's favorite invention, and the public loved it, too. Edison started to manufacture phonographs, and members of his staff developed an improved wax compound for the cylinders. To extend the life of the blunted needle, they developed an artificial jewel for its tip. Edison stayed with cylindrical records until 1912. Emile Berliner, a German-born American, patented the flat phonograph record in 1904. Flat-disk records were more compact and immediately began to replace

Smithsonian Institition Photo No. 9082

One of Edison's earliest phonographs

cylinders. Edison eventually had to adopt the more practical disk records. In all, Edison manufactured phonographs for more than 40 years. Ironically, Edison himself was almost deaf from boyhood on.

Edison was strongly independent and received countless medals during his life. He once joked that he had to measure them by the quart. After 13 years of marriage, his first wife died in 1884. He married again two years later. He had a total of six children. One son, Charles, became Secretary of the Navy in 1939 and Governor of New Jersey in 1941. Still, Edison wasn't much of a family man, and he spent most of his time at the laboratory. Work remained his greatest pleasure.

Edison had three close friends: naturalist John Burroughs, tire manufacturer Harvey Firestone, and automobile manufacturer Henry Ford. The four spent many vacations car camping in the Smoky Mountains and in other rustic settings. Starting in 1901, Edison regularly spent February and March at his winter home in Fort Myers, Florida. His friends often visited him there during the cold winter months, and Firestone planted a banyan tree that still grows on Edison's Florida grounds. For the 1929 golden anniversary of Edison's electric light, Ford moved Edison's Menlo Park laboratory to Greenfield Village, Ford's large public museum in Dearborn, Michigan.

Old age slowed Edison down but did not stop him. He received patents right up through the last year of his life. To pay their final respects to the world's most prolific inventor, tens of thousands of people waited in a cold New Jersey drizzle when Edison died.

References and Resources

A Streak of Luck—The Life and Legend of Thomas Alva Edison by Robert Conant, Seaview Books, 1979.

The Engineer by C. C. Furnas, Joe McCarthy, and the editors of Time Life Inc., 1966.

American Invention and Technology by Mitchell Wilson, Bonanza Books, 1960.

Dictionary of American Biography, Charles Scribner's Sons Publishers, 1932; with supplemental updates.

National Cyclopedia of American Biography, James T. White and Co. Publishers, 1891; with supplemental updates.

McGraw-Hill Encyclopedia of Biography, McGraw-Hill Publishers, 1973.

Asimov's Biographical Encyclopedia of Science and Technology by Isaac Asimov, Doubleday & Co. Publishers, 1964.

Alexander Graham Bell

THE most valuable patent in United States history is number 174,465. It was issued in 1876 to a 29-year-old who had immigrated to America from Scotland. The patent was for the telephone. Today, there are almost 500 million telephones in use throughout the world, and Alexander Graham Bell's name will always be associated with the telephone.

Bell was born in a comfortable three-story house that we would now call a townhouse. The second of three sons, his parents named him Alexander after his grandfather, and he later adopted the name Graham after a family friend. Family members usually called him Graham. Both his father and grandfather were recognized professionals in the field of vocal physiology. Bell's father taught hearing-impaired people to speak, and he wrote several textbooks on the topic. He called his technique *visible speech*. Bell's grandfather was a professor of elocution at the University of London. Bell's mother was a sensitive musician and painter who helped him develop an appreciation for both hearing and music. He played music by ear and at one time considered a career in music.

During his early years, Bell's mother taught him at home. He eventually decided to follow his father's career path. He entered a Scottish academy at the age of 10, and by 20 he had received the finest university education available in Great Britain. Bell started working with his father in London and became his partner in 1869. In this context, he carried out experiments to determine how vowel sounds are produced. This started his interest in electricity.

Then, disaster uprooted his family. Bell's younger brother died of tuberculosis in 1867, then his older brother in 1870. Local physicians warned that Graham was show-

National Portrait Gallery, Smithsonian Institution

Born:
March 3, 1847, in Edinburgh, Scotland

Died:
August 2, 1922, in Baddeck, Nova Scotia, Canada

ing signs of the disease and was at risk. His father had recently returned from the United States and Canada where he had been lecturing on speech articulation. He had found the weather there more pleasant than that in London, and he received greater professional recognition in America. Sacrificing a well-established career, the father moved the family to Canada. He chose to settle near Hamilton, Ontario, which he felt would provide a healthy climate for his surviving son. He was correct, and Graham soon fully recovered his health.

A principal at a Boston school for the hearing impaired requested a demonstration for her teachers on how to use visible speech. The younger Bell went in his father's place and spent three months at the school. He also visited other schools in the area. Due in part to his courteous manner, the demand for his services increased and he opened a school for teachers. Highly respected by his peers, Bell subsequently received an appointment as professor of vocal physiology at Boston University. He enjoyed life in Boston and met a young deaf woman whom he married in 1877. He became an American citizen on November 10, 1882.

Bell did some private teaching and was particularly successful with the son of Thomas Sanders, a wealthy leather merchant. To show his gratitude, Sanders offered to subsidize evening experiments Bell conducted in rooms he had rented on the top floor of a boarding house. Between 1873 and 1876, Bell worked along three related lines: making speech visible on paper (he called this making a *photoautograph*), a multiple telegraph, and an electric speaking telegraph. Bell found that he lacked the technical skill needed to make parts necessary for his experiments. He hired Thomas Watson to assist him. The two men became close friends, and Watson eventually received a share in the telephone patent as payment for his work.

Replica of the world's first telephone. Bell spoke down into the large opening.

Bell said that the theory behind electrical transmission of the voice came to him while he was vacationing at his parents' home in Ontario in 1874. Putting the theory into practice presented a problem. But, Bell knew that Joseph Henry, first organizer of the Smithsonian Institution, had some knowledge in this area. Bell visited Henry in Washington, D.C., and Henry advised him that he was on the right track, that he should not yet publish his incomplete results, and that he should file a patent as soon as he could. Encouraged by the aging Henry, Bell worked even more diligently on

The first commercial telephones, in 1877, used the same opening for both speaking and listening.

the project. His patent application described a transmitter that had a short platinum wire attached directly to a diaphragm. As speech caused the diaphragm to vibrate, the wire moved up and down in a weak acid solution. When the wire went deeper, the resistance decreased. As the wire rose, the resistance increased. This meant that the sound controlled the current passing through the wire. The apparatus looked like a metal glass, set on a small metal frame, over a small coil of wire. On March 10, 1876, the telephone transmitted its first complete intelligible sentence. Bell shouted down into the mouthpiece of their experimental telephone: "Mr. Watson, come here. I want to see you." Watson was in another room but heard the sentences clearly.

Bell set up a display of his new telephone at the 1876 Centennial Exposition in Philadelphia. It failed to attract much attention until the Brazilian emperor, Dom Pedro II, requested a demonstration. Bell had set up schools for the hearing impaired in Brazil and Dom Pedro recognized him. Dom Pedro listened at the receiver and exclaimed, "It talks!" Newspapers reported the event the following day, introducing the telephone to the public. Bell improved on his patented transmitter and receiver, and the Bell Telephone Co. came into existence in 1877. Passage of a year's time found 3,000 telephones in use and the first telephone exchange opened in New Haven, Connecticut. Alexander Graham Bell found himself rich and famous before he turned 30.

Bell's technical work in telephony ended completely in the early 1880s. He cheerfully admitted that keeping up with the rapidly changing technology did not appeal to him. However, many claimants came forward to contest his patent, and Bell became involved in about 600 court cases. The United States Supreme Court upheld all of his claims. The court declared Bell the discoverer of the only way that speech could be electrically transmitted.

The Scottish-born Bell had a summer home built on Cape Breton Island in Nova Scotia, which means "New Scotland." He maintained an interest in technology and used his remaining 45 years in many different ways. Bell financed the early stages of Albert Michelson's experiment to measure the speed of light. Michelson went on to become America's first scientific Nobel Prize winner in 1907. In 1883, Bell helped to establish and financed the first 12 years of *Science*, which is now a principal scientific journal. He served as president of the National Geographic Society from 1896 to 1904. He founded the Aerial Experiment Association with Glenn Curtiss and others. Bell's fertile mind helped produce the first airplane to make a public flight, in 1908, and the first to fly in the British Empire. He built a twin-engine hydrofoil boat that held the world's speed record for 10 years at 70.86 mph. He invented an iron lung and even investigated rocket propulsion. Bell considered himself a teacher first, and he continued to work with hearing-impaired people. Helen Keller, a close friend, dedicated her autobiography to him.

The first transcontinental telephone line was established in 1915 between New York and San Francisco. During opening ceremonies, Bell repeated his famous line to Thomas Watson on the West Coast: "Mr. Watson, come here. I want to see you." Watson humorously answered that he would be glad to come, but that it would take him a week to do so.

Bell often proudly proclaimed that he was an American by choice rather than by accident of birth. His grave stone in Nova Scotia reads: "Died a Citizen of the U.S.A."

References and Resources

Alexander Graham Bell, a pamphlet produced by AT&T, dated July 1979.

Those Inventive Americans, National Geographic Society, 1971.

Inventing: How the Masters Did It, by Byron M. Vanderbilt, Moore Publishing Co., 1974.

"Hello to History" by William Grimes, *New York Times News Service*, 7 March 1992

Dictionary of American Biography, Charles Scribner's Sons Publishers, 1932; with supplemental updates.

National Cyclopedia of American Biography, James T. White & Co. Publishers, 1891; with supplemental updates.

McGraw-Hill Encyclopedia of Biography, McGraw-Hill Publishers, 1973.

Asimov's Biographical Encyclopedia of Science and Technology by Isaac Asimov, Doubleday & Co. Publishers, 1964.

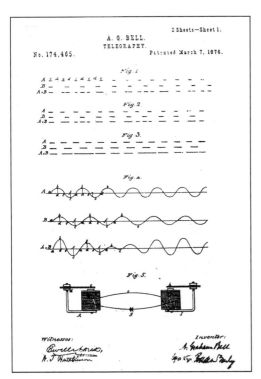

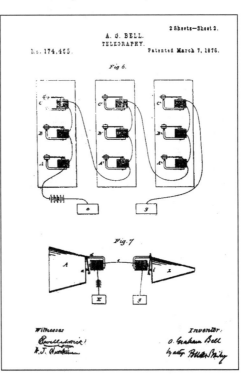

Bell's patent for the telephone is the most valuable ever awarded. His later telephone patents were primarily refinements of his original one.

Lewis Latimer

Born:
September 4,
1848, in
Chelsea,
Massachusetts

Died:
December 11,
1928, in
Flushing,
New York

MOST people know that Thomas Edison made the incandescent lamp practical. However, many others contributed to improving the lamp to make it an affordable and durable consumer product. One such person was Lewis Latimer. He invented the first inexpensive and practical method for manufacturing carbon filaments and securing them to metal wires. Edison employed Latimer and so respected his opinion that Latimer often represented Edison in legal proceedings that took place in the early years of the electrical industry.

Latimer's father escaped from slavery in Virginia in the 1830s and settled in the Boston area. While Latimer was still a child, his father left the family. Latimer went to work at the age of 10 to help support his mother and three siblings. He had received little formal education. Latimer did the best he could to earn money through odd jobs and selling newspapers. After the Civil War broke out, he enlisted in the Union Navy at 16. He served on the side-wheeled steamer *U.S.S. Massasoit* and saw action on the James River in Virginia. After his honorable discharge in 1865, Latimer found employment with Crosby and Gould, patent attorneys in Boston. He had no related work experience, and he started out as an office boy. It was a fortunate turn of events because the job introduced him to inventions and inventing. In his spare time, Latimer taught himself drafting from library books and he practiced the principles with a used set of instruments. Noticing that he was a self-starter and willing to learn new skills, Crosby and Gould moved him up through the ranks. He was promoted to drafter and then chief drafter.

In his new position, Latimer prepared the drawings of inventions that went to the Patent Office in Washington. He worked in a building that was close to a school where Alexander Graham Bell conducted speech experiments. The two apparently became friends, and Bell used the offices of Crosby and Gould to patent the telephone. He specifically asked that Latimer prepare the drawings and descriptions for his 1876 telephone patent application.

During this period, Latimer received the first of his own several patents. The title of his 1874 patent was "Water Closets for Railroad Cars." This invention met with only limited success, but it launched Latimer on a career as an inventor.

Looking for a hardware-oriented position, Latimer found employment in 1880 with the United States Electric Lighting Co. in Bridgeport, Connecticut. The company's owner was Hiram Maxim, a prolific inventor whose best-known invention may have been the machine gun. Maxim also worked with gasoline engines and steam engines, and he had considerable experience with arc lighting. He wanted to extend his expertise to incandescent lighting and was emerging as Thomas Edison's most serious rival.

In his first significant project with Maxim, Latimer and co-worker Joseph Nichols investigated methods to attach metal conductors to fragile lightbulb filaments. The two developed a carbon filament with flattened ends that could be pinched with copper- or platinum-plated terminals. Copper wires connected the terminals to a metal base. With all components enclosed in a glass globe, the lightbulb worked like a modern incandescent lamp.

In developing his most important patent, Latimer conducted experiments that resulted in improved carbon filaments. Edison used bamboo strips that he curved and exposed to high heat in the absence of air. The result was a filament of almost pure carbon that glowed when electricity passed through it. Latimer's longer-lasting filaments came from textiles clamped under pressure between sheets of cardboard. The cardboard had grooves to hold the filament and flatten its ends to serve as electrical connections to the lamp base. Both the cardboard and the textile in the clamped assembly had the same rate of expansion. The assembly was placed in an oven and baked. The pre-shaped textile turned into a carbon filament that was stronger and longer lasting than Edison's strip of bamboo.

Latimer's methods proved so successful that Maxim had him set up an incandescent lamp department in Maxim's factory in Montreal. To communicate with the French-speaking workers, Latimer taught himself the language in record time. He found that he had to instruct the workers in all the processes for making Maxim lamps, including glass blowing. It took several months before the factory moved into full production. At that point, the public was still uncertain how to best use the new electric lamps, and Latimer's were primarily used to illuminate railroad stations.

After attending the Paris Exposition in 1881, Maxim never returned to the United States. Edison's display at the exposition completely overshadowed his, and Maxim

decided to drop out of the lighting field. He settled in England, became a British citizen, was knighted by King Edward VII for his technical accomplishments, and died in 1916 at the age of 76.

Latimer moved to the Olmstead Electric Lighting Co. and then to the Acme Electric Light Co., both in the New York City area. He began his association with Edison in 1883 as a drafter and engineer in an office at 65 Fifth Avenue. A few years later, he began a series of frequent appearances as an expert witness on Edison's behalf before the U.S. Board of Patent Control. At the time, there was no national policy concerning the use of direct current (dc) or alternating current (ac) electricity. Edison had a great deal of dc-generating equipment, and he wanted the entire country to standardize on direct current. George Westinghouse, realizing the technical advantages of alternating current, just as strongly favored ac. Latimer testified

The filament in this lamp was manufactured using Lewis Latimer's patented technique.

on the issue to the Board of Patent Control, which attempted to establish standards.

Latimer also supervised the installation of electric lamps in New York, Philadelphia, and London. He made a significant contribution to the infant industry by writing the first standard textbook on electric lighting: *Incandescent Electric Lighting*, pub-

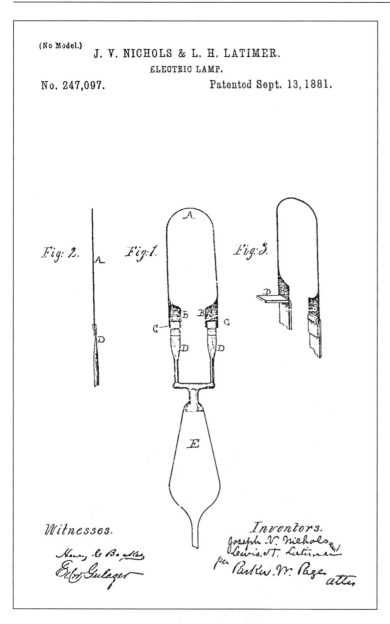

(No Model.)   J. V. NICHOLS & L. H. LATIMER.
                       ELECTRIC LAMP.
No. 247,097.   Patented Sept. 13, 1881.

Fig: 2.   *Fig: 1.*   *Fig: 3.*

Witnesses.   *Inventors.*

An early Latimer filament patent

pute. In 1896, Latimer left Edison to work as a drafter for the U.S. Board of Patent Control. He left that job in 1911 to become a full-time patent consultant. He retired in 1924.

Latimer was a member of the Edison Pioneers, a group of 28 technologists who had personally worked with Edison. Organized in 1918, the group held its annual meetings on February 11, Edison's birthday. An important year for the Pioneers was 1929, which marked the 50th anniversary of Edison's improvements to the incandescent lamp. It was called Light's Golden Jubilee, and the Edison Pioneers used the occasion to honor Latimer, who had died the previous year, along with Edison. The Pioneers recognized Latimer as the only black Edison Pioneer. Their official statement at the time of his death was: "Broad mindedness, versatility in the accomplishment of things intellectual and cultural, a linguist, a devoted husband and father, all were characteristics of him, and his genial presence will be missed from our gatherings."

Latimer was pleasant and well liked, and he was a man of many talents. Not only did he receive at least seven patents, but he was an amateur poet. On his 75th birthday, friends had his work printed and published in a 25-page booklet titled *Poems of Love and Life*. Latimer taught mechanical drawing to immigrants at the Henry Street Settlement in New York before illness claimed his life at the age of 80.

References and Resources

Black Pioneers of Science and Invention by Louis Haber, Harcourt Brace, 1970.

A Streak of Luck by Robert Conot, Seaview Books, 1979.

The Real McCoy: African-American Invention and Innovation by Portia P. James, Smithsonian Institution, 1989.

lished in 1890. He published it around the time that he transferred to Edison's seven-person legal department, where he served as chief drafter for patents under legal dis-

Benjamin Holt

THE word *bulldozer* brings to mind an off-road piece of equipment with a large scraper blade in front. A bulldozer moves easily over rough terrain because it has a track-laying system. The vehicle lays down its own track to spread its weight over a large area, which keeps it from getting stuck. Farmers used the first successful track layer on 20-ton tractors they operated on the soft, rich soil of northern California. Benjamin Holt and his three brothers built it in the course of trying to make a maneuverable agricultural power unit that had a large ground-contact area. Holt developed a pair of crude wooden crawlers and successfully tested the world's first practical track-laying tractor on Thanksgiving Day in 1904.

Four Holt brothers were born into a Concord, New Hampshire, family that had a sawmill that processed hardwoods for wagon construction. Concord's popular wagons and coaches, first made in 1813, carried passengers and mail throughout the entire New England area. Charles was the oldest son, followed by William, Ames, and, finally, Benjamin. The three older brothers moved to the San Francisco area in 1864, where they founded C. H. Holt and Co., which did business in hardwood, lumber, and wagon materials. They primarily dealt with structural applications such as axles, wheels, and frames. They had hardwood from their home state shipped west by cargo ship, and they dried it in the arid climate near Stockton, California. Benjamin stayed in New Hampshire to handle that end of the family business.

The Holt brothers soon organized the Stockton Wheel Co., and in 1883 Benjamin moved west to manage the company. The factory had cost $65,000 to construct. For power, it used a single 40-horsepower

Courtesy of the Caterpillar Tractor Co.

Born:
January 1, 1849, in Concord, New Hampshire

Died:
December 5, 1920, in Stockton, California

Corliss steam engine that had been manufactured in Providence, Rhode Island. All its machinery was belt driven by the Corliss engine. Production in the first year of operation totaled 6,000 wagon wheels and 5,000 carriage bodies. Among their more popular wheel sizes was a 10'-diameter model. Redwood loggers used two of these, connected by a strong 10' axle. The loggers would fasten a large log to the axle and pull it from the forest with a team of horses.

Many people who came to California during the Gold Rush of 1848 did not, as they had hoped, become instant millionaires. Instead, they found livelihoods farming wheat fields in the northern part of the state. Land was plentiful in the mid-1800s and the huge farms required large numbers of people and horses to harvest the crops. One farm was 36,000 acres in size, and

California ranked sixth in wheat production among the states.

Benjamin proved to be the most technically competent of the Holt brothers, and he soon expanded the company into the manufacture of farming equipment. He bought patent rights to some equipment and enlarged the factory to accommodate up to 300 employees. The company sold its first huge combine, a combination harvester and thresher, in 1886. It had a 14' cutting bar and was pulled by 18 horses. The largest combine the Holts built had a 50'-long cutting bar. (A 20' cutting bar is now considered large.) Combines were expensive combinations of gears, belts, and shafts that required as many as 40 horses to operate. Even a slight provocation, such as gear noise or a bee sting, could cause a stampede that damaged parts and required costly repairs. That problem and the difficulty of controlling so many animals made obvious the need for a more compact power source.

Holt built his first experimental steam-powered tractor in 1890. It had a 24'-long frame and developed 60 horsepower from a single 11"-diameter, 12"-stroke piston. Customers could order it equipped to burn wood, coal, or oil as fuel. When loaded with its 675 gallons of water, it weighed 48,000 pounds and rode on large metal wheels. In spite of their weight and awkward size, Holt's tractors were popular because they could harvest large fields for one-sixth the cost of horse-drawn combines. Although

they were designed for farming use, foresters bought them to haul redwood logs where there were no roads. Holt claimed his standard engine could haul 40 to 50 tons at 3 mph, and at half the cost of using horses. The tractors were extremely powerful and useful, but they were so heavy they often got stuck in the soft soil. Holt unsuccessfully tried to eliminate the problem by using large wheels. One tractor had wheels 7-1/2' in diameter and 6' wide—resulting in a 46'-wide tractor. The tractor was expensive, difficult to transport, and difficult to maneuver in the field. Holt experimented with multiple wheels until he decided to try a track-laying technique.

The use of tracks on moving machinery was not new at the time that Holt made his first attempt. Well over 100 worldwide patents had already been issued. However, all the designs were mechanical failures that did not work well in the field. Since most of the patents were British, Holt traveled to England in 1903 to investigate the courses of their development. He used his knowledge along with the company's expertise in design, metallurgy, and testing to develop a practical track layer. His 1904 crawler tractor proved a success from the beginning, and Holt soon introduced models under the Caterpillar trademark. Company photographer Charles Clements had observed that the tractor crawled like a caterpillar. Holt responded, "Caterpillar it is. That's the name for it!" The first production Caterpillars had a track frame on each side that measured 30" high x 42" wide x 9' long. The tracks were 3" x 4" redwood slats. Holt sold his first steam-powered tractor crawlers for $5,500.

Holt started developing gasoline-powered tractors in 1906. Gasoline engines offered the advantage of producing more power per pound since they did not have the added weight of the heavy boiler water needed for steam engines. The first 40 hp gas-powered models went into production in 1908. The company sold 28 of them for use in building a 233-mile aqueduct to supply water to the city of Los Angeles. The most popular gas-powered tractor was the Model 75, manufactured a few years later. It weighed 24,000 pounds and had a 75 hp engine.

The older Holt brothers realized that Benjamin had insight into mechanical devices

Courtesy of the Caterpillar Tractor Co.

One of Holt's original track-laying tractors working a field in northern California

that they lacked. By 1905, his brothers had either died or left the area, and Benjamin managed the factory by himself. His company became enormously profitable by making tracked vehicles for farming, road construction, and the military. Before the outbreak of World War I, 2,000 Caterpillar tractors were in service in more than 20 countries.

Holt was a quiet and unassuming man who loved his work. He was happiest when experimenting at the factory with whatever mechanical problems faced him at the time. He took out several patents. Holt's factory workers liked him, and he left a trust fund for former employees who found themselves in financial difficulties. He died in 1920, but his wife lived until 1952 and served as a regent of the University of the Pacific for 25 years. In 1925, the Holt Co. merged with one of its competitors, the C. L. Best Co., and took the name Caterpillar Tractor Co.

One noteworthy modern vehicle that uses the track-laying concept is the bulldozer. The precise origin of the word *bulldozer* is obscure and appears to be lost to history.

References and Resources

Benjamin Holt—The Story of the Caterpillar Tractor edited by Walter A. Payne, University of the Pacific, 1982.

Caterpillar—Century of Change, Caterpillar Tractor Co., 1984.

"Holt Caterpillar Tractor Designated International Lankmark," in *Mechanical Engineering*, June 1981.

Information from Holt trade journals stored at the Ford Archives, Dearborn, MI.

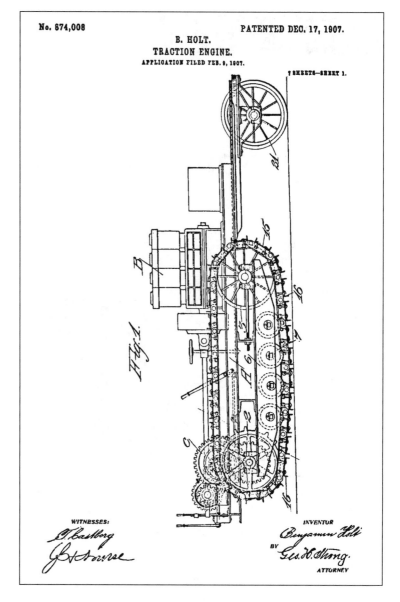

Holt's original track-laying patent

Francis Edgar Stanley and Freelan Oscar Stanley

Francis Edgar Stanley Born:
June 1, 1849, in Kingfield, Maine

Died:
July 31, 1918, in Newton, Massachusetts

Freelan Oscar Stanley Born:
June 1, 1849, in Kingfield, Maine

Died:
October 2, 1940, in Estes Park, Colorado

IN the late 1800s, people who reached the peak of New Hampshire's Mount Washington had to take a 10-mile dirt road that had a 12 percent grade. The first automobile with an engine powerful enough to make the climb was an 1899 Stanley steamer. FO Stanley and his wife used the car to take a leisurely two-hour journey to the peak. The engine in that $650 car was the same basic design as the one used in a race car that established a 1906 speed record of 127 mph. Both cars were manufactured by twin brothers Francis E. and Freelan O. Stanley.

The Stanley twins, known simply as FE and FO, were born on a farm in western Maine. They graduated from high school and then vocational school, where they learned woodworking. Both enjoyed whittling and for a while earned a living by making violins. FE also discovered that he had artistic talent and built up a portrait business. He moved to Lewiston where he entered the business full time, becoming a leading New England portrait photographer. He and FO began to experiment with photographic dry plates and organized the Stanley Dry Plate Co. in 1883. Their plates were so good that they came into general use throughout the United States and in several foreign countries. The brothers built a plant to manufacture them in Newton, Massachusetts, in 1890 where better railroad facilities were available.

Despite their docile appearances, the Stanley brothers loved to drive fast. That was what originally attracted them to steamers—steamers could outrun anything on the road. FE and FO often had contests between themselves to see who could drive the fastest between their factory in Newton and Lewiston. They experimented with steam power in their spare time. With only minimal knowledge of steam engine technology, the brothers decided they could build a better product than the ones then available. They established the Stanley Motor Carriage Co. in 1897 and hired workers to construct one steamer that year. However, they did not employ patternmakers for the casting molds. The Stanleys' experience with woodworking allowed them to carve their own patterns for engine castings.

The Stanley brothers built two more cars in 1898 and went into full production in 1899. They made 200 cars that year and bought an old bicycle factory next door to their photographic plate company. Within weeks, magazine publisher John Brisben Walker approached them with an offer to buy their business. Walker was lured by the backlog of hundreds of orders for Stanley steamers, and he offered 10 times what the Stanleys had invested. The twins could not turn down the offer. Walker established the Locomobile company and

The look-alike Stanley twins posed in a new steamer in 1899. That was their first year of full production.

made a steamer almost identical to the Stanley steamer.

Two years later, Locomobile decided to make gasoline-engine vehicles, and the Stanleys bought back their original company. They sold their photographic plate company to George Eastman in 1904 and renewed their interest in automotive production. Their factory became America's first successful automobile company, and Stanley steamers remained in production until 1927.

The Stanley steamer did not need a gearbox because steam engines develop large amounts of torque at low engine speed. FE was the primary designer of the engine. It had two horizontal side-by-side cylinders with staggered double-acting pistons. Because of the staggered pistons, the engine started immediately when boiler pressure was applied. The arrangement eliminated the hand starting that gasoline engines required. Cranking an engine by hand was the most feared aspect of motoring, because the frequent backfires that occurred during a start could cause a broken bone.

Excellent at business and tireless workers, the Stanleys enjoyed all aspects of automobile production and sales. They did not advertise in newspapers or magazines. Instead, they set up special racing cars for high-speed runs and let their steamer publicize itself through success in demonstrations, road races, and hill climbs. FE drove

the brothers' first racing car in 1903 in Readville, Massachusetts, and set a track record of almost 60 mph. For most racing events, however, their driver was Fred Marriott, the head of the Stanleys' maintenance department. Marriott drove a modified Stanley steamer in two memorable high-speed runs.

Their best-known racing car, the *Rocket*, resembled an inverted red canoe mounted on four bicycle wheels. On top, it had only an opening for the driver and a large steam exhaust pipe. Its simple rear-mounted 30 hp, 750 rpm engine (shown below) had a bore of 4-1/2" and a stroke of 6-1/2". The handle in the middle altered steam flow to allow the car to travel in reverse. Stanley steamers sold to the public carried a 16-gallon kerosene tank and a 20-gallon water tank, and they operated at boiler pressures up to 600 psi. Racing engines that used gasoline burners under wire-wrapped boilers were typically uprated to 1,300 psi.

Marriott drove the *Rocket* in January 1906 at Daytona Beach, Florida. Following a

Smithsonian Institution Photo No. 34258

This two-cylinder steam engine powered the 1906 Stanley steamer *Rocket* to a world speed record of 127 mph.

seven-mile accelerating run, he established a world speed record of 127.659 mph for the measured mile. The Stanleys wanted to exceed that speed the following year. With

Marriott again driving, their speeding car was almost silent except for a faint whine from its slowly rotating engine. When it passed the marker at the beginning of the measured mile, it hit a depression in the sand. With its smoothly covered under side, the car acted like the wing of an airplane. It rose in the air and sailed above the ground for about 100 feet. When it dropped back down, it was dashed to pieces by its own built-up momentum. The car's heavy boiler broke free and rolled 1,000 feet along the beach. The *Rocket* was a total loss. The badly injured Marriott fully recovered and lived for almost 50 more years. An informal timing rig showed that the car had traveled at 190 mph. The unofficial measurement was unverified, though, and the car had no speedometer. Badly shaken by the near-disaster, FE and FO never built another race car.

The almost inseparable twins had few, if any, personal vices, but they did enjoy practical jokes. Both wore identical full beards, dressed alike, and tried to confuse people whenever they could. In one trick, FO would take off very fast in his car a few minutes before FE. After FO was stopped by a police officer for speeding, FE would slowly and solemnly drive by, identical in all respects other than speed to FO and his car.

During one high-speed drive between Newton and Lewiston, FE came across two wagons stopped in the road as he crested a hill. He swerved the car into a ditch and was killed. This tragedy, in 1918, was almost more than FO could endure. He retired and moved to a hotel he built in Colorado. Without the energetic Stanley twins to provide vigorous leadership, the company failed.

The last production Stanley steamer was built in 1927. It was the final copy of over 60,000 vehicles to bear the Stanley nameplate. This was the largest number of steamers produced by any company. FO died in 1940. Not until 1985 did another steamer officially exceed the 30 hp *Rocket*'s 1906 speed record.

References and Resources

"The Stanleys and Their Steamer" by John Carlova in *American Heritage*, February 1959.

The Stanley Steamer and Other Steam Cars by Nick Taylor, Bellerophon Books, 1980.

Pictorial History of the Automobile by Phillip Van Doren Stern, Viking Press, 1953.

Materials at the Ford Museum Archives, Dearborn, MI.

Dictionary of American Biography, Charles Scribner's Sons Publishers, 1932; with supplemental updates.

National Cyclopedia of American Biography, James T. White and Co. Publishers, 1891; with supplemental updates.

A drawing for one of the Stanleys' patents for a photographic dry plate manufacturing machine is at right. At left is one of many the brothers received for steam-powered motor cars.

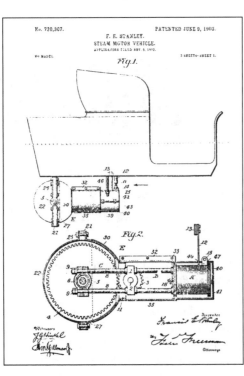

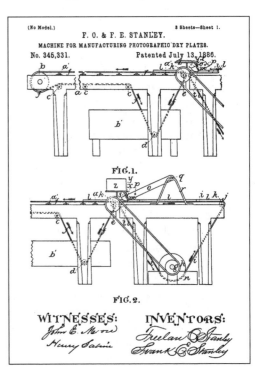

Edward Weston

The Electrical World, June 1888

Born:
May 9, 1850, in
Shropshire,
England

Died:
August 20,
1936, in
Montclair,
New Jersey

DIGITAL meters are so common today that we might not appreciate the measurement problems encountered by nineteenth-century electrical pioneers. All they had available were delicate galvanometers that made only comparative readings. They did not read in volts, amperes, or ohms. Galvanometers could not be moved during a test because the earth's magnetic field affected them. Thunderstorms and even the metal nails in shoes upset meter readings. The problem so exasperated Edward Weston that he took time from his busy life as a generator manufacturer to invent the world's first practical direct-reading voltmeter in 1886.

Weston was born in a brick farmhouse in a small town 150 miles northwest of London, England. His grandfather was a well-to-do farmer and his father was a respected mechanic. His family moved to the dynamic industrial city of Wolverhampton when Weston was 9. There, for the first time, he saw steel companies, foundries, and gas works. The school he attended introduced him to the exciting new field of electricity. He conducted textbook experiments at home using glass jars, sulfuric acid, and small pieces of copper and carbon. Yet his parents saw no future in his work with electricity, and they obtained a medical apprenticeship for him at 16. As an apprentice, Weston gained a knowledge of chemistry that would help him later in life, but he decided to leave the field of medicine after three years. While traveling by train to London, a chance meeting with a talkative and persuasive American tourist made him consider moving to the United States. Three weeks later, in May 1870, Weston spent practically all of his money for a steamship ticket to New York.

His chemistry background helped Weston secure employment with the American Nickel Plating Co. At the time, plating voltage came from clumsy and troublesome batteries that could produce only a thin and poorly bound layer of nickel. Weston developed a dynamo, or direct current generator, that produced higher and better-regulated electrical current than batteries could. This was the first time anyone had used a dynamo for electroplating, and the dynamo soon entirely replaced batteries in the process. The patent Weston took out at age 22 formed the basis for a successful electroplating partnership he established with one of his customers, Charles Theberath.

Income from this partnership allowed Weston to continue his work on dynamos, and he soon developed one for arc lighting that proved to be far superior to anything offered by his competitors. It included his invention of laminated pole pieces and cores that increased efficiency enormously—from 45 percent to 85 percent. Weston added other innovations to improve voltage regulation and soon opened the Weston Dynamo Electric Machine Co. in Newark, New Jersey. America's first commercial dynamo factory, it manufactured four bathtub-sized dynamos a day. Each sold for about $500. Weston held many patents related to arc lighting, such as the ones for the first copper-coated carbons that were universally used. He designed and sold complete lighting systems. His products were so highly regarded that Weston won the contract to illuminate the Brooklyn Bridge when it

opened in 1883. The four lines of arc lamps that he suspended on what was then the highest structure in New York became something of a tourist attraction. They remained in place for 15 years, until incandescent lights replaced them.

Weston was also deeply involved with incandescent light production. He developed an improved pump for removing air from a glass globe. In 1885, he invented a way to coat weak carbon filaments with dense carbon to strengthen them and to provide a predictable resistance. He did this by sending high currents through filaments inside a container filled with natural gas. The heated filaments became coated with carbon from the natural gas. The process was called *hydrocarbon flashing*, and no successful carbon filament lamp was ever made without it.

Weston's decision to build a direct-reading voltmeter followed a week-long electrical experiment at the Franklin Institute's well-equipped generator laboratory in Philadelphia. He had expected the experiment to take only one day and he felt frustrated by the lack of proper meters. To that point, some inventors had unsuccessfully tried to make meters by using the heat generated from current flow. Others had tried to use magnetic effects by pulling two electromagnets together. Neither of these approaches worked well. Thomas Edison built the first electrical power plant in 1883 near Wall Street in New York. To make a crude ammeter he hung a nail from a string and positioned it near the electrical supply line. Different current flows caused magnetic effects that pulled the nail near the wire. Edison made adjustments based on this crude measurement.

Weston decided to expand on an 1881 French patent for an unsuccessful meter designed by Jacques Arsene D'Arsonval. The French inventor used a small coil of wire suspended by a filament inside a permanent magnetic field. A small amount of electricity sent to the coil converted the wire to an electromagnet. The two magnetic fields interacted, causing a slight rotation of the coil. A dial connected to the coil moved over a calibrated scale. The idea was good in theory, but D'Arsonval's specific design proved impractical. Nonetheless, the moving coil in electrical meters that have dial

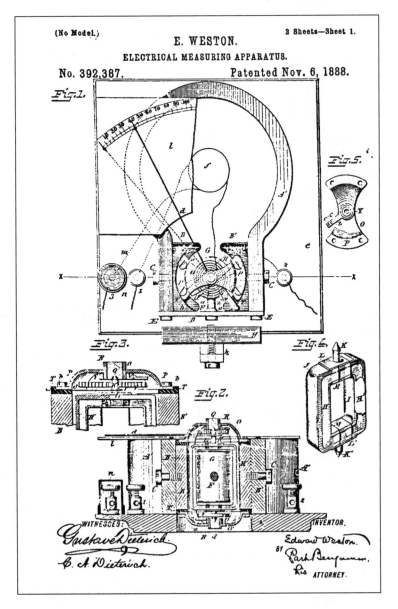

Weston's voltmeter patent used a D'Arsonval meter movement.

indicators is called a D'Arsonval meter movement.

Weston determined that the fundamental flaw of the French patent lay in the shape of the magnetic field surrounding the coil. The coil had to be completely encircled, and Weston was the first person to find a way to make permanent magnets in any shape. That was the key to a practical D'Arsonval meter movement. Weston spent two years perfecting his moving coil voltmeter before starting production in 1888. The 100 volt dc meter that he called Model One was the first portable voltmeter ever made. Weston carefully manufactured it with jeweled bearings, finely drawn coil wire, and nonmagnetic springs to provide a balance torque for the coil. The meter was an immediate success with schools, colleges, power companies, and electric equipment manufacturers. With the success of his voltmeter, Weston eventually saw his factory grow to 15 buildings on a 12-acre site.

Weston's catalog listed voltmeters with code names to avoid confusion when orders were sent by telegraph. He sold a 150 Vdc Reprint, a 150/300 Vdc Reptatus, and a 600 Vdc Requital. Each cost about $70 and was accurate to 1/4 percent. Weston invented the shunt resistor for ammeters, and his factory's production soon included ammeters, ohmmeters, and wattmeters, in addition to the voltmeters. He was the first in the electrical industry to use Bakelite for meter cases. Over the years, his meters took gold medals at seven international expositions.

Weston bought a large house in Newark for his wife and two sons. A two-story private laboratory he built in his backyard had modern tools for physical, chemical, and metallurgical research. Weston's residence was so complete that *Scientific American* described it as a "house of wonder." The recipient of 334 patents and a member of many professional organizations, Weston was a charter member of the American Institute of Electrical Engineers and later served as its president. The photograph on page 109 came from the 1888 announcement of his presidency, when Weston was 38. Weston also helped found the New Jersey Institute of Technology, and he received honorary doctorate degrees from McGill University in Montreal, Princeton University, Stevens Institute of Technology, and the University of Pennsylvania. He enjoyed collecting rare electrical books and autographs. Weston died of natural causes at the age of 86 while he cruised on his yacht in Long Island Sound after watching a boat race.

References and Resources

Measuring Invisibles, Weston Electrical Instrument Corp., 1938.

Edward Weston: Inventor–Scientist–Industrialist, Henry Berring, 1942.

Newark Evening News, 21 August 1936.

The Electrical World, 2 June 1888.

Weston Electrical Measuring Instruments–Catalog 15.

Trade journal information from Ford Museum Archives, Dearborn, MI.

Dictionary of American Biography, Charles Scribner's Sons Publishers, 1932; with supplemental updates.

National Cyclopedia of American Biography, James T. White and Co. Publishers, 1891; with supplemental updates.

Charles Hotchkiss Norton

Born:
November 23, 1851, in Plainville, Connecticut

Died:
October 27, 1942, in Plainville, Connecticut

Norton Co. Archives, Worcester Historical Museum

Norton with his first production grinder in 1901. This very machine is on display at the Henry Ford Museum in Dearborn, Michigan.

LIGHTLY constructed grinders with 1/2"-thick wheels did most of the metal-finishing work required in nineteenth-century factories. Unlike cutting tools such as lathes and milling machines, those grinders removed only small amounts of metal. However, grinders became a valuable high-volume manufacturing tool with Charles Hotchkiss Norton's introduction of his large lathe-like grinder in 1901. His was the first production grinder used on a factory floor, and Norton is often identified as the originator of precision production grinding.

Norton was born in a clock-manufacturing area of Connecticut. His father was a cabinetmaker for the Whiting and Royce Clock Co. His mother worked for the same company painting clock dials. Norton attended the local public schools and served apprenticeships in several local machine shops. At the age of 15, he joined his father and uncle at the Seth Thomas Clock Co. in Thomaston, Connecticut, where he performed odd jobs. Recognizing his reliability, aptitude, and inventiveness, the young

Norton's supervisors soon promoted him to machinist. He received additional promotions to foreman and then to manager of the department that made tower clocks. During his 20 years at the factory, he became familiar with methods for mass producing precision parts. The grinders he used were only suitable for slow finish work. Norton found that he had some ideas about production grinding that other company leaders did not like. He decided to look for a company that would allow him to work on developing the grinder's full potential.

Norton took his skills to the Brown & Sharpe Manufacturing Co. in Providence, Rhode Island. Joseph Brown was an expert in grinding, and he encouraged many talented people to join his company. Like Norton, he had started his career in a clock-making factory. Norton hired in as an assistant engineer and became Brown & Sharpe's expert in cylindrical grinding machines. Such machines finished curved surfaces rather than flat ones. One of Norton's major accomplishments was the design of an internal grinding attachment. He also developed a special machine to grind triple air cylinders for the Westinghouse Air Brake Co.

At the time Norton began his modifications, the production grinder was in a state of transition. It was no longer used only for sharpening tools and finishing surfaces. It aided in the manufacture of small metal parts for clocks and sewing machines and showed potential for use in the rapid production of high-precision parts. Norton added a variety of controls to expand the machine's versatility, but Brown & Sharpe still used grinders only for light manufacturing. To show that grinders could accurately manufacture and finish larger items, Norton built machines with big grinding wheels that made it unnecessary to traverse the workpiece.

Norton's experimental grinders took heavier cuts, and they required more rigid construction. His was a radical design for the time, and Norton tried to persuade his supervisors to offer such machines for sale. They disagreed because they thought it impossible to control cuts to thousandths of an inch with a grinding wheel. Frustrated by Brown & Sharpe's unwillingness to innovate, Norton left in 1890. He moved to Detroit to work with the newly formed Leland, Faulconer, and Norton Co.

Henry Leland was one of the pioneers of American automobile manufacture, and he wanted to find new methods of production. He had worked with Norton at Brown & Sharpe. Robert Faulconer put up $40,000 capital to start the company, and Norton served as its technical expert. The company prospered and Norton received broad experience in the design and construction of production machine tools for automobile parts. In 1895, after an argument over a milling machine, Norton left to work for a small company in Bridgeport, Connecticut. A year later, he returned to Brown & Sharpe.

During his second stint at Brown & Sharpe, Norton worked on production machines for large automobile drive parts. He designed plunge grinders that made just one pass of the grinding wheel. The new grinders required more power, higher speeds, heavier cuts, and stronger construction. Norton worked out designs that made it possible to produce highly accurate contoured work at high rates of production. He said that he wanted a "machine to utilize more power during a shorter period of time . . . to secure the product in a shorter time for labor." Norton's revolutionary production ideas again met with opposition—as he described it, they "nearly caused a riot." Brown & Sharpe emphasized manufacture of smaller items. Norton left the company again in 1900 to establish the Norton Grinding Co. in Worcester, Massachusetts. He wanted to manufacture machines that would make large precision parts.

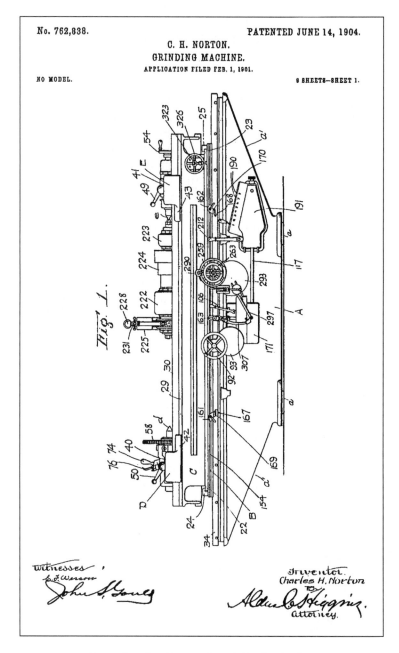

Drawing for Norton's original grinder

Norton picked Worcester because it was the location of the industry's largest manufacturer of grinding wheels, Norton Emery Wheel Co. Neither the company nor its operators were related to Charles Norton. Norton Emery Wheel did provide some financial backing as a way to expand its abrasives market, though the two companies remained independent until 1919.

With other investors, Norton put up funds and rented a manufacturing area in the basement of the factory. The veteran machinist immediately started to work on his ideas. Within months, the handful of employees at Norton Grinding Co. produced a huge machine unlike anything seen before. Most other grinders weighed up to 3,000 pounds and required 2 hp electric motors, but Norton's grinder weighed 9,500 pounds and its deep cuts required a 15 hp motor. Norton's grinder could handle 18"-diameter workpieces up to 8' long and 1,200 pounds in weight. More important, it could maintain an accuracy of 0.00025" over the entire workpiece. At half the diameter of a human hair, that accuracy was four times better than the previous 0.001" industrial standard. The photograph on page 112 shows Norton standing next to his very first machine, which he sold to the Hoe Printing Press Co. of New York City in 1901. Norton bought it back in 1931, and it is now on display at the Henry Ford Museum in Dearborn, Michigan.

At $2,500, the Norton grinder was relatively expensive, and it did not find an immediate market. The target industry that Norton had in mind was locomotive manufacturers, but railroad shops showed no interest. Much of the company's income came from machine shop work—particularly on automobile crankshafts—that it did for others. The company did not make a profit, and its owners unsuccessfully tried to sell out to a twist-drill manufacturer in 1904.

Grinder sales only increased after automobile manufacturers began to view the tool as essential to their fledgling industry, which demanded a high volume of precision parts. Norton's grinder cut the time required to finish a Ford Model T engine crankshaft from 5 hours to 15 minutes. It finished rear axles at the rate of one per minute. Henry Ford soon ordered 35. By 1927, Norton's seven-acre factory and 1,000 employees had manufactured 68,000 grinders that were in use throughout the world.

An impatient and overbearing man, Norton was sometimes difficult to get along with. He married three times and had two daughters. Norton wrote a book on grinding and was a frequent contributor to such journals as *American Machinist* and *Iron Age*. Over the course of his lifetime, he received more than 100 patents. He stopped actively participating in his company after it merged in 1919 with Norton Emery Wheel Co., though he retained the title of chief engineer until he was well into his eighties. Norton retired to his hometown and contributed in a civic-minded way to many projects. Recalling his early work life, he donated Seth Thomas tower clocks to the town library and a church.

References and Resources

Family Firm to Modern Multinational by Charles W. Cheape, Harvard University Press, 1985.

Norton Grinder display at Henry Ford Museum, Dearborn, Michigan.

Norton Company at 100 Years, pamphlet produced by Worcester Historical Museum, Worcester, MA 1985..

Dictionary of American Biography, Charles Scribner's Sons Publishers, 1932; with supplemental updates.

National Cyclopedia of American Biography, James T. White and Co. Publishers, 1891; with supplemental updates.

Jan Earnst Matzeliger

The only portrait photograph of Jan Matzeliger and one of only two photos ever taken of him

Born:
September 15, 1852, in Paramaribo, Suriname

Died:
August 24, 1889, in Lynn, Massachusetts

NEAR the end of the nineteenth century, the 185 shoe factories in Lynn, Massachusetts, produced half the total number of shoes made in America. Much of that manufacturing dominance resulted from a remarkable shoe-assembling machine invented by a young African-American, Jan Matzeliger. Working single-handedly in an unheated apartment, he produced an invention that enriched American industry by billions of dollars and created work for tens of thousands of people.

Matzeliger was born in Suriname, a country on the northeast coast of South America, in 1852. His father was a Dutch engineer in charge of his government's machine works in the capital city of Paramaribo. Matzeliger's mother was a slave from a nearby plantation, who traced her ancestry to west Africa between Senegal and Angola. Matzeliger's father arranged a machine shop apprenticeship for his son, which lasted until the lure of the sea drew the young man from home at the age of 19. Matzeliger left Suriname, never to return. He took with him a small jar of nutmeg seeds and coffee beans grown in Suriname, preserved in alcohol, that he kept for the rest of his life.

Following two years of service on a merchant ship, the Dutch-speaking Matzeliger entered the United States at Philadelphia. The unrivaled mecca at that time for African-Americans, Philadelphia boasted a black-owned-and-operated hospital, black newspapers, several of the largest black churches in the country, and some of the foremost black musicians, artists, and entertainers in the world. Arriving during a severe economic downturn in 1873 and unable to speak English very well, the soft-spoken Matzeliger could not find employment as a machinist. He held several unremarkable jobs before taking an apprenticeship in a shoe-making shop.

While in Philadelphia, Matzeliger occasionally visited the U.S. 1876 Centennial Exposition in Fairmount Park. He visited the Shoe and Leather Building more than once, and there he enthusiastically discussed the possibility of better work opportunities in Lynn, Massachusetts. He left Philadelphia in 1876, as he had left Suriname, only looking forward.

Matzeliger arrived in Lynn that winter almost empty handed. Previous experience with a shoe-stitching machine helped him find a job operating one at the M. H. Harney factory. To increase his knowledge, he bought some technical books and a secondhand set of drafting instruments. At work,

Matzeliger noticed that one group of boastful employees rarely passed up an opportunity to proclaim their singular importance in the shoemaking process. They were the lasters. *Lasting* is the shaping and fastening of the upper part of a shoe to the inner sole, an intricate operation that seemed impossible to mechanize. Forming the leather required much hand manipulation, especially near the compound curves at the heel and toe. It was a slow process and an efficient laster could complete only 50 to 60 pairs of shoes per day. Other shoe parts that were made using machines piled up to wait for the lasters.

Matzeliger decided to give close attention to the project of inventing a lasting machine. He was skilled, intelligent, creative, and ambitious, and he wanted others to recognize those qualities in him. He saw creating a seemingly impossible invention as his path to recognition. This potential mechanical genius unknowingly found himself in the right place at the right time.

For several years, after putting in a 10-hour work day at the factory, Matzeliger spent his evenings considering new ideas. To analyze the possibilities, he put them down on paper with his drafting equipment. Since he had no family or friends close by, encouragement for this complicated task came only from Matzeliger himself. Fabrication of a metal model would require a suitable working space and access to machine tools. Matzeliger left the M. H. Harney factory to work as a maintenance

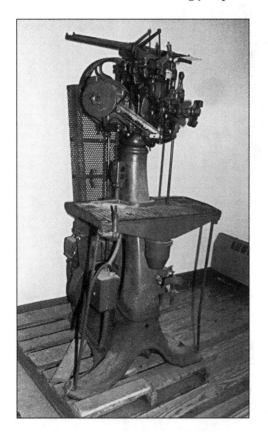

An early-twentieth-century version of Matzeliger's shoe-lasting machine. A laster hand held the shoe and turned it as pleating and tugging were done automatically. The angled metal strip on the left delivered tacks that were automatically driven into the shoe.

machinist at the nearby Beal Brothers factory. He also received permission to use the company's machine tools for his own projects.

Matzeliger searched junkyards and factory cast-off piles of broken machinery for good parts: forgings, gears, pulleys, levers, and cams. He spent much of his time altering existing parts to fit his requirements. It's not surprising that he had some battles with depression and became particularly discouraged during this period. An engineering group that had all the machining talent money could buy had recently failed in an attempt to make a lasting machine. Matzeliger told himself for the thousandth time that the invention was, for him, much more than just a unique combination of intricate iron and steel shapes.

Modification went only so far, and Matzeliger had to spend money to fabricate several specialized parts using his employer's machine tools. While denying himself proper food, rest, and warmth, Matzeliger put in almost two years of unaided effort to produce his machine. It was a crude prototype but quite capable, nonetheless, of the most difficult lasting task, pleating leather around a toe. Matzeliger filed for a patent in 1882. Even by modern standards, his 15-page patent is detailed and complex. It's what we would expect from a large corporation, not from a self-supporting and unproven immigrant working on his own.

As most successful inventors discover eventually, the question of financing is critical. Matzeliger found help from local businessmen Charles H. Delnow and Melville S. Nichols, but they asked a steep price for their financial assistance. They promised to support Matzeliger in exchange for two-thirds of all profits. Matzeliger agreed.

Generally shaped like a large drill press, the lasting machine was ready for a factory demonstration run on May 29, 1885. Its main working component was a single pincer that resembled the thin and bent jaws from an ordinary pair of pliers. A worker placed an inner sole and a leather upper in the machine. The pincer grabbed and pleated the leather, and other parts automatically hammered tacks until the shoe was finished one minute later. Those who saw the demonstration couldn't believe their eyes. Matzeliger's first preproduction model worked five times faster than hand lasting.

It perfectly lasted 75 pairs of hard-to-make women's shoes.

Delnow and Nichols negotiated with other investors and formed the Consolidated Hand Method Lasting Machine Co. in 1885. The company bought patent rights from Matzeliger for an amount of stock worth something over $15,000. By the next year, 225 workers manufacturing lasting machines at the Beverly, Massachusetts, plant could not keep up with the demand. So popular was the Matzeliger lasting machine that between 1885 and 1925, virtually every shoe factory in America had at least one. In the hands of a competent operator, it could last as many as 700 pairs of shoes a day. Shoe prices dropped by half.

Matzeliger's personal life took a turn for the better while he was working on the factory demonstration machine. Some members of an active youth group at the North Congregational Church spoke to officials about membership for Matzeliger. Church officials accepted him, and Matzeliger quickly immersed himself in church activities.

Matzeliger earned just a fraction of the money realized by some of his financiers. However, his happiest years followed his decision to give up control of his patent. He now had pleasant surroundings, good friends, a certain degree of financial security, and the recognition he had sought for so many years. He filled his days with work on an improved tack-delivery system and finishing the design of another machine. Matzeliger received five patents altogether, but three came posthumously.

Years of self-deprivation had taken their toll on the tireless Matzeliger's health. His weakened body was more susceptible to contracting illnesses and diseases. He was diagnosed in 1886 as having tuberculosis. Despite intensive medical treatment, Matzeliger became bed ridden and died in 1889, just a few weeks before he turned 37. He left about a third of his estate to the church, which used the money 15 years later to pay off its mortgage. Matzelinger's jar of nutmegs and coffee beans was never accounted for.

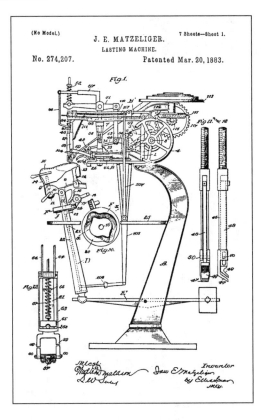

The machine shown in Matzeliger's patent drawing was never constructed as shown. Matzeliger modified it, producing a machine resembling the one shown on page 116.

References and Resources

Jan Matzeliger and the Shoe Lasting Machine by Robert A. Smith, master's thesis, University of Massachusetts, undated (approximately 1983).

The Hidden Contributors by Aaron E. Klein, Doubleday, 1971.

"Jan Earnest Matzeliger and the Making of the Shoe" by Sidney Kaplan, *The Journal of Negro History*, January 1955.

Black Pioneers of Science and Invention by Louis Haber, Harcourt, Brace & World, 1970.

"Against All Odds" by Dennis Karwatka, *American Heritage of Invention and Technology*, Winter 1991.

The Negro in Pennsylvania, 1639-1861 by Edward Raymond Turner, Arno Press, 1969.

"First of the Automated Lasters" by Arthur D. Anderson, Jr., in *Boot and Shoe Recorder*, June 1969.

Dictionary of American Biography, Charles Scribner's Sons Publishers, 1932; with supplemental updates.

Elihu Thomson

Hall of History

Born:
March 29,
1853, in
Manchester,
England

Died:
March 13,
1937, in
Swampscott,
Massachusetts

MANY factories use electric welding to permanently fasten metal pieces together today, employing robots to do the job. Industrial robots use electricity to join metal in a manner almost identical to that first demonstrated by 23-year-old Elihu Thomson in the autumn of 1876. Every auditorium seat was filled during the last of his five lectures at the Franklin Institute in Philadelphia. Thomson first charged a Leyden jar (capacitor) with a static voltage generator. He discharged the Leyden jar through the secondary wires of a transformer instead of the primary wires. The voltage in the secondary wires induced a large current flow through the primary windings. The high current produced an arc that melted and fused the barely touching primary leads. The leads had welded together.

Thomson was born in the industrial city of Manchester, England, where his father was a textile mill mechanic. An economic depression in 1857 forced the Thomson family to consider its alternatives. Thomson was five when his family moved to Philadelphia, the industrial center of America at the time. The older Thomson found steady employment as a maintenance engineer at a sugar machinery company. Thomson's parents always encouraged his interest in reading and science. That encouragement was instrumental in his completing elementary school at the age of 11. Too young for high school, Thomson then spent two years conducting electrical and chemical experiments at home.

Thomson was an excellent student, and he graduated from Central High School in 1870. Six months later, the school offered the teenager a position teaching chemistry, physics, and electricity. Thomson became friends with fellow teacher Edwin Houston, who was only seven years older than Thomson. The two men decided to work together on inventions. Their first successful one was a machine that separated cream from milk using centrifugal force. Their small income from royalties allowed them to buy and experiment with electrical devices. They specialized in dynamos, direct current (dc) generators. Dynamos produced electricity for arc lights used in factories and on public streets. Thomson and Houston had some difficulty testing their designs because no indicating meters existed at that time. The two men had to make measurements with galvanometers and Wheatstone bridges in a variety of complex circuits. They eventually constructed several 500 volt, 750 rpm dynamos for the 1,200 and 2,000 candlepower lamps used in street and factory lighting.

In 1879, by winding three overlapping armature coils, Thomson developed the world's first three-phase alternating current (ac) generator, or alternator. Through a simple change in connections, it could provide dc electricity through a commutator or ac electricity through slip rings. The more efficient alternators began to compete with dynamos. Production of ac required less mechanical power from steam engines than did production of dc. Thomson and Houston sold their first three-phase alternator to a bakery in Lynn, Massachusetts. It was optionally wired as a dynamo and sold as part of a complete arc-lighting system. The sale led to other contracts and the two partners opened an electrical manufacturing factory in Lynn. Thomson acted as the chief engineer of the Thomson-Houston Co.

The company gained great prominence and soon dominated the electrical manufacturing industry. By 1888, customers were using 358 Thomson-Houston dynamos and 44,417 arc lamps. The Thomson-Houston Co. employed 3,800 people in 20 buildings on a 23-acre site. Besides dynamos and alternators, Thomson-Houston also manufactured motors, electrical distribution systems, and equipment for electric railways. During the early 1880s, Thomson patented such inventions as shaded-pole electric motors for household appliances and automatic current regulators for transformers.

He also patented air- and oil-cooled transformers and a wattmeter. Always interested in safety, he devised the grounded secondary of a transformer as a way to save lives. In 1883, Thomson conducted the world's first efficiency tests of a dynamo at the Franklin Institute. The Thomson-Houston Co. merged with the Edison General Electric Co. in 1892 to form the General Electric Co. For the rest of his life, Thomson remained General Electric's consultant in technical matters and patent litigation.

Electric welding has been called Thomson's greatest contribution to industrial advancement. For many years, though, his numerous electrical interests and manufacturing responsibilities kept him from fully investigating electric welding. In 1885, Thomson built a demonstration transformer and reversed the coils as he had done in his 1876 experiment. The secondary side consisted of a single ring of 1" × 4" copper bar with ends that protruded to serve as as terminals. The primary side consisted of many windings of wire wrapped around a copper ring. The entire doughnut-shaped device was about two feet in diameter and weighed 1,000 pounds. Thomson's welder combined pressure with heat, which came from the metal's resistance to the flow of current. The pressure came from clamps on the ends of the copper ring. Thomson's welder easily fused 1"-diameter steel rods in a few seconds.

Thomson took out a patent on his welder in 1886 and organized the Thomson Electric Welding Co. to manufacture it. Thomson welders resembled metal lathes. Roebling Iron Works in Trenton put his first commercial welder in operation in 1888. In describing the welder's functioning, a U.S. Ordnance Department report that year stated that current flows "sometimes reach 50,000 amperes." Thomson demonstrated his

Hall of History

Elihu Thomson with his first electric welder

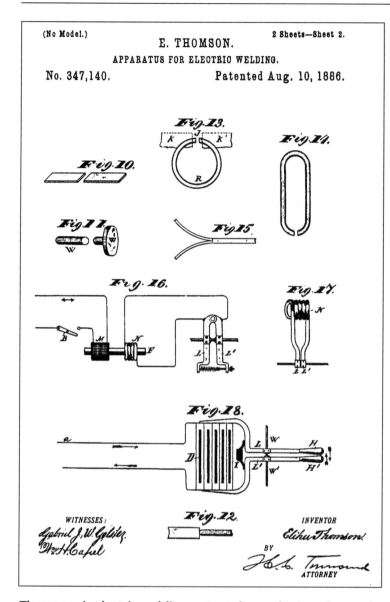

(No Model.)

E. THOMSON.

APPARATUS FOR ELECTRIC WELDING.

No. 347,140. Patented Aug. 10, 1886.

2 Sheets—Sheet 2.

Thompson's electric welding patent shows the transformer in Fig. 16

welding equipment at the 1889 Paris Exposition. The U.S. commissioners called it "one of the few recent developments of an important character in an entirely new direction." Thomson later exhibited 12 machines at the 1893 World's Columbian Exposition in Chicago. The largest had a 60 kilowatt capacity. However, Thomson usually demonstrated a smaller 300 volt ac, 1,000 watt unit. It easily welded 1/4"-diameter rod. The exhibit won a gold medal.

The International Electrical Congress was held at the 1893 exposition. With delegates from 10 countries, the congress reached final agreement on the international units of the ohm, volt, ampere, coulomb, joule, watt, and henry. The congress chose Thomson, the best known of the six American delegates, to serve as its chairman. The group also selected Thomson's wattmeter as the exposition's standard reference.

An excellent and captivating speaker, Thomson was equally comfortable before groups of children or scientists. He was very active in a dozen professional societies, serving as an officer several times. He wrote many articles for scientific and technical journals. His development of electrical welding was only one aspect of an extensive career that saw him gain world renown as an electrical expert. He accumulated a remarkable total of 696 U.S. patents—second only to Thomas Edison's 1,093. Thomson received 17 international awards and decorations, as well as honorary degrees from five colleges, including Harvard and Yale. He served as president of the Massachusetts Institute of Technology from 1920 to 1922.

Thomson was the foremost expert in the electrical manufacturing field, yet he had a pleasant manner, a trait often seen in people of high professional attainment. His hobbies included color photography and astronomy. He made the 10" lens for his own refracting telescope. He also enjoyed playing a pipe organ he had in his home at Swampscott, near Lynn. Thomson and his first wife had four sons. His first wife died in 1916, and he remarried a few years later. Thomson had many significant technical accomplishments, his peers liked and regarded him highly, and he lived a long life. Still, Thomson's name is little known today, and it appears in few technical references.

References and Resources

Beloved Scientist by David Woodbury, McGraw-Hill, 1944.

Electricity at the Columbian Exposition by J. P. Barrett, R. R. Donnelley & Sons, 1894.

Information from Henry Ford Museum Library, Dearborn, MI.

Dictionary of American Biography, Charles Scribner's Sons Publishers, 1932; with supplemental updates.

National Cyclopedia of American Biography, James T. White and Co. Publishers, 1891; with supplemental updates.

Ottmar Merganthaler

Smithsonian Institution Photo No. 32896

Born:
May 11, 1854, in Hatchel, Germany

Died:
October 28, 1899, in Baltimore, Maryland

IT was so hard to print books in the nineteenth century that in the 1880s only 76 American public libraries had more than 300 volumes in their collection. Parents handed down school books to their children, and magazines were few, thin, and expensive. The largest daily newspapers were limited in size to eight pages because all type was set one letter at a time, exactly as it had been done for 400 years. A German immigrant's complex 1886 invention greatly speeded up the printing process. Ottmar Merganthaler's Linotype was such a remarkable machine that Thomas Edison called it the "eighth wonder of the world."

Merganthaler's father was a village schoolmaster in Germany and his mother was the daughter of a schoolmaster. He was brought up in an academic setting, but his family had a limited income. Like many nineteenth-century technologists, Merganthaler showed an early interest in mechanical devices. Before he had entered his teens, he had repaired the town clock after the local clockmaker gave up on the task. Merganthaler wanted to study engineering or science, but his parents wanted him to teach school. He resisted the idea and reached a compromise by agreeing to take a clockmaker apprenticeship as a 14-year-old. He also attended night classes to expand his technical knowledge. Merganthaler considered his work on clocks the most useful work he ever performed. He said, "Above all, watchmaking taught me precision. . . . I realized that if a [watch] was to work, it must be considered as a whole, that each part had to be perfect in itself and also harmonize with every other." That experience helped him later in life, when he spent years working on the fiendishly complex Linotype.

The Franco-Prussian War of 1870-71 encouraged many Germans to leave their homeland. Following completion of his apprenticeship, Merganthaler was among the 125,000 who emigrated in 1872. A cousin of his, August Hahl, who lived in Washington, D.C., offered him a job. The cousin even advanced Merganthaler the necessary travel money.

The goal of all inventors is to obtain a patent, and in the 1870s a model was required for patent applications. Washington, D.C., was the center of the patent model industry and Hahl owned a machine shop that specialized in making models. He also made measuring instruments for the emerging field of electrical technology. Because of his clockmaking experience, Merganthaler adapted well to his new job. He made rapid progress in his new profession. Hahl even kept him on the payroll when a downturn in the national economy mandated a move to Baltimore.

In August 1876, shortly before Merganthaler became an American citizen, an inventor approached him with the plans for a kind of typewriter. The machine used lithographic techniques to transfer an entire page of text. Constructing the model introduced Merganthaler to the printing industry's fruitless efforts to develop an automatic typesetting machine. More than 200 inventors over a period of 50 years had tried to patent a typesetter. The author Mark Twain went bankrupt in the late 1880s while financing one designed by James Paige that had 18,000 parts. Merganthaler began to work on an automatic typesetter in his spare time after hearing of a reward. The New York City newspapers offered $500,000 for a machine that would save at least 25 percent of the work of hand composition.

Merganthaler and Hahl began a partnership in 1878 that lasted five years. Then, Merganthaler decided to establish his own machine shop. There was plenty of patent and instrument work to go around, and Merganthaler's business prospered. He had not lost interest in inventing a printing machine and he spent every spare minute pursuing the idea. Merganthaler felt challenged by the machine's mechanical complexity. He had an unusual advantage over

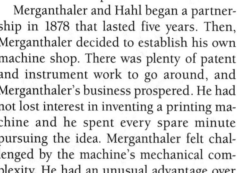

This 1915 Linotype is quite similar to the one Merganthaler invented in 1886.

others with the same objective: Merganthaler had no background in printing and could approach the problem from a fresh perspective. Where others tried to duplicate the hand motions of a human typesetter, Merganthaler focused on molds. He worked on a technique for casting an entire line of type at once.

Merganthaler's first important invention came in 1883. He called it the First Band Machine. About the size of a large refrigerator, the machine had a series of vertical bars, with the alphabet and other special characters on each bar. When the operator typed one letter, a bar would descend to bring the character to a certain level. After a line of type was assembled, a papier-mache strip was pushed into the line. It produced a one-line mold, or matrix. When all the mold strips for a single page were assembled in a frame, molten metal was poured into all of them at once. This produced a completed printing plate.

Unfortunately, the machine was not a commercial success, and Merganthaler made only a few of them. To pay for its high cost, the rate of composition had to be several times faster than what people could do by hand, and the First Band Machine wasn't that fast. Merganthaler's financial backers grew concerned that he had greater interest in producing a perfect machine than in producing a workable one. It was a valid assessment on their part because Merganthaler was a perfectionist with what was typically considered a German's eye for precision. He had abandoned friends when he thought their ideas were wrong, and he occasionally went into debt when he neglected the responsibilities of his business.

July 26, 1884, is often cited as the birthday of the Linotype machine. On that date, Merganthaler demonstrated his Second Band Machine to a small group of potential purchasers. Its major improvement was the elimination of the papier-mache operation. Long thin brass bars with individual type molds dropped into alignment with others at the touch of a letter on the 90-key keyboard. Hot metal pressed against the line to form a slug, and several slugs combined to make a page. The operation was not perfect—people still had to perform right justification by hand, for example, and the machine was quite expensive. However, Merganthaler's financial backers were encouraged by the results and provided the money for the first production Linotype. On July 3, 1886, a portion of the *New York Tribune* newspaper was set with a Merganthaler experimental typesetter. Whitelaw Reid, the publisher, saw the machine at work and exclaimed, "Ottmar, you've done it . . . a line o' type." That was the casual christening of the most potent machine of its age. The newspaper purchased 12 of the new machines, and before long the first hundred were in use.

A printing boom soon began. More people were hired at higher wages for shorter hours as newspapers increased in number and size. Cost dropped from 3¢ for an eight-page newspaper in pre-Linotype days, to 1¢ or 2¢ for many more pages after Merganthaler's invention. Within 20 years, daily newspaper circulation in America had increased from 3.6 million to 33 million. Because of Merganthaler's invention, the magazine industry emerged, and schools all over the nation could buy inexpensive books. The illiteracy rate dropped from 17 percent to 5 percent. By 1900, there were over 8,000 Linotypes operating throughout the world.

Merganthaler became wealthy, but he never lost interest in his invention. He devised more than 50 patented improvements over the next few years. He received awards from the Franklin Institute in Philadelphia and Cooper Union in New York. Constant work and anxiety had undermined Merganthaler's health, though, and he contracted tuberculosis while in his forties. He moved to Deming, New Mexico, in hope of improving his health. There, an unfortunate fire in 1897 destroyed his home, technical papers, and an autobiography he had started. Against the advice of physicians, Merganthaler returned to Baltimore where he died at the age of 45.

References and Resources

Mechanisms of the Linotype and Intertype by Oscar Abel and Windsor Straw, Brookings Lebarwarts Press, 1961.

"Merganthaler's Wonderful Machine" by Michael Scully, *The Reader's Digest*, March 1953.

Publications provided by Merganthaler Linotype Co.

Dictionary of American Biography, Charles Scribner's Sons Publishers, 1932; with supplemental updates.

National Cyclopedia of American Biography, James T. White and Co. Publishers, 1891; with supplemental updates.

McGraw-Hill Encyclopedia of Biography, McGraw-Hill Publishers, 1973.

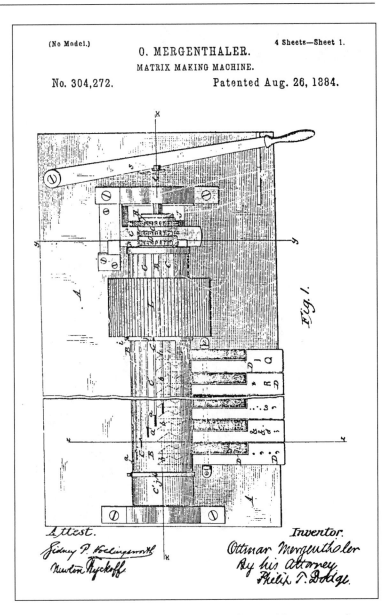

One of Merganthaler's early patents for making a matrix, or group of lettters

George Eastman

Born:
July 12, 1854,
in Waterville,
New York

Died:
March 14,
1932, in
Rochester,
New York

Courtesy of Eastman Kodak Co.

Formal portrait of George Eastman, taken around 1884

THE small hand-held cameras that most amateurs use for taking personal photographs did not originate in the twentieth century. George Eastman introduced the world's first conveniently sized, mass-produced camera intended for use by the public in June 1888. It came loaded with 100 exposures. After taking all the pictures, the purchaser returned the entire camera to Eastman's factory. For $10, the photographs were developed and printed, and a fresh roll of film was inserted. Eastman marketed his camera as the No. 1 Kodak.

Eastman went to work at age 14 to support his widowed mother and two sisters, when his father died unexpectedly. His first job as a messenger boy for an insurance company paid just $3 per week. Eastman later took work as a junior clerk in a bank in Rochester, New York.

When he was 24, Eastman took his first vacation, a photographic trip to Mackinac Island, Michigan. At the time, the simplest photographic process available used wet plates of glass. A chemically cleaned glass plate was coated with a sticky substance called a collodion. Next came a wet, light-sensitive silver salt emulsion. The operation had to be carried out in a completely dark tent. Using a special light-tight holder, the photographer placed the wet plate in a large camera. The exposed plate had to be developed before it dried. For $94, Eastman bought the necessary equipment, which included a large tripod-mounted camera and a dark tent. Glass plates, chemicals, tanks, several plate holders, and some miscellaneous items rounded out his supplies. Learning to use the equipment cost him $5.

Eastman became very absorbed in photography and wanted to simplify the complicated process. Particularly interested in making a dry emulsion, he spent evenings conducting experiments in his kitchen. Most earlier investigations of dry emulsions were done in England, and to learn about them Eastman read every issue of the *British Journal of Photography* that he could obtain. Forty years had passed since the French inventor Louis Daguerre introduced his daguerreotype technique for recording images. However, no U.S. citizen had ever made a significant contribution to the technology of photography.

Initially, Eastman just wanted to simplify picture taking for his own enjoyment. However, he soon considered the possibilities of producing dry plates for the professional market. He worked tirelessly during his free time. Eastman dreaded the potential poverty he felt could overtake his family, as had occurred when his father died. He invented a process for mass producing dry photographic plates in 1879. Traveling overseas with drawings and specifications, he obtained his first patent in England. The sale of his patent rights for $2,500 provided enough money to establish a U.S. factory, and Eastman left his job at the bank. His dry-plate business soon soared.

While looking for a less-heavy and more flexible support for his emulsion, Eastman experimented with paper. Professional photographers did not like the product. The paper's grain was reproduced in the print after removal of the emulsion from the paper during development. Eastman then decided to test the amateur market. He invented a camera the public could use, becoming the first manufacturer to do so. With the single venture of the No. 1 Kodak, Eastman brought amateur photography into being.

Eastman was the first person to practice the modern techniques of large-scale production at low cost for a world market. The Kodak was loaded with a long roll of flexible film. A popular slogan of the time that Eastman created was: "You push the button, we do the rest." Such an idea was unheard of at a time when average people thought photography was an advanced hobby only for those who had considerable knowledge of chemistry. The public loved the new camera and made Eastman an extraordinarily wealthy man.

Professional photographers did not take kindly to amateur photography. Eastman did not feel particularly concerned, and he always thought of himself as an amateur who took a cumbersome procedure and simplified it. By the mid-1890s, his cameras and emulsion development service had expanded several times but still could not keep up with the demand.

Eastman made up the word "Kodak" as a trade name for his camera. He once explained, "I devised the name myself. The letter K had been a favorite with me. It seemed a strong, incisive sort of letter. It became a question of trying out a great number of combinations of letters that made words starting and ending with K. The word Kodak was the result." The Eastman Kodak Co. was incorporated in 1892 with a capitalization of $35 million.

Eastman was one of the first commercial users of celluloid as an emulsion backing. Celluloid was invented by the American John Wesley Hyatt in 1869. Eastman's photographic film—for the first time a photographic medium could properly be called "film"—was manufactured by spreading a celluloid solution on a 200'-long by 42"-wide glass table. The smooth transparent celluloid remained with the emulsion after developing, eliminating the delicate emulsion-stripping operation. This flexible, strong, and transparent film made motion pictures possible. Its development was so important to the film industry that the word "celluloid" has been used to describe motion pictures.

Eastman always felt the need to share his good fortune in ways that reflected his social views. Most of his monetary gifts went

Courtesy of Eastman Kodak Co.

This first-ever amateur camera was named the No. 1 Kodak. Casually called the Kodak, 100,000 were manufactured between 1888 and 1896.

to colleges, particularly ones with dental clinics. He wanted children to benefit from early dental care so they could have "a better chance in life with better looks, better health, and more vigor." Because his best technical assistants came from the Massachusetts Institute of Technology (MIT), he anonymously gave a total of $20 million to that school. On just one day in 1924, he gave away a total of $30 million to the Hampton Institute, MIT, the Tuskegee Institute, and the University of Rochester. Dental clinics in Brussels, London, Paris, Rome, and Stockholm also received his financial support. In all, he gave away his entire personal fortune, estimated at between $75 and $100 million.

Eastman extended his generosity to his employees by declaring a wage dividend in 1912. It amounted to 2 percent on all wages received over the previous five years. He developed other employee benefit programs such as a medical department, high-quality lunchroom facilities, shorter hours, and the sale of company stock at reduced rates. By the 1920s—long before employers typically offered such benefits—Eastman had established a retirement plan, life insurance, and disability benefits for his employees.

Eastman succeeded to such a degree in promoting responsible managers that by 1932 his direction was no longer required at the Eastman Kodak Co. Also, he could not understand the details of his company's chemical research into such advanced products as color film and improved amateur cameras. A lifelong bachelor, his large home had not had a first lady since his mother's death 25 years earlier. Eastman felt he was too old and ill to carry on. He wrote on a piece of paper, "My work is done, why wait?" before taking his own life in 1932.

References and Resources

Technology in America by Carroll W. Pursell, Jr., MIT Press, 1983.

American Science and Invention by Mitchell Wilson, Bonanza Books, 1960.

"George Eastman" by O. N. Solbert, in *Image—The Journal of Photography of the George Eastman House*, November 1953.

A Brief History, a pamphlet from the Eastman Kodak Co., Rochester, New York

Dictionary of American Biography, Charles Scribner's Sons Publishers, 1932; with supplemental updates.

National Cyclopedia of American Biography, James T. White and Co. Publishers, 1891; with supplemental updates.

McGraw-Hill Encyclopedia of Biography, McGraw-Hill Publishers, 1973.

Asimov's Biographical Encyclopedia of Science and Technology, by Isaac Asimov, Doubleday and Co. Publishers, 1964.

Frederick Winslow Taylor

Smithsonian Photo No. 61600-C

Born:
March 20, 1856, in Philadelphia, Pennsylvania

Died:
March 21, 1915, in Philadelphia, Pennsylvania

AMERICAN factories in the mid-nineteenth century were inefficient and wasteful of their own most valuable asset: the efforts of their workers. Early factories did not analyze manufacturing techniques to determine the easiest and best way to perform each task. Supervisors based their work quotas on guesses, rather than on evaluations of different ways of making a product. The first person to develop universally accepted techniques for improving production techniques was Frederick Taylor. His methods allowed employees to manufacture better products with less effort and thus to improve productivity and raise their incomes.

Taylor was born in Philadelphia into a financially comfortable family. His father was a lawyer and his mother was an active social organizer. She educated Taylor at home until his early teens, when he went to Europe for formal education. After almost four years overseas, Taylor returned home and entered Exeter Academy in New Hampshire to prepare for Harvard Law School. He was a popular student and his teammates elected him captain of the baseball team. He graduated after two years but never made it to Harvard. A temporary but severe case of eye strain kept him from reading the fine print common in law books. As a remedy, his physician recommended manual work. For a person of his social standing, Taylor took the unusual step of going to work as an apprentice at the Enterprise Hydraulic Works in Philadelphia. The company manufactured pumps, and Taylor quickly learned the patternmaker and machinist trades.

Taylor enjoyed production work and decided to stay with it. In 1878, he changed jobs and went to work as a common laborer at the progressive Midvale Steel Co. By studying at night, in 1883 Taylor earned a degree in mechanical engineering from the Stevens Institute of Technology located in Hoboken, New Jersey. Managers at Midvale soon recognized his technical talents and gave him a series of promotions. He advanced to foreman at the age of 22, then to chief draftsman, and director of research. He became chief engineer, virtually heading the entire production operation, in only six years. His gift for understanding machinery made him an ideal assistant for the company's mechanically minded president, William Sellers.

Taylor was a slender and intense young man from an upper-class background. He frequently found himself the target of threats from the people who worked under him. He was generally unaffected by such confrontations, but they did make him think seriously about production methods. He noticed that different workers used different techniques to complete the same job. Taylor became the first supervisor to focus his attention on workers instead of on the machines they operated. Within a few years, he established his reputation in a field that is now known as scientific management, or the Taylor system. Scientific management is a system of developing standard ways of doing particular jobs. Taylor reasoned that by scientifically studying and timing every manufacturing step, a manager could obtain information useful for establishing fair and reasonable production rates. A pioneer in the area of time and motion study, Taylor

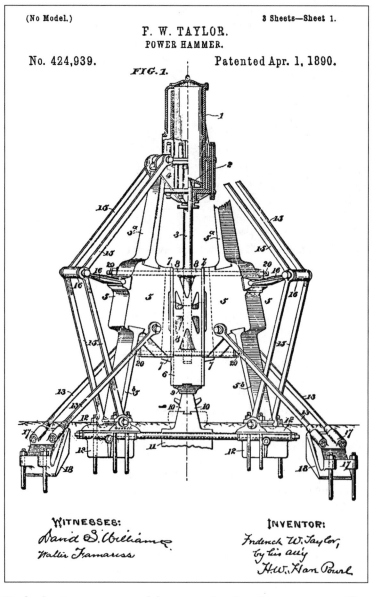

(No Model.)   3 Sheets—Sheet 1.

F. W. TAYLOR.
POWER HAMMER.

No. 424,939.   Patented Apr. 1, 1890.

FIG. 1.

WITNESSES:
David S. Williams
Walter Framarss

INVENTOR:
Frederick W. Taylor,
by his att'y
H. W. Hau Pourl

Taylor's steam-powered hammer for forging was once the largest in the world.

was moving into risky territory. In the factories and machine shops of the 1880s, antagonism between management and labor was common.

In his first major industrial research, Taylor studied a skilled machinist and his machine. He measured the effects of changes in shafting, machine speed, the quality of raw material, and the type of cutting tool. He determined that the individual machinist should not be responsible for sharpening tools. Managers could reduce downtime by having a special group of workers perform that task. One by one, Taylor studied the jobs in the plant and made recommendations for improvements. Operators received detailed instruction sheets that showed them how to do their jobs. The Midvale experiments yielded dramatic improvements in productivity. After 12 years at Midvale, Taylor left so that he could spread the information and methods he had learned to other companies. He opened a consulting business called the Manufacturing Investment Co. His business card described his service as: "Systematizing Shop Management and Manufacturing Costs, a Specialty."

Taylor's system had to be customized for each company. In one of his books, *The Principles of Scientific Management*, he tells a story from his experience working with Bethlehem Steel Co. Laborers there lifted and carried 92-pound pig-iron castings up a ramp and into a freight car. Each person carried about 12 tons per 10-hour day. Taylor noted that workers often had to line up and stop on the ramp as those ahead of them dropped their loads in the freight car. He determined that merely holding the 92-pound load required almost as much effort as walking with it. Taylor developed a system that told the workers when to pick up the load, when to carry it, and when to rest without a load. The system improved the daily average to 47 tons per worker without producing undue fatigue. The employees who participated in the new program received a 60 percent pay increase. Their pay went from $1.15 per day, a fair wage at the time, to $1.85.

Analyzing a machine shop operation in 1898 put Taylor on the trail of his most important invention, high-speed steel. While studying self-hardening steels, Taylor and J. Maunsel White developed a method for hardening chrome tungsten steel alloy without making it brittle. The improved tool steel more than doubled machine productivity. The Taylor-White process is still used throughout the world. In all, Taylor received over 100 patents. His most dramatic came in 1890 for the largest successful steam hammer ever built in America.

Taylor's efficiency programs required reorganization of departments and the use of new methods to replace comfortable old ones. Both of these functions were hard to accomplish, and Taylor became unpopular among his contemporaries. Also, he was a poor public speaker and frequently difficult to get along with. He could be blunt, impatient, and demanding. His revolutionary ideas, combined with his personality and background, made people reluctant to accept his recommendations. Although everyone knew Taylor's ideas were right, production changes came slowly. Among his best-known technical supporters were Frank and Lillian Gilbreth. They and others founded the Society to Promote the Science of Management. Following Taylor's death in 1915, they changed its name to the Taylor Society.

Taylor and his wife adopted three children, and starting in 1901 he made more time for his family. He had by this time developed a well-respected reputation and had become prosperous. Taylor went into semi-retirement, offering his services free of charge to those he wanted to work with. He built a house on an 11-acre estate in the Chestnut Hill section of Philadelphia and renewed his interest in sports. He designed life jackets for canoeing with his family before they were commonly used for sport boating. Taylor and his brother-in-law Clarence Clark won the first U.S. lawn tennis doubles championship in 1881 in Newport, Rhode Island. Taylor's special racket had an unusual curved handle. He also designed improved putting greens for golf, a new golf driver, and a two-handed putter that swung between the legs.

At the age of 59, Taylor died of pneumonia, a common killer at the time. He had lived to see his efficiency system capture the imaginations of American and foreign companies. His books were translated into all major Asian and European languages. In 1918, the French government required the use of several Taylor system features in factories under its control. Vladimir Lenin also strongly suggested its use in Russian factories.

References and Resources

Frederick W. Taylor—Father of Scientific Management by Frank Barley Copley, Augustus M. Kelley Publishers, 1923.

"Frederick W. Taylor" by Fritz Hirschfeld, in *Mechanical Engineering*, August 1980.

"Automating the Worker" by Joseph Gies in *American Heritage of Invention and Technology*, Winter 1991.

Dictionary of American Biography, Charles Scribner's Sons Publishers, 1932; with supplemental updates.

National Cyclopediaof American Biography, James T. White and Co. Publishers, 1891; with supplemental updates.

Albert Blake Dick

Photo courtesy of A.B. Dick Co.

Born:
April 16, 1856,
in Galesburg,
Illinois

Died:
August 15,
1934, in
Chicago,
Illinois

IF you say the word *mimeograph* to a teacher, the teacher probably will think of a motor-operated machine that rapidly makes many copies of classroom materials. However, the first mimeograph machine made just one copy at a time in a manner similar to silk screening. Albert Blake Dick invented the first successful mimeograph in 1887.

Dick received a typical elementary and high school education. In his first job out of school, he worked for a manufacturer of agricultural equipment in his hometown. He stayed there for five years, beginning to establish himself in the business world. Dick also worked for John Deere in Moline, Illinois, and finally wound up in Chicago, in his late twenties. There, he established a successful lumber company.

To communicate with mills and lumber yards, Dick developed the idea of sending a daily inquiry sheet. Responses to the sheet gave him up-to-date information about where he could obtain needed lumber sizes. He would typically send out 50 or more identical, hand-written letters. Although Christopher Sholes had invented a practical typewriter in 1868, American business people still relied heavily on handwriting as their basic communication method. Dick wanted to find a simple way to make multiple copies in an office environment.

Dick tried several ideas, but his successful solution followed a casual experiment he conducted at his desk. He had just eaten a piece of candy wrapped in waxed paper. He placed the paper over a file and pulled a nail over the paper. Dick held the paper up and saw that it was perforated along the line made by the nail. He reasoned that if he could force heavy ink through the holes and onto a sheet of paper, he could duplicate the line. At this early stage, he only considered the duplication of handwriting.

Dick still needed to develop a suitable file-like plate and to make a durable wax stencil master. After solving these problems, he was ready to apply for a patent. In conducting the necessary patent search, he discovered that Thomas Edison had tackled a similar problem. Edison had an existing patent for a vibrating electric pen that made a series of holes in a wax master. The pen had a small low-voltage dc motor at its top that caused its pencil-sized pointed steel shaft to vibrate 8,000 times a minute. A person writing with the device would make a series of holes in a wax master, much the same as in Dick's method. Ink was rolled through the master onto a sheet of paper to make the copy. While Edison's invention was only moderately successful, it is particularly noteworthy because it was the first product with an electric motor to go into production.

Edison and Dick met, liked each other from the start, and became lifelong friends. They had no trouble developing an agreement on the mimeograph. Edison provided some initial financing and invented a device for making the wax masters. Although the use of Dick's flat-bed, file-like surface was essential to the invention's success, he emphasized Edison's name on the mimeograph label. Labels of the early models read: "The Edison Mimeograph, Originally Designed and Patented by Mr. Thomas A. Edison, Made By A. B. Dick Company, Chicago U.S.A." The word *mimeograph* originated in the Greek words *mime* (to copy) and *graph* (to draw).

To use the mimeograph, an office employee placed a stiff wax master over a fine file-like plate, or sheet, of specially frosted glass. The person then hand wrote a message on the master with a metal-tipped stylus. Each written line or word created many holes in the master. The holes converted the wax master to a stencil. The stencil was lifted from the plate and placed on a sheet of paper. The employee rolled an inked, hard-rubber roller over the stencil. That forced ink through the many small holes and made a single copy. The process was repeated for as many copies as necessary. Each stencil could make up to several hundred copies.

Dick aggressively marketed the Edison-Dick mimeograph, as the product was originally called. His company made mimeographs in an eight-story building on the corner of Lake and LaSalle Streets in Chi-

Early mimeograph duplicating hardware and supplies

cago. Within five years, the company had 1,700 employees.

The original mimeograph used a handwriting technique instead of a typewriter for two reasons. Early masters were stiff and could not bend to fit into a typewriter. Also, they were not strong enough to withstand the impact of the keys. Experimental masters shredded during typewriter tests.

Dick accidentally discovered a stronger master material while buying a pair of shoes. The shoes came wrapped in soft, long-fiber paper. Dick thought that such paper might make a suitable carrier for the wax on the master. Dick's idea was similar to the one George Eastman had when he used paper in 1884 as a carrier for light-sensitive emulsion in cameras used by amateur photographers. Dick experimented with different papers and ultimately developed his own made from the fibers of a particular species of hazel bushes. The bushes grew only in high mountains on islands off the coast of Japan. Dick coated the paper with an improved wax made from seven parts paraffin to one part ordinary lard. Both sides were sealed with a thin layer of elastic varnish. The sandwiched combination was flexible and yet strong enough to resist the impact of typewriter type. Typing compressed the special wax away from the paper, exposing clean holes that allowed ink to pass through freely. Typewriters became more popular in businesses and schools, and the mimeograph offered rapid duplication.

Label on an early mimeograph

Hand-rolled copies could be made at the rate of only a few copies per minute. It wasn't until 1900 that Dick developed a rotary mimeograph machine. The frame of the flat bed was bent into the shape of a half cylinder, similar to that found in modern mimeograph machines. Ink passed through the stencil from inside the cylinder. The hand-cranked device did not revolve continuously. It rocked back and forth as each sheet of paper was fed into the machine. Four years later, Dick introduced the Model 75, the first completely rotary-type mimeograph machine.

Dick served as a trustee of Lake Forest College, was a board member of several banks, and participated in many civic activities. Widowed in 1885, he married a second time. He had a total of five children. He named one of his sons Edison, in honor of Thomas Edison. Although Dick held many patents associated with mimeographic duplications, he often referred to Edison as the originator of stencil duplication. Dick was the head of his company for 51 years. Few organizations can duplicate that record for continuous leadership.

References and Resources

Materials from the A. B. Dick Co., Chicago, IL, circa 1934 and 1949.

National Cyclopedia of American Biography, James T. White and Co. Publishers, 1891; with supplemental updates.

Granville Woods

BLACK Americans have made significant contributions to our society while going about their professional lives. The U.S. Patent Office generally did not keep records of an inventor's race, yet through 1900, at least 104 black Americans received more than 375 patents. Many of their inventions were as important as those of better-known technologists. Yet, if past inventors of all races are generally forgotten today, this is especially true of black inventors.

Black American technologists have always been innovators and discoverers. Their contributions are all the more remarkable considering the discouraging social and political barriers they frequently encountered. We know little about many of them because they received only limited publicity. Very few wrote biographies, and detailed information about their lives is scattered. No better example of this can be offered than the sketchy records of the life of Granville Woods, a genius in the field of electricity.

Woods was born in central Ohio, and he attended elementary school for a few brief years. He started working in a machine shop at the age of 10, and he did his best to educate himself in the evening through private tutoring. A voracious reader throughout his life, he was, for the most part, self-taught. At age 13, he learned that metal rails connected the Atlantic and Pacific Oceans, and he read everything he could find about railroads. He left home at 16 and moved to Missouri to work first as a fireman and then as a locomotive engineer for the Iron Mountain Railroad. He enjoyed all aspects of railroad work and developed an interest in telegraphy. Telegraph lines followed the rail lines, and Woods learned all he could about electricity and electrical transmission of information.

Born:
April 23, 1856, in Columbus, Ohio

Died:
January 30, 1910, in New York, New York

Woods held many different jobs in his late teens and twenties. From his work with the railroad, he moved to a steel mill in Springfield, Illinois, and then to a machine shop in New York City. Just before he turned 22, he signed up for a four-year tour aboard the British steamer *Ironsides*. Between 1882 and 1884, Woods worked for the Danville and Southern Railroad. During the evening, he worked on new ideas related to his work, and he received his first patent in early 1884. It was for an improved steam boiler furnace that used less coal than conventional boilers did. Receiving the patent encouraged Woods to strike out on his own. Throughout his working life, he had saved part of his wages, and in 1884 he had enough money to establish a business. He and his brother Lyates opened a machine shop in Cincinnati. They called it the Woods Electric Co.

It was a small company that produced specialty items for its customers. The Woods brothers made such things as gears, generators, and tools. They repaired pumps, measuring instruments, and household items. Woods worked on electrical devices and took out his second patent 1884. It was for a highly efficient telephone transmitter that used a flexible diaphragm and carbon particles. A person's voice caused the diaphragm to vibrate and press against a small box of carbon particles. When the particles came close together, they conducted electricity quite well. When they spread apart, they conducted electricity only weakly. The action produced a series of strong and weak

electrical currents that followed the sound patterns of a person's voice. This method made the telephone more practical. Woods sold the patent rights to the American Bell Telephone Co. of Boston, without a requirement that his name be used with the transmitter. That decision was probably a mistake, but it was a pattern Woods always followed. It is the main reason that Woods is not well remembered.

Selling patents provided Woods with money that supported further experiments at the machine shop. Some of his customers included the General Electric Co., Westinghouse Electric and Manufacturing Co., and the American Engineering Co.

Most of Woods's work was in the field of electricity. This was an emerging technology that tended to attract the brightest and most capable technologists. Woods's best year was 1887, when he received seven patents. He designed a regulator for electric motors that permitted the user to vary the speed without using energy-robbing resistors. The regulator proved so effective that it produced an energy savings of 40 percent. Woods's most sophisticated invention was the induction telegraph, a system that allowed communication between a moving train and a railroad station. It worked by laying an electrical wire on the ground between the rails. Another wire was suspended underneath a railroad car that carried telegraph equipment. The second wire hung 10" above the first and parallel to it. The moving train transmitted telegraph messages by sending electrical impulses to the wire suspended from the car. Those impulses induced a current in the receiving wire between the rails. The telegrapher at the railroad station picked up the dots and dashes of the induced current. The technique permitted both sending and receiving messages on a moving train.

Apparently influenced by the success of Thomas Edison, Woods reorganized his company to manufacture his own inventions. However, he did not have the proper tooling and went back to selling his patents. Woods wanted to make electricity practical for transportation, and many of his approximately 50 patents reflect that interest. In 1888, he worked on a system of electrically driven street cars for mass transportation in cities. The cars drew their power from

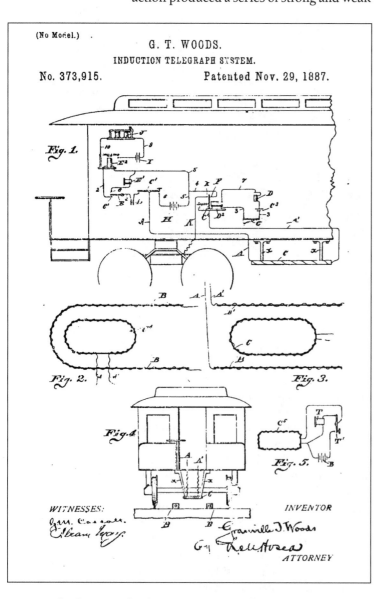

Loops of wire attached to a moving railroad car picked up telegraph signals from a wire between the rails.

an overhead line. Using electricity eliminated the clouds of smoke and soot from steam engines operating in cities. One of Woods's inventions that continues to modern times is the third-rail power pickup on subways and urban commuter trains. Subways draw electricity from a protected power rail outside the two original tracks. Woods received a patent for it in 1901. He received patents for electromagnetically controlled air brakes on trains and automatic circuit breakers for operator safety. Having an expansive mind, Woods also patented an egg incubator, a small train for use in amusement parks, and improved techniques for constructing tunnels. Around 1890, he sold his share of the business and moved to New York City.

Shortly before his death, Woods was practically penniless, but the reason is unclear. He had succeeded as an inventor and machine shop owner and had never before experienced financial difficulties. His later financial problems may have resulted from the types of inventions he worked on. Woods did not work on small consumer-type products but on large transportation systems. He often confronted powerful business people and politicians. People have speculated that the manager of the American Engineering Co. stole some of Woods's patents in 1892.

As a result of defending his work to the public, Woods may have been charged with libel. He spent a short time in jail. The related legal defense all but forced him into bankruptcy, and he never fully recovered. He died of a stroke in 1910.

Woods never married, and little is known of his personal characteristics. The drawing on page 133 is the one most commonly connected with him, though it is of uncertain origin. Like Edison, Woods devoted his technical career to invention. Also like Edison, his inventions came primarily in the field of electricity. In an October 1974 proclamation, Ohio governor John Gilligan recognized Woods as "the black Edison." It was a fitting tribute to an unsung genius of electricity.

References and Resources

The Real McCoy: African-American Invention and Innovation by Portia P. James, Smithsonian Institution Press, 1989.

Black Pioneers of Science and Invention by Louis Haber, Harcourt, Brace, & World, 1970.

Eight Black American Inventors by Robert Hayden, Addison-Wesley, 1972.

American Black Scientists and Inventors by Edward S. Jenkins and others, National Science Teachers Association, circa 1975.

Nikola Tesla

Born:
July 9, 1856, in
Smiljan,
Croatia

Died:
January 7,
1943, in
New York,
New York

Smithsonian Photo No. 80-16573

Nikola Tesla at age 29

A 28-year-old Croatian immigrant reached New York City in the summer of 1884. He had just 4¢ in his pocket and many ideas in his head. The young man thought that he could easily use alternating current (ac), then in its infancy, to power electric motors. Nikola Tesla made the use of ac practical. We sometimes associate his name with the Tesla coil used in high-voltage, high-frequency electrical demonstrations. His most important contributions, however, involved the design of practical ac motors, alternators, and transmission equipment.

The fourth of five children, Tesla was born in a small village in what was then called Austria-Hungary. His birth was said to have come during a thunderstorm at the stroke of midnight. His father was a clergyman. His mother could neither read nor write, but she had an excellent memory and inventive skill in developing household devices. Tesla was close to his mother and credited her as the source of his creative ability. Static electricity and mechanical items fascinated the young man. He recalled stroking the back of a cat to produce a shower of crackling sparks. He also remembered building a tiny motor powered by June bugs that he attached to a cross on a spindle.

In the classroom, the tall, slender Tesla was an outstanding pupil, especially in mathematics. Without using pencil and paper, he often arrived at and blurted out the correct answers to complicated problems. After graduating from elementary school, Tesla moved in with an aunt and uncle in the larger town of Karlovac for his high school years. Many of his ancestors had had military or religious careers, and Tesla's father hoped that he would follow their lead. Then, Tesla came down with a serious case of cholera shortly after graduating from high school. When it looked as if he would die, his father tried to rouse him by granting him permission to attend a technical school. Tesla recovered, spent a year rebuilding his strength, and entered the polytechnic institute in Graz, Austria.

The school had obtained a new direct current (dc) generator, or dynamo. The dynamo fascinated Tesla, and he spent many hours analyzing its operation. Noticing that its commutator caused a great deal of sparking, Tesla pondered the possibility of eliminating those electrical losses. His unusual intellectual powers allowed him to mentally design and test ac electrical devices. His instructors paid little attention to his ideas, which they thought were fanciful perpetual motion machines.

After receiving his degree, Tesla moved to Budapest to work as a draftsman. He again developed a grave illness and while recovering worked out designs for ac motors in his head. His few friends did not know how to respond to Tesla's seemingly strange comments which emerged from his mental testing of motors. After recovering from his illness, he redesigned dynamos and developed automatic regulators for an Edison plant in Paris. The job gave him contacts in America, and he decided to take advantage of the more challenging opportunities available abroad.

After arriving in New York, a letter of introduction got Tesla a position with Thomas Edison at his Pearl Street electrical generating plant in Manhattan. Tesla was a cultured man, while Edison was quite folksy. Yet, regardless of their differences, Tesla's work impressed Edison. Because Edison wanted to promote the use of dc power generation, he offered Tesla $18 per week plus a $50,000 bonus to significantly improve dynamo efficiency. Tesla took up the challenge, and he worked at it more than 16 hours a day, seven days a week, for several months. When he solved the problem at hand, Edison refused to pay the promised bonus. Edison said that Tesla obviously did not understand American humor. Angry and upset, Tesla quit on the spot. In 1912, when Tesla was offered the Nobel Prize in physics to be shared with Edison, he refused the honor because of his lingering anger toward Edison.

Tesla worked for several electric companies and experimented with ac motors and alternators in his spare time. He took out 12 patents in 1888, from his lifetime total of more than 100. He presented his ideas to the American Institute of Electrical Engineers and met with George Westinghouse. Unlike Edison, Westinghouse was committed to alternating current. However, he was having problems developing suitable motors and alternators. The devices covered by Tesla's patents filled the void and the two men made a deal. Tesla received $60,000 plus $2.50 for every horsepower of motor or generating capacity that Westinghouse sold. Tesla used the money to open his own private laboratory. Around that time, he also became an American citizen.

Westinghouse underbid Edison's company to win the contract to illuminate the 1893 world's fair in Chicago. This was the first fair to use electric lighting. After assembling 24 500-horsepower alternators, the smartly dressed Tesla gave demonstrations at the Westinghouse exhibit. He showed off an electric clock, fluorescent tubes, and huge noisy sparks from electric coils. His

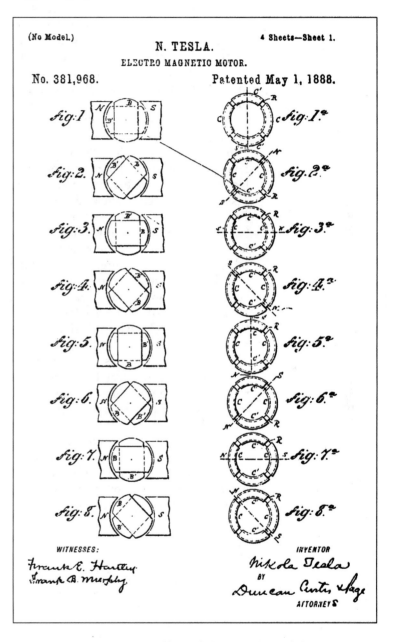

A Tesla ac motor patent showed the rotation of the armature.

motors originally operated from an ac frequency of 133 cycles per second. Finding that to be too high, he experimented until he came up with 60 cycles per second. That frequency was low enough to operate motors and high enough to eliminate lamp flickering.

The same year, Westinghouse won the contract to build three alternators at Niagara Falls. They would make up the world's first large hydroelectric generating plant. Three huge turbines were connected to 5,000 horsepower two-phase alternators designed by Tesla. The system went on-line in 1895, and a 22-mile ac transmission line soon carried power to Buffalo, New York. The plant was completely operational in 1902 with 21 alternators. By itself, it produced more electrical power than that generated in 31 states. Tesla's patents formed the basis of the entire power generation and transmission network.

In his ac-dc battle with Edison, Westinghouse spent large sums of money, bringing his company close to bankruptcy. He asked Tesla to modify their financial arrangement. Tesla agreed to sell his patent rights for $200,000. He was then at the height of his fame and felt he would get more money from other sources in the future. This was not a wise decision, but Tesla did not trust financial advisors. Lowering the royalty payments he received would have easily saved Westinghouse and still made Tesla a millionaire in a few years.

Tesla's pet project was the atmospheric transmission of electrical power. He worked on techniques to transmit power through the air for motors and lights. As part of that effort, he first worked on wireless communication. In 1897, he transmitted a wireless message over a distance of 25 miles. He patented and built a successful model of a radio-controlled ship in 1898. He was constructing a 187-foot tower on Long Island in 1901 just as Guglielmo Marconi sent the first wireless signal across the Atlantic Ocean. Tesla calmly commented, "Let him continue. He is using 17 of my patents." The U.S. Supreme Court agreed. In 1944, the justices voided Marconi's wireless patent in favor of a 1900 Tesla patent.

Tesla was clearly an underappreciated technical genius who had extraordinary powers of analysis and invention. But he was also an arrogant man who had little tact, had no friends, never married, and was almost uniformly disliked. Late in life, he became enamored with pigeons and spent hours a day feeding them. He often brought them into his New York apartment, where he died alone in 1943.

References and Resources

"Seeking Redress for Nikola Tesla" by Eliot Marshall, *Science*, 30 October 1981.

"Nikola Tesla" by Kenneth M. Swezey, *Science*, 16 May 1958.

"The Work of the World" by Curt Wohleber, in *American Heritage of Invention and Technology*, Winter 1992.

Dictionary of American Biography, Charles Scribner's Sons Publishers, 1932; with supplemental updates.

National Cyclopedia of American Biography, James T. White and Co. Publishers, 1891; with supplemental updates.

McGraw-Hill Encyclopedia of Biography, McGraw-Hill Publishers, 1973.

Asimov's Biographical Encyclopedia of Science and Technology, by Isaac Asimov, Doubleday & Co. Publishers, 1964.

Michael Idvorsky Pupin

THE U.S. Patent Office noted a significant increase in patent applications during 1924. Officials there credited the increase to the publication of Michael Pupin's autobiography, *From Immigrant to Inventor*, the previous year. A true rags-to-riches story about a poor Serbian-born genius in the field of electricity, it apparently encouraged many would-be inventors to make patent applications. The book was even more remarkable because Pupin won the 1924 Pulitzer Prize in biography for it. It was the only award of its kind ever received by a person whose career was grounded in technology.

Pupin was born to an illiterate but intelligent farm couple. His father served several terms as mayor of his small village and his mother strongly encouraged him in his studies. Pupin received his elementary education in Idvor, but he went to high school in a larger town nearby. His teacher introduced the young Pupin to electricity by conducting small demonstrations and explaining Benjamin Franklin's kite experiment. During summers at home, Pupin helped herdsmen at night with their oxen. They communicated with each other by using a long knife inserted deeply into the soil. Tapping on the knife's wooden handle sent vibrations through the ground. The technique gave Pupin his introduction to sound transmission.

While in his early teen years, Pupin made himself politically conspicuous by speaking out in favor of a new and rising feeling of nationalism. This activity brought him difficulties with some of the people around him. An earlier chance encounter with a traveling American couple had introduced him to some of the values considered important by many in the United States. Pupin concluded that Americans must hold loftier

Library of Congress

Born:
October 4, 1858, in Idvor, Austria-Hungary

Died:
March 12, 1935, in New York, New York

ideals than those he saw around him. In 1874, following his father's death, the 15-year-old Pupin decided that his future lay across the Atlantic Ocean.

Pupin sold his clothes and books to buy a steamship ticket. He boarded in Hamburg and arrived in New York City 14 days later. He landed with 5¢ in his pocket and the clothes on his back. He could not speak English. He quickly found a job with a Delaware farmer who happened to be in New York. Pupin worked on the farm for a few years and started taking English lessons from the farm owner's daughter. He later moved to a cracker factory on Cortland Street in New York, while acquainting himself with American customs and traditions. He roomed above the cracker factory with a German student named Bilharz who admired Pupin's desire to learn. Bilharz taught Pupin to read and write English, and later to read Greek and Latin. Pupin particularly enjoyed books on advanced mathematics and read each one several times.

Through dogged perseverance, Pupin prepared himself to apply for admission to Columbia University in 1879. He passed his entrance examination with honors and received a scholarship. Pupin involved himself so much with life in his new country that his classmates voted him class president his junior year. The week that he graduated from college in 1883, he became a naturalized citizen of the U.S. He then studied electricity further in England and Germany. Pupin returned to Columbia to become an

instructor in the university's newly established electrical engineering department. He and Francis Crocker comprised the department, which had almost no equipment and no budget. The two men raised funds by giving lectures to business people and lawyers who had an interest in electrical industries. Pupin remained at Columbia for the remainder of his 39-year professional life.

The idea for Pupin's best-known invention came to him as he thought about a string with a weight on it. He knew that a disturbance set up in a loaded string does not die out as quickly as a disturbance in one that is not loaded. In his autobiography, Pupin said that what he learned with the herdsmen in Idvor about sound conducted through the ground helped him understand the weighted-string analogy. In the transmission of sound over telephone wires, particles are also set in motion, just like the string. Pupin thought that an electrically loaded transmission line would be more efficient than an unloaded line. Using that theory, he tackled the problem of telephone and telegraph transmissions that weakened and distorted as they traveled down a wire. Pupin did much theoretical work and experimentation to solve the problem. He determined that inductance coils, properly sized and strategically located along the phone lines, would greatly reduce the problem. The coils, spaced two to five miles apart and resembling wire-wrapped doughnuts, were called *pupinized lines* in Europe and *Pupin coils* in America. Pupin's discovery allowed people to hold intelligible conversations over distances as great as 1,000 miles. The Bell Telephone Co. bought his patent in 1901 and used it to make long-distance telephoning practical.

Pupin also did a great deal of work with medical X rays and made the first X-ray exposure in America in early 1896. It was of the hand of a young attorney who had been wounded by a shotgun blast. The X ray showed about two dozen shotgun pellets. By placing a fluorescent screen on top of the photographic plate, Pupin reduced long exposure times to just a few seconds. The fluorescent screen came from Pupin's close friend Thomas Edison.

Another of Pupin's discoveries involved the tuning of oscillating currents for radio reception. Every radio uses such a circuit

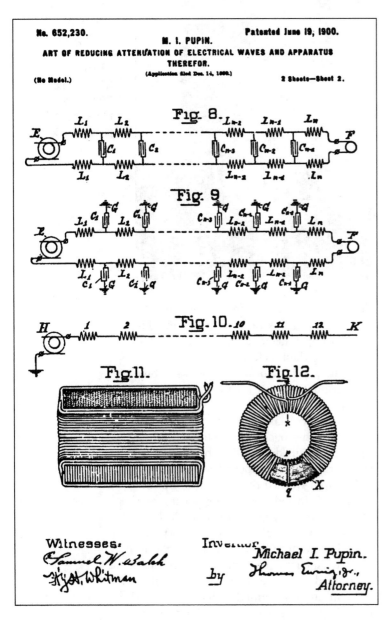

A patent drawing related to Pupin coils

to allow selecting the signal from only one station while excluding all others. Pupin was the first person to use the term "electrical tuning."

While working on his inventions, Pupin also taught electrical engineering courses. One of his students was Edwin Armstrong, who invented the frequency modulation (FM) system for radio transmission in 1939. He and Pupin jointly received a patent for a high-frequency vacuum-tube oscillator. Two of Pupin's students won Nobel Prizes. Robert Millikan won the award for physics in 1923 and Irving Langmuir won for chemistry in 1932.

Pupin married Sarah Jackson in 1888. Eight years later, he contracted tuberculosis. While caring for him, his wife also contracted the disease and died. A heart-broken Pupin moved to a farm in Connecticut to complete his recuperation. A friend presented him with a pair of horses on the condition that Pupin train them. Working with the horses brought Pupin out of his depression, and he returned to work several months later. Pupin bought the Connecticut farm and built a large home resembling a Serbian medieval landlord's house. After his death, it became the home of his only child, his daughter Varvara.

Much like Albert Einstein, Pupin worked in an area of technology that the average person could not understand. Still, in their times, both Einstein and Pupin were widely considered to be great men who deserved respect and recognition. Pupin received 34 patents, and he wrote 68 technical articles and 4 books. He received 5 medals and 18 honorary college degrees, 2 from European colleges.

Pupin was a large and generally healthy man who enjoyed hard work and athletic activity. He was an eloquent public speaker, with an upbeat personality and much social grace. Although he was a naturalized American citizen, Pupin never forgot his heritage. He organized an immigrant society and helped provide temporary housing for others from his homeland. He also helped to publish a newspaper of interest to immigrants. During World War I, Pupin represented the Serbian branch of the Yugoslavian government. He died on the 61st anniversary of the day his ship had left Hamburg. The Pupin Physics Laboratory at Columbia has a bronze plaque that honors him as "a true guide to the perplexed."

References and Resources

From Immigrant to Inventor by Michael Pupin, Charles Scribner's Sons, 1923.

Smithsonian Book of Invention, Smithsonian Institution, 1978.

Dictionary of American Biography, Charles Scribner's Sons Publishers, 1932; with supplemental updates.

National Cyclopedia of American Biography, James T. White and Co. Publishers, 1891; with supplemental updates.

McGraw-Hill Encyclopedia of Biography, McGraw-Hill Publishers, 1973.

Asimov's Biographical Encyclopedia of Science and Technology, by Isaac Asimov, Doubleday & Co. Publishers, 1964.

George Washington Gale Ferris

Chicago Historical Society Photo No. 10257

George Ferris at age 33

Born:
February 14,
1859, in
Galesburg,
Illinois

Died:
November 22,
1896, in
Pittsburgh,
Pennsylvania

THE words *Ferris wheel* usually bring to mind the modern, two-person-per-open-seat, 40'- to 45'-tall vertical wheel found at amusement parks and local fairs. The first one was far more dramatic. Installed at the World's Columbian Exposition of 1893 held in Chicago it was a huge 264'-tall, 36-car ride that many called "the big wheel." It could carry 1,440 passengers. The brainchild of George Washington Gale Ferris, the wheel drew more attention than the exposition's serious cultural displays.

Ferris was born into a prominent family in northeastern Illinois. When he was five years old, his family moved to Carson City, Nevada. The youngster often spoke of wanting to build bridges someday. His parents sent him at age 16 to a military school in Oakland, California, so he could learn discipline and the basics of engineering. Ferris then went to Rensselaer Polytechnic Insti-

tute in Troy, New York, graduating with a degree in civil engineering.

In his first job, the tall and slender Ferris helped to establish 3-1/2 miles of narrow-gauge railroad lines outside New York City. He also laid out 78 miles of track in West Virginia. A man who always looked for new challenges, Ferris became general manager of the Queen City Coal Mining Co. in West Virginia. He designed and built a coal trestle and three 1,800' tunnels. Ferris then worked for several bridge companies, developing a reputation for his knowledge of concrete work. He then moved on to work for the Kentucky and Indiana Bridge Co., helping to build bridges near Wheeling, West Virginia, and over the Ohio River at Pittsburgh, Pennsylvania, Cincinnati, Ohio, and Henderson, Kentucky.

Anticipating that builders would soon construct bridges using steel in place of iron, Ferris developed the profession of testing materials. He became an expert in the properties of structural steel. He opened a consulting firm in Pittsburgh, the steel center of America. His firm advised companies on forging steel and evaluating it for new uses. Ferris also specialized in inspecting the manufacture of structural components for safety and durability. Ferris was only 26 when he started his testing firm, which had several employees.

Ferris's active involvement with the big wheel began in 1890 after he attended an informal meeting in Chicago for architects and engineers. The meeting was hosted by Daniel H. Burnham, the construction chief for the exposition intended to commemorate the 400th anniversary of Christopher Columbus's journey to the New World. Burnham encouraged meeting participants to design and build a unique structure for the exposition that would rival Gustave Eiffel's 984' tower at the Paris Exposition of 1889.

Ferris had designed his wheel five or six years earlier for professional recreation. He first showed it to friends and business associates over dinner a few weeks before the meeting with Burnham. They advised Ferris against going ahead with the project. Ferris disagreed, considering the exposition just the right setting. He presented his design to the exposition evaluation committee, which also proved reluctant to grant the concession. Committee members feared that the huge wheel might turn into a monstrosity that did not reflect the dignity of the occasion. Their consultants predicted that the heavy wheel would collapse on itself. Undaunted, Ferris continued his negotiations and finally received a concession in December 1892. The exposition's opening date was May 1893, and its site was near Chicago's Museum of Science and Industry.

Mid-winter construction began with the pouring of a foundation of eight 20' x 20' concrete footings, kept warm with steam to permit proper curing in the cold weather. Ferris traveled to nine different steel and iron suppliers to locate enough materials for his wheel. It ultimately weighed over 1,200 tons and required 175 freight cars to deliver its thousands of parts. The massive 33"-diameter, 45'-long hollow axle was the largest piece of steel ever forged. After workers mounted the axle on its 140'-high supports in March, assembly of the wheel began. In spite of the wheel's circular appearance, every piece of structural metal in it was straight. It had no curved pieces.

Much of the wheel consisted of structural iron, but its spokes were 2-9/16"-diameter rods that had special turnbuckles and clevises to permit tightening. The 30'-wide circular structure was not much different from a bicycle wheel. Ferris correctly theorized that the lower tensioned spokes would support the upper spokes, making the wheel function like a perpetual arched bridge.

This was a revolutionary idea, and no one had ever calculated the stresses for such a structure. With the wheel only partially built, a storm with winds of up to 72 mph occurred on the night of April 21-22. The wheel survived the storm without damage. To assure the public of the wheel's safety,

promoters often repeated that story during the exposition.

Two 1,000-horsepower steam engines, located in 4'-deep pits, turned the wheel. Operators used one of the 30"-bore, 48"-stroke engines at a time, while holding the other in reserve. Power was transferred to the wheel using two chains similar to bicycle chains that had links so large that their pivot pins were more than five inches in diameter. The wheel used a 60 psi Westinghouse air brake. The wheel revolved under perfect control, and it drew an excited response from all who saw it.

The Ferris wheel's official opening date of June 21 came 51 days after the exposition opened. On that day, all 36 elegant en-

The first Ferris wheel at the 1893 World's Columbian Expositon in Chicago

closed pendulum cars, each with 40 plushly upholstered swivel chairs, were in place. Successful test runs had been made. Ferris, his wife Margaret, city officials, the Iowa state band, and other guests took the first official trip. Operators loaded six cars at a time from 8 A.M. to 11 P.M., and people stood in line to pay an exorbitant 50¢ for a two-revolution, 20-minute trip. The big wheel operated flawlessly from the first day it took passengers. By the time the exposition closed in early November, the $400,000 wheel had shown itself to be a complete financial success. Paid admissions totaled 1,453,611 people.

The wheel was dismantled in 1895 and moved a few miles north, to a location just two blocks from Lincoln Park and near a busy trolley line. Despite lively promotional campaigns, the wheel lost money in its new location and went bankrupt. The Old Truck scrap metal firm bought it at auction in 1903 for $1,800. Instead of scrapping the wheel, the buyer sent it to St. Louis for the 1904 Louisiana Purchase Exposition. There, receipts from its use could barely pay for the necessary steam-engine fuel. The owners of the world's largest toy dynamited it for scrap in 1906. Legend has it that they buried the 40-ton axle in St. Louis's Franklin Park because no one knew how to cut it up.

However, the axle has never been located.

George Ferris held no patents on the wheel. Since he died of tuberculosis in 1896, he did not see this unpleasant end to his creation. Ferris's wheel may have been the last great technical triumph of the nineteenth century. In recognition of his achievement, Rensselaer Polytechnic Institute proclaimed 1981, the 100th anniversary of Ferris's graduation, "The Year of the Ferris Wheel."

References and Resources

The Ferris Wheel: An Engineering Wonder, Rensselaer Polytechnic Institute Archives, undated (circa 1981).

"George Ferris and His 'Big Wheel,'" *Chicago Magazine*, March 1981.

"The Big Wheel," *Engineer*, vol. 5, 1965. (Published by University of British Columbia.)

"George Ferris's Wheel: The Great Attraction of the Midway Plaisance," *Chicago History*, Fall 1977.

Unreferenced clippings from the Chicago Historical Society.

Dictionary of American Biography, Charles Scribner's Sons Publishers, 1932; with supplemental updates.

National Cyclopedia of American Biography, James T. White and Co. Publishers, 1891; with supplemental updates.

Herman Hollerith

Smithsonian Institution Photo No. 060700

Born: February 29, 1860, in Buffalo, New York

Died: November 17, 1929, in Washington, D.C.

THE expanded use of computers in education, business, and industry might lead some to think that automated information retrieval is a modern innovation. It's not. The first system to store and analyze large amounts of data was invented in 1887. Herman Hollerith developed tabulating machines that could read and interpret information stored as holes in punched cards. Previously, French textile weavers had used punched paper and thin wood to automate the weaving of intricate fabric designs. Mathematicians had tried to make calculating machines using the same principle. However, it was Hollerith who first produced a practical information retrieval system that was the predecessor of electronic computers.

Hollerith was the seventh child of German immigrants. Raised for the most part by his widowed mother, he moved with his family to New York City at age 9. Hollerith's mother supported herself and her children by making women's hats. Hollerith graduated from Columbia University with a degree in mining engineering at the age of only 19, and his first job involved assisting one of his former teachers. William Towbridge had the responsibility of tabulating data for the 1880 United States' census. He assigned Hollerith to compile data on the statistics of manufacturers. The job had little to do with mining, but it paid $600 a year.

The project led Hollerith to Washington, D.C., where, on one occasion, he had dinner with a young lady and her family. Her father, John Billings, was a specialist at the Census Office. He discussed with Hollerith the desirability of having a machine that would do the routine work of tabulating populations and other statistics. Billings speculated that the time required to conduct a complete census analysis by hand could take over 10 years. Counting by making marks with a pen worked fine for the first census of 1790, when the U.S. had only four million residents and census takers asked only four questions. Ninety years later, the U.S. population had multiplied by 12 times and citizens had to answer dozens of questions on the census. The 1880 census would take seven years to complete, and a more efficient tabulation method was an absolute necessity. His chance encounter with Billings started the 20-year-old Hollerith thinking about a tabulating machine.

Finishing his duties with the 1880 census, Hollerith accepted a teaching job at the Massachusetts Institute of Technology in 1882. It gave him more time for experimentation, as well as the opportunity to talk with others about the field of applied electricity.

His first serious attempt at creating a tabulating machine involved the use of a strip of paper with holes punched in it. Hollerith ran the paper over a metal drum and made contact through the holes to operate a counter. He liked the design because it was an automatic feed system. Hollerith patented his design, but never went into production with it because it proved difficult to make changes or locate data in long tapes.

After finding that he disliked teaching, Hollerith moved to St. Louis, where he worked for a short time on electrically controlled air brakes for trains. While traveling for work, he often noticed railroad conductors punching several holes in tickets. The holes were used for identification as a hedge against theft by vagrants who might try to resell the tickets. Hollerith wrote: "The conductor . . . punched out a description of the individual, as [having] light hair, dark eyes, large nose." These "punch photographs" gave Hollerith the idea he needed.

Hollerith moved to the Patent Office in 1884 and spent his spare time working on his tabulating machine. He worked for more than three years on different techniques, finding the use of punched cards the most versatile. A pin could be slipped through

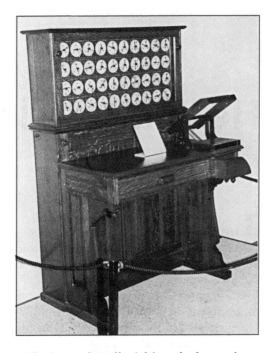

Full view of Hollerith's tabulator, in a museum display. The hand-operated card punch is on the desk at the right.

the punched hole into a tiny cup of mercury to complete an electrical circuit. Counting was automatic and registered on circular dials. When Hollerith was ready to build a prototype, he asked his brothers and sisters for financial help. None believed in his invention, and he received no assistance. After that rebuff, he had little contact with his siblings. He obtained the needed money in small amounts from many other investors.

Hollerith's tabulation method had to compete with two others for the 1890 census contract. The others would have used the conventional method, in which clerks worked with tally sheets, colored paper, and colored pens. Hollerith's technique was so unusual that officials decided to test it with Baltimore's 1887 death records. The cards were punched with a train conductor's ticket punch. Hollerith recorded age, sex, and cause of death in grid squares printed on thousands of cards. His battery-powered tabulator completed the analysis in a few days instead of the several weeks required by hand tabulation. Amazed at the system's speed, officials asked Hollerith to repeat the process for New Jersey and New York City. He did so, and won the contract for the 1890 census.

Hollerith's keypunch machine rests on the working surface of his battery powered tabulator. The dials in the background recorded totals as the punched cards were fed into the tabulator.

Hollerith ordered cards the same size as dollar bills, which allowed them to fit into file drawers used by banks. Instead of using a single-hole hand punch, Hollerith invented a keypunch machine. The photograph on page 146 shows one on the working surface of a tabulator that could handle up to 40 pieces of information per card. Hollerith started with an initial 30 machines that the Western Electric Co. built for $1,000 each. Up to 100 women during the day and 100 men at night punched information into the cards. Workers fed cards individually into the machines, and the dials behind the keypunch registered totals. It took Hollerith only six weeks to arrive at a figure of 62.5 million as a rough count of the U.S. population. When the final tabulations came in just two years later, the actual total was 63,056,000. The entire process had consumed only one third of the time it was estimated to take.

The following year, Canada, Norway, and Austria used Hollerith's equipment for their censuses. Russia's first-ever census was also tallied on Hollerith equipment. Hollerith attended the International Statistical Institute in 1895 in Bern, Switzerland. Over the next several years, he adapted his machines to handle statistical data. He found an expanded market and was soon making equipment for business, industry, and education.

Hollerith established the Tabulating Machine Co. to manufacture machines and sell punch cards. Not forgetting how he got started, he offered Billings a share in the business. Following the lead of George Pullman, who rented—rather than sold—his fancy railroad cars, Hollerith rented his machines. Within a few years, hundreds of companies were renting Hollerith punched-card tabulators. He sold the company in 1911 for an estimated $2 million. In 1924, its name changed to the International Business Machines Corporation.

In his lifetime, Hollerith was granted 38 patents and became a wealthy man. He took pleasure in the gold medal his tabulator received from the French government in 1889. He also received the prestigious Elliott Cresson medal from Philadelphia's Franklin Institute in 1890. He lived with his wife and six children in expensive houses in the Georgetown section of Washington, D.C., about a mile from the White House. He

owned four automobiles, a yacht, and country acreage. Because he was born on February 29 of a leap year, he had only 17 birthdays in the course of his lifetime.

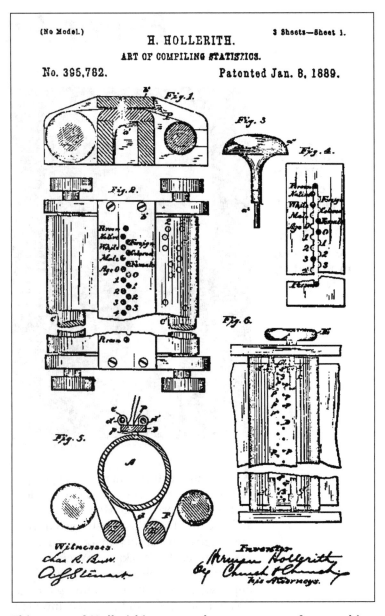

This page of Hollerith's patent shows a process for punching holes in paper, a stage of processing data.

References and Resources

Those Inventive Americans, National Geographic Society, 1971.

Machines—LIFE Science Library by Robert O'Brien, Time Inc., 1964.

Dictionary of American Biography, Charles Scribner's Sons Publishers, 1932; with supplemental updates.

Elmer Ambrose Sperry

Smithsonian Institution Photo No. 42732

Born:
October 12, 1860, in Cortland, New York

Died:
June 16, 1930, in Brooklyn, New York

FOR many centuries, mariners depended on magnetic compasses to direct them safely to their next port of call. However, the iron and steel used in ships constructed during the nineteenth century made such compasses unreliable, making navigation less accurate. In 1911, Elmer Sperry significantly improved the directional compass for the first time in a thousand years. He invented a practical motor-operated gyrocompass for ships and airplanes. Sperry organized his first company at the age of 19, and he accumulated more than 400 patents during his lifetime.

Sperry was born in a small town in the Finger Lakes region of New York state. His father worked in timber production. His mother died shortly after his birth, and his grandparents raised him. Early on, Sperry showed an aptitude for mechanical design. During his school years, he took every avail-able opportunity to visit the small factories and shops near his home. He often said that his high school science teacher opened his mind to the technical world. At 14, he invented a swiveling headlamp for locomotives to provide illumination as a train rounded a curve. Although the lamp was not a commercial success, it gave Sperry early exposure to inventing and patenting. Through an arrangement made possible by the Young Men's Christian Association (YMCA), Sperry visited the 1876 Centennial Exposition in Philadelphia as a teenager. There, he first saw modern technical equipment and developed an interest in arc lighting. Sperry called the visit his most memorable boyhood experience, and it determined the direction his career would take.

Sperry casually attended nearby Cornell University for a year or two after graduating from high school. While at Cornell, he constructed an automatically regulated and intensely bright arc lamp. He connected it to a dynamo, or generator, of his own design that produced the necessary electricity. Showing interest in the lamp, a local manufacturer financed Sperry's continued work. An improved model was so successful that Sperry built a large dynamo for the city of Syracuse and earned enough money to start his own company. In early 1880, he established the Sperry Electric Co. in Chicago. The factory opened on the day Sperry turned 20. A number of cities used Sperry's arc lamp and dynamo combinations for area lighting. The lamps guided air-mail planes during landing and along flight paths. Sperry's lamps also permitted the construction of larger movie houses. Older, less-efficient lamps did not produce enough light to illuminate a large screen evenly. An arc lamp that Sperry introduced in 1918 was five times brighter than any produced by his competitors. It served as the standard searchlight used throughout the world by the military and other organizations.

In the mid-1880s, Sperry turned his attention to the use of electricity for coal mining. He established the second of his eight companies devoted to the manufacture of dynamos and of electric cutting and transporting equipment. From electric locomotives for mining, it was just a short step to street railway cars. Sperry founded the Sperry Electric Railway Co. in Cleveland, Ohio, in 1890. He continued to obtain patents on both new equipment and improvements to existing equipment. He sold his factory to the General Electric Co. in 1894.

Sperry possessed the unusual combination of inventive ability and good business sense. He worked productively for nearly 50 years in several different technologies. Companies he established also manufactured electrically powered automobiles, batteries, compound diesel engines, and industrial chemicals. However, Sperry is best remembered for the gyrocompass.

An early model of Elmer Sperry's aircraft gyrocompass for an automatic pilot is on display at the National Air and Space Museum.

Military use of his arc lamp as a searchlight put Sperry in contact with people interested in the control of ships. Metal ships affected readings on magnetic compasses, making precise navigation difficult. Sperry's gyrocompass used the natural stability of a rapidly rotating disk to point in one direction. The gyrocompass proved more accurate than a magnetic compass. A magnetic compass uses the earth's magnetic field and indicates magnetic north. A gyrocompass, however, can be calibrated to always point true north. It is not affected by metal, nearby magnetism, nor the pitching motion of a ship. Sperry began work on the project in 1896 and soon found that he had to make hardware to the finest tolerances attainable. Perfection of the gyrocompass was a tedious and expensive 15-year project, but Sperry liked challenging technical problems. His companies developed a reputation for coming up with techniques that others would not even attempt. Though Sperry had thousands of workers, he often discussed machining problems directly with individual employees.

Through his insight and the skill of his workers, Sperry combined electrical and mechanical technologies and made a practical gyrocompass. It required a manufacturing sophistication unmatched by anything else that would come along before the space age. The U.S. Navy tested Sperry's gyrocompass in 1911 on the large battleship USS *Delaware* out of the Brooklyn Naval Shipyard. The test was a complete success, and the navy adopted the gyrocompass almost immediately. The impeccably dressed Sperry frequently gave human names to his inventions. He coupled the gyrocompass with an automatic steering mechanism and called the resulting instrument "Metal Mike." The name stuck for many years.

Two of Sperry's three sons, Lawrence and Elmer, Jr., built an airplane and taught themselves to fly while still in high school. Unlike his brothers and sister, Lawrence did not want to attend college. He much preferred flying and working at his father's company. Lawrence saw the gyrocompass as the potential heart of an automatic pilot system. He took a Curtiss flying boat with an experimental control system across the Atlantic by ship in 1914. France had offered

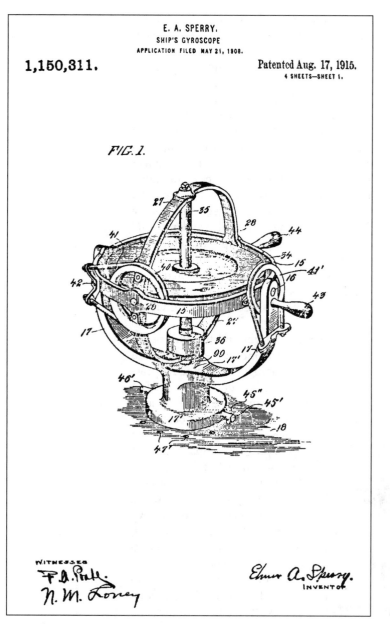

E. A. SPERRY.

SHIP'S GYROSCOPE

APPLICATION FILED MAY 21, 1908.

1,150,311.

Patented Aug. 17, 1915.

4 SHEETS—SHEET 1.

FIG. 1.

WITNESSES

F. A. Pratt.
N. M. Loney

Elmer A. Sperry.
INVENTOR

Sperry's first gyrocompasses were used on ships.

a 50,000-franc prize for a stable airplane. The Sperrys were among 53 entrants. They won on technical merit, and the pilot, Lawrence, could not help impressing the crowd with some low-level hands-off flying. Still, the automatic pilot was crude and in its infancy. Nine years later, while continuing his work to improve it, Lawrence died when his plane crashed into the English Channel. In 1933, a Sperry automatic pilot installed in Wiley Post's *Winnie Mae* allowed Post to make the first solo flight around the world.

Scientist Albert Michelson put to good use Elmer Sperry's knowledge of intense light sources and high-speed rotation. Michelson was America's first Nobel Prize winner in the sciences, in 1907. Michelson used a Sperry-built eight-sided mirror and arc lamp in 1926 to make the most accurate determination of the speed of light at that time. His measurement of 299,796 km/second differs only by 0.0012 percent from the value accepted today. The project sent Sperry all over the world, and he shared much of his data with Hantaro Nagaoka, a highly respected Japanese scientist. Through this connection, Sperry developed a keen interest in promoting better understanding between the people of America and Japan. He devoted much time in his later years to this work.

Sperry received many technical honors and awards from the U.S., France, Japan, and Russia. Stevens Institute of Technology, Northwestern University, and Lehigh University awarded him honorary degrees. He served as president of the American Society of Mechanical Engineers and co-founded the Institute of Electrical Engineers. Throughout his life, Sperry expressed gratitude to the YMCA for giving him the opportunity to visit the Centennial Exposition. He left the organization $1 million in his will.

References and Resources

Industrial Explorers by Maurice Holland, Harper & Brothers, 1928.

"Tribute to a Scientist" in *Science Teacher Magazine*, October 1960.

Modern Americans in Science and Invention by Edna Yost, Frederick A. Stokes & Co., 1940.

Science and the Instrument Maker: Michelson, Sperry, and the Speed of Light by Thomas Park Hughes, Smithsonian Institution, 1976.

Dictionary of American Biography, Charles Scribner's Sons Publishers, 1932; with supplemental updates.

National Cyclopedia of American Biography, James T. White and Co. Publishers, 1891; with supplemental updates.

Asimov's Biographical Encyclopedia of Science and Technology by Isaac Asimov, Doubleday & Co. Publishers, 1964.

George Washington Carver

From the collections of Henry Ford Museum and Greenfield Village, Negative 12237

George Washington Carver's college graduation photograph, taken when he was 33

Born:
in 1861, Diamond Grove, Missouri

Died:
January 5, 1943, in Tuskegee, Alabama

BIOTECHNOLOGY is a relatively new area of technology that involves the practical application of biological products. The first American biotechnologist was born into slavery and went on to use his considerable intelligence to achieve an international reputation. With quiet persistence, George Washington Carver identified hundreds of new products obtainable from pine cones, pecans, peanuts, and other crops. Those items fell under a wide range of uses from foods like mayonnaise and cheese, to construction materials like synthetic marble and wallboard.

George Carver was born a slave on a Missouri farm owned by Moses and Susan Carver. The exact date of his birth is unknown. Carver's father died in a farming accident before his birth, and his mother raised him alone for the first three years of his life. Then, outlaws kidnapped Carver, his mother, and his brother. Moses Carver sent out a search party to locate the group, and exchanged a race horse as ransom for the young Carver and his brother. Carver's mother was not heard of again. At the time of the rescue, Carver was quite ill with whooping cough. The illness affected his voice and he spoke in a high pitch for the rest of his life. Whooping cough was the beginning of a long battle with poor health that kept Carver from manual labor. Because of his physical limitations, he had time to learn to read and to develop an interest in biology. His ability to produce healthy plants prompted Carver's peers to call him the "plant doctor."

Freed after the Civil War and looking for education, Carver left home during his early teens. He traveled around the Midwest for several years, alternating farmwork with school attendance. He was about 24 when he completed high school in Minneapolis, Kansas. To avoid being confused for another Carver on the same mail route at the time, he added "Washington" as his middle name. He farmed for a few more years and then applied for admission to Simpson College in Indianola, Iowa. There, he paid his way by cooking at a hotel. Carver studied piano and art for a year until an art teacher, Etta Budd, discovered his abilities with plants and flowers. She contacted her brother, who was an agriculture professor at Iowa State College in Ames. Carver gained admittance there in 1891.

Carver had come to the right college. Two of his professors were excellent instructors who would each later become U. S. secretary of agriculture. They were James Wilson, who served under Theodore Roosevelt, and Henry Wallace, who served under Calvin Coolidge. Carver was a superb student who graduated at the top of his class, and he also excelled in painting. His sketch of the flower Yucca Gloriosa won a first prize at the World's Columbian Exposition in Chicago in 1893. The formal photograph

National Portrait Gallery, Smithsonian Institution

Painting of George Washington Carver, completed near the end of his life when he was 81

shown on page 151 was his yearbook picture from 1894, the year he graduated from Iowa State.

Because of Carver's outstanding academic performance, the college offered him an agricultural position. During the next three years, Carver operated the college's greenhouse, worked on plant parasites, and took classes for his master's degree. He collected more than 20,000 plant parasite specimens, and several were named in his honor.

Carver received statewide recognition in horticulture and was cited in many scientific papers. He made many presentations at state meetings.

In 1896, Carver received both his master's degree and the attention of Booker Taliaferro Washington. Washington headed the Tuskegee Normal and Industrial Institute in Tuskegee, Alabama. He invited Carver to establish a Department of Agriculture at Tuskegee. There was no equipment, not even a classroom bell, and Carver was offered an annual salary of just $1,500. Washington knew what he was asking and told Carver, "I cannot offer you money, position, or fame. . . . I offer you in their place hard, hard work, the task of bringing a people from poverty and waste to full manhood." Tuskegee attracted Carver because he believed the school's industrial approach to education could help solve the post-Civil War economic problems faced by poor southern farmers. Carver showed a lifelong indifference to money, and the salary seemed of little concern. He accepted Washington's challenge and began a legendary 47-year career at Tuskegee.

Carver was an unusual researcher. He never participated in professional meetings, he did not publish his findings in standard journals, and he received only three minor patents, all after he had reached his sixties. He preferred to deliver information to where he felt it could do the most good. Consequently, he held monthly conferences and tours of the college. He wrote simply worded bulletins directed at the semi-literate farmers of the period. His 44 bulletins carried such straightforward titles as "How to Grow the Peanut and 105 Ways of Preparing It for Human Consumption." China, India, Albania, and other countries soon adopted his techniques.

Much of the South's soil was worn out by farmers growing a single crop of either cotton or tobacco. Carver went by horse-drawn wagon from farm to farm, offering advice on restoring the soil's fertility. This teaching method was first called the "movable school" and, later, the "Jessup wagon," after a sponsor named Morris Jessup. Carver encouraged the farming of peanuts and sweet potatoes because both grew well in the South and improved soil quality. Peanuts originally came from South America and early on were almost unknown in the United States. After a particularly severe insect attack from the 1890s to the 1910s, Carver found farmers more accepting of his advice to change their crops.

The new crops had limited markets, however, and Carver felt obligated to find new ones. Working alone in his laboratory, as he preferred, he developed 325 new products from peanuts. They included face powder, shampoo, linoleum, wood stain, soap, ink, coffee, and even peanut-butter cookies. His research revolutionized agriculture, and by 1940, peanuts had become the South's biggest cash crop. Even today, the U.S. is the world's largest exporter of peanuts.

Carver's 118 products derived from sweet potatoes included flour, candy, shoe polish, glue, and rubber. He developed 75 new products from pecans. He obtained more than 500 dyes from 28 kinds of plants. He made synthetic marble from wood shavings, carpets from okra stalks, and wallboard from pine cones. Carver's imagination seemed boundless. U.S. and foreign governments regularly asked him for agricultural assistance. Thomas Edison and Henry Ford frequently tempted Carver with offers of a private laboratory and an annual salary as high as $100,000. He turned them down.

Likable, modest, small in stature, and eccentric in dress and mannerisms, Carver once appeared before a Congressional Committee wearing an old green suit. He commented, "They want to hear what I have to say. They will not be interested in how I look." The 1950 Nobel Peace Prize winner, Ralph Bunche, described Carver as "the least imposing celebrity the world has ever known."

Carver did have a quick sense of humor. One of his students glued the wings of a fly onto the body of a mosquito and asked Carver to identify it. The teacher quickly fired back, "It's a humbug."

Carver never married. At the time of his death, 18 schools had been named after him, he had received many awards, including admission to Great Britain's prestigious Royal Society for the Encouragement of Arts, and he had received two honorary doctorates. He donated his life savings of $60,000 to Tuskegee Institute. In 1951, the United States government established the George Wash-

---

Patented June 9, 1925. **1,541,478**

UNITED STATES PATENT OFFICE.

GEORGE W. CARVER, OF TUSKEGEE, ALABAMA.

PAINT AND STAIN AND PROCESS OF PRODUCING THE SAME.

No Drawing.   Application filed June 13, 1923. Serial No. 645,199.

To all whom it may concern:

Be it known that I, GEORGE W. CARVER, a citizen of the United States, residing at Tuskegee, in the county of Macon and State of Alabama, have invented certain new and useful Improvements in Paints and Stains and Processes of Producing the Same, of which the following is a specification.

The invention relates to paints and stains, and has as an object the provision of a process for producing paints and stains from clays. Clays are found in many sections of the country of a variety of colors, and by a proper choice of color there may be produced by the process of the invention a large variety of colors of pigments, fillers and stains for treating wood or other materials.

To carry out the process of the invention the desired clay having a high percentage of iron is treated by any of the well known processes for refining the same and reducing it to a finely divided condition. A desirable composition for a clay to be treated by the process of the present invention is 5.6% peroxide of iron and 16.7% aluminum.

While a clay testing as above described and substantially free from lime or any similar alkali is suitable for the carrying out of the process, yet a higher iron content will vary the effect only by improving the result.

To reduce the clay to a gelatinous condition the same is treated with acid. For this purpose taking as a basis a quantity of 25 pounds of clay free from sand or other objectionable substances, 25 pounds of commercial sulphuric acid and 25 pounds commercial hydrochloric acid may be added to the clay, with three pounds of clean scrap iron of any kind, iron turnings being a desirable form for the iron. The clay and iron are put into an acid-proof vessel which is capable of withstanding heat, as for instance a porcelain vessel. The acids are added with enough water to make a thin paste. The substance is then boiled slowly, with frequent stirring, until the iron is dissolved, and the whole mass assumes a uniform color.

Water free from alkali is then added sufficient to substantially double the volume, when the solution is well stirred and allowed to settle for about five minutes, for the purpose of settlement of coarser portions. The material remaining in suspension with the liquid is then decanted into shallow acid-proof vessels and the remaining coarse and insoluble material is thrown away.

The material thus secured is utilized as a base for subsequent steps, the nature of which, as well as the nature of the clay first taken for treatment may be chosen to vary the color of the resultant products.

As a variation of the above process the nitric acid may be added with the sulphuric and hydrochloric, but it is found that slightly inferior results are thus obtained. Moreover copperas may be substituted for the scrap iron with, however, probably not such fine results.

For use as a wood filler or stain, clay of a desired color may be treated with the acid as above described, and the thus secured gelatinous clay is found to strike into the wood fiber and to produce an exceedingly smooth surface, giving a color thereto dependent upon the color of clay chosen for treatment, thereby acting as a filler and stain with the single application. It is found that a filler made as thus described becomes very hard when dry and enables the wood to take a high polish. Moreover specimens of wood which have been thus treated are found, after twenty years, to be brighter and more beautiful than when first treated. For this use the iron scrap may be omitted if desired.

The material thus described as a compound filler and stain, may be dried and mixed with linseed oil or its equivalent as a pigment to provide a paint. If desired to be darkened to a slight extent some good grade of carbon or lamp black may be added.

When the above acid treatment is carried out utilizing a micaceous clay of the variety of shades which occur in the Southern States a sheen results that has not to my knowledge been secured by heretofore used artificial mixtures.

I claim:

1. The process of producing pigment or the like which comprises boiling clay and metallic iron with acid and separating the coarser particles therefrom.

2. The process of producing pigments or the like which comprises boiling a mixture of clay and scrap iron with a mixture of sulphuric and hydrochloric acid, and separating the coarser particles therefrom, the color of clay utilized being chosen in accordance with the color desired in the finished product.

GEORGE W. CARVER.

---

ington Carver National Monument on 210 acres of the southwest-Missouri farm where Carver was born.

References and Resources

George Washington Carver, Mercer Publishing Corp., 1988.

Dictionary of American Biography, Charles Scribner's Sons Publishers, 1932; with supplemental updates.

National Cyclopedia of American Biography, James T. White and Co. Publishers, 1891; with supplemental updates.

McGraw-Hill Encyclopedia of Biography, McGraw-Hill Publishers, 1973.

Asimov's Biographical Encyclopedia of Science and Technology by Isaac Asimov, Doubleday & Co. Publishers, 1964.

Henry Ford

Ford Motor Co.

Born:
July 30, 1863,
in Dearborn,
Michigan

Died:
April 7, 1947,
in Dearborn,
Michigan

AFTER two years of evening work, Henry Ford rolled his first motor car out of his Detroit garage in 1896. No one realized that the small box-shaped vehicle would be the first of tens of millions to display Ford's name. The Ford Motor Co., which Ford established in 1903, was no different from the 150 other companies struggling at that time to enter the emerging motor car industry. However, Ford's philosophy set him apart from the others. At a time when a motor car was considered a luxury item, Ford wanted to provide personal transportation for everyone. His affordable Model T made automobile transportation available to ordinary people.

One of eight children, Ford was born on a farm that is now part of Dearborn, Michigan. His formal education included eight years of attending two rural schools. Ford disliked farmwork, preferring to work with machinery instead. He became a machine-shop apprentice at 16 and later worked for a ship-building firm. Ford also serviced steam engines on tractors and occasionally returned home to work on the family farm. His natural curiosity led him to work on engines in his spare time. Like many others, Ford was trying to build a lightweight, reliable, and powerful gasoline engine suitable for use in a motor car.

Ford worked full time as a night engineer at a local electrical generating plant owned by the Edison Illuminating Co. There, he first met Thomas Edison. Ford's supervisor arranged the meeting, which the abrupt Edison later said he promptly forgot. Ford, 16 years younger and an unknown inventor, greatly admired Edison and never forgot the meeting.

Shortly after its completion, Ford sold his two-passenger, 500-pound motor car for $200. Because of the sale, he persuaded several investors to support his after-hours engine work. Ford's next handmade car featured fully enclosed mechanical parts, as well as a chain-and-sprocket transmission. That vehicle helped establish Ford's reputation as an automotive pioneer. After two false starts as a motor car manufacturer, the 40-year-old Ford organized the company that was literally to put America on wheels.

Ford brought out his first production car, the Model A, in 1903. It had an eight-horsepower, two-cylinder engine and cost $850. Ford sold 1,700 in 15 months. To increase profits, Ford's investors wanted him to build more expensive cars. The investors also worried that Ford put too much of the profits toward increasing the size of his factory, an unusual idea at the time. Ford answered the investors' criticism by buying out their shares. In 1907, he held over 58 percent of the company's stock and could manufacture the Model T, the car he believed the country needed.

Ford designed the Model T over a three-year period with two company engineers, C. Harold Wills and Joseph Galamb. Influenced by his farming background, Ford made sure the car would be suitable for use in rural America. The simple 20 hp, 4:1 compression ratio, four-cylinder engine had no self-starter, generator, water pump, oil pump, or fuel pump. Almost anyone could repair it. The pedal-controlled transmission combined the functions of clutch and gearbox in one simple unit. The 1,000-pound car had two forward speeds and reverse. Its top speed was 45 mph and fuel consumption was 28 mpg. Its light weight and high 30"-diameter wheels allowed it to roll easily over deep ruts. High-strength-alloy steel axles and frames held up well under constant abuse. Model Ts often went where roads did not exist, and many saw service as trucks and tractors.

The car was in such demand, that for a few years, more Model Ts were made than all other American automobiles combined. Ford was the first automobile manufacturer to concentrate on a single model with a standard chassis made of interchangeable parts. His company manufactured more than 15 million Model Ts between 1908 and 1927. The car brought farmers and city dwellers together, uniting the nation like nothing before it. In 1957, Ford biographer Allan Nevins called the Model T the greatest single vehicle in the history of world transportation.

To increase production without decreasing quality, Ford introduced the moving assembly line. Although he was not the first to use an assembly line, his idea of having the product move while workers attached parts to it was new. It dramatically increased production. The first components made on a moving assembly line were Model T magnetos, in 1913. Production time dropped from 20 minutes per magneto to 5 minutes. Overhead conveyors, gravity slides, endless belts, and other devices transported the necessary materials. Parts came to the employees, rather than having the employees move to the parts. Such a network required specialized machinery and Ford was in an ideal position to design and buy the new equipment. He had the profits to pay for it and

his company manufactured a product without annual model changes. Ford's factory was the largest in the world and soon produced one drive-away Model T every two minutes, complete except for the body. Ford offered more cars for sale than anyone ever had.

Ford was also responsible for establishing the eight-hour work day. In 1913, his company had 15,000 employees and paid a minimum daily wage of $2.34 for nine hours of work. It was a rate comparable to that paid by other companies. Early in 1914, however, Ford increased the minimum to $5 per day for eight hours of work. The daily schedule went from two 9-hour shifts to three 8-hour shifts. Ford also announced that his company would share its profits with the workers. The news caused a mild panic as people rushed to seek employment at the company. The $5 day made it possible for every one of Ford's employees to buy a car. Ford's new approach worked. The year af-

Ford Motor Co.

The first moving assembly line was established by Henry Ford in Highland Park, Michigan.

ter the wage increase, the company made more profit than it had the previous year.

A holder of 161 patents, Ford was as much an inventor as president of a huge manufacturing organization. He acquired enough wealth to buy all his company's stock in 1919. The company was solely owned by the Ford family until 1956 when stock was made available to the public.

Ford's concern for human welfare prompted him to establish the Ford Foundation, the world's largest philanthropic organization, in 1936. Ford was a complex man who was well known to the public. Hardly a day went by without mention of Ford in the newspapers. Reporters sought his opinion on a variety of different topics.

Ford rekindled his association with Edison in 1912. A mutual friend arranged a meeting and Ford asked Edison to design a battery, starting motor, and generator for the Model T. From that time on, the men were close friends. To honor Edison and others, Ford built a 260-acre open-air museum that he named Greenfield Village in Dearborn in 1928. Ford moved all of Edison's laboratory buildings from Menlo Park, New Jersey, to Greenfield Village. Along with almost 100 other historic buildings, Edison's buildings are now open to the public. The adjacent Henry Ford Museum contains many one-of-a-kind technical items, such as the still-operational boxy quadricycle that Ford built in 1896.

References and Resources

Ford: The Times, the Man, the Company by Allan Nevins and Frank Ernest Hill, Scribner, 1957.

Henry Ford by John Rae, Prentice Hall, 1969.

The Public Image of Henry Ford by David Lewis, Wayne State Press, 1976.

Ford: The Men and the Machine by Robert Lacey, Little Brown & Co., 1986.

Dictionary of American Biography, Charles Scribner's Sons Publishers, 1932; with supplementary updates.

National Cyclopedia of American Biography, James T. White and Co. Publishers, 1891; with supplementary updates.

McGraw-Hill Encyclopedia of Biography, McGraw-Hill Publishers, 1973.

Asimov's Biographical Encyclopedia of Science and Technology, by Isaac Asimov, Doubleday & Co. Publishers, 1964.

Charles Martin Hall

ON a Monday evening in November 1936, NBC aired a special radio program called "Voice of Progress." It included a broadcast from a new DC-3 airplane flying at several thousand feet. During one part of the program, Charles Kettering read a short list of names of some important American technologists. Most were familiar, like the Wright brothers, Alexander Graham Bell, and Thomas Edison. Yet, one name was less well known than the others: Charles Martin Hall. One year out of college and barely in his twenties, Hall had developed an efficient process to produce large quantities of aluminum from its raw ore. Before his discovery, it took slow chemical reduction to obtain small amounts of aluminum. In 1884, the largest piece ever made was the 9"-high, 100-ounce, pyramid-shaped casting used to top the Washington Monument. It was worth so much money that it had been displayed at Tiffany's, a famous New York jeweler.

Hall's father, a minister, moved his family to Oberlin, Ohio, when Hall was 11. One of seven children, Hall enjoyed chemistry and dreamed of making great inventions that could benefit humanity. He had the advantage of receiving a good basic education and he attended Oberlin College, as did all of his siblings. One of his favorite teachers was Frank Jewett. A graduate of Yale University, Jewett had studied chemistry in Germany and taught for four years at the Japanese Imperial University in Tokyo. On one occasion, he remarked in a chemistry class that anyone who found an efficient process for producing aluminum in commercial quantities would become rich, famous, and a benefactor to the world. Jewett's chance statement stirred Hall's imagination and started him looking for such a process.

Smithsonian Institution Photo No. 47904A

Born:
December 6, 1863, in Thompson, Ohio

Died:
December 27, 1914, in Daytona Beach, Florida

Jewett knew Hall from a few years earlier when Hall came to the college to buy glass tubing and test tubes. He allowed Hall to use his private laboratory to learn more about chemistry.

Another of Hall's professors was Elisha Gray, who taught electricity. Like Alexander Graham Bell, Gray had invented a serviceable telephone. Four years earlier, he had arrived at the patent office a few hours after Bell, thus losing his chance to patent the telephone. This cautionary story impressed on Hall the importance of timeliness, keeping records, and establishing witnesses. Hall's older sister Julia became his witness, as well as his advisor and lifelong correspondent.

Although the most plentiful metal on earth, aluminum is found only as part of chemical compounds. In Hall's day, it was difficult to separate aluminium from its ore.

In the 1800s, aluminum was worth $115 per pound and classified as a semiprecious metal. Hall started working on a technique to obtain aluminum from ore, while in college. The December 6, 1884, ceremony that placed the aluminum cap on top of the Washington Monument as a lightning conductor particularly impressed him. That date was Hall's 21st birthday, and he redoubled his after-hours work on aluminum extraction.

After graduation, Hall worked almost around the clock in a woodshed behind his home on Oberlin's East College Street. Initially, he duplicated many previously unsuccessful experiments. The one that finally worked occurred on February 23, 1886. Hall

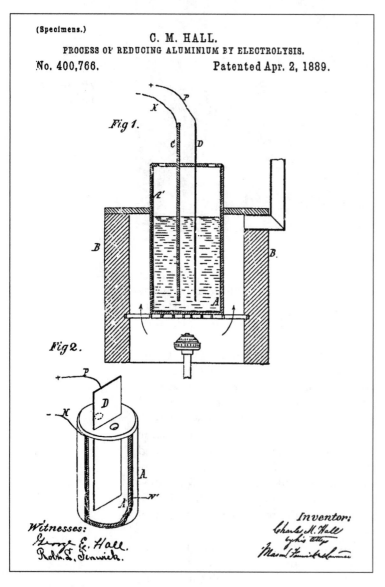

(Specimens.)

C. M. HALL.
PROCESS OF REDUCING ALUMINIUM BY ELECTROLYSIS.
No. 400,766.   Patented Apr. 2, 1889.

Fig 1.

Fig 2.

Witnesses:
George E. Hall.
Robt. S. Fenwick.

Inventor:
Charles M. Hall
by his atty.

Hall's first patent for producing aluminum

made a carbon-lined clay crucible capable of withstanding very high temperatures. He placed ground cryolite and alumina into the crucible, which had two carbon rods connected through a switch to a bank of home-made batteries. The cryolite, a soft whitish mineral from Greenland, served as the electrolyte that helped pass the electrical current. Alumina was the raw ore. With the switch open, Hall heated the crucible with a blowtorch until the mixture inside melted. He then closed the switch and passed electrical current through the molten mass for two hours. According to his patent, a 4 volt to 6 volt supply was satisfactory. Hall opened the switch and poured the red-hot liquid into an old skillet. When it solidified, he broke up the material with a hammer and found a dozen small globules of aluminum. He had his sister witness the event and with great excitement showed the metal to Jewett that very afternoon. Jewett encouraged Hall to apply immediately for a patent. Hall worked at improving his process and filed for his basic patent a few months later. The brief three-page patent that was issued in 1889 soon launched an entire new industry. Hall went on to make a fortune estimated at $30 to $50 million.

A French inventor, Paul Heroult, independently discovered the same technique at almost exactly the same time. For that reason, the method is sometimes called the Hall-Heroult process. In an interesting twist of fate, not only did Hall and Heroult develop the same process within weeks of each other, but both were born in 1863 and both died in 1914. There was no personal rivalry between the two men. When Hall received the Perkin Medal in 1911, Heroult came to America to attend the ceremony and congratulate him.

Like many nineteenth-century inventors, Hall encountered problems when he tried to locate financial backing for the construction of his factory. Many investors felt reluctant to trust their resources to a young, unproven, boyish-looking amateur chemist. Two potential investors backed out at the last moment, and Hall spent a year working with a third before he decided not to get into aluminum production. Finally, a fourth investor followed through. The small Pittsburgh Reduction Co. used Hall's process, producing about 50 pounds of aluminum per day in November 1888. The company made 10,000 pounds during its first year of operation and reached 15 million pounds in 1907, when it changed its name to the Aluminum Company of America (Alcoa). Hall's 1886 electrolytic process produced aluminum at $1 per pound. By 1914, additional improvements reduced the cost to 18¢ per pound.

With aluminum finally in production, Hall had one unusual difficulty: There was no significant demand for the metal. Its strength, corrosion resistance, light weight, heat transfer properties, and electrical conductivity were not critical to other late-nineteenth-century technologies. Cooking utensils were the first major items made from aluminum, but it wasn't until the introduction of metal aircraft that manufacturers used the metal in large quantities.

Hall never married. He was an ardent piano player who maintained a boyish appearance all his life. The photograph shows him at 42. He moved his home to Niagara Falls to be close to the giant factory he built to take advantage of cheap and clean hydroelectric power. Professor Jewett's chance remark did result in Hall becoming rich and famous, and Hall always credited Oberlin College with giving him his start in life. On his death in 1914, he bequeathed Oberlin $16 million. His sister taught at Berea College in Kentucky, and Hall left that school $5 million. Every year, the Aluminum Association offers $10,000 in the Charles Martin Hall Award competition for student-written technical papers on a subject related to aluminum.

Jewett outlived his protégé. At Jewett's 50th Yale class reunion, all present were asked to summarize their career. Jewett rose to tell them about Hall. He began by saying, "My great discovery has been the discovery of a man."

References and Resources

"Silver from Clay" by Robert Friedel, in *American Heritage of Invention and Technology*, Spring 1986.

Dictionary of American Biography, Charles Scribner's Sons Publishers, 1932; with supplemental updates.

National Cyclopedia of American Biography, James T. White and Co. Publishers, 1891; with supplemental updates.

Asimov's Biographical Encyclopedia of Science and Technology, by Isaac Asimov, Doubleday & Co. Publishers, 1964.

Charles Proteus Steinmetz

General Electric Company

Charles Steinmetz (birth name: Karl August Rudolph Steinmetz) working at his desk in 1923

Born:
April 9, 1865,
in Breslau,
Germany

Died:
October 26,
1923, in
Schenectady,
New York

ELECTRICITY was the most sophisticated emerging technology during the nineteenth century. The use of electricity for mechanical power was a particularly challenging field. Direct current (dc) for electric motors was commonly used, but alternating current (ac) was less well understood. An immigrant who gained worldwide recognition for his work in electricity stood just 4' tall, was hunch-backed, and had misshapen legs. Yet, the disadvantages of poverty and a crippling deformity did not keep him from being recognized as a technical genius. More than any other single person, German-born Charles Steinmetz was responsible for establishing the United States' early leadership in the field of electricity.

Steinmetz was born in Breslau, Germany, a city that is now called Wroclaw in present-day Poland. In spite of his deformities, he had remarkably good health and he had a

relatively normal childhood. His father headed the printing department in the local railroad office. Steinmetz's mother died during his first year, and his grandmother, who spoiled him badly, raised him.

It was obvious that Steinmetz had a keen technical mind. After he graduated from high school, his father sent him to the University of Breslau, instead of considering an apprenticeship. During his years at the university, Steinmetz never missed a class. He took lengthy class notes and often did independent investigations at home. Although his father encouraged him to attend college, he could not offer much financial help. Steinmetz made money by tutoring and doing odd jobs. It took him six years to complete his studies. He always selected the most difficult technical subjects. During his last year at the university, he specialized in six major subjects: electrical engineering, mathematics, physics, chemistry, astronomy, and medicine.

In Steinmetz's time, students at European universities commonly joined one or more outside societies. Steinmetz enjoyed the personal contacts. Because he thought that there was much social injustice in the world, he affiliated himself with the Social Revolution Party in the late 1880s. As student members of the group grew more politically active, they found themselves under suspicion. When the authorities arrested about 40 of

Steinmetz's friends, he knew he would soon join them. Shortly after he completed his university studies, he hurriedly left home on the morning he was to be arrested. He was 24 years old, and he never saw his family again.

Secretly arriving in Zurich, Switzerland, Steinmetz became friends with Oscar Asmussen. Asmussen was wealthy, and he offered to pay Steinmetz's boat fare to America. When the two men arrived in New York, immigration officials at first wanted to return the penniless Steinmetz to Europe. He spoke no English and thus could not defend himself verbally. However, when Asmussen showed a large amount of money, telling the officials that it belonged to both of them, they allowed Steinmetz to enter the U.S.

Steinmetz found work in Yonkers, New York, with the electrical inventor Rudolph Eickemeyer. Eickemeyer was developing dc electrical motors and electrical machinery. He found Steinmetz's keen technical mind to be of great help and set him up with a laboratory. Steinmetz began working on the problem of hysteresis, the loss of electrical motor efficiency caused by alternating magnetism. The laws of power loss were unknown, and many people did not believe hysteresis existed. No one had been able to measure it. Using existing data, Steinmetz applied high-level mathematics to show that it did exist. He also demonstrated how to measure and reduce hysteresis. He presented his results to the American Institute of Electrical Engineers in 1882 and became an immediate sensation in technology. He showed people how to deal with the complicated effects that resulted from the use of ac. The methods Steinmetz used were so complete that a motor designer who understood them could hardly make a mistake.

Steinmetz had found a country that accepted him as he was, and he felt comfortable in America. Shortly after arriving, he had learned the language so well that he spoke with only a slight accent. He became an American citizen in 1894 and changed his first name to Charles. His middle name, Proteus, was his college nickname. It came from Greek mythology and referred to someone who could quickly change character.

The General Electric Co. (GE) was formed in 1892. It began through the con-

solidation of the Edison General Electric Co. in Schenectady, New York, and the Thomson-Houston Electric Co. in Lynn, Massachusetts. Its main offices were in Schenectady. Those in charge at GE wanted to obtain as much talent in the field of electricity as they could. They invited Steinmetz to join their staff, but he refused. He did not want to turn his back on the employer who gave him his start in America. In its most important action in the nineteenth-century, GE offered to buy Eickemeyer's company with the understanding that GE would also receive Steinmetz's services. Everyone agreed and Steinmetz soon moved to Schenectady, where he remained for the rest of his life.

After Steinmetz's arrival at the company, GE established research laboratories. They were the first company-sponsored industrial research facilities in the U.S. While still in his twenties, Steinmetz joined as a member of the calculating department. He soon be-

Steinmetz's summer cabin is on display at Greenfield Village in Dearborn, Michigan. This is the first section he had built in the 1890s and it was originally on stilts. Three other rooms were later added to it.

came a consulting engineer. That position allowed him to come and go as he pleased, and he held it from then on. Although well liked and highly respected, he did work that almost no one could understand. Through the publication of 10 technical books, Steinmetz gradually made ac electricity less mysterious. He showed the profitability of applying advanced mathematical methods to practical electrical problems. Over his lifetime, he obtained 195 patents, and his methods are now universally used in ac equipment design and calculations.

Steinmetz conducted much of his theoretical work at a cabin he had built on a tributary of the Mohawk River. He would often work there for weeks at a time. He typically wore a bathing suit and a faded red sweater, which he did not change for even the most important visitors. After a day in his canoe, he once wrote, "It was a hot sunny day with almost no wind, and I sat in the sun and calculated instances of condenser discharge through an asymmetrical gas circuit." As with Isaac Newton and Albert Einstein, the public did not understand Steinmetz's work. However, everyone acknowledged and respected his technical contributions.

Although Steinmetz had completed the necessary academic work, the University of Breslau had never granted his degree. He felt pleased when Union College in Schenectady awarded him an honorary Ph.D. in 1903. From then on, Steinmetz used the title of "doctor." He also received many other forms of recognition. One of the more unusual was his election as head of the local board of education for two terms.

Steinmetz's favorite hobbies included photography, music, and bicycling. He also enjoyed botany, particularly work with desert plants, orchids, and ferns. He had a large greenhouse attached to his house. He rarely traveled, preferring to spend time near home. Steinmetz frequently smoked foul-smelling cigars and gave the immediate impression of being gruff and unapproachable. Yet, just the opposite was true.

Steinmetz loved children, though he had no family of his own. In 1905, he legally adopted the family of his young lab assistant, Joseph Hayden. Hayden, his wife, and their three children shared Steinmetz's large rambling home on Schenectady's Wendell Avenue. Steinmetz died of heart failure shortly after returning with the Haydens from a tour of the West Coast, his first long vacation trip.

References and Resources

Recollections of Steinmetz by Emil J. Remscheid, GE Co., 1977.

The Life of Charles Proteus Steinmetz by Johnathan Norton Leonard, Doubleday Publishers, 1929.

"The Mentor" by John Winthrop Hammond, *Charles Proteus Steinmetz*, May 1925 (Vol. 13, No. 4). (Supplied by GE, Schenectady, NY.)

Dictionary of American Biography, Charles Scribner's Sons Publishers, 1932; with supplemental updates.

National Cyclopedia of American Biography, James T. White and Co. Publishers, 1891; with supplemental updates.

McGraw-Hill Encyclopedia of Biography, McGraw-Hill Publishers, 1973.

Asimov's Biographical Encyclopedia of Science and Technology by Isaac Asimov, Doubleday & Co. Publishers, 1964.

Orville and Wilbur Wright

National Air and Space Museum

Orville and Wilbur Wright, in about 1908

NEAR the dawn of powered flight, many would-be inventors tried to build stable flying machines. Most wanted one that would have the same stability as a wagon or a ship. Early inventors generally thought that a flying machine would require pilot action only during a change of direction or altitude. Few thought of an airplane as being similar to a bicycle, though both are unstable machines. A pilot, like a cyclist, makes constant flight adjustments to maintain control. Unlike wagon drivers or ship operators, airplane pilots and cyclists must learn to operate their equipment just to maintain equilibrium. These similarities were apparent to the Wright brothers, who made their living as bicycle mechanics. They experimented for four years before their engine-powered *Flyer* lifted from the sand near Kitty Hawk, North Carolina, on Thursday, December 17, 1903, at 10:35 A.M.

Wilbur and Orville Wright were among five children raised in a close but disciplined family. Their father was a minister and their mother was a college graduate who regularly encouraged the boys' inventive activities. She herself developed several minor household inventions. Although Wilbur was four years older than Orville, the two were inseparable. They grew up in Dayton, Ohio, and attended elementary school together.

While in high school, Orville built a printing press and started a small business. The brothers later launched a neighborhood weekly newspaper named the *West Side News*. Orville tended to be mechanically active, while Wilbur was more thoughtful and deliberate. Their differences in working style and personality helped them during their experimental airplane work.

The Wright brothers' interest in the airplane started when their father gave them a rubber-powered toy helicopter in 1878. They enjoyed it tremendously and built a larger model. Although the one they built was identical except in size, it did not fly properly. People had not yet come to grips with scaling factors in aircraft design, and the Wrights were puzzled. Even as they opened their bicycle shop in 1892, they remained casually interested in flight.

In the Wright brothers' day, bicycling was a popular form of transportation and there were millions of bicycles on the road. U.S. production of bicycles in 1890 was 1.2 mil-

Orville Wright
Born:
August 19, 1871, in Dayton, Ohio

Died:
January 30, 1948, in Dayton, Ohio

Wilbur Wright
Born:
April 16, 1867, in Millville, Indiana

Died:
May 30, 1912, in Dayton, Ohio

lion. The Wright brothers had highly developed mechanical aptitudes, though they lacked formal technical training. Of all the Wright children, Wilbur and Orville were the only ones who did not graduate from high school or college.

The brothers lived at home with their parents and their only sister, Katherine. The Wright Cycle Shop was 1 of 14 bicycle shops in Dayton, and together the Wright brothers earned about $2,500 per year. Because bicycle repair was seasonal, they had free time during the cold winter months. The highly publicized death of German aeronautical engineer Otto Lilienthal during an 1896 glider flight focused their attention on the problems of flight. The brothers discussed the topic at great length. Having the proper

provide roll control on their gliders, they used wires to pull down the trailing edge of the wings. They developed this idea after carefully watching birds in flight. They called their development *wing warping*. Today, airplane designers use ailerons, which follow the same principle.

In spite of having some limited successes, the Wright brothers received no encouragement from family or friends. After obtaining advice on wind flow from the National Weather Service, they went to Kill Devil Hills sand dunes in North Carolina in September 1900. They traveled by train, with their disassembled 16' test glider. The trip was something of a vacation, and the brothers lived in tents for about six weeks while they flew in the glider. It was the first one they

Orville Wright piloted the *Flyer* during the first flight of a powered airplane. Others had been working on flight, and the confident Wrights had a photographer on site to take this picture and prove their success.

tools and space, their shop was well set up for experimental work. Their bicycle repair skills were also perfect for the task at hand. Some elements of bicycle technology transferred directly to the *Flyer*, which they named after one of their hand-crafted bicycles.

The brothers gathered all the scientific data they could. Available information was sketchy because aeronautics was not a well-established technology. The Wright brothers' first glider was a small one with a 5' wing span. It flew successfully in 1899 and greatly encouraged their efforts. From then on, they were unstoppable and often worked to total exhaustion. They correctly determined that Lilienthal had crashed due to a lack of control, especially during roll. To

built to carry a person, and it had limited success. The brothers returned in 1901 for more test flights on an improved glider. However, it did not have the lift necessary to carry a pilot and an engine. The brothers concluded that the published tables of air pressure over wing air foils must have been incorrect.

Back in Dayton, the brothers conducted tests on over 200 wing models in a small wind tunnel they built. The tests provided the world's most accurate data for lift, drag, and center of pressure. The information the Wright brothers acquired helped them design the most efficient wing ever built. They tackled the problem of flight systematically and built their last human-carrying glider in 1902. In all, they made several thousand glider flights over a period of four years. They taught themselves how to build and how to control an aircraft. After many flight tests, the Wright brothers were ready to try powered flight.

Unable to locate a suitable engine, the brothers built one. Partly relying on the expertise of machinist Charles Taylor, they spent much of 1903 working on the liquid-cooled engine. Their four-cylinder engine developed 12 horsepower at 1,200 rpm and weighed 152 pounds. They packed the engine along with a freshly built 40' airplane and left by train for Kill Devil Hills in September 1903. A series of bad storms and minor defects delayed their flight until December 17. Then, winning the toss of a coin, Orville acted as the pilot. The plane's engine started easily and turned two rear-mounted pusher propellers through a chain-and-gear assembly. The Wright brothers were so confident about the 750-pound plane that they showed no obvious surprise when it lifted from the ground and flew 120 feet in 12 seconds. The world's first controlled and powered flight was witnessed by only five other people. The photograph they had taken that day has been reproduced more often than any other in history.

The Wright brothers continued their experiments at a 70-acre field near Dayton owned by Torrence Huffman, a friend. They went into the business of building airplanes for sale in America and Europe. Neither brother married. After their mother died in 1889, they lived in the family home on Hawthorne Street with their father and sister. Their older brothers, Reuchlin and Lorin, had moved away. Although the Wright brothers were generally prosperous, they did not attain great wealth. Wilbur died of typhoid in 1912. Though Orville said little about it, he obviously felt heartsick. He sold the company in 1915 and last flew as a pilot in 1918. He continued to work on aviation matters the rest of his life, though primarily as a follower rather than a leader. People often referred to him as the elder statesman of the air.

When Neil Armstrong and Edwin Aldrin made the first manned trip to the moon in 1969, they carried pieces of wood and fabric from the *Flyer*. Those pieces are on display at the Air Force Museum in Dayton. The Flyer hangs over the entrance lobby of the National Air and Space Museum in Washington, D.C.

References and Resources

Wright Brothers by Omega G. East, National Park Service, 1961.

The Wright Brothers by C. H. Gibbs-Smith, Her Majesty's Stationery Office, 1963.

Those Inventive Americans, National Geographic Society, 1971.

"How the Bicycle Took Wing" by Tom D. Crouch, in *American Heritage of Invention and Technology*, Fall 1987.

Dictionary of American Biography, Charles Scribner's Sons Publishers, 1932; with supplemental updates.

National Cyclopedia of American Biography, James T. White and Co. Publishers, 1891; with supplemental updates.

McGraw-Hill Encyclopedia of Biography, McGraw-Hill Publishers, 1973.

Asimov's Biographical Encyclopedia of Science and Technology, by Isaac Asimov, Doubleday and Co., 1964.

August Charles Fruehauf

Born:
December 15, 1868, in Fraser, Michigan

Died:
May 16, 1930, in Detroit, Michigan

Courtesy of the Fruehauf Corp.

August Fruehauf, at the age of 57

TRUCKS provide the most important means of moving manufactured goods because they can go from door to door. Trains, airplanes, and ships do not have that advantage. Trucks can operate anywhere that roads exist, and they haul 75 percent of America's industrial products. No one knows who invented the first truck, but the vehicle began appearing in the 1890s as a modified motor car. At that time, though, trucks were not commonly used for hauling because unpaved roads were so poor. In 1904, there were only 700 trucks in the United States, but today there are over 30 million. About 1.5 million are semitrailers quite similar to the first one produced by August Fruehauf in 1914.

Fruehauf (he pronounced it "Free Hof") was born on a farm near Detroit, Michigan, to parents who had come from Germany.

He had 10 siblings. Fruehauf's father was a trained blacksmith and machinist, who instructed his son in the basics of working with metal. Fruehauf also received a basic education at a local elementary school. He left school at 14 to work at a sawmill where his father served as maintenance engineer. Like many rural youths of the late 1800s, Fruehauf left the family farm to seek his fortune elsewhere. He found work as a blacksmith apprentice for Fent and Sons in a nearby town. While making a delivery, he met Louise Schuchard at a general store. They married in 1890 and eventually had five children.

Fruehauf opened his first blacksmith shop in a converted feed store. After just a few years of operation, a fire destroyed the shop and badly burned his wife as she saved her pet horse. The family moved to Detroit where they rented a combination home and blacksmith shop. It too was destroyed by fire. Fruehauf set up a third shop in 1899 and stayed there for 13 years. The building had a ramp leading to a loft where Fruehauf built and repaired wagons. He quickly developed a reputation as an excellent blacksmith and carriage builder. The business prospered, and Fruehauf soon needed more space.

In a vacant lot across the street, Fruehauf constructed what was then described as the finest brick blacksmith shop in the United States. The building was two stories high, about 40' wide, and could house 60 horses at one time. With its large glass windows and airy feel, the beautiful building looked more like a department store than a blacksmith shop. The sign on its front stated: "August C. Fruehauf—Manufacturer of Trucks and Wagons." At that time, people thought of a truck as a wheeled wagon or carriage, and a truck was usually pulled by a horse.

Fruehauf had a well-established reputation as both a horseshoer and carriage builder. In 1914, his staff numbered eight and included his 16-year-old son, Harry. That year, wealthy Detroit lumber dealer Frederic M. Sibley came to see Fruehauf about a hauling problem. Sibley had a summer home on a small lake in Michigan's Upper Peninsula, and he wanted to move his new boat there. People commonly used horses and wagons for such hauling, but that would require many days on the road. Sibley wanted Fruehauf to design a device that would allow him to use his Ford Model T roadster to haul the boat.

Fruehauf and his close working associate Otto Neumann designed a coupler they thought could do the job. They started with a four-wheeled trailer and added a short vertical wooden pole to act as a connecting link between the trailer and roadster. To improve steering, they removed the trailer's

Fruehauf advertised his new product with the statement: "A horse can pull more than it can carry . . . so can a truck." It took the public several years to realize that a truck could tow a rolling load that is heavier than the one it could carry. Fruehauf's early advertisements appeared in national lumber journals, and other lumber yards ordered semitrailers. Fruehauf then introduced his product in other trade publications, vocational magazines, and newspapers. The new method of haulage quickly spread to many different businesses.

Within two years, orders came in so rapidly that Fruehauf had to operate both day and night shifts to try to fill them. In another two years, orders were still arriving faster than semitrailers could be constructed. Sales reached $150,000 in 1918, and Fruehauf decided to construct another building and establish the Fruehauf Trailer Co. He named his good friend Otto Neumann as factory manager.

One of the earliest semi-trailers connected to a Ford Model T truck in 1918. Harry Fruehauf is looking out the back window.

Courtesy of the Fruehauf Corp.

two front wheels. They called the vehicle a *semitrailer*. The new trailer successfully transported Sibley's boat to his lake, and Sibley asked Fruehauf to build another for use in his lumberyard. He asked that the second trailer have a flat floor. The new and stronger one that Fruehauf built proved to be both practical and efficient. It had a platform chassis with stake sides. The trailer featured sturdy wooden spoked wheels with hard-rubber tires, wagon springs, and a better coupling device. The improved semitrailer worked better than anyone had expected.

Fruehauf built trailers for specific purposes, using such designs as enclosed vans for small manufacturers and ground-hugging carryalls for heavy construction equipment. He manufactured the first refrigerated units for food transportation. Rated at four or six tons of payload, his first units hauled bulk ice cream in metal cans. After workers loaded the ice cream, they opened a trap door in the van's roof. Crushed ice and salt entered the trailer, fell over the cans, and kept the ice cream from melting.

Fruehauf designed jacks with wheels on their ends for front trailer supports. Workers could raise or lower the jacks as a trailer was coupled or uncoupled. The company also developed a reversible four-wheel trailer. It could be pulled from either end, and, with large cylindrical tanks installed, it was heavily used by the petroleum industry. Ernest Hartwick invented a fifth wheel in 1919 and transferred the patent to Fruehauf. Hartwick's fifth wheel coupled the tractor, or towing vehicle, to the trailer. It set over the rear axle of the tractor to support it on turns and improve control of the truck. In 1926, Fruehauf made an automatic version of his semitrailer. It allowed using the engine's power for coupling and uncoupling the trailer.

A large, pleasant, and informal man, Fruehauf preferred to be called Gus. He closely involved his family in the trailer business. During the early years, his wife painted trailers. Later, she became the purchasing agent and then vice-president of the company. Fruehauf started the company in partnership with his son Harvey, who became president when Fruehauf died in 1930. The photograph on page 167 shows another son, Harry, looking out the back of a Model T truck. An early Fruehauf semitrailer is on public display at the Henry Ford Museum in Dearborn, Michigan.

References and Resources

Fruehauf's History, Fruehauf Corp., undated (circa 1985).

"Transport Topics," *National Newspaper of the Motor Freight Carriers*, June 15, 1959, pages 1-5.

International Directory of Company Histories edited by Thomas Derdak, St. James Press, 1988.

Alice Hamilton

THE first American to investigate dangerous substances used in factories was not a fierce-looking, hard-bitten government employee. That person was a gracious, slightly built woman who greatly disliked conflict. Alice Hamilton gained an international reputation as America's first investigator of ailments that resulted from industrial conditions. She helped to establish the professional field of industrial medicine.

Hamilton was the second of five children. Her parents moved to Fort Wayne, Indiana, when she was six weeks old, and she grew up on her grandmother's estate. Her father had a part interest in a wholesale grocery business, and her mother encouraged all the children to be independent and choose their own career path. Hamilton's family had deep roots in Indiana. Many leading citizens came to her home as she was growing up. She received her early education at home from her parents and a tutor. She spent her last two years of secondary-level preparation at a school in Connecticut. Over her family's objections, she chose to pursue a career in medicine, and received her M.D. from the University of Michigan in 1893. Hamilton did four years of internship work and advanced studies in such widely separated cities as Minneapolis; Boston; Washington, D.C.; and Munich and Leipzig, Germany.

Finding herself uncomfortable working directly with patients, Hamilton took a position as professor of pathology at the Woman's Medical School at Northwestern University in 1897. During almost 40 years in the Chicago area, she lived at Jane Addams's Hull House. Named for benefactor Charles Hull, it was a settlement house for uneducated immigrants who entered the city seeking employment in the many area

The Schlesinger Library, Radcliffe College

Born:
February 27, 1869, in New York, New York

Died:
September 22, 1970, in Hadlyme, Connecticut

factories. The move to Hull House plunged Hamilton into a world of poverty, trade unionism, and social activism. Her new life was far removed from the protected environment of her youth. It was at Hull House that Hamilton saw firsthand the health problems associated with working in factories that used toxic materials in an unsafe manner. The many years she spent at Hull House were rich in human contacts, and they established her life's work in industrial medicine. Women's Medical School at Northwestern closed in 1902, and Hamilton went to work for a local bacteriology laboratory. Encouraged by the director, she published scientific papers, studied at the Pasteur Institute in Paris, and became active in Chicago's medical circles. Her investigation into the spread of a typhoid fever epidemic in 1902 brought Hamilton wide acclaim. She showed that the fever was carried by flies and further spread through a break in a major water pipe that allowed sewage to enter the water supply. Public pressure resulted in a complete reorganization of the Health Department under a new chief. Illinois Governor Charles Deneen later appointed Hamilton to a commission that investigated industrial poisons. At that time, there were no occupational safety laws, no medical records to investigate, and no effective factory inspection systems. The American Medical Association had not devoted a single meeting to the subject.

Hamilton had to start somewhere. Working tirelessly, she followed rumors, searched hospital records, and visited workers in their homes. Many felt reluctant to discuss their industrial environments for fear their employers would retaliate. Yet, Hamilton's calm manner had a reassuring effect, and she succeeded in accumulating the data she needed. Her surveys early in the twentieth century resulted in the passage of Illinois state laws dealing with factory working conditions. The laws covered industrial safety measures, medical examinations, and worker compensation. They were milestones on the road to improved working conditions, and many other states soon followed the lead of Illinois.

As supervisor of the Illinois Occupational Disease Commission, Hamilton was the first person to combine modern laboratory techniques with field study. Because of her pleasant, nonthreatening personality, she managed to conduct her investigations without antagonizing employers or employees. She never called herself a reformer. Hamilton was a well-regarded scientist who based her recommendations on carefully obtained data, not unfounded opinion. Sites she investigated included companies involved with mining, rubber, paint, gasoline, steel, munitions, radium, denatured alcohol, and mercury. Without resorting to government intervention, she persuaded many company leaders to add safety features to their operations. She believed that unsafe conditions resulted from ignorance, rather than simply from a motivation toward higher profits.

In 1912, Hamilton traveled to Brussels, Belgium, to report on industrial conditions in America at the International Congress on Occupational Accidents and Diseases. Her brilliant analysis drew the attention of lead-

ers in the U.S. Department of Labor. On her return to Illinois, she was asked to undertake similar investigations for the federal government. Her first target was the industrial use of lead. She found dusty processes conducted in poorly ventilated facilities and no protective equipment for workers. Hamilton went from industry to industry, making recommendations for improvement. Following her suggestions, the Pullman Railroad Car Co. reduced the level of lead in the paint it used. Ailments dropped from an incidence of 109 out of 489 employees in 1912, to 3 out of 639 employees in 1913. By 1916, Hamilton was the leading American authority on lead poisoning and one of only a handful of specialists in industrial diseases.

After World War I, the medical profession gained interest in industrial diseases, and laws forced reluctant plant owners to make their factories safer. Hamilton then became less of a pioneer and more of a consultant. She still did field studies, but compared with her earlier investigative work, she described her later efforts as more like attending Sunday school. She said that improvements in factory working conditions resulted from compensation laws, increased medical concern, and voluntary cooperation between business and government.

Hamilton's duties kept her in Washington, D.C., for long periods of time, but Hull House remained her permanent home until 1919 when she moved to Hadlyme, Connecticut. She continued to stay at Hull House for several months each year until the death of Jane Addams in 1935. Hamilton was associated with Florence Sabin, who researched tuberculosis and was the first woman elected to the National Academy of Science. Hamilton also knew Marie Sklodowska Curie, Polish co-discoverer of radium and polonium, and she maintained relationships with the wives of U.S. presidents and members of the cabinet. Hamilton generally shunned publicity. She preferred to make her point by studying and reporting on a company's processes with scrupulous honesty and persistence.

When Harvard University appointed Hamilton to its medical school faculty, she became Harvard's first female professor. She was astonished at the offer, because at that time Harvard did not even admit women students. She taught only six months per year so that she could continue her work as a special investigator for the U.S. Department of Labor. In one of her major field studies, she investigated the rayon industry and its use of carbon disulfide. Hamilton's analysis prompted the passage of Pennsylvania's first compensation law for occupational diseases. Her book *Industrial Poisons* (1925) was the first American text on industrial medicine, and it established her as a leading worldwide authority on the subject. She wrote many technical articles and other books, such as her autobiography, *Exploring the Dangerous Trade* (1943).

A living legend in her advanced years, Hamilton received numerous honorary degrees and awards. In an interview on her 100th birthday, she recalled the grim time when thousands of workers were crippled by poisons in dozens of industries. She had played a large role in eliminating such workplace hazards. However, the only acknowledgment Hamilton gave to herself came in a comment she made on her 88th birthday: "For me, the satisfaction is that things are better now and I had some part in it."

References and Resources

Notable American Women edited by Barbara Sicherman and others, Harvard University Press, 1980.

Women Pioneers of Science by Louis Haber, Harcourt Brace Jovanovich, circa 1975.

Dictionary of American Biography, Charles Scribner's Sons Publishers, 1932; with supplemental updates.

National Cyclopedia of American Biography, James T. White and Co. Publishers, 1891; with supplemental updates.

McGraw-Hill Encyclopedia of Biography, McGraw-Hill Publishers, 1973.

Lee De Forest

Born:
August 26,
1873, in
Council Bluffs,
Iowa

Died:
June 30, 1961,
in Hollywood,
California

Smithsonian Institution Photo No. 52213

Lee De Forest during a broadcast of the Metropolitan Opera about 1910

Early radio signals were transmitted from point to point and consisted only of dots and dashes. Average people had difficulty deciphering Morse code, and early radio was not a source of entertainment. It was Lee De Forest's inventive genius that transformed radio transmission to accommodate both voice and music. In 1907, De Forest invented the triode, the first vacuum tube that could faithfully reproduce audible sound. Most people think that Guglielmo Marconi invented the radio, but he did not. Marconi invented wireless telegraphy. De Forest invented radio. His audion plucked voice and music from the air and delivered it to the human ear.

When De Forest was six, his minister father became the first president of Talladega College in Alabama. Talladega was a newly founded college for children of former slaves. As a boy, De Forest grew up in the midst of racial tension that he could not understand. He had few friends, and his imagination led him to books on mechanics. The young De Forest constructed wooden models of such things as steam locomotives and blast furnaces. During part of the summer of 1893, he worked at the World's Columbian Exposition in Chicago. The time he spent at the exposition's Machinery Hall persuaded him to pursue an education in science and technology. His father had hoped he would become a minister.

The following autumn, De Forest received a scholarship and enrolled in Yale University at New Haven, Connecticut. Although he started out in mechanical engineering, he took one of the first courses on the subject of electricity ever offered at a university in the United States. De Forest earned a doctorate degree, writing his dissertation on the reflection of radio waves. He worked at several different electrical-related jobs, but he did not like any of them. After that, Chicago's Armour Institute provided him with a small teaching salary and laboratory space for working on his experimental devices. Then, just three years out of college, De Forest persuaded several stock promoters to establish the American De Forest Wireless Telegraphy Co. He demonstrated that his equipment could transmit a dot-dash signal at least six miles. The U.S. government, which wanted to gain independence from foreign wireless companies, gave

De Forest several contracts. Also, a fruit company decided to build a chain of his radio stations between Costa Rica and Panama. De Forest's company built 90 stations before he discovered that executives were mishandling company funds. He left the company and started another. De Forest repeated this pattern of establishing one company after another several times during his life.

In the early 1900s, wireless communication used Morse code, a series of dots and dashes generated by powerful sparks. The sparking required the use of six large, heavy electrical condensers. A typical one-ton condenser fit inside a 2' x 7'-long wooden box. Glass plates and kerosene filled each box. De Forest set out to simplify and improve the bulky system, which had the danger of producing shocks and fire.

De Forest worked on methods for improving vacuum-tube diodes. He set up an experimental station at the 1904 World's Fair in St. Louis. It included a 300'-tall antenna, the tallest structure at the fair. When he succeeded at sending wireless messages to Chicago, De Forest received the grand-prize medal for general excellence in wireless telegraphy. In 1906, he sent a 1,000-word message from Coney Island to Ireland—a distance of 3,400 miles. More than 570 of the words were received. It was the first such transmission since Marconi's transmission of three dots in 1901.

Like most electrical investigators, De Forest was searching for a more sensitive detector. He wanted to invent a device or circuit that would receive transmissions from long distances. After much experimental trial and error, De Forest placed a zigzag-shaped piece of nickel wire between the anode and cathode of a diode. He called the wire a *grid*. With proper circuitry, the three-element tube amplified Morse code far better than any diode could. De Forest called his tube the audion, or *triode*, and took out a patent in 1907. It was the prototype for billions of radio tubes that followed. De Forest did not appear to understand the capabilities of the triode. The theories he proposed were incorrect. Not until five years later did he realize the triode's most significant feature: It could amplify voice.

Using complicated electrical connections, De Forest produced a feedback circuit and generated musical tones. The tones could be varied to transmit and receive audible sound. Availability of De Forest's feedback circuit allowed the creation of the broadcast industry, and wireless communication was no longer limited to transmitting Morse code. De Forest also discovered that he could connect the output of one triode to the input of another. Through such a staging technique, several triodes could amplify weak signals.

Instead of point-to-point transmission, De Forest was more interested in *broadcasting* radio signals. (The term broadcasting comes from farming and refers to "spreading widely" in planting seed.) Thirteen years before the first radio station went on the air, De Forest arranged a broadcast of New York Metropolitan Opera singer Enrico Caruso. However, the early equipment was not up to the task, and the sound was almost inaudible. De Forest's concept was far ahead of its time.

An early production model of De Forest's audion

De Forest worked during a period when most people were unsure of the existence of electrons. No one quite understood how the audion worked, and some people claimed they had previously discovered

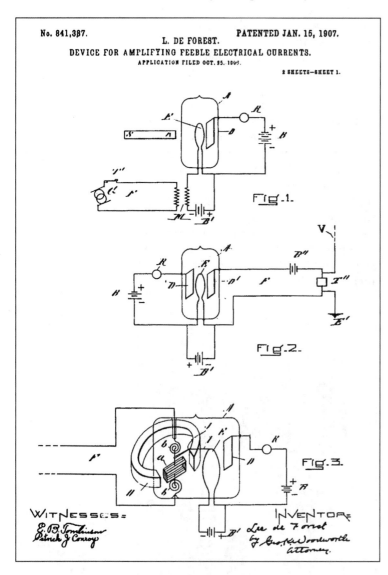

No. 841,387.   PATENTED JAN. 15, 1907.
L. DE FOREST.
DEVICE FOR AMPLIFYING FEEBLE ELECTRICAL CURRENTS.
APPLICATION FILED OCT. 25, 1906.
2 SHEETS—SHEET 1.

Fig. 1.

Fig. 2.

Fig. 3.

WITNESSES: INVENTOR:

De Forest's audion spawned an increase in radio communication.

De Forest's feedback circuit. Those two factors resulted in one of the longest patent battles in history. The two main combatants were De Forest and Edwin Armstrong. In 14 years of court battles, De Forest won seven times and Armstrong won six times. It was not until 1934 that the U.S. Supreme Court finally decided in De Forest's favor.

During the lengthy court proceedings, his audion made fortunes for others, helped create the Radio Corporation of America (RCA), and brought a new form of entertainment to the public. De Forest received little wealth or fame, and much unhappiness, as a result of his invention.

De Forest had pioneered sound transmission, but he ran into legal or financial problems at almost every stage of his work. Whenever he tried to manufacture or market his inventions, he encountered lengthy patent suits. While in his fifties, De Forest changed his strategy. He devoted himself to invention and then sold his rights to others. Only in his later years did he find contentment.

De Forest married four times. His fourth and happiest marriage, in 1930, was to silent-movie star Marie Mosquini. She shared his enjoyment of music, poetry, and camping. De Forest spent little time in the laboratory during his later years. He preferred to listen to music from the large high-fidelity phonograph he built for his own use. He received more than 300 patents over the course of his lifetime, with the last granted when he was 83. Many were commercially successful, but the triode had by far the greatest importance. It was one of this century's greatest inventions. Late in his life, De Forest called his audion "the granddaddy of all the vast progeny of electronic tubes that have ever come into existence."

References and Resources

Empire of the Air by Tom Lewis, Harper Collins Publishers, 1991.

Those Inventive Americans, National Geographic Society, 1971.

American Science and Invention by Mitchell Wilson, Bonanza Books, 1960.

Dictionary of American Biography, Charles Scribner's Sons Publishers, 1932; with supplemental updates.

National Cyclopedia of American Biography, James T. White and Co. Publishers, 1891; with supplemental updates.

Asimov's Biographical Encyclopedia of Science and Technology, by Isaac Asimov, Doubleday & Co. Publishers, 1964.

Charles Franklin Kettering

ONE early-twentieth-century technologist is often compared to Thomas Edison. What Edison did for the advancement of electrical technology, Charles Kettering did for the advancement of transportation technology. Kettering invented the automotive self-starter, helping to make the automobile a product for average consumers, not just one for enthusiasts. He developed the two-stroke-cycle diesel engine for use on locomotives and ships. His many patents included improvements to air-cooled aircraft engines. As a philanthropist, Kettering helped establish a cancer research organization. He also cofounded the Sloan-Kettering Institute with Alfred Sloan, president of the General Motors Corporation.

Kettering's childhood was not much different from that of other youngsters who lived in rural areas at the time. He attended local schools and did many daily farm chores. Although not a spectacular student, he graduated from Loudonville High School with above-average grades. Kettering immediately became a teacher in a one-room schoolhouse, saving his money to attend college. In the summer of 1896, he entered the College of Wooster in Ohio planning to study ancient languages. While there, he heard of engineering courses at other colleges and became fired with enthusiasm about technology. However, chronic eye problems forced him to leave Wooster. He then attended school on and off, graduating finally from the Ohio State University in 1904 with an engineering degree. It is said that when he received his diploma, Kettering immediately threw it away because he did not want to consider his education ended.

Kettering's first job after leaving Ohio State was in the inventions department at

General Motors Corp.

Charles Kettering at the age of 82

Born:
**August 29,
1876, in
Loudonville,
Ohio**

Died:
**November 25,
1958, in
Dayton, Ohio**

the National Cash Register Co. (NCR) in Dayton. At the time, the company was a source of ideas and leaders for American industry. Kettering's first assignment was to develop an electrical drive for cash registers. Experts considered the task impossible in practical terms because it would require using a motor as large as the cash register itself. However, Kettering knew that he could overload a motor if it ran for only a short time. One year out of college, he used that idea to build the first practical electric cash register. Fifty years later, the electric drive remained basically unchanged from the one in Kettering's original model.

After five productive years, Kettering left NCR to organize his own company. He named it formally the Dayton Engineering Laboratories Co., calling it Delco for short.

At General Electric's Research Laboratory, Charles Kettering (right) at 65 attempts to pull apart experimental magnets given to him by the lab's director, William Coolidge.

Kettering's electrical work at NCR led him to investigate the shortcomings of automotive electrical components. First, he tackled the battery ignition system. The system in use at the time had a high-drain vibrator circuit that provided a stream of sparks for ignition. Kettering invented the breaker-point ignition system to substitute just one spark for ignition. The new system increased battery life from an original 300 miles to 2,000 miles. The breaker-type system first went into production on some 1909 Republic automobiles. Eventually, manufacturers used it on all automobile engines for more than 60 years, until the electronic ignition gained popularity in the 1970s.

Henry Leland was the general manager of Cadillac Motor Co. He mourned the death of a close friend, Byron Carter, who had died of complications caused by a broken jaw he received while crank starting an engine. Leland encouraged Kettering to use his knowledge to develop an electric self-starter. To build a relatively small electric motor that would start a gasoline engine, Kettering applied the same logic he used at NCR. After much work and testing, he shipped an experimental automobile to Cadillac in 1911. The car was damaged in a garage fire a few weeks later. At the time,

Kettering was bed ridden with a badly broken leg, which he had injured while testing an experimental car. Ignoring medical advice, he took a train to Detroit and repaired the damaged starter with his leg in a cast. The Delco-made starter went into production on 1912 Cadillacs. Many people view Kettering's invention of the electric self-starter as the key to making the automobile a true consumer product. It freed drivers from worrying about the dangers of crank starting. Although electric starters were not the only reason for the increase, North American automobile production soared from 181,000 in 1910, to 1,525,600 in 1916.

Having gained great wealth from his previous inventions, Kettering sold Delco in 1916 to open a research laboratory. The first problem he took on was the challenge of eliminating engine knock in high-compression engines. Knock, or detonation, is an erratic combustion during the power stroke that can damage internal parts. Technologists thought the cause was the new ignition system or carbon particles inside the engine. Production engines typically had a compression ratio of 4:1, and Kettering looked toward 7:1 as a ratio that would develop more power and improve fuel economy. Working with Thomas Midgley, Kettering found that gasoline was the problem. Adding a small amount of a little-known chemical, tetraethyl lead, eliminated the problem. Labeled *ethyl*, *premium*, or *high performance*, the new gasoline became available in 1923.

Another of Kettering's outstanding contributions to transportation was the development of the two-stroke-cycle diesel engine. He began work in 1929 on a lightweight high-speed diesel engine for small ships, buses, trucks, and locomotives. It was a complex engine, and the project was unusually time consuming and difficult. The key problem was injecting the precise amount of fuel, at exactly the right time, and against high-compression pressures. Kettering's solution was an improved fuel injector. Two 12-cylinder, 11,000-pound, 1,000 hp, 750 rpm engines powered the Chevrolet exhibit at Chicago's Century of Progress World's Fair in 1933. The engines were quite troublesome and required considerable after-hours maintenance. (Kettering's adult son Eugene, who supervised the exhibit, often said that the only item not needing constant repair was the oil dipstick.) Nonetheless, the display encouraged Ralph Budd to use 8-cylinder versions of the engines in his new streamlined Zephyr trains. The Zephyrs led a renewal of passenger train travel during the 1930s. By 1938, orders for diesel-electric locomotives exceeded orders for steam locomotives.

Henry Ford had complained that while he could build a car in two minutes, it took two hours for the car's black paint to dry in an oven. Other colors required even more time. Kettering took up the challenge, and in 1922 he developed a lacquer that dried in minutes. He also made improved bearings, lubricants, and transmissions. Kettering worked on special alloys for use in pistons, valves, camshafts, and brake drums. After more than 140 patents, he closed out his career working on automotive-type gas turbine engines.

Kettering received 32 honorary doctorate degrees and many major professional honors, including a special one established in his honor by the joint engineering societies. In his own time, Kettering was acknowledged as America's greatest living inventor. He was a large, pleasant, eloquent man. He had a gift for making technical topics understandable to everyone, and he found himself in great demand as a speaker. Between September 1942 and July 1945, he told a series of five-minute radio stories on the topics of invention and technology. The stories were broadcast at the intermission of General Motors Symphony of the Air.

A master of the short statement, Kettering once said, "I concentrate on the future because we will spend the rest of our lives there." He never retired from industrial research, continuing to work until the year of his death.

References and Resources

Boss Kettering: Wizard of General Motors by Stuart Leslie, Columbia University Press, 1983.

Adventures of the Inquiring Mind, General Motors, 1957.

"Charles Franklin Kettering," mimeographed biography from General Motors Technical Center, Detroit, MI, 1976.

Dictionary of American Biography, Charles Scribner's Sons Publishers, 1932; with supplemental updates.

National Cyclopedia of American Biography, James T. White and Co. Publishers, 1891; with supplemental updates.

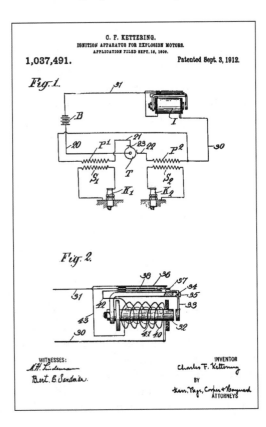

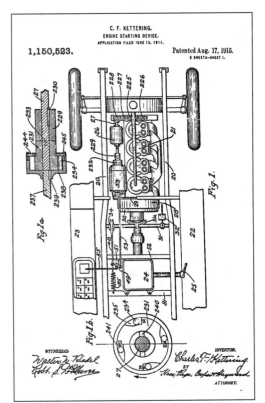

Kettering's fertile mind created the automotive breaker-type ignition system (left). He also patented the first practical self-starter for automobiles.

Garrett Augustus Morgan

Garrett Morgan (left) in a firefighting demonstration around 1920. Two firefighters wear Morgan safety hoods.

Born:
March 4, 1877,
in Paris,
Kentucky

Died:
July 27, 1963,
in Cleveland,
Ohio

MANY technologists have indirectly saved lives through the application of their inventions. Consider, for example, Alexander Graham Bell's telephone, which allows people to call others for help, or Benjamin Franklin's lightning rod, which protects homes against fire. However, few technologists take part in heroic actions in which they use their own inventions. One exception was Garrett Augustus Morgan. In 1916, disregarding his own safety, he used his newly patented safety hood to rescue the only two survivors from a smoke-filled construction tunnel under Lake Erie.

Morgan was the seventh of 11 children born to freed slaves who were farmers in Paris, Kentucky. His grandfather was Confederate Colonel John Hunt Morgan, who commanded a volunteer cavalry unit called Morgan's Raiders. As was typical of the period, Morgan received only an elementary school education. He left home at 14. After working for a short time in Cincinnati, he

hopped a freight train to Cleveland. He got off with only 10¢ in his pocket. Morgan had previously worked as a handyman, and he used that experience to find work repairing sewing machines in a clothing manufacturing factory. He received recognition in the *Cleveland Plain Dealer* newspaper as the only machine adjuster to understand the intricacies of weavers, zigzags, lock stitches, buttonholers, and hook-and-eye machines. He devised accessories for sewing machines, such as a belt fastener that increased a machine's efficiency. Morgan enjoyed the work and stayed with it for many years.

Then, in 1907, Morgan opened his own sewing machine sales and repair shop. He spent time at home searching for an effective needle lubricant. Rapidly moving sewing machine needles scorched sensitive fabrics. Instead of a needle lubricant, Morgan discovered a cream that would straighten curly hair. The product became the basis for the G. A. Morgan Hair Refining Co., which Morgan organized in 1913. Influenced by the styles of the time, some people felt that straight hair improved their appearance. Morgan's company was moderately successful, and it provided him with a financial base that gave him time for inventing. The company was a family affair that once employed all three of Morgan's children, as well as several grandchildren. The production area was in a building behind his home on Harlem Avenue. Morgan himself used his company's products for most of his life.

Though he only patented a few inventions, Morgan worked on many. The Morgan safety hood was the first of his two significant inventions. Morgan irritated his eyes in the course of filling a pepper box at home, and this set him to wondering how workers processed pepper in factories. Morgan started to work on a way to make a cloth helmet that would allow someone to work in a room filled with irritating fumes, smoke, or gases. His design was not a gas mask in the modern sense, but it functioned in a way similar to one. A sturdy canvas hood rested on the shoulders of the wearer, who could view the surroundings through two squares of mica, a transparent mineral. In a smoke-filled room, a large trailing tube picked up fresher air from the floor. If necessary to get fresh air, the wearer could place the end of the tube outside a window. A dampened sponge in the tube helped filter the air. The wearer exhaled into another tube inside the hood, and the exhaled air came out the top of the hood through a one-way valve. The hood proved particularly useful in smoky fires, so Morgan targeted fire departments and chemical companies as potential purchasers. He charged $25 for the hood, and he often personally demonstrated its use.

For such demonstrations, Morgan would ignite a mixture of tar, sulfur, and oily rags in a small room. With theatrical poise, he would then casually walk into the dense smoke wearing his safety hood. He often remained in the smoke for a half hour or longer. Fire department officials were usually impressed enough to buy several safety hoods. Morgan manufactured them himself at a small but thriving clothing manufacturing shop he established in 1909. Later, Morgan and several prominent business people

organized the National Safety Device Co. to manufacture the hood. It was more popular than hoods produced by competitors because it weighed only 3-1/2 pounds, and a user could put it on in seven seconds and remove it in just two. More than 500 fire departments adopted Morgan's hood. He had earlier sold $10 shares in his invention to members of the black community. Those who invested profited handsomely when the stock rose in value to $250 per share over the course of two years.

Morgan's improved Style Two hood featured a 20-minute air supply in a bag pressurized to 17 psi. He used the Style Two in the Lake Erie disaster at Crib No. 5. On July 25, 1916, methane gas exploded in a water-

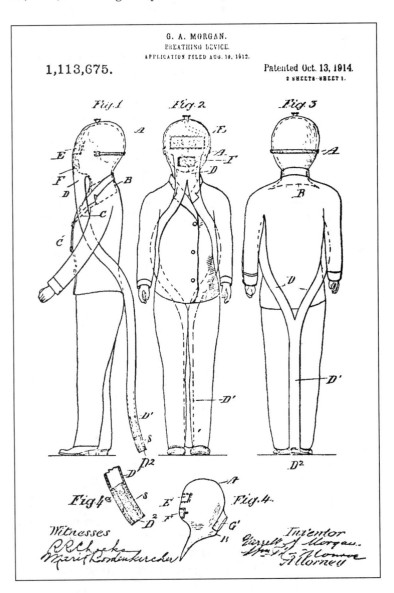

Morgan's hood preceded the gas mask.

intake tunnel being built from an artificial island five miles off the shore of Cleveland. Eleven men had been working in the tunnel. Morgan, his brother, and a neighbor arrived by boat at 4 A.M., bringing several hoods with them. They descended more than 220 feet into the smoke-filled tunnel to search for survivors after two earlier rescue parties, totaling 10 men, failed to return. Only two of the people they brought out in their four trips into the tunnel survived. The disaster claimed 19 lives.

Neither Morgan's heroic efforts nor his safety hood received acknowledgment in official accounts of the accident. The racial climate at that time may well have played a part in the lack of attention Morgan and his invention received. Whatever the reason, Morgan gave up further work on improving his safety hood.

In the early 1920s, Morgan witnessed an automobile collision at a street intersection.

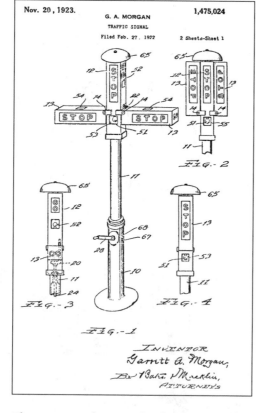

Morgan's traffic signal had arms that extended and retracted. It was the first to use the colors red, yellow, and green.

The event made enough of an impression that he began work on his second significant contribution to technology, the traffic control signal, or stop-and-go light. Mor-

gan's 1923 invention, like others before it, was manually operated and had arms that swung out. The words STOP and GO appeared on them. Morgan's patent had one important feature the others lacked: an intermediate position. Of it, Morgan wrote, "My invention . . . enables a director to . . . [stop] the movement thereof in all directions momentarily just prior to allowing traffic to move in any one direction."

Thus, although Morgan's traffic control device did not resemble modern stop-and-go lights, he did develop the concept behind the cautionary yellow light found on modern traffic signals. Because his patent model included red, green, and yellow plastic inserts, he sometimes receives credit for inventing the tricolor traffic signal. Morgan sold his patent rights to the General Electric Co. for an impressive $40,000.

Always active in the community, Morgan was a longtime member of many black civic organizations. He established the *Call and Post* newspaper in 1920 to voice minority concerns, and he unsuccessfully ran for Cleveland's city council. Although he lost money during the Great Depression of the 1930s, his granddaughter remembered him as a happy man. She noted that he was also outspoken and quick tempered.

Morgan developed glaucoma, which left him almost blind for the last 20 years of his life. His tombstone has a carefully carved traffic signal. Morgan's original wooden prototype traffic signal is on public display at Cleveland's African American Museum, along with one of the three original Morgan safety hoods still in existence. During the summer of 1991, Cleveland commemorated the 75th anniversary of Morgan's heroic action at Crib No. 5.

References and Resources

Documents from the Western Reserve Historical Society, Cleveland, OH.

"Guardian of the Public Safety: Garrett A. Morgan and the Lake Erie Crib Disaster" by William M. King, *Journal of Negro History*, circa 1988.

"The Heritage of Garrett Augustus Morgan" by Tracy Morgan Melamed (Morgan's granddaughter), *Lakeview Cemetary—The Heritage*, Spring 1991.

Ole Evinrude

ON a pleasant summer day at the lake, you can often see people fishing from boats. Most use reliable and convenient outboard motors. Ole Evinrude made the first practical one in 1907. His engine's cylinder was horizontal, with a vertical crankshaft and driveshaft. It had a horizontal flywheel and a set of bevel gears. Evinrude used a gearbox in a submerged lower unit to rotate the direction of power. All outboards today have basically the same features as the one he first built.

Evinrude was five when his farming family moved from its native Norway to southern Wisconsin. Evinrude's parents were poor, and his education ended at the third grade. Evinrude did not enjoy farming, preferring to work on mechanical devices. His first major project was a sailboat that he constructed at age 16. For a modest fee, he carried sightseers on Wisconsin's Lake Ripley. Through this enterprise, he saved enough money to pay his room and board when he moved to the city that year. Evinrude walked 20 miles to Madison and found employment as an entry-level machinist at the Fuller & Johnson Farm Machinery Co. He later moved to the steel mills of Pittsburgh and then to a tool company in Chicago. Finally he settled in Milwaukee, working as a patternmaker for E. P. Allis Co.

In his spare time, Evinrude worked on designing and constructing single-cylinder engines. His first used natural gas. When he started an engine one evening in the basement of his boarding house, it pulled so much gas from the pipes that all the building's gaslights went out. Evinrude had a polite and humble manner, and his landlady readily accepted his apology. He hoped to construct standard engines for the emerg-

Outboard Marine Corp.

Born:
April 19, 1877, in Christiana, Norway

Died:
July 12, 1934, in Milwaukee, Wisconsin

ing horseless carriages. His design was good enough that a small company agreed to manufacture them. Evinrude felt encouraged by an order for 50 engines from the federal government. At that time, he had not even considered designing an outboard motor.

One day in 1906, Evinrude went on a Sunday picnic with a young woman named Bess Emily Cary, whom he would soon marry. The two had rowed to an island on Okauchee Lake with several friends. After lunch, Bess asked Evinrude to row back to shore for some ice cream. An unexpected shift in the wind slowed him down on the return leg. Even though Evinrude was a large and strong man, the trip took so long that by the time he reached the island the ice cream had melted. The shy Evinrude felt quite embarrassed. The next day, he started work on an outboard motor.

Cameron Waterman first used the term

outboard in a patent he took out in 1905. Waterman used a bicycle-type chain to connect a Glenn Curtiss motorcycle engine to a propeller. Waterman established a company to make his outboard, but people showed little interest in it.

Evinrude worked for about a year on his idea for a two-stroke-cycle boat motor. He carried it to the Kinnickinnic River in 1908 with Bess's two brothers. After operating the motor, he felt that it needed some modifications. Around that time, Evinrude and Bess eloped. She humorously called his in-

Early model production outboard motor. The handle at the top is for turning the flywheel to start the motor. The metal label reads "Evinrude Detachable Row Boat Motor."

Outboard Marine Corp.

vention a coffee grinder. Evinrude made some changes to the outboard motor and received a patent. He lent the motor to a friend who was so impressed with its performance that he convinced 10 other people to order one. Evinrude made those 10, selling each for $62. An order for 25 more soon followed. In 1909, Evinrude left his job to form the Evinrude Motor Co.

The engines Evinrude built used a battery ignition system and developed about 1-1/2 hp at 1,000 rpm. They weighed 55 pounds and could average about 5 mph in a fishing boat. Evinrude also came out with a reverse, by making a gear housing that

turned 180 degrees. Evinrude attributed much of the Evinrude Motor Co.'s success to his wife, Bess. Ole functioned as designer, builder, and master mechanic. Bess served as business and advertising manager. Her first advertisement read: "Throw Away the Oars! Buy an Evinrude Detachable Rowboat Motor!" The company sold 1,000 motors during its first year and 2,090 in 1911. Evinrude motors cost $65 to $70 each, but income from them proved insufficient to pay the bills. Then, Oluf Mikkelsen, a Danish-born clerk in a New York office, saw an Evinrude ad. Attracted by the Scandinavian name, he convinced his supervisor to buy a few motors and send them to Denmark. The response from overseas was overwhelming, and it saved the budding company. In time, Mikkelsen became Evinrude's chief export agent.

The company employed up to 300 people at a time, and the husband-wife team worked together closely, until Bess became ill. They decided to sell out in 1914 for $137,500. Evinrude agreed to stay out of the outboard motor business for five years and allowed the purchaser to continue using the name Evinrude Motor Co.

At a time when paved roads were few, Ole, Bess, and their only child, Ralph, took a long-distance camping trip in a converted Packard. Hoping that a better climate would help improve Bess's health, they headed for the Pacific Ocean, with the 1915 Panama-Pacific International Exposition in San Francisco as their target. The family did other traveling as well, and Ole designed a cabin cruiser named *Bess Emily*. The family used it on the Great Lakes.

Bess fully recovered, and Evinrude began to design a new engine in his spare time. By now the five-year prohibition against setting up an outboard motor business had passed. Still, the loyal Evinrude discussed his ideas with the purchaser of his company. Evinrude had a two-cylinder engine in mind. The Evinrude Motor Co. was making a profit, and its owner declined the offer. Ole and Bess took their life savings of $40,000 and started Elto Outboard Motor Co. in 1920. Bess coined the name Elto from Evinrude Light Twin Outboard. The Elto product was the first practical twin-cylinder outboard to use lightweight aluminum instead of iron and steel. It was also the first to exhaust combustion gases through the propeller hub. The engine developed 3 hp at 1,400 rpm. It weighed 47 pounds—27 fewer than its closest competitor, an Evinrude Motor Co. 2 hp single-cylinder engine. The Elto offered full tilting and a waterproof ignition system. It sold for $135. The 1921 Elto outboard was the first to feature a fully encased and streamlined lower unit. The new company was an unqualified success. Elto sold 11,000 outboards in its first three years of production.

Early outboard motors had been designed for fishing, and none was rated at more than 4 hp. By 1925, boat racing was growing popular, and racing enthusiasts wanted more power. In 1928, Evinrude brought out the first four-cylinder outboard, the Elto Quad. Rated at 18 hp, it was the first outboard to power a boat to more than 60 mph. The next year, Elto sold a total of 59,000 outboard motors. Ole and Bess continued to work closely until Bess left the company in 1929. When she died in 1933, Ole was heartbroken. He died a year later.

Evinrude's 1909 outboard motor was dedicated as a National Historic Mechanical Engineering Landmark in 1981. It was the first consumer product to receive that recognition. The prestigious Science Museum in London, England, has even put an early Evinrude on display.

References and Resources

Ole Evinrude and the Old Fellows by Gordon MacQuarrie, Outboard Marine Corp., 1947.

"The Evinrude Story," in *Boat and Motor Dealer*, April 1984.

"Throw Those Oars Away," in *Mechanical Engineering*, November 1981.

"The Outboard Motor, Its History and Development," Outboard Marine Corp., Milwaukee, WI (undated).

Glenn Hammond Curtiss

Smithsonian Institution Photo No. 42731B

Glenn Curtiss at about the age of 35

Born:
May 21, 1878,
in
Hammondsport,
New York

Died:
July 23, 1930,
in Buffalo,
New York

THE Wright brothers were the first people to fly in a controlled, powered, heavier-than-air machine. However, it was the engine-building genius of the slender and solemn Glenn Hammond Curtiss that established the American aircraft industry.

When Curtiss was only six, his father died. His grandparents raised him and his sister. Curtiss finished elementary school and went to work in Rochester, New York, as a messenger boy. He seemed to have a passion for speed, and he greatly enjoyed using bicycles on his new job. He soon returned to Hammondsport, eventually opened a bicycle shop, and took up bicycle racing. During the next three years, Curtiss won every bicycle race he entered, until he lost at the state fair in 1901. He then turned

to something speedier, opening a motorcycle shop in 1902.

Curtiss ordered a rough casting for an engine, and it arrived without either instructions or a carburetor. After getting the single cylinder operating in a motorcycle, Curtiss ordered a larger set of castings. Seeing that it was too heavy to make a practical engine, he decided to manufacture engines himself. Curtiss made and sold motors, motorcycles, and accessories. He raced his own motorcycles and in 1903 won the national championship at Yonkers. In 1904, he established a speed record for two-cylinder engines of 67 mph at Daytona Beach, Florida. That record stood for more than seven years.

Curtiss had no thoughts about aviation until Thomas Baldwin visited him. Baldwin had used a secondhand Curtiss engine in a dirigible to win a prize at the 1904 St. Louis World's Fair. Baldwin was impressed by it and asked Curtiss to build other engines for his lighter-than-air flying machines. Curtiss agreed, and he went on to help Baldwin with propeller designs. He also accompanied Baldwin to many demonstrations at fairs and expositions. Curtiss once took the controls and said he had finally discovered a thrill greater than that of speed: flying.

Alexander Graham Bell had been conducting flight tests since the 1890s at his summer home in Nova Scotia. He bought a Curtiss engine in 1905 and used it for testing purposes. The 60-year-old Bell invited Curtiss to assist him in Nova Scotia in 1907. Along with Bell and three others, Curtiss agreed to form the Aerial Experiment Association (AEA). He would act as director of experiments. One of the other members was Lieutenant Thomas Selfridge, who would become aviation's first fatality while riding as Orville Wright's passenger in 1908.

The AEA's simple objective was to get an airplane into the air. Curtiss learned much about aeronautics from Bell. One of their early experimental aircraft lifted from the frozen surface of Keuka Lake, near Hammondsport. Bell had alerted the press and many people witnessed the flight of the *Red Wing* in March 1908. Flying 318 feet, it made the first public flight of a heavier-than-air flying machine.

Unlike the secretive Wright brothers, Curtiss and the AEA were far more open with the public and the press. As publicity continued, the Wright brothers protested Curtiss's use of movable ailerons for roll control. They claimed that use of the ailerons infringed on the *wing warping* technique described in their patent. Thus began a series of unpleasant and unfortunate confrontations. The dispute did not end until the government intervened in 1917.

Like all pioneer pilots, Curtiss taught himself to fly. He received the world's first pilot's license from the Federation Aeronautique Internationale in France. Curtiss also operated a school for aspiring pilots. He taught Blanche Scott, America's first woman aviator, to fly. By the spring of 1909, the AEA had reached the end of its planned duration. Curtiss drifted away from the others, although he continued to maintain friendly relations with them.

Curtiss built a plane and entered it in the first International Aviation Meet at Reims, France, in 1909. The only American entrant, he raced against the world's best aviators. Curtiss won at an average speed of 47 mph. He returned home with a trophy, $15,000 in prize money, and orders for both planes and engines. The 1965 motion picture *Those Magnificent Men in Their Flying Machines* was based on that event. The American pilot portrayed by actor Stuart Whitman was patterned after Curtiss.

Curtiss then began to establish his reputation as a flying-boat builder. He fitted an experimental airplane, named *June*, with floats and attempted to lift off from Keuka Lake in 1908. This was the first attempt of its type, and it failed. Curtiss attracted the attention of the Navy, which supported his efforts to make a flying boat. After many experiments and much study, he succeeded in taking off and landing on water in Janu-

ary 1911 in San Diego Bay. To break the suction of the water, he used a stepped hull—a design feature still in use today.

The *London Daily Mail* newspaper offered a $50,000 prize to the first aviator to cross the Atlantic. To do so, Curtiss lead the effort to construct the twin-engined flying boat *America*. The plane was almost ready for flight when World War I broke out. The flight was canceled and the airplane was used by the Royal Air Force for submarine patrol duty. After the war, Curtiss continued to work on the project for the Navy. He built the four-engined NC-4 ("NC" standing for Navy-Curtiss) flying boat that made the first airplane flight across the Atlantic Ocean. The plane was commanded by Lieutenant Albert C. Read. He and a crew of five took off from Halifax, Nova Scotia, in 1919 and landed in Lisbon, Portugal, 12 days later. A series of strategically located boats allowed the plane to put down for rest and fuel. NC-4 is now on public display at the Naval Aviation Museum in Pensacola, Florida.

Soon after the transatlantic flight, Curtiss's interest in aviation waned. This may have been caused by his aileron-wing warping court battles with the Wright brothers. Though not a villain in this situation, Curtiss was sometimes perceived as one. In an unusual move, the government gave the Wright brothers and Curtiss each $2 million in 1917 and declared that they could use each other's patents. World War I was in progress, and the government thought that too much technical talent and

The OX-5 V8 engine was Curtiss' most popular and well-known early aircraft engine.

potential was being wasted in the courtroom.

During his late thirties, Curtiss did little flying and spent most of his time dealing with manufacturing. He built both engines and airframes. His most successful engine was a 90 hp liquid-cooled V-8 that he called the OX-5. It became world famous as the power plant of the JN-4 airplane. Called the Jenny, this training plane was often flown by barnstorming pilots who entertained the public during the 1920s. More than 2,000 Jennies were sold as government-surplus trainers. Curtiss's company also built the 225 hp air-cooled radial engine used in Charles Lindbergh's Spirit of St. Louis in the first solo crossing of the Atlantic.

During the 1920s, Curtiss began to lose interest in his company. With his wife and son, he lived the life of a wealthy man in their large home in Garden City, Long Island. He experimented with streamlined travel trailers, improved automobiles, and

speedboats. Curtiss died after an operation for appendicitis, just a few months after the formation of the Curtiss-Wright Corp.

References and Resources

"Man in Motion" by Carrie Brown, *American Heritage of Invention and Technology*, Spring/Summer 1991.

The NC-4–The First Transatlantic Flight, Naval Aviation Museum, Pensacola, FL (undated brochure).

Glenn Hammond Curtiss, Glenn Curtiss Museum of Local History, Hammondsport, NY (undated brochure).

Dictionary of American Biography, Charles Scribner's Sons Publishers, 1932; with supplemental updates.

National Cyclopedia of American Biography, James T. White and Co. Publishers, 1891; with supplemental updates

McGraw-Hill Encyclopedia of Biography, McGraw-Hill Publishers, 1973.

Curtiss's patent for a flying boat featured a stepped hull on the floats to allow takeoff with the low-powered engines of the era.

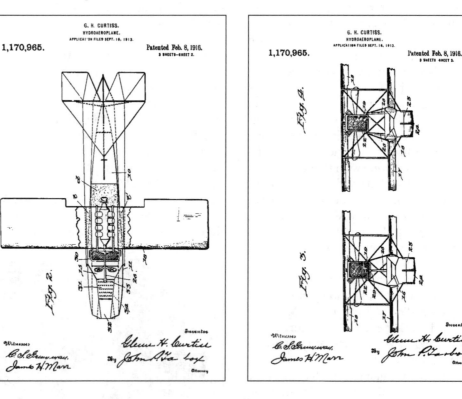

Lillian Evelyn Moller Gilbreth

Born:
May 24, 1878, in Oakland, California

Died:
January 2, 1972, in Phoenix, Arizona

During Henry Ford's teenage years, a child was born who would later be called by some "the most amazing American woman." A pioneer in the field of motion study, Lillian Gilbreth found ways to save motion in factories and offices long before universities offered courses on the subject. She developed work methods that increased industrial production. She helped to establish the industrial engineering profession. She and her husband had 12 children, two of whom wrote a book about the Gilbreth family's experience titled *Cheaper by the Dozen.*

Gilbreth was born into a California merchant family. Because she was very shy, she did not start first grade until the age of nine. Consequently, she was always the oldest in her class. She earned a degree in literature from the University of California at Berkeley in 1902 and had the honor of being the first female commencement speaker in the school's history. Gilbreth met her future husband while she was in Boston in 1904 making arrangements to work on a degree in psychology. Frank Gilbreth was 10 years older than Lillian. He was an outspoken building contractor who had started work in his teens as an apprentice bricklayer. Soon after meeting, the unlikely pair married and Lillian found herself in a totally new environment. Instead of being involved with art and literature, she found new interests in production and efficiency. In 1914, she wrote a book titled *Psychology of Management.* Often asked if he was related to the book's author, Frank's standard answer was, "Only by marriage."

During the early years of her married life, Lillian remained in Frank's shadow. While she was retiring, he was dynamic, professionally well established, and filled with

new ideas on scientific management. Scientific management uses measurable characteristics to establish production goals. Frank dropped his construction business to devote full time to motion study. One of his clients was a company located near Brown University in Providence, Rhode Island. Brown's president had an interest in psychology and its application to industrial management. Lillian worked on the project and received her Ph.D. in psychology in 1915. The husband-and-wife team then established Frank B. Gilbreth, Inc., to develop a specialty in motion study and to change work habits in ways that eliminated useless steps. It was one of the first production management firms in the world. The Gilbreths moved from Providence to Montclair, New Jersey, to be close to the New York headquarters of many companies. They wrote five books together, including *Fatigue*

Study, published in 1916, and *Applied Motion Study*, published in 1917.

As a highly successful team, the Gilbreths improved work environments for the handicapped and developed efficient work techniques for the construction industry. They developed process charts and motion picture techniques to analyze work methods. They attached lights to the hands of workers and photographed them. Then, they made three-dimensional wire models of the hand paths to help in determining a more efficient motion. The Gilbreths recommended such innovations as rest periods, improved working conditions, and encour-

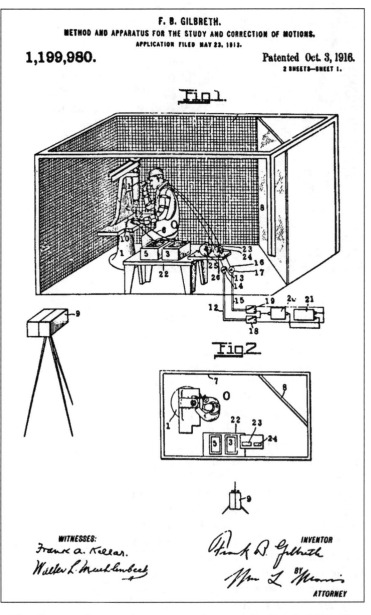

The first motion study patent, taken out by Frank Gilbreth

aging positive attitudes to boost morale and productivity. One of their early investigations concerned bricklaying. By using new methods, they could improve a worker's production to an average of 350 bricks per hour, without any additional effort. Previously, only the fastest people could lay 120 bricks per hour. Frank was a heavy man, and he once humorously said he grew interested in motion study when he realized how often he moved his own 250 pounds to lay one brick.

Lillian came from a family of 10 children, but it was Frank who wanted a dozen. Of the potential problems involved in raising that many youngsters, he said, "We teach management, so we will have to practice it." The couple eventually had six sons and six daughters. Their lifestyle was different from the average family. The Gilbreths had family council meetings to discuss pets, the purchase of new furniture, and other domestic matters. They developed a division-of-labor method, and chores went to the lowest bidder. Frank expected all the youngsters to know the alphabet forward and backward, so they could look up a word in a dictionary by moving in either direction. To avoid wasting time in the bathtub, he instructed the children in the fastest way to take a proper bath. When a neighbor asked Frank why he had so many children, he replied that they were cheaper by the dozen.

Frank served as a major in World War I with the Army Corps of Engineers. After the war, his military service and civilian specialty flooded the Gilbreths with work from overseas, and especially from Germany. Frank helped to establish the International Management Congress in Prague for the purpose of sharing information on American methods of production. He was preparing to attend its first meeting in 1924, when he unexpectedly died at a railway station. Knowing how important the organization was to her husband, Lillian went in Frank's place three days later. Her appearance provided a rallying point for the organization's members and greatly helped advance the international management movement. After returning home, Lillian assumed the presidency of the consulting firm and continued to operate the business for the next 45 years.

Encouraged by others at the Prague meeting, Gilbreth opened a motion-study school in her large home. The first class had eight students, all employees of large industrial firms and three of them from overseas. Enrollment grew and Gilbreth continued the private instruction until universities accepted and began to offer scientific management as an approved program of study. She developed many insights and at various times served on the faculty of the New Jersey Institute of Technology, Rutgers University, the University of Wisconsin, and Purdue University.

Throughout a long and varied career, Gilbreth's accomplishments touched many different aspects of her life. She designed the single-surface efficiency kitchen, improved box-stacking techniques in warehouses, and developed the secretary's chair to improve back support for office workers. Gilbreth improved efficiency in companies that made automobiles, soap, and shoes. She even analyzed surgical techniques, golf swings, and the arrangement of silverware on a table. During World War II, she served on many education committees, such as the Committee on College Women Students and various others for the War Manpower Commission.

Gilbreth served on national committees under presidents Hoover, Roosevelt, Eisenhower, Kennedy, and Johnson. Those committees dealt with production, civil defense, and rehabilitation of the handicapped. During one particularly active year, Gilbreth visited 16 countries, making presentations to 42 technical organizations and civic groups. A frail but dynamic woman, she once said that she preferred to save her time and spend her energy. At the age of 88, she represented the American Institute of Industrial Engineers at a worldwide industrial conference in Rotterdam.

Frequently introduced as the First Lady of Engineering, her awards were many and varied. Gilbreth was the first woman elected to the National Academy of Engineering. She received 23 honorary college or university degrees. Countless professional organizations presented her with honorary memberships and awards. They included the American Society of Mechanical Engineers, the Society for the Advancement of Management, and the American Society of Engineering Education. A pleasant and soft-spoken woman, she almost never raised her voice. People often described her as a friendly person whom everyone trusted. She died in retirement at the age of 93.

References and Resources

"Dr. Lillian Moller Gilbreth, 1878-1972" by Nancy S. Reynolds, in *Industrial Engineering*, February 1972.

"The Gilbreths" by Fritz Hirschfeld, in *Mechanical Engineering*, November 1980.

Motion and Time Study by Ralph Barnes, John Wiley, 1958.

Life Science Library: Machines by Robert O'Brien, Time Inc., 1964.

Note: The Smithsonian Institution, Washington, DC, has an *Annotated Index of the Gilbreth Stereo Slide Collection* (Acc. 318949 Cat. 334998). It contains 2,250 glass slides from the Gilbreth's work between 1910 and 1924, as well as views of the Gilbreth family, travels, and friends.

Robert Hutchings Goddard

National Portrait Gallery, Smithsonian Institution

Painting of Robert Goddard based on a photograph taken at his Roswell, New Mexico, workshop

Born:
October 5, 1882, in Worcester, Massachusetts

Died:
August 10, 1945, in Baltimore, Maryland

OUR transportation systems use five internal combustion engines to move people or cargo. Two are named after their inventors, Rudolf Diesel and Felix Wankel. Of the remaining three—gasoline, gas turbine, and rocket—one was developed by an American. Robert Goddard fired the first successful liquid-fueled rocket on March 16, 1926, in Worcester, Massachusetts.

An only child, Goddard grew up in financially comfortable circumstances near Boston. His father was part owner of a small business that made industrial knives for textile and furrier companies. His mother had tuberculosis and was an invalid. Two books ignited his lifelong interest in rocketry: *The War of the Worlds* by H. G. Wells's and *From the Earth to the Moon* by Jules Verne. Both

had a great impact on Goddard's career choice. Goddard said that the books "gripped my imagination tremendously . . . and [the] means of accomplishing the physical marvels set forth kept me busy thinking." Goddard graduated from Worcester Polytechnic Institute and later earned a doctorate in physics from Clark University. With a firm background in science, he put his technical knowledge to work building rockets during a successful but sometimes lonely career.

Goddard spent his first year after college at Princeton University, working on the theory of rocket propulsion. He envisioned using a fuel of liquid hydrogen and liquid oxygen (LOX) as an oxidizer. (The Space Shuttle's three main inboard engines use the same propellants.) Then, Goddard developed tuberculosis. When doctors told him that he had only two weeks to live, he returned home to Worcester. There, Goddard slowly recovered. Working as little as one hour a day, he took out two patents during his period of convalescence. One covered three broad claims to rocketry. The first claim was combustion chamber and nozzle design. The second dealt with propellant flow into the combustion chamber. The third claim covered multistage rockets.

After his recovery, Goddard took a teaching position at Clark. He made efficiency tests on nozzle-equipped steel rockets fueled with powder, a solid propellant. In need of financial assistance, he applied to the Smithsonian Institution for a $5,000 grant. He sent with his application a 70-page document he had written, titled *A Method of Reaching Extreme Altitudes*. The Smithsonian had published it two years earlier, and Goddard used it to strengthen his request. The document outlined his test results and hinted at space flight with a rocket-powered craft. At the time, to the general public "space" meant the moon. Goddard was unfortunately labeled "the Moon Man" by the popular press. He was dumbfounded and unprepared for such undeserved sarcasm. Goddard considered himself a properly credentialed scientist who taught at a respected university—and his publication bore the Smithsonian's stamp of approval. Goddard received the Smithsonian grant, but the negative publicity caused him to distrust reporters forever.

World War I interrupted Goddard's space-flight work, and he put time into weapons development with associate Clarence Hickman. They built a small recoilless rocket that weighed 5 pounds and was fired from a tube 2" in diameter and just over 5' long. The military did not use the rocket in World War I, but eventually, during World War II, it saw use as the bazooka.

After World War I, Goddard returned again to Clark to continue his research. He abandoned solid propellant work in 1921. He correctly reasoned that liquid propellants were more suitable for space flight and concentrated on gasoline and LOX. He had trouble making pumps for the supercold -300° Fahrenheit LOX and used gas pressure to force propellants into the combustion chamber. Building a small supporting frame, he made a flight attempt on December 30, 1925, at a cousin's farm. Although the engine fired and trembled in its supports, it did not lift from the frame. Two more failures followed before Goddard's successful, noisy 1926 rocket rose 41' in the air and reached 60 mph. This was the first flight of a liquid-fueled rocket. Goddard's wife, Esther, took the picture shown at right of Goddard with his rocket. The exhaust nozzle was at the top, with the gasoline and LOX in the lower section.

Goddard continued static tests and sent up a larger rocket in 1929. The first instrument-carrying rocket, it carried a barometer, thermometer, and small camera. The engine fired for more than 18 seconds and made much more noise than Goddard's other rockets. After more unfavorable publicity, officials ordered Goddard to stop conducting tests in Massachusetts. Fortunately, Charles Lindbergh had an interest in

Goddard's work, and he convinced philanthropist Daniel Guggenheim to provide financial support. Goddard received a leave of absence from his teaching duties and moved his operation to Roswell, New Mexico, in 1930. He stayed there for most of the next decade.

Goddard conducted a total of 103 static tests and 38 successful launches with rockets that became steadily larger and more powerful. All of his last 26 rockets flew. His rockets attained speeds up to 550 mph and heights of 9,000'. Although he had four assistants, he was essentially a lone wolf who preferred to work on his own. His engines required higher propellant flow rates than pressurized tanks could provide. No one could build the turbine-driven high-speed

Robert Goddard with the world's first liquid-fueled rocket, just before firing in March 1929

pumps he needed, so Goddard made his own. To steer the rocket, he used a gyroscope-controlled, rudder-like device that deflected exhaust gas to one side or the other. Goddard's mind knew no bounds. He accumulated 214 patents, including ones for multistage rockets, planetary landing tech-

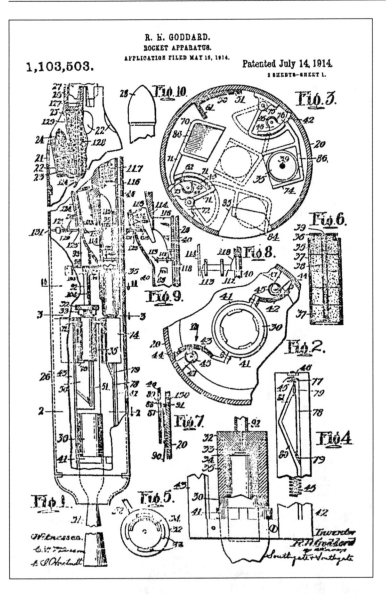

Goddard's rocket patents were quite detailed.

went back to solid-fueled units. Unlike the American government during the 1930s, Germany showed considerable interest in Goddard's work. It built the liquid-fueled V-2 rocket with technology that originated in Roswell, New Mexico. The V-2 carried a 2,200-pound warhead to targets in England and other countries. Germany built more than 5,000 of the long-range V-2s. After World War II, the surviving V-2s became the foundation of the U.S. space program.

Goddard was a dreamer with a sense of destiny, who reread *The War of the Worlds* at Christmastime every year. He died in 1945 in Baltimore, near the army's missile-testing site at Aberdeen. *The New York Times* belatedly published a retraction of the mocking editorial about Goddard that it had published many years earlier. The retraction was printed July 17, 1969, when the American Apollo XI spacecraft was on its way to making humanity's first moon landing. The Apollo spacecraft was lifted from Earth by a three-stage Saturn V booster rocket that burned liquid propellants. If the space age could be said to have started with one person, that person was clearly Robert Goddard.

References and Resources

History of Rocketry and Space Travel by Wernher Von Braun, Thomas Y. Crowell Publishers, 1966.

Robert Goddard—Space Pioneer by Anne Perkins Dewey, Little, Brown, and Co., 1962.

"The Dream of Yesterday Is the Reality of Tomorrow" by Roger Bruns and Bryan Kennedy, in *American History Illustrated*, Summer 1989.

"God Pity a One-Dream Man" by Richard Rhodes, in *American Heritage*, June/July 1980.

Dictionary of American Biography, Charles Scribner's Sons Publishers, 1932; with supplemental updates.

National Cyclopedia of American Biography, James T. White and Co. Publishers, 1891; with supplemental updates.

McGraw-Hill Encyclopedia of Biography, McGraw-Hill Publishers, 1973.

Asimov's Biographical Encyclopedia of Science and Technology by Isaac Asimov, Doubleday & Co. Publishers, 1964.

niques, and reentry. So complete was his investigation of rocket-powered flight, that no rocket today lifts off anywhere in the world without using one or more devices originally patented by Goddard. Almost single-handedly, Goddard developed rocketry from a vague dream to a dynamic branch of modern technology.

During World War II, the army asked Goddard to work on liquid propellants for rocket-assisted takeoff (RATO) units on airplanes. However, Goddard's experience was in long-range rockets and the RATO work wasted his talents. His heart was not in the project, and the rockets with which he experimented never worked well. The army

Lloyd Raymond Smith

HIGH factory production rates are certainly not a modern development. In 1921, a fully automatic American factory was making automobile frames at the rate of one every eight seconds. The factory's automatic riveting machines strongly resembled modern robotic welders. The groundwork for this plant was laid by Charles Smith, who emigrated from England and opened a Milwaukee machine shop in 1874. He financed his shop with money that he had saved from his work as a machinist. Twenty years later, Smith was the world's largest supplier of bicycle parts. Following a series of corporate reorganizations, his son Arthur Oliver Smith formed the A. O. Smith Co. in 1904. However, it was Charles's grandson Lloyd Raymond Smith who was most responsible for the success of the family business. Under his direction, the A. O. Smith Co. went on to develop the first fully automatic automobile frame factory. It was the only one of its kind in the world. Smith's employees called it "the Mechanical Marvel."

Arthur Oliver Smith was born near Milwaukee in 1859. With his two older brothers, he helped his father expand the C. J. Smith and Sons Co. After spending several years in the building contracting business, he joined his father in 1896. Arthur had shown some business sense and was the one most responsible for the company branching out into making tubular bicycle frames. He developed the technology to manufacture brazed steel tubing after repairing a small stand for a shoe manufacturer. The manufacturing equipment was designed and built under Arthur's supervision. The tubes the Smiths produced were much lighter and stronger than the solid iron that many bicycle manufacturers used. Having good products to offer, a pleasant personal-

A.O. Smith Automotive Products Co.

Born:
August 21, 1883, in Chicago, Illinois

Died:
December 22, 1944, in Milwaukee, Wisconsin

ity, and a positive outlook on life all helped Arthur to secure large orders. The company also prospered because of the bicycle's enormous popularity. Bicycles were cheap, fast, and fun. In 1897, four million people regularly rode bicycles in America.

Charles liked bicycles and rode one almost every day from his home to the company on Clinton Street. Even though he was president of the company, he carried his lunch to work in his jacket pocket. When Charles sold the business to another bicycle manufacturer, Arthur remained as manager. His two oldest sons, George and Charles, Jr., left the family business to form independent companies. A few years later, in 1904, Arthur bought back the company and changed its name to the A. O. Smith Co. That was the same year his father died.

With the company's background in making metal tubes for bicycle frames, Arthur investigated the possibility of manufacturing bent metal automobile frames. The solid structural metal used in cars was quite heavy and wooden frames wore out quickly. A. O. Smith Co. made the first American-built pressed steel frames for the Peerless Motor Car Co. in 1902. Orders soon arrived from Cadillac, Packard, Locomobile, Waverly Electric, and other automobile

A.O. Smith Automotive Products Co.

The heart of the automatic frame plant were the air-operated riveters. Looking like huge birds, they were officially known as Smith Type C Riveting Presses. Note the slotted floor that allow the riveters to be repositioned for different frame shapes.

manufacturers. The company made frames for Cadillac starting in 1903 and ending in 1990 when Cadillac cars no longer used separate frames. The Smith-Cadillac connection was one of the longest supplier-com-

pany relationships in U.S. automotive history.

Henry Ford traveled to Milwaukee in 1906 to talk with Smith about a contract for his Model N automobile. Ford wanted 10,000 frames in four months—an almost impossible request. Ford wanted to discuss it face to face with Smith. The contract would require producing about 100 frames every working day, while Smith's factory was at the time making only 10 to 12 frames per day. Nonetheless, Smith agreed. Since he could not manufacture thousands of frames so rapidly using existing technology, he completely retooled his factory. Smith built a new frame assembly line, and Ford received his order on schedule.

Smith's company prospered and moved to a new building on 27th Street in Milwaukee, where it built frames for 39 automobile companies. The customers included Fiat in Italy and Austin in England. Smith's new factory was among the first to have safe, brick-enclosed stair wells. It also had fire walls and many fire-hose stations. In 1905, Arthur's son, Lloyd Raymond Smith, left his engineering studies after three years at the University of Wisconsin to join the company as an apprentice. Employees commonly called him L. R., and his family called him Ray. He worked at many jobs over the years and became the company's president following his father's death in 1913.

Annual U.S. automobile production stood at 1.5 million in 1916. L. R. saw the need to make more frames for less money, to keep the company in business. He told his engineers to design a completely automatic plant. He wanted a factory that would take sheet steel and automatically cut, shape, and fasten it.

The plant was designed on paper 10 times, and an 84-page related patent was issued in 1921. It took six years, $8 million, and a new 129,000-square-foot building to ready the production line for a test run in May 1921. L. R. felt so nervous that later he could not remember whether he or an associate had thrown the switch to start the machinery. Uncut sheet steel entered the beginning of the line and went through 552 separate mechanical operations. Once in-process frames filled the line, a finished frame emerged from the line's end every eight seconds. On its first day, the line operated for just under two hours before operators shut it down because it had consumed all the available raw material. Two city blocks long, the line had five basic sections: cutting and shaping, side bar assembly, crossbar assembly, final assembly, and painting. It was because of its complexity and well-ordered operation that the employees called it the "Mechanical Marvel."

Chain-driven carriages transported the in-process frames. Air-operated nailing guns received rivets from hoppers in the floor and rapidly shot them into drilled holes. The rivets were formed in the jaws of riveting machines that resembled the open beaks of huge birds. Air pressure closed the jaws, fastening each rivet with 20 tons of force. Each automobile frame used about 100 rivets. The riveting machines were adjustable, and a specially slotted floor allowed repositioning them for different frames. It took only 6 to 12 hours for the 200 employees to change dies and reset tooling for a different run. Production soon reached 10,000 per day, and the A. O. Smith Co. produced better frames at lower cost. The company was the world's largest frame manufacturer, making more than all its competitors combined.

The layout of the production line was strikingly similar to that found in modern factories. The adjustable riveting machines resembled industrial robots. Another simi-larity to current factories was the ability to shut down the entire line from any workstation. In operation until June 1958, the A. O. Smith Automatic Frame Plant was designated a National Historic Mechanical Engineering Landmark in 1979 by the American Society of Mechanical Engineers. A. O. and L. R. Smith were both inducted into the Automotive Hall of Fame in 1988.

L. R. was strongly civic minded, and he established a private vocational school that eventually became part of the Milwaukee public school system. He also financed the 50-bed Columbia Hospital and Milwaukee's Children Hospital. He served on numerous boards of directors. As was the case with both his father and grandfather, L. R. had outside interests that included music, reading, and fishing.

References and Resources

Automatic Assembly—The Next Manufacturing Development by A. W. Redlin, assistant works manager. (Reprinted from *Factory and Industrial Management*, January 1929, and provided courtesy of A. O. Smith Co., Milwaukee, WI.)

10,000 Automobile Frames a Day, May 1979. (Provided by A. O. Smith Co., Milwaukee, WI.)

From Rivets to Atoms, undated. (Provided by A. O. Smith Co., Milwaukee, WI.)

Clessie Lyle Cummins

Courtesy of C. Lyle Cummins, Jr.

Clessie Cummins in 1930, at age 42

Born:
December 27, 1888, in Honey Creek, Indiana

Died:
August 19, 1968, in Sausalito, California

RUDOLPH Diesel invented the compression-ignition engine in 1894 in Augsburg, Germany. Shortly afterward, a U.S. citizen, Clessie Lyle Cummins, established a reputation as one the world's best diesel engine developers. He manufactured engines primarily for trucks and boats, and he had 33 patents to his credit. Cummins put diesel engines on American highways in 1932. That was when the first commercial U.S. diesel-powered truck delivered food to stores in California's San Joaquin Valley. Built in 1920, Cummins's first engine was a horizontal desk-sized single-cylinder 6 hp stationary engine intended for farm use. However, Cummins aspired to be the first to use the diesel engine in road transportation.

Cummins spent time around machinery from an early age, because his father operated a barrel-making factory. At the time, wooden barrel hoops were made from elm. Having a nearby supply required frequent family moves. Frustrated by having to change school many times, Cummins completed only elementary school. However, his education didn't end at the eighth grade. He remained an avid reader his entire life and continued to educate himself.

Cummins became a machine shop apprentice and then worked as an inspector for Marmon Automobile Co. in Indianapolis. He was often pressured to allow questionable automobiles to pass inspection. Cummins left to work for W. G. Irwin, the leading banker in Columbus, Indiana. He served as chauffeur and mechanic for the Irwin family's Packard. Thus began a life-long friendship between Cummins and three generations of the Irwin family.

At 22, Cummins decided to take an adventurous boat trip with a brother-in-law. They planned a journey down the Ohio and Mississippi Rivers in a homemade 16' boat equipped with a 4 hp gasoline engine. The spark-ignition engine caused so many problems that Cummins returned thinking about producing small diesel engines for boats. Diesels are compression-ignition engines that use the heat of air compressed by the piston to ignite kerosene fuel. Early designs were also known as "oil engines."

Irwin agreed to provide the necessary financial backing for a machine shop that would do contract work while Cummins worked on his project. With World War I in progress, the bulk of their early income came from making gun parts for the army. After the war, Cummins founded the Cummins Engine Co. in an old cereal mill. Using inexpensive second-rate industrial machinery, the company specialized in the manufacture of low-horsepower, high-speed diesel engines. This was quite a technical undertaking since Cummins's competitors were building engines about the size of a small bedroom. Many textbooks at the time authoritatively stated that 600 rpm was the highest possible rotating speed. Experts considered that the limit for proper burning to take place in the combustion chamber.

Cummins proved the textbooks wrong and built engines for shrimp boats and yacht-sized river boats, as well as for stationary power uses. Among his innovations was the development of an improved fuel-injection system. His company was the first U.S. high-speed diesel manufacturer to design and build its own fuel system. Many early diesels used a blast of compressed air to force fuel into the engine. Cummins always used more reliable mechanical methods. He tested more than 3,000 different designs over a four-year period. Most of his patents were for improved fuel-injection systems. His one- to six-cylinder engines were rated from 1-l/2 hp to about 100 hp, at 800 rpm to 2,200 rpm. Cummins made the first diesel with totally enclosed working parts. The U.S. Lighthouse Bureau, one of his first customers, bought four-cylinder engines to generate electrical power.

While demonstrating an experimental engine installed in a boat on the Ohio River, Cummins once ran out of fuel several miles downstream from his destination. He knew that the fuel line extended up a short distance from the bottom of the tank to keep water out of the pump. He cautiously added a small amount of water to raise the fuel level, started the

engine and continued on to home port. The next day, a Chicago newspaper mistakenly reported that the new engine operated on water!

The Cummins's company had come close to profitability when the Great Depression destroyed its traditional markets. Irwin told Cummins on December 15, 1929, that the company would have to close its doors on January 1. Acting quickly, Cummins decided to enter the road transportation market. Within only a few days, he placed a huge four-cylinder, 1,200-pound, 50 hp marine engine in a 1925 Packard limousine. The Packard was the largest secondhand car Cummins could find on short notice. His creation was the first U.S. diesel-powered automobile, and Cummins drove it to the

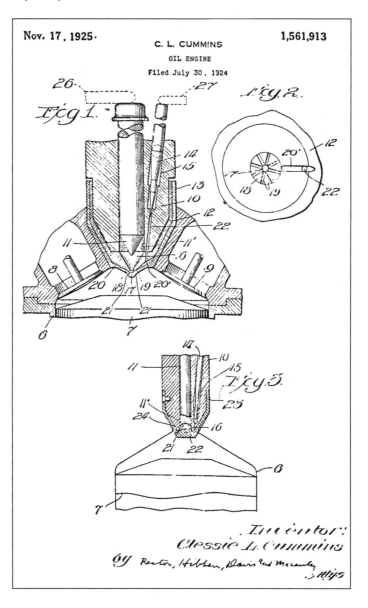

Many of Cummins's patents dealt with fuel injection systems for diesel engines. During the 1920s, injection systems were changing from the use of compressed air to mechanical techniques.

New York Automobile Show. He left Indianapolis on January 4 and arrived January 6 at 3:37 P.M. Cummins averaged 26.4 mpg and his fuel cost only $1.38—which made for good publicity during the Great Depression. That act of desperation saved Cummins's company.

Cummins initiated a series of spectacular demonstrations during what is called his "Barnum and Bailey Days." He spent five strenuous years of circus-like exploits with race cars, trucks, buses, and automobiles. He set speed, endurance, and economy records to prove the capabilities of the diesel engine for road transportation. For example, he personally established the first official diesel speed record of 80.36 mph in 1930 at Daytona Beach, Florida. He drove a loaded truck from coast to coast in 1931 using only $11.22 worth of fuel. To publicize engine durability, Cummins and another person completed a remarkable 14,600-mile nonstop two-week drive around the Indianapolis 500 track. One of his diesel engines was in the nonstop race car that finished twelfth in the 1930 Indianapolis 500 Mile Race. For such ventures, he typically used a four-stroke, six-cylinder, 125 hp, 1,500 rpm truck engine. It became his most popular production model.

The physical and emotional strain of keeping his company going through three near collapses that occurred during the introduction of diesel-powered trucks was quite severe. Cummins took a year off, and he eventually left company operations to others. He later spent World War II as director of the Internal Combustion Engine Division of the War Production Board, for which he was paid $1 per year. He never cashed the paychecks.

Cummins moved to California during the 1950s and opened a small shop near his home. During that period, he and his youngest son developed the Jacobs engine brake retarder. It converted a truck engine into an air compressor for downhill speed control. Because of complicated personal and financial relationships, it was named for the Jacobs Manufacturing Co. That company is the world's largest manufacturer of drill chucks. The first production retarders left the factory in 1961. The American Society of Mechanical Engineers declared the Jacobs retarder a National Historic Mechanical Engineering Landmark in 1985.

At the time of Cummins's death, diesel engines powered more than 60 percent of heavy-duty trucks in the U.S. To honor Cummins's contribution to developing high-speed diesel engines, the Society of Automotive engineers posthumously awarded him its coveted Horning Memorial Award.

References and Resources

C. Lyle Cummins, Jr., personal correspondence.

Internal Fire by C. Lyle Cummins, Jr., Society of Automotive Engineers Press, 1989.

Diesels from the Woodshed by C. Lyle Cummins, Jr., Society of Automotive Engineers, April 1970.

"Clessie Cummins, Imagineer" by C. Lyle Cummins, Jr., in *Diesel Car Digest*, First Quarter 1978.

Cummins Engine Company, Inc.—History, Cummins Engine Co., Columbus, IN, October 1980.

Newsweek, 2 September 1968 (page 57); short obituary.

New York Times, 20 August 1968 (page 41); short obituary.

SAE Update, 15 October 1988, Society of Automotive Engineers.

Igor Ivanovich Sikorsky

Smithsonia Institution Photo No. 78-16302

Born:
May 25, 1889, in Kiev, Ukraine

Died:
October 28, 1972, in Easton, Connecticut

LEONARDO da Vinci's expansive technical mind led him to be the first to analyze the helicopter. However, 500 years ago, da Vinci could never have made a full-size model that worked. Helicopters are aerodynamically complex and require powerful lightweight engines. Over the years, many people had tried to build one, and some met with minor success. But it was Igor Sikorsky who built the first practical and controllable helicopter in 1939. Wearing his trademark fedora hat, he made the first flight and many later ones in the VS-300.

Sikorsky was born in the Ukraine. His father was a respected doctor of psychology, who provided a comfortable life for his family. Sikorsky was a weak child. Because he was subject to hemorrhages, his parents kept him from playing outdoors with other children. He spent his free time reading about the inventions of da Vinci and the Wright Brothers. He developed an interest in aviation that continued throughout his long life.

Sikorsky graduated from the Kiev Institute of Technology in 1908 and went to work at the aviation factory of the Russian Baltic Car Works. In those days, people considered anything that rose from the earth something of a success. One of Sikorsky's coworkers made a comment that he remembered all his life: "To invent a flying machine is nothing. To build a flying machine is little. To make a flying machine fly is everything." During his spare time in 1909, Sikorsky tried to build his first helicopter. Sponsored by a loan from his sister Olga, it was powered by an Anzani three-cylinder 25 hp engine. The helicopter had two rotors that turned in opposite directions, one above the other. It vibrated badly and never showed any sign of lifting from the ground. Sikorsky left helicopter work and spent the next 30 years working on fixed-wing aircraft. He designed his first biplane, the S-1, shortly after his first attempts with the helicopter. It proved unsuccessful.

Just before World War I, Sikorsky worked for the Russian government on bomber aircraft. He succeeded in designing and building the world's first four-engine aircraft in 1913. Because of its size, he named it *Le Grand*. He personally piloted the airplane during its first flight. With an enclosed cabin for the pilot, the 9,000-pound biplane had a huge 92' wingspan. It had four engines paired back to back. The airplane was the prototype for 75 giant bombers that Sikorsky's company manufactured for the army.

With the beginning of the Russian revolution in 1917 and the resulting great disruption to society, Sikorsky decided to leave his homeland. He moved to the United States, where he saw more opportunities for technical trailblazers. He was disappointed to find the American aircraft industry in a state of decline, and he could not locate a job. After World War I ended, there was no need for military airplanes, and commercial aviation was just entering its infancy. Sikorsky barely kept himself alive by privately teaching mathematics and other subjects to other recent immigrants. He joined a Russian science group and in 1923 used a $1,000 loan from the group to organize his own company. Also through the group, he met his wife, Elizabeth Semion.

Sikorsky's fabric-covered VS-300 is displayed at the Smithsonian's National Air and Space Museum. It was the first practical helicopter. The display includes the hat Sikorsky wore when piloting his helicopter.

He used an old chicken house on Long Island for his office and factory. Sikorsky shopped in junkyards to locate materials for use in constructing an experimental airplane. Sikorsky and 14 part-time employees built the twin-engine S-29A ("A" for America) biplane outdoors. When he ran out of money, Sikorsky used the partly built airplane to persuade others to invest in his company. Several employees climbed on board for the maiden flight. Too kindhearted to remove them, Sikorsky nearly met with disaster when the overloaded and underpowered airplane lost height and crashed. Undeterred, Sikorsky and his employees rebuilt the plane and replaced its engines with recently overhauled eight-cylinder Liberty engines. The subsequent success of the experimental S-29A put Sikorsky's young company on its feet. Its first income was $500 earned for transporting two pianos from New York to Washington, D.C. The 14-passenger production S-29 cruised at 100 mph and was the first twin-engine airplane that could fly with only one engine operating.

Sikorsky went on to build popular flying boats for Pan American World Airways. His 1927 S-38 carried 10 passengers at 130 mph. Ten different airlines used Sikorsky planes, and they pioneered airline travel routes to Central America. Business was so good that Sikorsky opened a large plant in Stratford, Connecticut. His much larger S-40 was the original long-range clipper that inaugurated regular scheduled air service between North and South America. Charles Lindbergh piloted the plane's first flight in 1929. With four 575 hp Pratt & Whitney Aircraft engines, it carried 40 passengers up to 700 miles between fuelings at 115 mph. Pan Am asked Sikorsky to build a super clipper, and the result was the S-42. It had a 3,000-mile range at 150 mph and made the first sched-

National Air and Space Museum

In 1940, Connecticut commissioner of aeronautics Lester Morris presented Sikorsky (in pilot's seat) with the first official license to pilot a helicopter in America.

uled crossings of the north Atlantic. For years, the still larger S-44 held the record for the fastest flight to Europe. Sikorsky's flying boats were in demand, and his company prospered during the 1930s. Yet, the helicopter was always in the back of his mind.

Sikorsky knew that many talented people had attempted to construct a practical helicopter and failed. Although he had not built one in years, he filed for a patent in 1931 and received it in 1935. He led the design team at his company, the Vought-Sikorsky Division of United Aircraft Corp. The VS-300 had a single three-blade main rotor that was 28' in diameter. A four-cylinder 75 hp Franklin air-cooled engine provided power. Five V-belts carried power from the engine to a transmission that used truck gears. The transmission shaft connected directly to the main rotor. A small single-blade vertical rotor at the tail kept the body from spinning with the main rotor.

Chains held the VS-300 near the ground for safety during flight testing. Sikorsky made the first jerky 10-second flight in 1939. The *Ugly Duckling*, as the helicopter was nicknamed, rose only a few feet from the ground. Each week's work brought new adjustments or modified parts. On May 15, 1940, the helicopter made its first unchained controllable free ascent. The experimental vehicle had just three instruments, all for the engine: oil pressure gauge, cylinder head temperature indicator, and tachometer. Its top speed was 50 mph.

A true flight pioneer, Sikorsky survived several crashes. In one particularly dramatic one, a helicopter's tail support broke and the small vertical rotor stopped. The helicopter rolled over and hit the ground sideways in a mass of wreckage. As in all his crashes, Sikorsky walked away with only minor cuts and bruises. Based on the VS-300's experimental flights, the government placed an order for R-4 helicopters to be used for rescue duties. The R-4 was the world's first production helicopter and 131 were manufactured.

Near the end of his life, Sikorsky felt certain that the helicopter's commercial potential had yet to be realized. He saw the VS-300 as an intercity carrier and all-purpose workhorse. General Jimmy Doolittle once

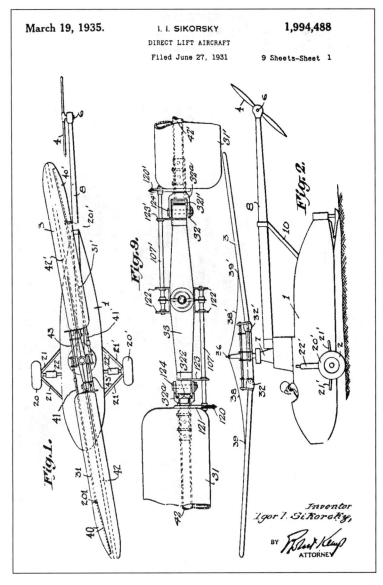

A drawing from an early Sikorsky helicopter patent

said, "Igor Sikorsky is a genius. His life and character exemplify those basic virtues and values which in today's complex society are sometimes forgotten. He is a gentle person who instinctively does the right thing."

References and Resources

The Story of the Winged-S by Igor Sikorsky, Dodd, Mead and Co., 1938.

Sky Pioneer—The Story of Igor I. Sikorsky by Robert Bartlett, Charles Scribner's Sons, 1947.

All about Helicopters by Jean Ross Howard, Sports Car Press, 1969.

McGraw-Hill Encyclopedia of Biography, McGraw-Hill Publishers, 1973.

Vladimir Kosma Zworykin

Smithsonian Institution Photo No. 79-11567

Born:
July 30, 1889,
in Murom,
Russia

Died:
July 29, 1982,
in Princeton,
New Jersey

TELEVISION may currently be the world's most influential media form. It has been with us since the National Broadcasting Co. (NBC) established the first regular U.S. telecasts in 1939. Like many electronic innovations, television has no clear-cut single inventor. But one American stands out as the person whose achievements were pivotal to television's development. He held more than 120 patents. His best known are patents for the iconoscope camera tube (*icon* means "image") and the kinescope picture tube (*kine* means "motion"). Russian-born Vladimir Zworykin's contributions were so important that he is often described as the inventor of television—a title he always rejected.

Zworykin was born in a small town 200 miles east of Moscow near the Oka River. His father owned and operated a fleet of river boats, and the young Zworykin helped him during school vacations. He learned basic electricity on river journeys by reading books and making observations. He eagerly repaired electrical equipment. He obviously had greater interest in electricity than in shipping.

After graduating from high school in Murom in 1906, he decided to study electrical engineering at the St. Petersburg Institute of Technology. This new environment was quite a change for a young man raised in the countryside. St. Petersburg was the second-largest city in Russia, a cultural center, and about 700 miles from Zworykin's home. He almost immediately met Professor Boris von Rosing, who was working on transmitting pictures by wire. Von Rosing was the first person to attempt transmission of an image by scanning the inside of a cathode-ray tube. He freely allowed Zworykin to assist him in his research. He felt that the future of television lay in the cathode-ray tube—not in the mechanical systems being investigated by others. Zworykin spent much of his time with von Rosing blowing glass to form photocells and amplifying tubes. He learned much during his years at the institute and stayed on after graduation as an assistant for a few more months. Zworykin then went to Paris and assisted in X-ray experiments until the outbreak of World War I.

Zworykin made his way back to Russia and joined the Russian Signal Corps. He served until 1918, much of the time working on wireless transmission equipment near the Polish border. The Russian Revolution followed on the heels of the world war, plunging Zworykin's country into chaos. He wandered for months to avoid arrest by competing armies. Finally, he made his way to the northern port city of Archangel. Pleading his case to an American official, he received a visa. He sailed to London and then on to New York, arriving in the United States in 1919.

Zworykin first took work as a bookkeeper for the financial agent of the Russian Embassy in Washington, D.C. He moved to Westinghouse Electric and Manufacturing Co.'s research labs in Pittsburgh the following year. On his first assignment there, he worked on new radio tubes and photoelectric cells. He went to the University of Pittsburgh at night, earning a doctorate in 1926. He had become an American citizen in 1924, the same year that he first demonstrated a television system.

Zworykin had applied for a patent the previous year for his iconoscope, or television transmitting tube. He showed Westinghouse executives the first flickering images from his experimental system. His method differed from the cumbersome mechanical system of whirling perforated disks that had dominated early television development. Of the demonstration, Zworykin later said, "I was terribly excited and proud. After a few days I was informed, very politely, that my demonstration had been extremely interesting. But it might be better if I spent my time

on something a little more useful." The same year, he patented his kinescope, or television receiving tube. The two components set the stage for a practical television transmitting and receiving system.

Unable to convince Westinghouse executives of the value of his inventions, Zworykin moved to the Radio Corporation of America (RCA) in 1929. He became director of its electronic research laboratory in Camden, New Jersey. Company president David Sarnoff encouraged Zworykin to develop the equipment necessary to make television practical. Himself a Russian immigrant from Minsk, Sarnoff provided Zworykin with everything he requested. In November, Zworykin demonstrated the first practical and completely electronic television system at a convention of the Institute of Radio Engineers. Over the next 20 years, RCA spent $50 million—a huge amount of money—perfecting a television system.

Zworykin and his staff worked diligently on the project. Their main concern was electronic sensitivity. They continually worked on producing more sensitive iconoscopes and kinescopes. For all its refinements, the modern television picture tube remains es-

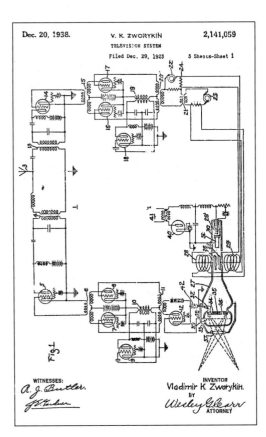

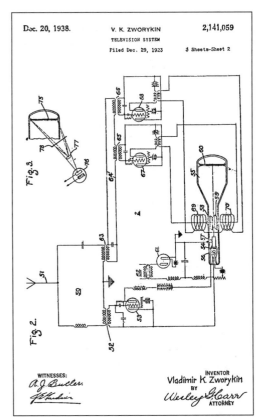

First two pages of drawings for Zworykin's television system patent. His design included both a transmitter (camera) and receiver (television). It was the first successful all-electronic system.

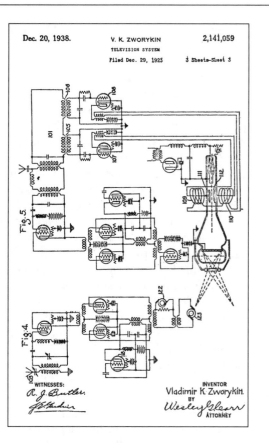

Final page of the television system patent drawings

Dec. 20, 1938.   V. K. ZWORYKIN   2,141,059
                            TELEVISION SYSTEM
                        Filed Dec. 29, 1925   3 Sheets-Sheet 3

WITNESSES:

                                                    INVENTOR
                                            Vladimir K. Zworykin.
                                                    BY
                                            Wesley Glenn
                                                    ATTORNEY

sentially the kinescope that Zworykin patented in 1924. RCA installed television sets in 150 New York City area homes in 1936 and began experimental telecasts. Felix the Cat, a popular cartoon character of the time, was the first image broadcast. NBC, a division of RCA, established regular telecasts in 1939.

Zworykin's other accomplishments included a color picture tube patent he took out in 1929. Using his knowledge of photoelectric tubes and image multipliers, he developed a rifle scope that allowed soldiers in World War II to see in the dark. Zworykin developed an electric eye that operated electric switches and automatically opened doors. He made vastly superior detector tubes for measuring radioactivity. He also worked on early computers. The photograph on page 202 shows him holding an experimental data-storage tube.

After the television system, Zworykin's next-most-important work was with the electron microscope. The microscope was his idea, though he and James Hillier worked on it as a team during the early 1940s. Instead of focusing an image of reflected light with lenses, electron microscopes focus electrons with electromagnetic fields. Zworykin and Hillier reduced the microscope's size from an experimental device that almost filled two rooms to a 16" portable model. Electron microscopes magnified as much as 200,000 times, while optical microscopes had a limit of 2,500. Their improvement allowed researchers to identify such incredibly small things as metallic grain structure or viruses.

Zworykin retired from RCA in 1954, but he kept an office at the RCA laboratories. He never wanted to retire from technology. Zworykin was a humanist and was keenly aware that inventions do not automatically serve the public interest. He wanted to stay involved so that he could express his opinions. What free time he did have went to his favorite pastimes of swimming, tennis, and woodworking. He and his wife, Katherine, kept an open house for their 5 children and 17 grandchildren. The younger people passed in and out of the Zworykin's Princeton home with erratic frequency. Zworykin died of natural causes the day before he turned 93.

In 1966, President Lyndon Johnson awarded Zworykin the National Medal of Science, America's highest scientific honor. It was the most significant of the 27 major awards he received, which included several honorary doctorates. A modest person with a well-developed sense of humor, Zworykin coauthored many books. They included *Television* (1940) and *Electron Optics and the Electron Microscope* (1945). He once said that his response to the statement "It can't be done" would always be "Want to make a bet?"

References and Resources

Those Inventive Americans, National Geographic Society, 1971.

American Science and Invention by Mitchell Wilson, Bonanza Books, 1960.

McGraw-Hill Encyclopedia of Biography, McGraw-Hill Publishers, 1973.

Asimov's Biographical Encyclopedia of Science and Technology by Isaac Asimov, Doubleday & Co. Publishers, 1964.

Vannevar Bush

IN selecting a radio station, adjusting a microwave oven, or checking time on a wristwatch, people often read numbers from a digital display. By contrast, some radios, ovens, and watches have just a few numbers permanently in place on a dial face. With an *analog* wristwatch, for example, you determine time by the position of the two hands. While analog wristwatches use position to arrive at a time, digital watches use counting. Computers can also be classified as either digital or analog. Digital computers use input from keyboards. Analog computers operate with input of quantities of things such as voltage or speed. Heating-system thermostats and speedometers work on this principle. All analog computers descend directly from the first one built by the lanky Vannevar Bush in 1930.

The grandson of a whaling-ship captain and the son of a minister, Bush attended Tufts College, where he earned two degrees in engineering. He received his first patent while he was still in school. It was for a profile tracer, a surveying machine that measured elevations as a bicycle-tired device rolled along the ground. The machine included servomechanisms and other components that Bush would later use in his analog computer. Bush so impressed his instructors with his profile tracer that they granted him a college degree based on the invention's complexity. After graduation, he took a $14-per-week job testing machinery for the General Electric Co. in Schenectady, New York. After a suspicious fire destroyed some equipment, the company suspected foul play. It fired several employees, including Bush.

Bush served in the U.S. Navy during World War I, conducting research on submarine detection. He also worked at a few

Smithsonian Institution

Born:
March 11,
1890, in
Everett,
Massachusetts

Died:
June 28, 1974,
in Belmont,
Massachusetts

other jobs before moving to the Massachusetts Institute of Technology (MIT), where he spent most of his professional career. Besides teaching at MIT, Bush served as the institute's dean of engineering from 1932 to 1938. He also acted as a consultant to many companies. He was a brilliant investigator and organizer. He founded several successful companies, including, with two other persons, the Raytheon Corp., which now employs more than 76,000 persons.

Bush was particularly interested in problems associated with electrical power transmission. His investigations led him to think about the value of a calculating device that could solve complex problems. While working to eliminate blackouts, Bush managed to solve one particularly complex problem. It took him several months. To shorten the time required for necessary calculations, Bush invented his computer in 1930, calling it a *differential analyzer*. Because he was so busy at the time, he did not patent the computer. The paperwork involved seemed too troublesome.

Bush was a highly intelligent person who was rather colorfully described as a "reedy

ware to use those concepts. He took several years to invent his totally mechanical analog computer. It used motor-driven shafts and gears to multiply, divide, and solve complicated problems. The heart of his inven-

Bush (at left in photo) worked with several colleagues at MIT to build, test, and regularly operate his analog computer. Inputs and outputs used tracings on the tables in the photograph.

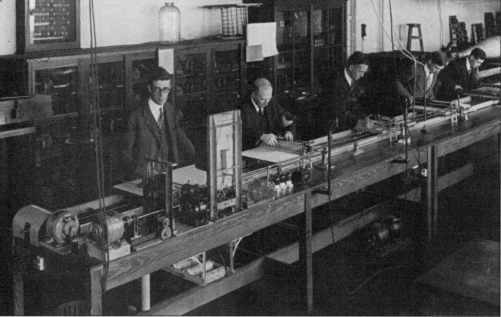

Smithsonian Institution Photo No. 58197

plain-spoken New Englander with a rustic grin and cracker-barrel drawl that concealed a mind of whiplash speed." With his expansive intellect, he could understand abstract mathematical concepts and visualize hard-

One of the six integrators used on Vannevar Bush's 1930 analog computer

tion was a disk rotated by an electric motor. A wheel rolled on top of the disk in much the same way that a phonograph needle tracks the surface of a record. The wheel's speed changed as it moved closer to the center of the disk. Bush called the disk an integrator, and he used six of them in his analog computer. The photograph at right shows one.

Long shafts interconnected six integrators and several small gear boxes. Like many other prototypes, the assembly was crude. It resembled something created using a huge Erector set. The photograph above shows Bush, at the far left, working on his computer in 1929. The other four men are working on the input/output tables, which resembled drafting tables. The computer was not easy to use and programming it took up to two days. Three or four people were stationed at the tables. They continually observed and adjusted input pointers to keep them on track. At the output tables, other operators made notations and recorded the graphical results. The output was not digital—it appeared only as graphs or lines on a piece of paper. Interpreting the results took great skill.

Bush's analog computer was quite influential in the technical community. It offered an impressive demonstration of the computational power of machines. Because the computer was a mechanical device, it was not 100 percent accurate. It typically achieved 98 percent accuracy—a level that was quite acceptable for technical calculations in 1930. Not knowing exactly how to describe the computer to average people, some experts described it as a "mathematical robot."

The U.S. Ballistics Research Laboratory in Maryland and the University of Pennsylvania each wanted one of the computers. Contracts were signed and two 20'-long analog computers were completed in 1935. They were the first contract-built computers in the world. Much more elaborate computers were constructed at MIT over the next 15 years. At present, analog computers are used in flight simulators to teach pilots to fly airplanes, in hospitals to monitor patients, and in industrial process control.

Besides the analog computer, Bush also invented a network analyzer to test the ability of power systems to perform under heavy loads. He modified vacuum tubes and produced new gaseous conduction devices. Once, when asked how many patents he had, Bush replied, "20 or 30."

Bush was an excellent organizer who served in several administrative capacities before, during, and after World War II. He was president of the multimillion-dollar Carnegie Foundation from 1939 to 1955. Between 1939 and 1941, he served as chair of the National Advisory Committee for Aeronautics, the predecessor to the National Aeronautics and Space Administration (NASA). He was also director of the Office of Scientific Research and Development from 1941 to 1946. In that position, he coordinated the wartime efforts of 25,000 science and technology workers involved with such complex projects as radar and atomic energy. After the war, he devoted his efforts to civilian control of atomic energy and to establishing the National Science Foundation in 1950.

There was also a light side to Bush's life, and he told some amusing stories in his 1970

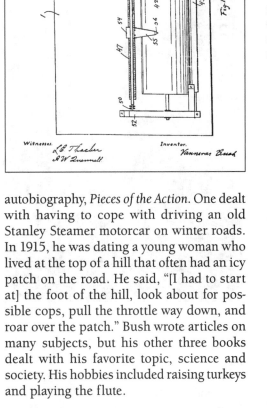

Bush's first patent was granted when he was in college. It measured ground elevations with a servo mechanism.

autobiography, *Pieces of the Action*. One dealt with having to cope with driving an old Stanley Steamer motorcar on winter roads. In 1915, he was dating a young woman who lived at the top of a hill that often had an icy patch on the road. He said, "[I had to start at] the foot of the hill, look about for possible cops, pull the throttle way down, and roar over the patch." Bush wrote articles on many subjects, but his other three books dealt with his favorite topic, science and society. His hobbies included raising turkeys and playing the flute.

References and Resources

Pieces of the Action by Vannevar Bush, William Morrow Publishers, 1970.

The Computer from Pascal to Von Neumann by Herman H. Goldstine, Princeton University Press, 1972.

Standard and Poor's List of Corporations, 1990.

Asimov's Biographical Encyclopedia of Science and Technology by Isaac Asimov, Doubleday & Co. Publishers, 1964.

Natonal Cyclopedia of American Biography, James T. White and Co. Publishers, 1891; with supplemental updates.

Edwin Howard Armstrong

Smithsonian Institution Photo No. 43614

Born:
December 18, 1890, in New York, New York

Died:
February 1, 1954, in New York, New York

IF radio communication has an unsung hero, it is certainly Edwin Howard Armstrong. He single-handedly developed the superheterodyne circuit, the basis for 98 percent of all modern radio and television receivers. Armstrong also developed many other useful circuits, but he is best known as the inventor of static-free FM radio. His *frequency modulation* principle is used not only in radios and televisions, but also in telephones, radar, and spacecraft communication networks. Armstrong lived an active life filled with discovery, invention, financial success, court battles, and, ultimately, tragedy.

During his teenage years in Yonkers, New York, Armstrong was fascinated by the new technology of wireless communication. After reading Guglielmo Marconi's book *The Boy's Book of Invention*, he decided to be-

come an inventor in the field of radio. In his room—overlooking the Hudson River and filled with crystals, coils, condensers, and resistors—Armstrong busied himself experimenting with electrical circuits. While still a student at Yonkers High School, Armstrong built a 125-foot-high antenna on his family's lawn. He had no fear of heights, and he would often climb the tower to make adjustments or just for fun. After graduation, he commuted by motorcycle to Columbia University, where he eventually earned a degree in electrical engineering. One of his teachers was Michael Pupin, developer of the radio circuit that made possible tuning in just one radio station at a time.

Under Pupin's influence, Armstrong made his first significant discovery while he was still in college. While mountain climbing in Vermont in the summer of 1912, he devised a regenerative circuit for use with the new audion radio tube. Returning to complete his senior year, Armstrong built the circuit and found that it greatly improved radio reception. The circuit permitted hearing distant stations without the use of headphones. He filed for a patent, but World War I intervened before his circuit could gain wide acceptance.

Armstrong received a captain's commission in the U.S. Army Signal Corps and went to France. He worked on developing a system to detect enemy aircraft from the high-frequency pulses emitted by their spark plug firings. At first, the firing frequency was too high to permit easy reception. Armstrong developed a circuit that lowered the frequency and then amplified it. Using an antenna on the Eiffel Tower in Paris, his eight-tube superheterodyne circuit worked superbly. (*Heterodyne* refers to the mixing of radio signals.) Although Armstrong developed his system too late to play a role in the war, the superheterodyne circuit could be used in ordinary AM (*amplitude modulated*) radio receivers. When Armstrong returned home with the rank of major, the Institute of Radio Engineers (IRE) gave a dinner in his honor. The IRE awarded Armstrong its first Medal of Honor. The medal recognized his status as the foremost expert in his field.

Armstrong was known as Howard to his friends, and in adult life he was almost totally bald. He lost his hair following an illness during his overseas wartime service. After the war, he continued to work at a Columbia University laboratory on circuits that improved the sensitivity of radio receivers. His work brought him in contact with the Radio Corporation of America (RCA), which paid him quite well for his patent rights. He became a millionaire during the 1920s. He also dated the secretary of RCA's president. It may have been the young woman, Marion MacInnis, who inspired Armstrong to scale the WJZ transmitting tower, 450 feet above New York's 42nd Street, in May 1923. He posed for several photographs, without safety gear. That stunt got him barred from the RCA offices for several weeks, but he married MacInnis the following December. His wedding present to her was a suitcase-sized portable superheterodyne radio, the first ever made. The couple drove Armstrong's new Hispano-Suiza convertible to Florida for a honeymoon and lugged the radio to the beach for the benefit of reporters and photographers.

Armstrong continued to work on FM radio in his laboratory. As the decade wore on, he found himself trapped in a corporate war to control radio patents. RCA, Westinghouse, American Telephone & Telegraph, and others all aimed to build large corporations based on the patents of different individuals. With 60,000 homes using radios in 1922 and projections for rapid growth, there was a great deal of money at stake. The number of homes with radios boomed to 2.75 million in 1925 and 14 million in 1930. Armstrong became involved in complex court battles that dragged on for years. In 1934, after 12 years of litigation in one particularly important suit, the U.S. Supreme Court handed down a verdict against Armstrong. It was a heavy blow to

him and his supporters. Many people felt the members of the Supreme Court based their judgment on a misunderstanding of the technical facts. Armstrong offered to return his Medal of Honor to the IRE but the institute refused to accept it. In a further show of support, the Franklin Institute weighed all the technical evidence and awarded Armstrong the highest honor in U.S. science, the Franklin Medal. Throughout all the years of testimony, he continued his work to eliminate radio static.

During the early 1930s, practically everyone thought that frequency modulation was useless for communication. Nonetheless, Armstrong felt that FM was the only solution. He had already decided there was no way to eliminate static from conventional AM radio transmission. Since RCA had heavy investments in AM transmitters and receivers, company officials finally asked Armstrong to remove his equipment from the space RCA provided for him in the Empire State Building. He moved to a large apartment overlooking the East River and personally financed his continuing experiments with FM. He field tested his efforts in 1933 during a violent thunderstorm and received static-free high-fidelity sound from 80 miles away. On July 18, 1939, Armstrong began broadcasting from the world's first FM

Hall of History Foundation, Schenectady, NY

Edwin Armstrong demonstrates his FM radio system in 1939. William Baker (rear) was head of radio research at General Electric.

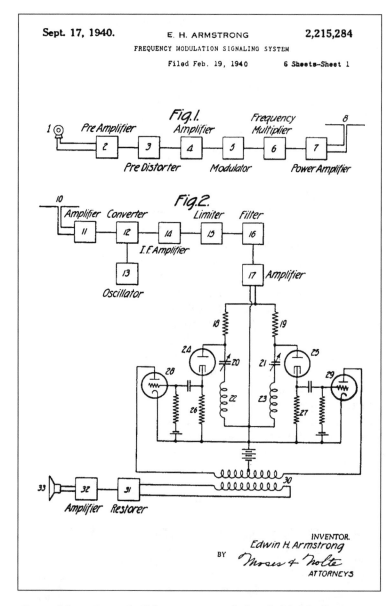

One of Armstrong's FM patents used simple block diagrams.

station, W2XMN, which he had built in Alpine, New Jersey, with his own money.

Once again, a war interrupted Armstrong's work. He spent World War II working on radar. After the war, RCA brought out its first FM receiver, which supposedly used a new circuit to eliminate static. The circuit was effective—and it was obviously an adaptation of Armstrong's patented circuit. Armstrong filed a suit against RCA. Although he was clearly in the right, he knew he couldn't win the legal battle. Regarding the situation, this man of few words said, "They will stall this along until I am dead or broke." RCA did stall, and Armstrong's legal fees steadily mounted. The financial and emotional strain proved more than he could bear. Armstrong took his own life in 1954.

Shortly after her husband's death, Armstrong's widow won $10 million in damages in 21 patent-infringement suits. The proceedings weren't completely closed until 1967, when the Supreme Court refused to review a lower court judgment against Motorola.

The International Telecommunications Union in Geneva, Switzerland, elected Armstrong to its roster of communication pioneers. His name appears with Marconi, Pupin, and Alexander Graham Bell. Today, there are about 5,000 FM stations in the U.S. All are testimony to the creative genius of Howard Armstrong.

References and Resources

Empire of the Air by Tom Lewis, Edward Burlingame Books, 1991.

The Smithsonian Book of Invention, Smithsonian Institution, 1978.

"Radio Revolutionary" by Thomas S. W. Lewis, in *American Heritage of Invention and Technology*, Fall 1985.

Dictionary of American Biography, Charles Scribner's Sons Publishers, 1932; with supplemental updates.

McGraw-Hill Encyclopedia of Biography, McGraw-Hill Publishers, 1973.

Asimov's Biographical Encyclopedia of Science and Technology by Isaac Asimov, Doubleday & Co. Publishers, 1964.

Donald Wills Douglas

THE best-known transport airplane in history flew just 10 months after design work on it began on the drafting board. Following the plane's first flight in December 1935, almost 11,000 DC-3s, or its C-47 military equivalent, were built. The airplane was the brainchild of Donald Wills Douglas, who headed a small company that had not previously built an airliner. He and his designers proposed a twin-engined airplane instead of the three-engine design specified in a widely distributed request by Transcontinental and Western Air (TWA). The resulting airliner was the first to make a profit carrying only passengers.

Douglas was born in a comfortable apartment in Brooklyn, New York. His father was a bank teller. While growing up, Douglas played the banjo and was captain of his high school football team. Airplanes had fascinated him ever since the Wright Brothers first flew in 1903. He felt especially impressed witnessing a flight by Orville Wright above Fort Myer, Virginia, in September 1908. The Wright airplane was the first ever ordered by the Army. Douglas entered the U.S. Naval Academy but found that the Navy had little interest in aviation. A year before graduation, he resigned. He completed his education at the Massachusetts Institute of Technology (MIT). While working at MIT after graduation, he helped build one of the first wind tunnels. A year later, while working in New Haven on a dirigible, he heard of a job opening in Los Angeles. Lured by the prospect of aviation work and a more pleasant climate, he accepted an offer from Glenn Martin to work on military airplanes. A few years later, at the age of 28 and with only $600 in savings, he started his own company in the rented back room of a barber shop. Within a year, Douglas

Photo courtesy of the McDonnell Douglas Corp.

Donald Douglas under the wing of a DC-4. The company he founded merged in 1967 with another started by James McDonnell.

had not only secured financial backing but designed and constructed the *Cloudster*, the first airplane to lift a useful load that exceeded its own weight. He sold a variation of the plane to the Navy for use as a torpedo bomber.

Douglas further showed his technical genius in 1924. That year, two of his Douglas World Cruiser floatplanes were the first to fly around the world, from Seattle to Seattle. They covered 27,553 miles in 175 days. Douglas founded the Douglas Aircraft Co. in 1928 and did well with mostly military contracts until the Great Depression began to squeeze all manufacturers. Douglas was operating out of an old movie studio in Santa Monica, California, when the two-

Born:
April 6, 1892,
in Brooklyn,
New York

Died:
February 1,
1981, in
Palm Springs,
California

page request letter from TWA arrived in 1932. Since Douglas Aircraft Co. was among the smallest aircraft companies, he moved quickly and was the first to contact TWA. After some assurances from Douglas, TWA ordered a prototype airplane for $125,000, with an option for 60 more at $58,000 each.

Douglas and his staff built an airplane with such innovations as a streamlined all-metal stressed-skin fuselage based on wind tunnel testing, engine cowlings that reduced drag, and retractable landing gear. The plane featured wing flaps, which had not previously been used on large airplanes, and dual-pitch propellers for efficient takeoff and cruise operation. The Douglas designers calculated that their airplane could even

a large wing spar inside the cabin. It is a feature used by every large airliner to this day.

When TWA officials saw the airplane fly in July 1933, it so surpassed their expectations that they immediately ordered 40. Douglas went into production with an improved 14-passenger DC-2. Both American and European airlines bought DC-2s, including KLM Royal Dutch Airlines, which bought 14. The airline, known in Holland as Koninklijke Luchtvaart Maatschappij, is the oldest commercial airline in the world. Only one DC-1 and about 220 DC-2s were manufactured before the enormously popular 21-passenger DC-3 made its debut as a potential sleeper airplane for overnight travel. All three airplanes were similar

An Eastern Air Lines DC-3 is on display at the Smithsonian's National Air and Space Museum in Washington, D.C. A Boeing 247 is below the DC-3. The two airplanes were early competitors. The tail of a Ford Trimotor is at the upper right.

take off with an 18,000-pound payload from an airport located at a 4,000'-high location using only one engine.

Named the DC-1 for the company name Douglas Commercial, the prototype was the first airplane to provide lush passenger comfort with a bright, attractive color scheme in the roomiest cabin of its period. It had large upholstered seats and individual reading lamps. The thick carpeting and sound insulation made the DC-1 quieter than a railroad passenger car. It was the first transport design that had the wing totally under the fuselage. This design eliminated the need for passengers to climb over

enough in appearance that only a critical observer could point out differences.

American Airlines had to fly a lengthy roundabout transcontinental route determined by air mail contracts. The airline asked Douglas to make a wider and longer airplane to accommodate 14 sleeper berths. The resulting larger fuselage could easily handle seven rows of three seats for day flights. The DC-3 was born. Variously called the *Gooney Bird*, *Dakota*, or *Skytrain*, the DC-3 was powered by two 1,000-horsepower Pratt & Whitney Aircraft R-1830 14-cylinder radial engines. Pratt & Whitney produced more of those engines in its East Hartford, Connecticut, plant than any other airplane engine in history: 173,618. When the DC-3 went into scheduled service between New York and Chicago in June 1936, it was the biggest airplane in the sky. With a 64-foot fuselage and a 95-foot wingspan, it was the equivalent in its time to today's jumbo jets. Yet, above all, the shiny aluminum airplane was economical. Its operating cost per passenger was 30 to 50 percent lower than that of any other airplane then in operation. By 1939, air travel had quadrupled, and DC-3s carried 75 percent of all passengers.

Before the DC-3 and its 170-mph cruising speed, commercial airplanes flew at 100 to 110 mph, barely faster than some railroad trains. The DC-3's range of 1,300 miles was far greater than the 200 or 300 miles of early wood-framed airplanes. It could more comfortably carry twice as many passengers in a much safer and stronger all-metal airframe. No DC-3 has ever been lost as the result of a structural failure. With only one or two exceptions, every first-line Allied military airplane in World War II used the DC-3 structure design.

The lean athletic Douglas was once described as a person "who dips into the future with the mind of a poet and the slide rule of an engineer." He received many honors, including the Guggenheim Gold Medal in 1940 for his contribution to commercial and military airplanes. In 1936, he received the Collier Trophy—one of aviation's highest honors—for his twin-engined commercial transport airplane. President Franklin Delano Roosevelt presented the trophy.

Douglas loved fishing and sailing. The photograph on page 211 shows him leaning on a propeller of a DC-4, a four-engined transport that went into service in 1942. He remained an honorary chairman of the McDonnell Douglas Corp. until his death.

A 1938 Northwest Airlines advertisement prominently features a DC-3.

References and Resources

"The Letter That Changed the Way We Fly" by Frederick Allen, in *American Heritage of Invention and Technology*, Fall 1988.

"Aerospace Engineering" by Tom Rhodes, in *History of the Airframe*, June 1989.

Around the World in 80 Years, McDonnell Douglas Corp., 1972.

Dependable Engines, Pratt & Whitney Aircraft, 1972.

Lore of Flight by Tre Tryckare, Cagner & Co., 1970.

Flight in America, 1900-1983 by Roger E. Bilstein, Johns Hopkins Press, 1984.

National Cyclopedia of American Biography. James T. White and Co. Publishers, 1891; with supplemental updates.

McGraw-Hill Encyclopedia of Biography, McGraw-Hill Publishers, 1973.

R. Buckminster Fuller

Born:
July 12, 1895,
in Milton,
Massachusetts

Died:
July 1, 1983, in
Los Angeles,
California

National Portrait Gallery, Smithsonian Institution

A twentieth-century technologist who had many different successful professions—including those of inventor, engineer, and architect—was also labeled an environmentalist, philosopher, and genius. His relatives shook their heads in disbelief when he announced that he planned to become a "problem solver on behalf of all humanity." No one thought he could possibly succeed in such an unusual undertaking. Yet, Richard Buckminster Fuller was a uniquely creative person compared by some to Leonardo da Vinci. Fuller received 28 patents and 47 honorary college degrees. He wrote more than two dozen books with unusual titles such as *Operation Manual for Spaceship Earth* and *Nine Chains to the Moon*. He also invented the geodesic dome, an elegant structure of honeycombed pyramids.

Fuller was born into a tea merchant family. He had crossed eyes and extremely poor vision. Spending summers as a child on Bear Island off the coast of Maine, he discovered self-education and invention. At eight, he designed a small boat-propulsion device that used motions modeled after those of a jellyfish. After attending a private high school, Fuller entered Harvard in 1913. He found it hard to adjust to strict academic and social requirements, and Harvard expelled him twice. He never graduated from college. He worked as an apprentice machine installer at a cotton mill in Quebec and then at a meat-packing plant in New York City.

At the outbreak of World War I, Fuller joined the Navy and served at sea as a junior officer. While in the service, he invented several devices, such as a boom that could flip over an airplane that crash-landed upside down in the ocean. After the war, Fuller worked as an architect for his father-in-law, James Monroe Hewlett. He designed 240 buildings over a period of several years, but his projects consistently lost money. Because of his inability to cope with the realities of financial considerations, he lost his job.

When a young daughter died of pneumonia in 1927, Fuller felt so despondent that he moved his family into a slum section of Chicago. He did not speak for almost two years. During that time, he began to develop radical theories of structural design. He had very little income and the family lived on his wife's small inheritance and small grants that Fuller occasionally received. When he emerged from his self-imposed solitude with his wife and a second daughter, he wanted to design and construct affordable housing using mass-production principles. He hoped to build assembly-line houses whose production rates would match those of automobiles. Fuller designed a house that he called the Dymaxion, a name that combines the concepts of "dynamic" and "maximum." His Dymaxion Corp. produced a $1,500 prefabricated dwelling that weighed only 3 tons, compared with a conventional house's 150 tons. The metal, cylindrically shaped house had four wedge-shaped rooms. It featured a modular bathroom with a fog-gun shower that used only one quart of constantly filtered water for a 10-minute shower. It was unveiled in 1929 at Chicago's Marshall Field and Co. department store. The Dymaxion house went on tour, and Fuller went with it. He lectured continually about a world with affordable technology-inspired housing for everyone.

The curved laminated-metal walls of his house did not require an internal framework. Workers could disassemble the house, put it into a tube 16' long by 5' in diameter, and easily move it to another site. A few 36'-diameter Dymaxion houses were built, but at the time the American Institute of Architects officially resisted all prefabricated buildings. Fuller's lifetime impatience with profit-motivated financiers also kept his design from making much of an impact.

Fuller also built three prototypes of a torpedo-shaped Dymaxion car in 1932. Using a standard Ford V-8 engine, it had front-wheel drive and rear-wheel steering. The car traveled at 120 mph, obtained 40 mpg, and had room for 11 passengers. Its efficiency resulted almost totally from careful aerodynamic design. Fuller exhibited the car at the 1933 Chicago World's Fair. However, a fatal accident unrelated to the car's design generated much unfavorable publicity, and the car never went into production.

The one invention most connected with Fuller is the geodesic dome. Fuller developed the design during the late 1940s. Using about 3 percent of the material needed for a conventional structure of comparable size, the simplest geodesic dome is a sphere composed of many pyramid-shaped tetrahedrons. Its unique design relies on two technical concepts. The first is that the sphere is the strongest shape for countering internal pressure. The second is that the tetrahedron is the strongest shape for countering external pressure. Therefore, the design—not the size of the structural members—is what produces enormous strength. No internal columns are needed to support

a geodesic dome, which results in large clear-span interiors. One of the most impressive examples is the 20-story 250'-diameter structure used at the U.S. pavilion of the Expo 67 held in Montreal in 1967. Now owned by the Canadian government, the 6.7 million-cubic-foot dome has no interior supports. Walt Disney's EPCOT Center in Orlando has a geodesic dome open to park visitors, which has appeared in some advertisements.

In 1952, the U.S. government considered geodesic domes that could be assembled on site in a few hours as enclosures for sites along the Arctic Circle. A team of engineers from the Massachusetts Institute of Technology (MIT) predicted that the domes would collapse in an 18-mph breeze. Instead, a full-size model withstood a 150-mph gale in an MIT wind tunnel before its concrete foundation pulled out of the ground. One survived 200-mph winds on top of New Hampshire's Mount Washington.

A geodesic dome house in South Carolina

Ford Motor Co. offered Fuller his first commercial contract for a geodesic dome in 1953. Ford wanted a 93' cover for a rotunda planned for use at the company's fiftieth-anniversary celebration. Ford gave Fuller only one month to design and build it. His dome had 19,000 plastic-covered aluminum struts, and it weighed not much more than a car. Ford executives were so sure the structure would collapse that they hired a wrecker to stand by ready to clear away the debris. Yet, the structure did not fail, and because of the prestige associated with the success of the Ford project, geodesic

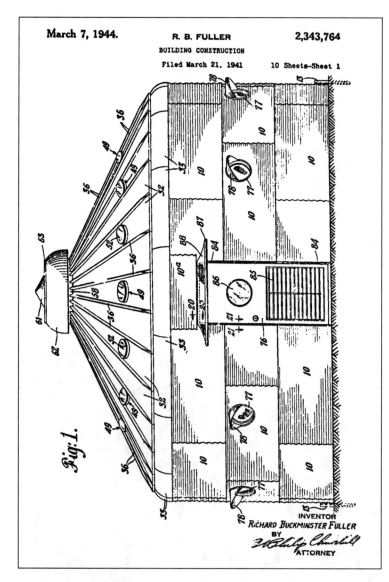

Patent drawing for Fuller's Dymaxion house

domes began to receive general acceptance. They are now recognized as a uniquely American contribution to architecture. Geodesic domes inspired by Fuller's ideas cover more ground area worldwide than the buildings of any other architect in history.

Fuller was an extremely popular college teacher at Southern Illinois University in Carbondale, and he lived in a geodesic dome house made of plywood. He traveled tens of thousands of miles each year on lecture circuits. The stocky and somewhat disheveled Fuller was just over five feet tall, and he wore thick-lensed, dark-framed glasses. A giant in the field of technology, Fuller lectured at more than 500 colleges and universities. *Time* magazine featured him on its cover in 1964. He received a gold medal in 1970 from the American Institute of Architects, for his contributions to architecture. That was the same organization that rebuffed his efforts on prefabricated housing in 1929.

Fuller believed that "man can do anything he needs to do" through the application of technology. When he died, he was eulogized as a "poet of industrialization." Just 36 hours after Fuller's death, his wife of 66 years also died.

References and Resources

"Who Was Buckminster Fuller, Anyway?" by Amy C. Edmondson, in *American Heritage of Invention and Technology*, Winter 1988.

"R. Buckminister Fuller Dead; Futurist Built Geodesic Dome" by Albin Krebs, *The New York Times*, 2 July 1983.

McGraw-Hill Encyclopedia of Biography, McGraw-Hill Publishers, 1973.

Wallace Hume Carothers

Library of Congress

THE world's first completely synthetic fiber with characteristics comparable to natural fibers was developed more than 50 years ago. Nylon is as important today as it was back then. In solid form, it is a strong, naturally slippery, abrasion-resistant material that people can form into bearings, gears, and sliding surfaces. Some of its other uses include textiles, recreational equipment, and automobile engine parts. It's even used to prevent asphalt roads from cracking. The international community has so completely accepted nylon that the word appears in almost every known language. The name came from combining parts of the words "nitrogen" and "Babylon." (Babylon was an ancient city noted for luxurious living.) Wallace Hume Carothers discovered this most useful synthetic material in 1934.

Carothers's father was a teacher at the Capital City Commercial College in Des Moines, Iowa. Because he was an educator, he made sure his son received a well-balanced education. Carothers covered a major part of his college expenses at Tarkio College in Missouri by teaching such varied subjects as accounting, English, and chemistry. He found he had an aptitude for chemistry, and he received all of his academic degrees in the subject. Carothers's college work was of such high quality that Harvard University offered him a teaching position. He accepted it because he viewed Harvard as an "academic paradise" for teachers.

Born:
April 27, 1896, in Burlington, Iowa

Died:
April 29, 1937, in Philadelphia, Pennsylvania

The E. I. du Pont de Nemours Co. had started as an explosives manufacturer. Around the time Carothers was teaching at Harvard, the company was diversifying into industrial chemistry. It was constructing a $115,000 organic chemistry laboratory in Wilmington, Delaware, and invited Carothers to organize the lab and head up organic chemistry research. Carothers found that he did not like full-time teaching, and he jumped at the opportunity. The prospect of working with state-of-the-art equipment and having high-quality assistants swayed him. The challenge of open-ended industrial research also attracted him, as did the $6,000 annual salary. He earned only $3,200 at Harvard. Carothers moved to Wilmington in January 1928.

Actually, du Pont at first had little interest in hiring Carothers. He was only 31 years old and had not yet established himself in the field of chemistry. To head its prestigious laboratory, du Pont wanted someone with a national reputation. The company had hoped to have 15 people at work in early 1928, but only Carothers took the offer. All the others were in the middle of projects that they did not want to leave. Although he became the department head by default, Carothers soon developed a national reputation and his contributions to twentieth-century chemistry came at break-neck speed.

During the nine short years he was at du Pont, Carothers and his department published more than 30 technical papers. They received about 70 patents. One early significant discovery was neoprene, the first synthetic material that could readily replace rubber. The research group produced its

Feb. 16, 1937.   W. H. CAROTHERS   2,071,250
                   LINEAR CONDENSATION POLYMERS
                         Filed July 3, 1931

Wallace H. Carothers. Inventor

By R. F. Miller
                                    Attorney

Carothers called this device a "molecular still."

somewhat-white first-ever sample on April 17, 1930. Unlike rubber, neoprene did not deteriorate when exposed to gasoline and oil. As a result, it found wide application in fuel hoses and gaskets used in automobiles, trucks, ships, and airplanes.

As with neoprene, Carothers's discovery of nylon resulted from careful and deliberate laboratory experiments. He was trying to develop what he called a super polymer, a very large organic molecule. To do that, he built experimental equipment to melt, mix, pressurize, and condense various materials. In his patents, Carothers referred to a "molecular still" to produce the experimental synthetic materials. Most of the materials melted at too low a temperature, making them unsuitable for clothing. For example, one material melted in warm water. When he knew he was getting close to his goal, Carothers tentatively named the target material 66, or nylon 66. Nylon was ultimately based on two organic chemicals, adipic acid and hexa-methylene-diamine. The two materials contained six carbon atoms each.

On May 23, 1934, after three years of work, Carothers himself made the first batch of nylon by squirting a 482° F chemical solution through the tiny end of a hypodermic needle. It had taken five weeks to prepare the compound. Carothers subjected the pliable filament to all the tests that he could think up. It passed with flying colors. More than $1 million of research had gone into the project. At that point, Carothers turned it over to the technologists and cost accountants who would decide how to manufacture nylon in large quantities.

Commercially produced nylon uses coal, water, and air as raw materials. A molten honey-like solution is forced through many tiny holes in a metal plate. The resulting fibers can then be twisted into rope or woven into rugs, parachutes, and other textiles. From 1 to more than 2,500 filaments are combined to make textile nylon yarn. Nylon was introduced to the public as toothbrush bristles in 1938. However, it did not draw worldwide attention until it was used to make nylon stockings in 1939. Nylon provided an inexpensive alternative to the silk stockings it replaced, and the public bought 64 million pairs that first year.

Carothers received many awards. His

most significant honor was election to the National Academy of Sciences in l936, as the first nonacademic professional in the organization. He was a modest man who shunned publicity. Although ill at ease in large groups, he was a witty conversationalist when among friends. Carothers was a well-rounded person who had interests in art, politics, music, and sports. He was an avid tennis player.

Clearly a potential Nobel Prize candidate, Carothers ranked at the very top of his profession. Nonetheless, he regularly suffered bouts of depression. In the mid-1930s, his depression grew worse. He became obsessed with the notion that he was a failure. He feared that he could not come up with another idea to match his discovery of nylon. (Probably no one could. Nylon is now ranked as one of the most significant discoveries of twentieth-century chemistry.) Carothers felt particularly upset when his sister died prematurely. Terribly depressed, he took his own life in 1937.

A postscript to Carothers' career occurred on April 6, 1938. A former colleague of his at du Pont's organic lab, Roy J. Plunkett, discovered an incredibly slippery solid that was chemically named tetra-fluoro-ethylene (TFE). Its existence was kept secret throughout World War II. TFE was the only gasket material that would contain the corrosive hexafluoride gas used to process uranium at Oak Ridge, Tennessee, for the atomic bomb. That gasket material is now a household word: Teflon. Used primarily for nonstick cookware and wire insulation, it is listed in the Guinness Book of Records as the slipperiest substance in the world.

References and Resources

"The Nylon Drama" by David A. Hounshell and John Kenly Smith, Jr., in *American Heritage of Invention and Technology*, Fall 1988.

"Nylon: 50 Years Old and Going Strong" by Kathy McWalter, in *Design News*, 4 July 1988.

American Science and Invention by Mitchell Wilson, Bonanza Books, 1960.

Name into Word by Eric Partridge, Books for Libraries Press, 1970.

Dictionary of American Biography, Charles Scribner's Sons Publushers, 1932; with supplemental updates.

National Cyclopedia of American Biography, James T. White and Co. Publishers, 1891; with supplemental updates.

McGraw-Hill Encyclopedia of Biography, McGraw-Hill Publishers, 1973.

Asimov's Biographical Encyclopedia of Science and Technology by Isaac Asimov, Doubleday & Co. Publishers, 1964.

Leopold Mannes and Leopold Godowsky II

Leopold Mannes Born: December 26, 1899, in New York, New York

Died: August 11, 1964, on Martha's Vineyard, New York

Leopold Godowsky Born: May 27, 1900, in New York, New York

Died: February 18, 1983, in New York, New York

Reprinted courtesy of Eastman Kodak Co.

Leopold Mannes (left) and Leopold Godowsky in their research lab at Kodak in 1932

CAREER technologists have not been the only ones to improve products and processes. A pair of classical musicians combined their technical talents in 1935 to develop the world's most popular color-slide film. American-born Leopold Mannes and Leopold Godowsky invented Kodachrome film at the Eastman Kodak Co. research laboratory in Rochester, New York.

The search for color-sensitive emulsion began during the nineteenth century. Early investigators took photographs of the same scene through colored filters, then projected superimposed images onto a wall through complementary filters. The projected image was a color rendition that used an additive process, because filters added the color. The emulsion that Mannes and Godowsky per-fected used a subtractive process. It was based on colored objects absorbing—or subtracting—some light rays and reflecting others.

Both Mannes and Godowsky were born into families with strong musical backgrounds. Mannes's uncle Frank Damrosch founded the Julliard School of Music, and Godowsky's father was a world-class pianist and composer. The two met at age 15 while attending the Riverdale Country School in New York City. They initially noticed each other because they shared the same first name. They soon discovered that they also shared interests in music, amateur chemistry, and photography. Mannes was to become a famous pianist and Godowsky would achieve equal fame with the violin. During their teen years, however, they were fascinated by attempts to devise a practical method for taking color photographs. Their meeting sparked a friendship and professional working relationship that lasted their entire lives.

Mannes and Godowsky conducted chemistry experiments in the bathrooms, kitchens, and pantries of their parents' New York City homes. The two friends did not know that hundreds of prominent scientists had been searching for a practical color process for some 50 years. Godowsky later said, "We were blissfully ignorant. Our physics instructor gave us a passkey to the [chemistry] laboratory and we spent a lot of time experimenting, boy fashion."

After graduating from high school, Mannes attended Harvard University and earned a degree in music. He also took many physics classes. Godowsky majored in chemistry and physics on the other side of the country, at the University of California. He started in Berkeley, where he played violin with the San Francisco Symphony Orchestra. He graduated from UCLA, where he played with the Los Angeles Philharmonic Orchestra.

After college, the two men began separate musical careers in New York City. Mannes taught music at the David Mannes College of Music, founded by his father and mother in 1916. The younger Mannes had a real talent for chamber music, and he received a Pulitzer Prize in music composition in 1925. Godowsky played with orchestras and continued studying music composition.

Mannes and Godowsky worked on the color-film project in their spare time. After several years of effort, they narrowed their investigations to an integral tripack: three layers of photographic emulsions on the same film base. The emulsion in contact with the celluloid film base was sensitive to red light. The next layer was sensitive to green light, and the top layer was sensitive to blue. To protect their interests, Mannes and Godowsky applied for patents. They received their first in 1924. Their experiments expanded, and they had to rent laboratory space. They paid for rent and supplies out of their earnings as musicians, but they soon realized that they would need financial assistance. In the late 1920s, they approached Kenneth Mees, a vice-president of Eastman Kodak and a strong supporter of photographic research. Mees agreed to provide some assistance in exchange for special considerations if they succeeded.

When George Eastman, the founder of Eastman Kodak, heard of Mannes and Godowsky's work, he wanted to buy the rights to their early patents. Eastman had a policy of paying a fair price for all patents dealing with photography. (Twin brothers F. E. and F. O. Stanley, for example, sold Eastman their patents for photographic dry-plate manufacturing machines. They used the proceeds to start their Stanley Steamer Motor Car Co.)

Because of economic hardship caused by the Great Depression, Eastman persuaded Mannes and Godowsky to join his company's research staff. He immediately paid each one $30,000 and offered an annual salary of $7,500. They started working in 1931 at a new research building with 12 technical assistants.

To measure critical development times in the complete darkness of a color darkroom, Mannes and Godowsky whistled the last movement of a classical music piece that

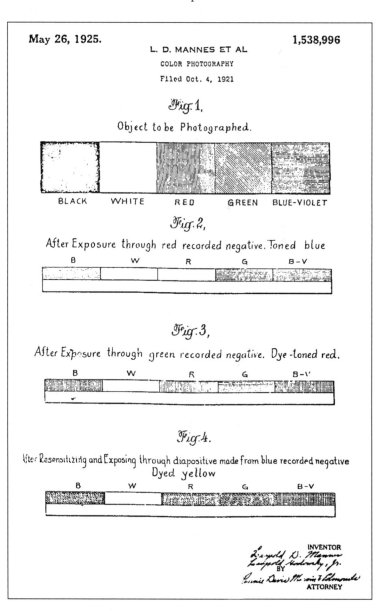

Diagram for film requiring dye toners

they both knew well. Strains of the *C-Minor Symphony* by Johannes Brahms, at a precise two beats per second, came from their darkroom almost every day. Their coworkers were not accustomed to such unusual lab activities, but the two Leos—as their friends called them—quickly earned everyone's respect. They accumulated a total of 40 patents, but Kodachrome remains their best-known invention. It was rated at a slow ASA (ISO) 10 when it first went on sale as 16 mm movie film on April 15, 1935. The following year, Eastman Kodak made it available for 35 mm still cameras. Kodachrome is still highly regarded for its sharpness, brilliance of color, lack of grain, and minimal color shift over time. Well-stored Kodachrome transparencies from the 1930s retain their beautiful color today.

Kodachrome is unique in that the colors seen after development are not part of the original tripack film. Kodachrome is the only color film that is black and white when exposed. Colors are added during development by a process called *dye coupling*. A dye coupler is a chemical that will react with a developed image to form a specific color. The first step is developing the film to obtain a negative, and then chemically reversing it to a positive. During three additional developments and color reversals, complementary colors of yellow, cyan (a greenish blue), and magenta (a purplish red) are introduced to the appropriate film layer. Silver is bleached away, leaving a color transparency. Amateur photographers cannot develop Kodachrome because it requires complex processing and quality control. In the late 1980s, only three dozen laboratories in the world could develop it.

Mannes and Godowsky left Kodak to return to concert music. However, the more inventive Mannes stayed with Kodak as a part-time consultant. He patented a sound track of gold in 1941 that improved the sound quality of color motion pictures. He also returned to teaching at his parents' music college.

Godowsky was a member of several prominent symphony orchestras, and he returned to professional violin playing. His father had been such a great pianist that the younger Godowsky took up the violin to escape his father's shadow. He even carried the influence of music into marriage. He married Frances Gershwin, the younger sister of George Gershwin, who composed such popular orchestra music as *Rhapsody in Blue*.

The two Leos were well rewarded over the years with royalties and the admiration of their peers. Almost 30 years after Kodachrome went commercial, international photographers had not forgotten Mannes and Godowsky. The two men received the Progress Award of London's Royal Photographic Society in 1964, the year that Mannes died. A reception at the George Eastman House in 1985 honored the fiftieth anniversary of Kodachrome's introduction to the public. At the opening, the Canterbury Brass Quintet performed separate musical pieces written by George Gershwin and Leopold Godowsky. After five decades of use, Kodachrome is a rare technical product in that it remains essentially unchanged.

References and Resources

The History of Photography by Beaumont Newhall, Museum of Modern Art, New York, 1964.

"Time Exposure" by Eaton S. Lothrop, Jr., in *Popular Photography*, February 1986 .

"Kodachrome Still a Leader in Color Film," in *Lexington (Kentucky) Herald-Leader*, 7 July 1985.

Dictionary of American Biography, Charles Scribner's Sons Publishers, 1932; with supplemental updates.

National Cyclopedia of American Biography, James T. White and Co. Publishers, 1891; with supplemental updates.

Margaret Bourke-White

Courtesy of Syracuse University with permission of the
Margaret Bourke-White Estate

MOST factory workers of the early twentieth century did not notice the beauty hidden in their industrial surroundings. Their workplaces were so familiar that most took no special notice of the dynamic visual impact of flowing steel. Few saw the symmetry in stacked airplane wings or the stark comparisons between people and the huge pieces of equipment they built. It took the trained and insightful eye of Margaret Bourke-White, one of the first industrial photographers, to isolate detail and record the visual drama of America at work.

This tall and strikingly handsome woman chose to add her mother's family name, Bourke, to her own while she was in her early twenties. Bourke-White's mother was a demanding person who expected her daughter to take the more challenging way to solve any problem. Her father was a would-be inventor and engineer in the printing industry. He once described his philosophy as "never leave a job until you have done it to suit yourself and better than anyone else requires you to do it."

Bourke-White graduated from Plainfield (New Jersey) High School and attended colleges in Michigan, Indiana, and Ohio. She earned a degree in biology in 1927 from Cornell in New York state. Bourke-White had a lifelong love of animals and expected to work with reptiles after college. She would occasionally take a pet snake with her to her classes. By the time she attended

Born:
June 14, 1904,
in New York,
New York

Died:
August 27,
1971, in
Stamford,
Connecticut

Cornell, her father had died, and to support herself she photographed buildings on campus. She used a 3-1/4" x 4-1/4" Ica Reflex camera that had a crack right through its lens and cost $20. She sold prints she made for income. That was the casual beginning of a lifelong career that would see Bourke-White never more than an arm's length away from a camera. She once said that if she hadn't had to work her way through college, she would never have been a photographer.

After graduating, Bourke-White moved to Cleveland to try her luck with professional photography. Fascinated by the city's manufacturing strength, she photographed factory buildings and other parts of Cleveland's industrial community. She was not the first person to take such photographs, but she is regarded as the first to avoid static representations of form. She gave her images a moving dramatic character. Bourke-White made machinery look so beautiful that one of her peers said she "transformed the American factory into a Gothic cathedral." A display of her prints at a local bank brought her to the attention of city leaders and resulted in a variety of new assignments. Her first serious industrial photographs were taken over a five-month period at the Otis Steel Corp.

At Otis, Bourke-White experimented with lenses, films, and magnesium flares to provide illumination for her slow ASA (ISO) 12 film. She produced a series of impressive images under challenging conditions. Although she took over 1,000 pictures with a large tripod-mounted camera, she only presented her best 12. The company presi-

This image of a 200-pound ladle was one that Bourke-White photographed at the Otis Steel Co.

dent liked the photographs and used them in a limited production magazine called *The Romance of Steel*. A few months later, the Associated Press ran a national article about Bourke-White's images. She was only 23, and the article was headlined: "Girl's Photographs of Steel Manufacture Hailed as New Art."

One of Bourke-White's technical contributions was the perfection of multiple-flash photography. Flashbulbs were not yet available so she burned magnesium in open pans. Her multiple-flash technique eliminated harsh high-contrast images such as those produced by a single flash. The magnesium pans had to be carefully positioned so that assistants could ignite them without showing up in the photograph. Synchronizing the lighting of several flashes at once proved a real challenge. Preferring cameras larger than 35 mm, Bourke-White's favorite was a 5" × 7" Corona View with Bausch & Lomb lenses. She used it to photograph miners, grain elevators, meat packing plants, oil refineries, electrical alternators, paper mills, watch factories, and countless other industrial subjects. People were routinely surprised to discover that the photographer was an attractive and fashionably dressed woman in her 20s.

A perfectionist, Bourke-White always spent a great deal of time setting up her shots. It was not unusual for her to place herself in life-threatening locations to obtain the best image. She moved in so close to the molten metal in a steel factory that the varnish blistered on her camera. Of one photograph, she wrote in her diary, "I am glad [it] is good because it was so exciting to go up and take it through the carbon monoxide gas on the top of the coke oven, with my guide posted at the foot of the steps to run up and catch me if I should keel over." The photograph on page 223 shows the 25-year-old Bourke-White with an early reflex camera. For dramatic effect, she positioned herself on the outside of the Chrysler building's sixty-first floor during construction of the building. (Years later, she had a studio located on that very floor.)

Bourke-White's reputation grew to the point where *Fortune* magazine offered her a position as its first staff photographer. She was the only one to receive a credit line in the first issue, February 1930. The finest photographic magazine in the country at the time, *Fortune* emphasized manufacturing. Bourke-White, its premier photographer, grew synonymous in the public's mind with industrial photography. Bourke-White also worked as one of *Life* magazine's original photographers and was responsible for both the cover picture and lead story in the magazine's first issue of November 23, 1936. Consistent with her industrial photography background, the cover image showed three huge concrete dam supports. Part of the $100 million Fort Peck Dam on the upper reaches of the Missouri River in Montana, each was about 100 feet tall. When she left *Life* more than 20 years later, Bourke-White had completed 284 assignments.

Early in her career, Bourke-White's images emphasized machinery, while the worker played a secondary role. At the time, this photographic style appealed to the public. By the mid-1930s, however, the Great Depression forced the country to pay closer attention to the problems of human beings. More and more, Bourke-White focused her lens on the workers. Then she slowly began to lean toward photojournalism. In *Life's* first issue, her cover photograph clearly demonstrated the technical might of America. However, practically all of her 16 photographs inside the magazine were of the *people* who were constructing the dam that appeared on the cover.

Bourke-White was a tireless and energetic worker who traveled with several assistants. She took 3,000 large-format photographs during several trips to Russia between 1930 and 1932. She was the first person to do a full documentary on that country's emerging technological strength. Her first book was the 1931 *Eyes on Russia*. It featured 40 of her pictures. Bourke-White was an excellent photographer of people. She demonstrated her talent by recording dramatically emotional images during World War II and the Korean War. "Maggie" to her closest friends, Bourke-White was briefly married two times. Her second marriage was to *Tobacco Road* author Erskine Caldwell. She died at her home in Stamford, Connecticut.

References and Resources

Portrait of Myself by Margaret Bourke-White, Simon and Schuster, 1963.

"Woman of Steel" by Vicki Goldberg, *American Heritage of Invention and Technology*, Spring 1987.

"Unforgettable Margaret Bourke-White" by Carl Mydans, *Reader's Digest*, August 1972.

Girls Who Became Artists by Winifred and Frances Kirkland, Books for Libraries Press, 1934.

Edwin Albert Link

Born:
July 26, 1904,
in Huntington,
Indiana

Died:
September 7,
1981, in
Binghamton,
New York

Link Flight Simulation Div.

COMPUTER-simulation games allow people to experience the sensation of flying high-speed airplanes and racing automobiles while avoiding the dangers involved in real-life experience. Modern full-size simulators train ship captains, locomotive engineers, astronauts, and pilots of commercial and military aircraft. The use of simulators began in 1929 when Edwin Link built the first trainer to provide ground instruction for new pilots. Commonly called the Blue Box—because it looked like a small blue box-shaped airplane—the Link trainer introduced flying to a half million World War II pilots.

Link's family moved from Indiana to Binghamton, New York, when he was six. His father had purchased a bankrupt player-piano company in Binghamton. Proving to have excellent business skills, Link's father formed the successful Link Piano and Organ Co. Link pianos soon appeared throughout New York and Pennsylvania. Then,

Link's parents separated and Link traveled with his mother to Illinois and California. He attended a series of vocational high schools where he studied carpentry, metalworking, and drafting. Link left school at 18 and went to work back at his father's company where he helped build, repair, and install air-operated theater organs. Link quickly learned about the compressors, valves, and bellows that would later make up the major operating components in his trainer.

Link took his first airplane ride in California as a teenager, and he quickly became hooked on aviation. The pilot of the plane was Sydney Chaplin, owner of an airfield and brother of the actor Charlie Chaplin. Link wanted to learn to fly, but the local airport charged an exorbitant $25 to $50 per lesson. Also, experienced pilots were often reluctant to trust their expensive machines to untrained pilots. To make up for his lack of flying time, Link repeatedly taxied a friend's airplane up and down the runway to get a feel for the controls. World War I pilots used the same technique, calling it the "penguin system." Before long, Link began wondering if he could construct a stationary device that would respond like an airplane while remaining safely on the ground.

In 1927, Link started building a flight trainer in his spare time in the basement of the organ factory. What he completed a year and a half later almost looked like a toy. His trainer was a small blue stubby airplane placed on top of a box and connected to the box by a large universal joint. A compressor in the box controlled air flow into four large bellows originally made for player pianos. Two of the bellows caused the tiny mock airplane to pitch up and down, and the other two caused it to move from side to side. An electric motor simulated the third dimension of flight, yaw, in which a plane turns around a vertical axis. The motor allowed a student pilot to turn the trainer in a complete circle.

The trainer's cockpit had standard airplane controls. The control stick varied air flow into the bellows through valves connected by a series of pulleys and levers. The rudder pedals controlled the electric yaw motor. Once in the trainer, the student pilot moved the controls and the stubby airplane responded just as a real airplane would. A fully instrumented dashboard gave simulated readings for altitude, air speed, and turn-and-bank angle. An instructor at a desk outside the box had a duplicate set of instruments for use in monitoring every move the trainee made. For navigation training, the pilot homed in on radio signals simulated by the instructor and transmitted over the headphones.

Link filed for a patent on the flight trainer and went into production in his father's factory. Unsure that he would find a large enough market in flight training, he considered an alternative use for his invention. Link titled his patent: "Combination Training Device for Student Aviators and Entertainment Apparatus." Since his family's business involved entertainment, Link gave serious consideration to using his invention for recreational purposes. Several amusement parks and penny arcades bought early trainers.

Link was a fully licensed pilot, and he opened a flying school with his older brother, George. His trainers allowed the brothers to teach people to fly for as little as one-third of what their competitors charged. Student pilots learned to fly in a simulated environment that duplicated a real airplane. The school turned a profit until the full force of the Great Depression made private flying a luxury that people could do without. The flying school went bankrupt, and for a while Link earned a living barnstorming, flying freight, and even flying an illuminated airborne sign. His big break came in 1934 when the Army Air Corps received a contract from the U.S. Post Office to fly mail over 14 air routes.

Air Corps pilots lacked experience in instrument navigation, and they flew an

aging fleet of reconnaissance planes and bombers. During foul midwinter weather, six planes crashed during one week, killing all six pilots. Another four were lost on a single day in March. The losses prompted the Air Corps to ask Link to demonstrate his trainer at the Newark airport that spring. As it turned out, the day was foggy and generally unfit for flying. Nonetheless, Link flew in from Binghamton, landing his Cessna without mishap. He told the officials present that he used the trainer to maintain his flying skills. The Air Corps immediately ordered 6 trainers at $3,400 each, and they took delivery on June 23. Japan bought the next 10, providing fuel for speculation that Japan's attack pilots who bombed Pearl Harbor had trained in Link trainers. Link formed the Link Aviation Co. in 1935. It

Link Flight Simulation Div.

Link trainer as it looked during the World War II era

quickly became a major manufacturer of aircraft equipment. At the beginning of World War II, 35 countries were using Link trainers. At the end of the war, trainers left Link's factory at the rate of one every 45 minutes.

Link loved aviation as a profession, but he also loved spending time outdoors on weekends and on vacations. In 1944, he designed and built a sectioned canoe that could be disassembled and carried in a private airplane. Link called his creation the Linkanoe, and he sold about 4,000 during its three-year production run.

Link never graduated from high school, but he received five honorary college degrees. He also received many awards from such organizations as Philadelphia's Franklin Institute, the Smithsonian Institu-

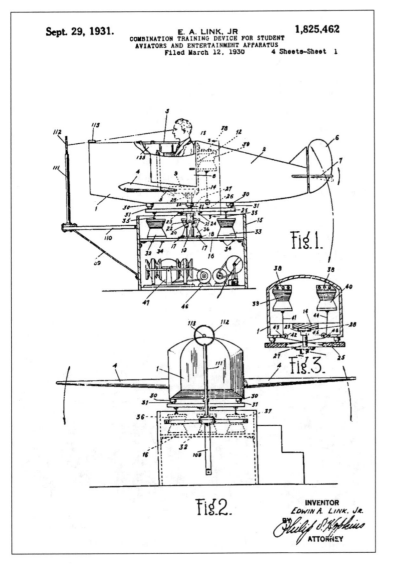

Sept. 29, 1931.   E. A. LINK, JR   1,825,462
                    COMBINATION TRAINING DEVICE FOR STUDENT
                     AVIATORS AND ENTERTAINMENT APPARATUS
                       Filed March 12, 1930   4 Sheets-Sheet 1

Fig.1.

Fig.3.

Fig.2.

INVENTOR
EDWIN A. LINK. JR.
ATTORNEY

Patent drawing shows how Link's trainer used compressed air.

tion, the Royal Aeronautical Society of London, and the International Oceanographic Foundation. He and his wife, Marion, established the Link Foundation in 1953. It made more than 120 grants to qualified organizations "interested in the mastery of the air and sea, and the development of energy resources and their conservation."

Following retirement from his company in 1954, Link began a second career in oceanography. From the deck of his research ship *Sea Diver*, he led many teams in exploring ocean depths around the world. Among his inventions were a submersible vessel, a submersible decompression chamber, an underwater television propulsion device, a heated diving suit, and an inflatable underwater living chamber. He held a total of 35 patents. In 1979, his submersible *Deep Diver* conducted the first underwater survey of the sunken Civil War ironclad USS *Monitor*. At his death, Link had homes in New York and Florida, and he was well known for his contributions to ocean explorations. Link may have finished his productive life with wet feet, but he started with his head in the clouds.

References and Resources

Linkanoe by Philip Carew, Roberson Center, Binghamton, New York, 1986.

The Story of the Link Orchestral Organ, Roberson Center, Binghamton, New York, circa 1968.

"The Plane That Never Leaves the Ground" by James I. Killgore, in *American Heritage of Invention and Technology*, Winter 1989.

"Edwin A. Link, 1904-1981," in *The Link Log*, September 1981.

Chester Floyd Carlson

IT seems hard to believe that people did not always think that many copies of documents were necessary. Today, there are more than 5 million copiers in use in America, which turn out an estimated 2,000 copies each year for every person in the country. In the 1930s, people didn't see a need for multiple copies, and it took more than 20 years for the first copier to reach production. Chester Floyd Carlson invented his copier in 1938. He was the last person who single-handedly developed a new product that spawned an entire industry. The first practical dry copier, the Xerox 914, was introduced to the public in 1960.

Carlson was the only son in a poor and sickly family. His mother's tuberculosis led the family to move often in search of a more healthful climate. Because he moved so often, Carlson developed very few friendships as a child. His father was a barber who became bedridden with a spinal disorder. At 14, Carlson provided his family's primary financial support. He rose before sunrise at their San Bernardino, California, home to wash windows and clean businesses. He earned $50 to $60 per month. He also worked summers on a farm and in a cement plant. Carlson later said that his early experience introduced him to the value of work and the discipline that goes with it.

Showing impressive determination not to give up, Carlson put himself through a local community college. There, he met an engineering teacher who encouraged him

Courtesy of the Xerox Corp.

In this 1965 photograph, Chester Carlson shows the materials he used in 1938 to make the first xerographic copy.

Born:
February 8, 1906, in Seattle, Washington

Died:
September 18, 1968, in New York, New York

to pursue photography and such outdoor activities as hiking and fishing. The teacher recognized Carlson as a brilliant student and pushed him to raise his goals. Carlson eventually graduated from the California Institute of Technology. He remained a lifelong friend of the teacher who inspired him.

Following graduation from Cal Tech, Carlson landed a $35-per-week position with Bell Telephone Laboratories across the country in New York City. He worked in Bell's patent department until he was laid off in 1933, a victim of the Great Depression. He found another job with P. R. Mallory Co., a manufacturer of electrical components. This was the most significant move in Carlson's life. At Mallory, he worked long hours checking and comparing patent drawings and text. At the time, the only two methods available for duplicating such complex documents were photography or redrawing and retyping. Carlson decided there had to be a better way.

Carlson had owned a printing press during his high school years and had a continuing interest in the graphic arts. He began his work on the dry copier by searching the technical literature. He found nothing that suggested that others were working on such a duplication process. However, Carlson did find information about photoconductivity. Some materials, such as sulfur, change electrical conductivity after exposure to light. Experiments that Carlson conducted in his kitchen produced unpleasant odors that spread throughout the apartment house where he lived. The daughter of the apartment's owner came to complain, but instead she became interested in Carlson and his work. They married in 1934.

Carlson needed more space to continue his nighttime experiments. He rented a small room at the back of a beauty shop operated by his mother-in-law in Astoria, New York. Although he could hardly afford it, he also hired an assistant, a German

The 1960 Xerox 914 was the world's first practical dry copier.

Courtesy of the Xerox Corp.

physicist named Otto Kornei who had just immigrated to the U.S. Carlson budgeted $10 per month for his research. Carlson and Kornei made their first successful experiment in 1938. Kornei darkened a room and rubbed a sulfur-coated zinc plate with a handkerchief to develop static electricity. He pressed the sulfur plate against a glass plate

that had words written on it and then exposed it to a bright light for about three seconds. Carlson then dusted the sulfur with yellowish lycopodium powder, a natural spore also known as club moss. He gently blew on the plate, removing the loose powder and leaving a temporary image. To make the image permanent, Carlson placed a sheet of waxed paper on the powder and heated it. The waxed paper held the world's first legible dry-copied image: "10-22-38 ASTORIA." Almost in disbelief, the men repeated the experiment several times. It succeeded equally well each time. To celebrate, the men put away the sandwiches they had brought with them and went to lunch at a nearby restaurant.

Carlson's patent was the first in the field. He called the process *electrophotography*. Since no one else was working on dry copiers, his patent was very broad based and gave Carlson many rights. Unsure of the project's direction, Kornei left six months later to take a corporate job. However, Carlson never forgot Kornei's help and generously rewarded him in later years with Xerox Corp. stock.

Carlson tried for five years to make a simple copying machine. He looked for a corporate sponsor, but more than 20 companies rejected his prototype. He was nearly broke in 1944 when an employee of Battelle Memorial Institute came to the Mallory Co. to discuss other patents. Battelle was a small research organization in Columbus, Ohio. Carlson engaged the Battelle representative in conversation, and he agreed to have technicians study Carlson's invention.

Battelle agreed to take over some of the design work, but soon spent the small $3,000 budget assigned to it. Batelle, too, went looking for corporate sponsors. Batelle met with rejection from everyone except the Haloid Corp., a manufacturer of photographic paper and other items in Rochester, New York. An agreement was reached in 1946 that gave Haloid a license to develop a copying machine based on Carlson's patents. The company figured that it would have to spend $25,000 per year in research on the device. Since it had earned only $101,000 in 1946, Haloid was taking a tremendous gamble.

Haloid introduced a crude and cumbersome copying machine in 1949 called the Xerox Model A. Its operation required 14 separate steps, and business and industry leaders did not accept it. The term *xerographic* comes from the Greek *xeros*, which means "dry," and *graphos*, which means "writing." The word was first used in 1947. Dozens of difficult technical problems with the copier awaited solution. The company experimented with other dry models before introducing the classic Xerox 914 in 1960. Its name came from the maximum size of copy it could make from a roll of paper, 9" x 14". Wildly successful, more than 200,000 of the freezer-sized 650-pound 914s were manufactured. Haloid had expected to make about 4,000. The 914s were never sold. Instead, the company leased each one for about $95 per month plus 5¢ per copy. The 914 could make seven copies per minute. The company's revenues went from $33 million in 1959 to over $500 million in 1966. Briefly called Haloid Xerox, the company changed its name to the Xerox Corp. in 1961.

The holder of 28 patents in xerography, Carlson always had faith in his abilities and never gave up. Though almost penniless in the late 1950s, he later received dozens of awards, including the 1964 Inventor of the Year Award and the 1966 Horatio Alger Award. Carlson had a net worth of $150 million by the late 1960s. He had a weak heart and painful arthritis later in life, and he spent his last years giving away $100 million. Most of his anonymous donations went to research and charities.

References and Resources

Xerox World–Special Issue: Chester Carlson's Invention, Fall/Winter 1988.

"Struggling to Become an Inventor" by Dean J. Golembeski, in *American Heritage of Invention and Technology*, Winter 1989.

"Chester F. Carlson, Inventor of Xerography" by Alfred Dinsdale, in *Photographic Science and Engineering*, January/February 1963.

"The Invention Nobody Wanted" by Don Wharton, in *The Kiwanis Magazine*, February 1965.

"Profiles: Xerox Xerox Xerox Xerox" by John Brooks, in *The New Yorker*, 1 April 1967.

Dictionary of American Biography, Charles Scribner's Sons Publishers, 1932; with supplemental updates.

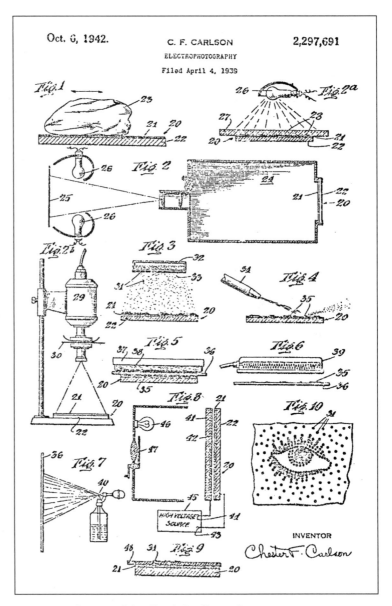

"Dry writing" originally took many steps.

Technology Overviews

Computers

**1700s to
1990s**

IT would be hard to imagine the world today without computers. The duties of these electronic workhorses include scanning bar code prices at grocery stores and monitoring hospital patients. Computers control machine tool operations in factories. They provide exciting simulation games and efficient word-processing capabilities. Their uses seem as boundless as a person's imagination. The digital computer is easily the greatest technological innovation of the twentieth century.

Unlike many other inventions, the computer has an origin that can be traced back to a single person: **Charles Babbage** (1791-1871). This wealthy Briton designed what he called an *analytical engine*. In an era before electricity, Babbage planned to operate his mechanical gear-and-lever device with a steam engine.

The Computer's Infancy

All twentieth-century computer pioneers acknowledged Babbage as the first in their field. Born near London, England, Babbage came from a wealthy family and did not have to work for his living. He took particular fascination in the lengthy tables of trigonometric and logarithmic functions. In Babbage's day, the tables were laboriously hand calculated and full of undiscovered errors. Babbage envisioned a calculator that would determine mathematical values and automatically print them.

Babbage spent his own money paying skilled machinists to make the necessary parts for a calculator he designed. He had more than 4,000 gears, levers, cams, and linkages made to exceedingly close tolerances. Many people throughout the world heard about the project. One was Joseph Henry, an American and the first head of

Charles Babbage's nineteenth-century demonstration calculator is displayed at the Science Museum in London. It operated by turning a crank at the top.

the Smithsonian Institution. Henry twice visited the inventor and wrote that Babbage, "more than any [person] who ever lived, narrowed the chasm separating science and practical mechanics."

Babbage never completed his calculator, but he did have a small demonstration model assembled in 1832. With 2,000 individual parts, it measured $72 \times 59 \times 61$ centimeters, one-seventh the size of the device Babbage designed. Powered by a hand crank, it operated faultlessly. It was the earliest automatic calculator. The beautifully made brass assemblage of gears, levers, cams, and rods looked as impressive as an elegant statue. It was the finest example of nineteenth-century precision machining. London's Science Museum now has it on display.

Babbage was a difficult person to work

with, and he upset many of the gifted machinists who worked for him. Even though Babbage had 12,000 parts made and he personally paid for almost all the work, he never saw the full-size calculator through to completion. His highly creative mind soon wandered toward making a computer.

Babbage's calculator processed numbers the only way it could, by adding or subtracting them in a particular sequence. Babbage wanted to make a more general-purpose machine that would perform mathematical tasks determined by the user. The procedure he developed in 1833 is identical to that used by modern computers. His computer design included five sections:

● An input device (punched cards, in Babbage's design).

● An arithmetic unit, to perform calculations.

● A programmable unit, to select the calculating sequences.

● Memory (gear positions).

● An output mechanism, such as a printer, plotter, or punched cards.

The idea for using punched cards came from **J. M. Jaquard**, who used them to control weaving patterns in his French textile looms. Babbage used small operation cards to specify arithmetical operations. Larger variable cards specified input data and controlled the location of the answers in the *store*, Babbage's word for memory. During the 30 years he worked on his computer, Babbage developed conditional branching, looping, and subroutines. All are important operations in modern computer programs.

In Babbage's era the word *engine* meant "device". He called his computer an *analytical engine*. The project turned out to be vastly more complex than Babbage's unfinished calculator. The accuracy requirements for the parts greatly strained nineteenth-century technology. The computer would have required about 200,000 parts, and Babbage designed it to be powered by a steam engine. Yet, once again, his personality got in the way of his invention and the analytical engine was never built. A demonstration model under assembly at the time of Babbage's death also went uncompleted.

Babbage was many generations ahead of his time, and he enjoys more widespread esteem today than he did during his lifetime. Calling Babbage a key computer pioneer is more than a casual comment.

Applying Electricity

Although Babbage originated computer technology, **Herman Hollerith** (1860-1929) built the first computer-like system. (See pages 145-147 for a profile of Hollerith.) One advantage he had over Babbage was that Hollerith worked during the electrical age and could take advantage of emerging electrical technology. He designed a tabulator for use in the 1890 U.S. census. Hollerith received the census contract after beating two competitors in a government test. One competitor, who used colored cards, took 55 hours to tabulate contest data. The other used metal tokens and took 44 hours. Hollerith's electrical machine did the work in just 6 hours.

A patent office employee in Washington, D.C., Hollerith worked on his tabulator during his free time. Like Babbage, he also used punched cards. The sections of his system included:

● A punch for indicating data on sturdy cards.

● A tabulator for entering and processing data.

● An output device of 40 clocklike counters.

Hollerith's early machines could only tally data and did not function as computers in the modern sense. However, his later machines had more advanced calculating designs. They generated statistical data for railroads, insurance companies, and steel mills. Hollerith's company evolved into the International Business Machines Corp. (IBM).

The Digital Age

The driving force behind modern digital computers was **Howard Aiken** (1900-1973), an engineering professor at Harvard University. As World War II loomed over the horizon, the pressure to build powerful calculators increased. Aiken approached IBM in 1937 with an idea for a computer. At the time, IBM manufactured telephone relays that could provide the rapid on-off switching required for binary arithmetic.

Aiken completed his big-as-a-house Mark I computer and first demonstrated it in January 1943. The huge machine was 51' long,

Smithsonian Institution

Howard Aiken inspects one of the paper tape input sections of the Mark I computer in about 1944. The switches on the wall were part of the programming technique.

Computers of the 1940s and 1950s

There is some question as to whether the Mark I was the first computer. A few early machines were dedicated calculators, potential computers designed for specific functions. The 1943 British Colossus was one example. It was a code breaker, though it had no internal memory. The 1941 German Z3 may have been a true programmable compu-ter. It was destroyed during World War II. With computer designs occurring so quickly during the early days of World War II, and with feelings of nationalism so strong during that period, differences of opinion arose. However, there is no doubt that the Mark I was the first American computer.

In 1946, the Mark I was moved to Harvard in Cambridge, Massachusetts. It remained in 24-hour use for 15 years. The next computing machine, ENIAC, was 1,000

8' high, and 2' wide. Built at IBM's headquarters in Endicott, New York, the computer weighed 50 tons and had more than 750,000 parts. Its 3,000 clicking relays sounded like a roomful of people knitting. The Mark I was probably the world's first programmable computer.

The Mark I's programs were loaded from a roll of punched paper tape. A story is told that a moth on the paper once shut down the system by covering some of the holes. Removing the "bug" allowed the program to continue. That is said to be the origin of the word *debug*, which refers to eliminating errors from a computer program.

The Mark I was mostly used to determine trajectories for shells fired from large U.S. Navy guns. By modern standards, it had little computational power. A 1/4"-square microprocessor chip could outperform the Mark I by a factor of over a million.

After the war, Aiken served as director of Harvard's new computational laboratory. He greatly influenced the creation of an academic environment that allowed the school to become an early leader in computer science. Harvard's Aiken Computational Laboratory is named in his honor.

Smithsonian Institution

The first all-electronic computer was ENIAC (Electronic Numerical Integrator and Calculator). One of its designers, J. Presper Eckert, is at the front left turning programming switches.

Smithsonian Institution

Programming on the ENIAC in the late 1940s was done by turning switches (right) and plugging in electrical cables (left).

times faster. It was built at the University of Pennsylvania in Philadelphia.

Computer professionals seem to delight in cryptic names. One such name was the 1945 ENIAC (Electronic Numerical Integrator and Calculator), the first electronic computer. **J. Presper Eckert** and **John Mauchly** headed ENIAC's design team. Like the Mark I, ENIAC was a huge machine. It had 18,000 vacuum tubes, weighed 50 tons, and took up more floor area than an average house. The computer used enough electrical power to supply a small city. Primarily used by the military, ENIAC could multiply a five-digit number by itself 5,000 times in a half second. However, the computer's memory capacity was low—it could store only about 20 words.

After the creation ENIAC, the computer revolution began in earnest. The IBM Electronic Discrete Variable Automatic Computer (EDVAC) of 1949 was the first stored-program digital computer. The first commercially successful computer was the 1951 Universal Automatic Computer (UNIVAC).

Manufactured by the Sperry-Rand Corp., it was the first computer used to predict a political victory. UNIVAC correctly selected Dwight Eisenhower over Adlai Stevenson for president in 1952. The first desk-sized computer was the 1956 E-101 from the Burroughs Corp.

So much activity followed, that it was hard to keep track of it all. Computer capacity and speed increased dramatically at the same time that size decreased. Large corporations built computers for other corporations. At this point, though, people found computers to be far too expensive for personal use.

Early programmers

Before the introduction of computers, all complex machines were externally controlled. Programming was a brand-new idea in the early 1940s. Programming made possible the creation of a machine with built-in intelligence, allowing it to operate on its own. Computer programming in those days included twisting dials, flipping switches, and connecting cables. Typewriter-like machines punched holes in paper for data entry. This was a complicated and highly technical operation. Few people knew how to do it. Even fewer could do it well. Those who could, were highly respected and thought of as magicians or wizards. Two of the earliest programmers were Grace Hopper and Adele Goldstine.

Grace Hopper was the first-ever pro-

Smithsonian Institution

Grace Hopper stands near one of the input sections of the Mark I computer in about 1944. She is holding a piece of paper tape used to input data.

grammer. A U.S. Navy officer in World War II, she programmed the Mark I by adjusting up to 1,400 dials and plugging in hundreds of cables. Data was read from a three-inch-wide strip of long punched paper tape. Hopper also wrote the manual of operation for the Mark I.

Hopper later played a major role in developing the most popular computer business language, Common Business Oriented Language (CO-BOL). Her subordinates affectionately called her "Amazing Grace." Before she retired in 1986, Rear Admiral Hopper was the highest-ranking woman in the U.S. Navy.

Adele Goldstine helped build the ENIAC. She was the only woman in an engineering design group of 14 people. When the $500,000 machine was built in 1945, she became one of its two chief programmers. ENIAC's first program took her two days to set up and only 20 seconds to run. Goldstine knew so much about the computer that she wrote its 301-page operations manual by herself.

Personal Computers

Computers of the 1950s and 1960s were large devices used only by companies and businesses. Most took up the space of two or more classrooms. Not until integrated circuits and microprocessor chips were developed did people see the desktop personal computer (PC) as a realistic possibility.

A Texas Instruments research engineer, **Jack Kilby**, made the first practical integrated circuit in 1959. It provided the equivalent of dozens of vacuum tubes in a space the size of a fingernail. Its earliest use was in handheld calculators. However, it was the invention of the quarter-inch-square microprocessor chip in 1971 that led to the creation of small PCs. A team at the Intel Corp. in California patented the first one, which Intel named the 4004. Each tiny chip had the equivalent of more than a million vacuum tubes.

Micro Instrumentation and Telemetry Systems (MITS) of Albuquerque, New Mexico, made the first PC, the little-known Altair 8800. **Edward Roberts** and **William Yates** designed it in the mid-1970s. They

named the computer after the *Star Trek* episode "A Voyage to Altair." It sold as a kit for $395 or came fully assembled for $650.

The Altair 8800 was not easy to use. It had no keyboard and no available software. All programming was done with switches,

Hopper stands near a magnetic tape input of a Remington Rand computer. She wrote the COBOL book in her hand.

using complex computer machine language. The Altair 8800's 256-byte (1/4K) memory was small. Although MITS sold several thousand, the company went out of business in 1979.

The Apple II

Two young men in their twenties invented the Apple II, the first widely accepted PC. **Steven Wozniak** and **Steven Jobs** established the Apple Computer Co. in 1976 in Cupertino, California. They introduced the $1,195 Apple II with a 16K memory in 1977. They chose the name Apple for their company because it was a simple word, and Jobs had once spent a summer picking fruit in Oregon. The Macintosh computer came out in 1984, and it was named after Wozniak's favorite type of apple.

The two Steves found a common interest in computers through meetings at the Homebrew Computer Club. Wozniak helped organize the club in 1975, and it is considered the first PC users' group. Jobs and Wozniak designed and assembled a

The prototype Apple personal computer was placed in a wooden case. It is on display at the Smithsonian Institution.

computer in 1976 that served as their Apple I prototype. To obtain money to market the computer, Jobs sold his Volkswagen and Wozniak sold his Hewlett-Packard calculator. They built the Apple I in Jobs's garage and sold it for $666. It was targeted at people with an interest in electronics and computers. Of the two men, Jobs had the better business sense and Wozniak was the real inventor of the Apple computer.

The Apple I was a well-received product, so the two young men easily found financing for their next computer. The Apple II came out in 1977. It made possible the purchase and use of a PC by the average person. The Apple II proved particularly popular for educational use, because of its low cost and the appropriateness of available software.

IBM developed floppy disks in 1970 and hard drives in 1973. Early Apples had used cassette tapes for storing programs and data. However, Apple also adopted the use of floppy disks and hard drives to improve the usability of its product.

Computer Software

Without software, personal computers would be about as hard to operate as the Altair 8800. People recognized this early on and worked to create programs that would make PCs more useful to the average person. One of the first pieces of useful software was the Formula Translation (FORTRAN) language developed by **John Backus** in 1957. Primarily used by engineers and technicians, FORTRAN was the first system to translate near-English into the computer's machine language.

Hopper's COBOL came out the next year, and it proved popular with the business community. However, casual users had difficulty with both FORTRAN and COBOL. Two Dartmouth University mathematics professors developed a still simpler programming language in 1964. **John Kemeny** and **Thomas Kurtz** came out with their Beginners All-purpose Symbolic Instruction Code (BASIC). They said they wanted a name "that was simple but not simple minded."

Daniel Bricklin invented VisiCalc, the world's first spreadsheet software, offering it for sale in 1979. With a price of $100 and availability only for the Apple II, it attracted attention slowly. Once business people realized its capabilities, however, VisiCalc sales zoomed. Many companies bought Apple II computers just to use that one program. All spreadsheet programs trace their heritage to VisiCalc.

Every PC requires a disk-operating system, a method for telling the computer how to operate. The most popular one is Microsoft Corporation's Disk Operating System (MS-DOS). Developed by **William Gates** in 1982, it quickly became the industry standard. Microsoft was founded by Gates and it was the first personal computer software firm.

The Value of Artificial Intelligence

Some people say that artificial intelligence is a contradiction in terms. Others call it a useful descriptor applied to a high level of computer operation. Both may be correct. However, it's important to remember that the computer, with its artificial intelligence, is only a tool. It will never rival the human mind for emotion or creativity. People dream about tomorrow. People form attachments to other people and to other creatures from all of nature's species. People can appreciate classical music, enjoy sporting activities, and visualize the entire universe in a simple flower. Though a very valuable tool for humanity, the computer can do none of those things.

References and Resources

Portraits in Silicon by Robert Slater, MIT Press, 1989.

The Making of the Micro by Christopher Evans, Van Nostrand, 1981.

How One Company's Zest for Technological Innovation Helped Build the Computer Industry, IBM corporate publication, 1984.

Charles Babbage and His Calculating Engines by Doron Swade, London Science Museum, 1991.

Babbage display, Science Museum, London.

Information Age display, National Museum of American History, Washington, DC, 1993.

Television

Twentieth century

John Logie Baird used this experimental apparatus to demonstrate a practical television system in 1926.

SOON after Samuel Morse invented his telegraph in 1844, technologists began to wonder if they could send images by wire. Placed in the proper order, a series of dots can produce a high-quality image. In the mid-1800s, early investigators did not know exactly how to accomplish their goal, but the idea eventually resulted in facsimile (fax) machines. Photographs were routinely sent over telephone lines as early as 1907.

The success of Alexander Graham Bell's 1876 telephone caused the champions of television to redouble their efforts. Unlike the transmission of a static image, a telephone sends dynamic audio signals as people speak them. Technologists imagined a system that would send video signals in real time. Even though no system was in place, some called the concept *electric vision* and the instrument the *telephonoscope*. Only a few years later, people were sending crude silhouette images over wire.

No single person can claim credit for inventing television. Dozens of people working in several countries made significant contributions to making television a practical method of communication. However, two people stand out above the others as central to its development. They were **John Logie Baird** of Scotland and **Vladimir Zworykin** (see pages 202-204) of the United States.

Early Attempts

The first people to investigate television worked on sending a single non-moving image over a wire. They did not try to transmit an entire picture but broke it into small sections. They sent these sections, one after another, in a precise order. At the destination, the pieces were reassembled, much as happens with a jigsaw puzzle. The idea of breaking a picture into smaller elements was important. It was the only practical way to send and reproduce a picture. The first person to develop a workable technique was a German, **Paul Nipkow** (1860-1940).

In 1884, Nipkow invented a process that used a revolving metal disk that had a series of holes. The holes scanned a picture and separated it into smaller sections. Known as *mechanical television*, this method formed the basis for most television processes used through the early 1930s. Nipkow's disk had 24 holes evenly placed in a shallow spiral near its circumference. An electric motor turned the disk at 600 rpm in front of a small picture whose image was to be sent to a television. A lens focused reflected light from the picture onto photocells behind the spinning disk. The cells translated the picture's image into a pulsing electric current.

To reproduce the image, Nipkow proposed using an identical rotating disk and an amplified light source. This was an ingenious idea that bore some similarity to the operation of motion picture cameras and film projectors. However, Nipkow could not build a complete system because he lacked the technology to do so. His biggest obstacle was that he had no way to amplify the power from the selenium photocells. The output image was not visible. **Lee De Forest** (see pages 172-174) remedied that problem with his triode tube in 1906.

Besides being an inventor, the Scottish-born **John Logie Baird** (1888-1946) was also a marketing wizard. He had keen interests in both developing a workable television system and getting the public interested in it. Using a Nipkow rotating disk, Baird became the first person to build a transmitter and receiver used in regular broadcast service. His was the only successful mechanical television system.

In 1926, Baird made the first public demonstration of television to 50 people in London. He used the experimental transmitting equipment shown in the photograph on the preceding page. Baird's spinning disk was a piece of cardboard with several holes that had lenses over them. The subject was a puppet head that Baird called Stooky Bill. The receiver used a spinning disk synchronized with the disk in the transmitter. During the demonstration, the image created by a faint pink glow from neon tubes in the receiver just barely resembled Stooky Bill.

Baird made a big show of presenting his equipment to London's Science Museum. He also did everything else he could to keep television in the news. In 1928, he sent the first television images across the ocean to New York. In 1930, he made the first demonstration of large-screen television, in London's Coliseum. He reproduced the image on a screen filled with neon lamps. The British Broadcasting Corporation (BBC) granted Baird's company a license, and Baird transmitted experimental television from 1929 to 1935. The audience was small, and the fuzzy images transmitted were usually head-and-shoulder shots of people talking during test transmissions. Baird did not broadcast any real programs. He estimated that no more than 30 sets received the images, and 20 of those were homemade. A

commercial Baird receiver, called a Televisor, is shown in the photograph below.

One major problem with the mechanical rotating-disk system was that it could only transmit low-quality images. Disks could not spin quickly enough. Baird's system transmitted low-definition signals, about 30 lines on a small three-inch screen. With such restrictions, fine details could not be reproduced. High-definition signals used from 343 to 525 lines on the screen and they required the speed that would be provided by electronics.

The Use of Electronics

The Nipkow disk showed technologists one way to send television images. However, the mechanical system could not scan

Baird's television receiver used a spinning disk and was called a Televisor.

quickly enough to transmit and receive high-quality moving images. Electronic systems did not suffer that shortcoming. Properly set up, an electronic scanner and receiver could operate at the speed of light.

In spite of their speed, electronic television systems still relied on the logic provided by the mechanical Nipkow disk. Cameras scanned objects with a rapidly moving electronic beam. The process worked the same way that a person's eyes work in reading a printed page. The electronic beam moved from left to right across the image, recording dots and empty space. Then, it returned rapidly to the left and scanned the next line. Early experimental systems scanned 343 lines. Transmitting equipment sent the pulses of dots along a wire or through the air. Electronic receivers rearranged the

Vladimir Zworykin's iconoscope was the first successful electronic television camera tube.

pulses and displayed them on a television screen.

At least that was the idea. It took a long time to move from theory to practice. The development of amplifier tubes by De Forest in America and **John Fleming** in England encouraged early investigators in their work on electronic television. Because of the complexity of developing a flying beam for a camera, early electronic television pioneers concentrated their efforts on amplifying the output. That was the route taken by **Boris von Rosing**, a professor at the St. Petersburg Institute of Technology in St. Petersburg, Russia.

Von Rosing and his young assistant, **Vladimir Zworykin** (1889-1982), experimented with a primitive amplifier tube. They used a mechanical disk transmitter and an electronic tube in the receiver. The transmitter comprised two revolving drums with many tiny mirrors attached. Von Rosing patented the design in 1908 and publicly

demonstrated it in 1910. The two investigators had to make almost every item in the system. Much of Zworykin's time went to the tedious task of glass blowing. Zworykin and von Rosing experimented with many different configurations to determine the best tube shape.

The system proved to be impractical because electronic amplifiers were still in their infancy. Zworykin and von Rosing's handmade tubes proved quite inefficient. World War I and the Russian Revolution soon ended their work. Yet, the project excited the young Zworykin. He continued doing related work at the College of France in Paris. Within a few years, Zworykin became more closely identified with electronic television than any other person in the world.

Zworykin arrived in New York in 1919 unable to speak English. He went to work in the radio-tube department of Westinghouse Electric Corp. in Pittsburgh. His assignments included improving the company's facsimile transmitters, as well as making a television camera and picture tube. Zworykin knew that some inventors were closing in on a practical design for a picture tube. Yet, none were close to a suitable electronic camera tube, one that would scan an image and break it into a series of dots. Zworykin decided to work on inventing one. He called his invention an *iconoscope*, meaning "image watcher." This was the most remarkable invention in the history of television. Every technical museum in the world has a Zworykin iconoscope on display.

The Iconoscope

Early technologists had calculated that high-definition television pictures would require more than six million impulses per second. A whirling Nipkow disk could not possibly spin fast enough to meet that requirement. (It would have to revolve about ten million times per minute.) Zworykin considered using electronic methods to accomplish the same objective.

The photograph of his iconoscope above shows a dark, rectangular, light-sensitive mosaic inside the glass tube. An electron gun, aimed at the mosaic, is at the bottom. It has wires coming out of the tube. This is how it worked:

1. A camera lens focused an image on the mosaic.

2. The electron gun sent out a narrow stream of electrons that scanned the mosaic. The electron gun made 343 passes in about 1/30 second.

3. A metal plate behind the mosaic absorbed the effect of the scanning and produced electrical impulses. The impulses were sent out on a wire just barely visible in the photo at the top right of the iconoscope.

4. Approximately six million electrical impulses left the iconoscope every second. Those pulses were characteristic of the image being focused by the camera lens.

Zworykin invented the iconoscope in 1923 and the *kinescope*, the television picture tube, in 1929. Westinghouse was unwilling to invest the necessary development money, so Zworykin moved to the Radio Corporation of America (RCA) in 1929. In November, he demonstrated the first practical and completely electronic television system at a convention of the Institute of Radio Engineers. It had both a transmitter and a receiver. RCA was so impressed with Zworykin and his invention, that the corporation spent $50 million over the next 20 years perfecting a practical television system.

The BBC introduced the world's first regular broadcast service, known as high-definition television, in England in 1936. The camera tube was an *emitron*, the British equivalent of the iconoscope. The television screens on the custom-made sets measured about 3" x 4", and the TVs cost from $750 to $1,100. The National Broadcasting Co. (NBC) started America's first scheduled service in 1939. In 1941, New York's WNBT became the first commercial television station.

Other Television Pioneers

Baird and Zworykin may have been television's biggest stars, but they were only part of a large team of dedicated players. Many other people struggled with the details of practical television transmission. They worked on improving the 5 to 10 percent efficiency of early iconoscope mosaics, designing more powerful amplifier tubes, and reducing the cost of television sets by finding simpler circuits. Any list of

important television technologists would include the individuals named below.

Charles Francis Jenkins (1867-1934) was the American equivalent of John Logie Baird. He held approximately 400 patents. Jenkins experimented with mechanical television images in 1890. He is best known for using Nipkow disks to transmit silhouette pictures from his Washington, D.C., workshop in 1925. He called his system *radiovision*.

Karl Braun (1853-1918) developed the first practical cathode-ray tube that could be used for electronic television reception. Braun was German. His 1906 invention was often called the *Braun tube*.

Alan Campbell Swinton (1863-1930) was an English scientist who proposed a television system in 1907 using a Braun tube. He did not build any hardware. Boris von Rosing took his idea one step further, constructing experimental apparatuses in Russia. Von Rosing patented the procedure.

Ernst Alexanderson (1878-1975) worked at RCA and at General Electric's research laboratories in Schenectady, New York. He held more than 300 patents for transformers, alternators, and televisions. He began tests on experimental television station W2XAD in 1928.

Philo Farnsworth (1906-1971) was an

Hall of History Foundation

As this GE publicity photo shows, television sets of the late 1940s had furniture-sized cabinets and small screens.

Philo Farnsworth invented a television camera tube that he called a "dissector."

Smithsonian Institution Photo No. 64079

Idaho-born inventor who had a practical system that rivaled Zworykin's. Instead of using an iconoscope, his system used what he called a *dissector*. Farnsworth patented his idea in 1930. Many television systems used Farnworth's design.

Allen DuMont (1901-1965) improved picture tubes at his DuMont Laboratories in New York. DuMont organized a commercial television station (WABD) and made the first television sets for sale to the public in 1939.

Peter Goldmark (1906-1977) was a Hungarian-born American who demonstrated the first practical color television system in 1940. Goldmark also developed long-playing, high-fidelity records.

References and Resources

4,000 Years of Television by Richard W. Hubbell, G. P. Putnam's Sons, 1942.

Television: The Eyes of Tomorrow by William C. Eddy, Prentice-Hall, 1945.

Television: Present Methods of Picture Transmission by H. Horton Sheldon, Van Nostrand Co., 1929.

Making of the Modern World edited by Neil Cossons, John Murray Publishers, 1992.

Manned Space Program

"**S**pace: the final frontier. These are the voyages of the starship *Enterprise*." With those words, William Shatner opened each episode of the 1960s *Star Trek* television show. The popularity of the series rested on its imaginative attempts to show what other beings may live in the universe. In an unrealistic-but-entertaining manner, the likable crew of the *Enterprise* took millions of people on weekly trips into space.

Since the beginning of recorded history, people have wondered about the sun, moon, stars, and planets. They made up mythological characters, such as Zeus and Mercury, and told stories of their travel through the heavens. Yet it was not until the dawn of the twentieth century that human beings seriously considered travel in space.

Only the United States and the Soviet Union (now Russia and other smaller nations) developed manned space transportation systems. Called the "Space Race," the early competition between the two countries lasted from about 1957 to 1969. American space pilots are called astronauts and their Russian counterparts are *cosmonauts*. *Astro* means "star" and *naut* means "sailor," so an astronaut is a "star sailor." *Cosmos* means "universe," which makes a cosmonaut a "universe sailor."

Pioneers in Rocket Design

The Russians were the first to place a human being in orbit around the earth. They were also the first to put up a satellite. Russia traces its national heritage in space exploration to **Konstantin Tsiolkovsky** (1857-1935), a high school physics teacher in the large city of Izhevsk. He became interested in the subject around 1895.

Before Tsiolkovsky, "rocketry" referred to the gunpowder-propelled missiles devel-

National Air and Space Museum

About 5,000 rocket-propelled V-2s were built by Germany during World War II. They used alcohol and liquid oxygen.

1900s to 1990s

oped by the Chinese in the 1100s. Often used by the military, solid-fueled rockets had no practical civilian application. By analyzing rockets, Tsiolkovsky determined that liquid propellants had advantages over the gunpowder type. Their thrust could be varied, and they developed more impulse (thrust multiplied by time). Tsiolkovsky wrote that the best combination was a fuel of liquid hydrogen (LH2) and an oxidizer of liquid oxygen (LOX).

Tsiolkovsky was right. Those propellants powered the upper stages of the *Saturn 5* rocket, which took Americans to the moon. LH2 and LOX also power the three main inboard engines on current Space Shuttles. One major disadvantage of LH2 and LOX is that they are supercold propellants. LH2 is -425° F and LOX is -300° F.

Because the technology of his era was not advanced enough, Tsiolkovsky never actually built a rocket. Yet, that did not stop him from developing reasonable designs for multistage rockets and for a space station. His fame as a rocket pioneer rests on a series of remarkable articles on rocketry that he wrote in 1911. Some people thought that rockets could not operate in the vacuum of space because the thrust would have no atmosphere to push against. That was incorrect logic, and Tsiolkovsky was the first to publish a clear explanation of how rockets worked.

The Russians wanted to acknowledge Tsiolkovsky by launching the world's first satellite on the one-hundredth anniversary of his birth, September 17, 1857. Although

A full size cutaway of a V-2 rocket engine is on display at the Deutsches Museum in Munich, Germany. The engine is quite similar to the one used to launch America's first satellite, *Explorer I*.

the satellite went up a few days late, *Sputnik I* was a perfect memorial to Tsiolkovsky.

In the early 1900s, Tsiolkovsky was an obscure Russian rocketry investigator. **Robert Goddard** (see pages 190-192) probably had not heard of Tsiolkovsky when he worked on liquid propellants in Massachusetts and New Mexico. He launched the world's first liquid-propellant rocket on his cousin's farm in 1926. Goddard was a superb scientific investigator and technologist. When a manufacturer could not supply a propellant pump that met his specifications, he designed one and helped his staff make it.

With financial assistance from the Smithsonian Institution and the Daniel Guggenheim Foundation, Goddard tested liquid-propellant rockets in New Mexico. Because of his technical insights and careful construction, his small test program proved quite successful and highly advanced. Although Goddard regularly took out patents, he could not persuade the U.S. government to support a larger rocket program. The newspapers even made fun of him because he wrote hypothetical descriptions of flights to the moon. When *Apollo 11* was on its way to the first moon landing in 1969, *The New York Times* belatedly apologized for unkind comments its writers had made many years earlier.

Goddard's experiments in the 1930s came to the attention of the *Verein fur Raumschiffahrt* (Society for Space Travel). The amateur rocketry club worked closely with the German army. It included Wernher von Braun among its members.

After Germany's defeat in World War I, the country was not permitted to conduct extensive experimental aviation tests. However, the peace treaty did not include rockets. During the 1930s, Germany became the secret world center for liquid-propelled rocket research. **Wernher von Braun** (1912-1977) was a young engineer from a city that is now Wyrzysk, Poland. In 1932, the German Army appointed him as a technical adviser to the rocket program.

Germany was preparing for war and von Braun worked on a liquid-propellant rocket named the V-2, for *Vergeltungswaffe*, or "Vengeance Weapon." Experimenting at the secret Pennemunde test facility on the Baltic Sea, von Braun and others perfected the world's first large liquid-propellant rocket engine. It used alcohol for fuel and an oxidizer of LOX. The engine developed 56,000 pounds of thrust and boosted the 46-foot V-2 to a speed of 3,500 mph. The rocket carried an explosive warhead. About 1,500 hit England during the war years of 1944 and 1945.

After World War II, von Braun and 112 others came to America and helped start the nation's rocket program. He became a U.S. citizen in 1955 and did most of his work in Huntsville, Alabama. The city was home to the U.S. Army's Redstone Arsenal, which developed solid rockets for military use. So many scientists, engineers, and technologists worked there that it was nicknamed "Rocket City, USA."

An alcohol-LOX engine called Redstone boosted America's first satellite, *Explorer I*, into orbit on January 31, 1958. Though modified in Huntsville, the engine was similar to the one used in the V-2.

Manned Flight

An important early goal called for placing a human being in orbit and safely returning that person to the earth. The Soviet Union achieved this goal first with **Yuri Gagarin**. He lifted off from the Baikonur Space Center in south central Russia in 1961 and made one orbit of the earth. The first woman in space was **Valentina Tereshkova**, a Russian who made 48 orbits in 1963.

The Soviets used a relatively simple booster rocket design. They strapped several small liquid-propellant rocket engines together. The Vostok launch vehicles that placed Gagarin and Tereshkova in orbit had 20 engines with a total thrust of 1.1 million pounds. The National Aeronautics and Space Administration (NASA) chose to cut back on the number of engines but use more powerful ones. Practically all American launch vehicles used from one to five main booster engines.

Large liquid-propellant engines are difficult to make. They require high-capacity propellant pumps, on-board gas turbine engines to drive the pumps, pressurized tanks, insulated lines and valves for the supercold propellants, and other specialized components. Solid-propellant engines are far simpler to make, but they are less reliable. In spite of their complexity, until the Space Shuttle Program, every Ameri-

can rocket rated for carrying people used only liquid propellants for the main booster engines.

Because the Soviet Union used smaller engines, it was not surprising that it was able to place a person in earth orbit ahead

Space Shuttles are launched into earth orbit by two strap-on solid rocket boosters and three liquid propellant engines.

of the U.S. Yet, it would have been difficult to boost a cosmonaut all the way to the moon by strapping more and more small engines together. So it was likely that an American astronaut would be the first person on the moon.

Because of early Soviet successes, however, the American public worried that the U.S. was losing the Space Race. In 1958, the government decided to manage the space program with NASA, a new nonmilitary agency. Its mission was to "contribute materially to the expansion of human knowledge of phenomena in the atmosphere and space." Wernher von Braun served as NASA's first director. Nine years later, the United States had all but won the Space Race. Through 1967, the U.S. had 388 successful launches (both manned and unmanned) compared with the Soviet Union's 239.

The U.S. Space Program

Named for the mythological Roman messenger of the gods, the six **Mercury Program** launches were America's first manned space operations. Mercury lasted from 1961 to 1963. The seven astronauts chosen for the program were the subject of a book and motion picture titled *The Right Stuff*.

The first astronaut in space was **Alan Shephard**. Flying alone in a spacecraft he named *Freedom 7*, Shepard was boosted into a 116-mile suborbital flight on May 5, 1961. Propulsion for the 15 minute flight was from a single Redstone rocket engine that developed 82,000 pounds of thrust. **John Glenn** became America's first orbiting astronaut on February 20, 1962. He made three 90-minute trips around the earth after being placed in orbit by a three-engine 367,000-pound-thrust Atlas booster. The program was more successful than anyone had expected and set the stage for the Gemini and Apollo Programs to follow.

During the Mercury Program, President John F. Kennedy showed his strong support for space research. He made an important and memorable speech at Cape Canaveral on May 25, 1961. Part of what he said was: "I believe this nation should commit itself to achieving the goal, before this decade is out, of landing a man on the moon and returning him safely to earth. No single space project in this period will be more exciting, or more impressive to mankind, or more important for the long-range exploration of space; and none will be so difficult or expensive to accomplish." President Kennedy's legacy was carried out eight years and eight weeks later. Americans **Neil Armstrong** and **Edwin Aldrin** landed on the moon and returned safely to earth.

Two astronauts went into earth orbit during each flight in the **Gemini Program**. Ancient astrologers believed the Gemini constellation was composed of twins and ruled by the planet Mercury. NASA used the name

to suggest that the program built on information and progress gained from the Mercury series, and that it would include two astronauts during each flight. The program lasted from 1965 to 1966.

Each launch used a twin-engine Titan II rocket with 430,000 pounds of maximum thrust. One flight, *Gemini 7*, kept astronauts in space for almost two weeks—far longer than any previous flight. Astronauts experimented with space walks, and they conducted important docking and rendezvous maneuvers. Information gathered during the nine Gemini missions was essential for a successful flight to the moon during the Apollo Program.

The **Apollo Program** was the most exciting in space-flight history. It was the only one designed to land human beings somewhere other than earth. Between 1968 and 1972, three astronauts either went into orbit or to the moon on each flight. In Greek mythology, Apollo was the god of light. He was the son of the goddess Leto and Zeus, king of the gods. NASA spent a long time evaluating the best technique for delivering people to the moon and returning them safely to earth. Constrained by the technology of the 1960s, NASA had to develop a complicated procedure:

1. A powerful rocket launched three astronauts into earth orbit.

2. After two orbits to verify system reliability, the astronauts fired a rocket to put them on a path to the moon.

3. Near the moon, they fired another rocket to slow their spacecraft and enter moon orbit.

4. Two astronauts entered an on-board lunar excursion module (LEM) and separated from the spacecraft. One astronaut remained behind while the others flew the LEM to the moon's surface.

5. After a day or more on the surface, the two astronauts fired another rocket, launching themselves toward the orbiting spacecraft. They docked and transferred to the spacecraft.

6. Firing still another rocket sent the three astronauts toward Earth, reentry, and pick up after the space craft parachuted into the Pacific Ocean.

Three astronauts were boosted to the moon by a 365-foot-tall launch vehicle named *Saturn 5*. With a total liftoff thrust of over 7.5 million pounds from five engines, it remains the largest and most powerful successful rocket ever built. Including main booster, flight control, and other rockets, each *Saturn 5* had almost 100 separate rocket engines.

The first manned flight of the *Saturn 5* came in 1968 when three astronauts orbited the earth for more than 10 days. The next flight sent astronauts around the moon without landing. To test systems, they looped around the moon and returned to earth. But the liftoff everyone was waiting for occurred on July 16, 1969. Neil Armstrong, Edwin Aldrin, and **Michael Collins** left for a landing on the moon on that date.

Armstrong and Aldrin landed the LEM and radioed back the first words ever sent from another world. "Tranquillity Base here, the *Eagle* has landed." The LEM was named *Eagle* and Armstrong and Aldrin touched down in a region called the Sea of Tranquillity. When Armstrong first set foot on the moon on July 20, he said, "That's one small step for man, one giant leap for mankind."

Another memorable flight was *Apollo 13*, launched April 11, 1970. When the astronauts on the flight were about 200,000 miles out in space, a small oxygen tank exploded in the service module. The damage was so severe that NASA canceled the flight's scheduled moon landing. Worse, it was uncertain whether astronauts **James Lovell**, **Fred Haise**, and **John Swigert** could return safely to Earth. NASA worked frantically to develop emergency flight procedures for the crew, and *Apollo 13* splashed down safely in the Pacific Ocean four days after the flight began. The exciting real-life adventure is shown in the motion picture *Apollo 13*.

Including lunar "fly-bys" like *Apollo 13*, *Saturn 5* rockets made nine flights to the moon. The last was in 1972. In spite of the complexity involved, no astronaut died or was seriously hurt during any of the Apollo flights. That record was also true during the Mercury and Gemini Programs.

Although moon landings were inspiring, they were inefficient and wasteful. In the Apollo Program, six million pounds of rocket, propellant, equipment, and astronauts left the Florida launch pad. Only 10,000 pounds of spacecraft and astronauts returned to earth. Consequently, NASA investigated the possibility of building a launch vehicle that could be flown much like an airplane. Investigation resulted in the Space Shuttle Program.

After years of research and flight testing, the stubby-winged Space Shuttle emerged. The first one to be flight tested was fastened to the top of a Boeing 747 jet liner in 1977. After being released during flight, the unpowered 100-ton shuttle glided back to a safe landing on a California runway. That shuttle was named *Enterprise*.

To suggest the work-like character of the shuttle and its many proposed launches, NASA used the term space transportation system (STS). The first powered shuttle flight on April 12, 1981, was commanded

National Portrait Gallery, Smithsonian Institution

Neil Armstrong (top) was the first person to set foot on the moon. Edwin (Buzz) Aldrin (right) was the second person. Michael Collins remained in lunar orbit during their landing. In this composite portrait, the *Saturn 5* launch vehicle is shown at the far left, the lunar excursion module is at the upper right, and spacecraft splashdown in the Pacific Ocean is shown at the bottom.

APOLLO XI ITEMS

WOODEN AND FABRIC ITEMS FROM THE WRIGHT "KITTY HAWK" FLYER WHICH MADE MANKIND'S FIRST POWERED, CONTROLLED FLIGHT ON DEC. 17, 1903.

THESE ITEMS WERE CARRIED TO THE SURFACE OF THE MOON FOR THE AIR FORCE MUSEUM BY ASTRONAUT NEIL A. ARMSTRONG ON HISTORY'S FIRST LUNAR LANDING, JULY 20, 1969.

Neil Armstrong carried items from the Wright brothers original airplane to the surface of the moon in 1969. This display is at the Air Force Museum in Dayton, Ohio.

by **John Young**. Over the next 10 years, 39 successful shuttle launches took place. With *STS-1*, Young made five orbital space flights, the greatest number made by any astronaut. Young also flew on *Gemini 3* and *10*, as well as *Apollo 10* and *16*.

Shuttles have three liquid-propellant inboard engines called SSMEs (space shuttle main engines). Using LH2 and LOX from a huge insulated central tank, each engine develops 375,000 pounds of thrust. Shuttles also have two strap-on solid rocket boosters (SRBs) that develop about 2.6 million pounds of thrust each. When all five engines fire during liftoff, the total thrust is about 6.5 million pounds.

Mission requirements vary from launch to launch. A typical launch might have four to six astronauts orbiting at 17,000 mph and 115 miles above the earth's surface. An astronaut opens the doors to a huge cargo bay that contains a communication satellite. A 50-foot electrically operated robotic arm controlled by the astronaut removes the satellite and releases it a safe distance from the shuttle. America's first woman astronaut, **Sally Ride**, helped design the robotic arm and tested it in orbit. She made her first Space Shuttle flight in June 1983. The first African-American in space was Lieutenant Colonel **Guion Bluford** in August 1983.

Shuttles can also carry a scientific labo-ratory. The laboratory allows experiments like surveying the earth's resources or conducting plant and animal experiments in the weightlessness of space. Studies are made on new techniques for making crystals for electronic applications. Shuttles operate only in earth orbit. They were not designed to go to the moon.

After orbiting earth for about a week, the astronauts fire small rockets to slow down the shuttle. It reenters the atmosphere and the pilot glides the unpowered shuttle toward a landing at Edwards Air Force Base in California or Cape Kennedy in Florida. The shuttle touches down at 220 mph, then rolls for a long distance to avoid overheating the brakes.

Is the Space Program Worthwhile?

Many people think America's space program provides an important national sense of identity. Although it is moderately expensive, it is an exciting high-visibility activity that has provided countless spin-off goods and services. New composite materials, improved medical services, and inexpensive personal computers are just a few examples.

However, space exploration is at the frontier of technology and some lives have been lost. Three astronauts died in a fire during a 1967 preflight test in the Apollo Program. Another seven people died in a 1986 Space Shuttle failure during launch. There will always be risks involved in the development of new forms of transportation and the exploration of emerging frontiers. That will be particularly true if we continue to strive to "boldly go where no man has gone before," as William Shatner suggested in his *Star Trek* introduction.

References and Resources

Apollo by Charles Murray and Catherine Bly Cox, Simon and Schuster, 1989.

To Space and Back by Sally Ride, Lothrop, Lee, and Shepard Books, 1986.

Space Shuttle by George Alexander, W. P. Brownwell, 1977.

Soviet Rocketry by Michael Stoiko, Holt, Rinehart, and Winston, 1970.

History of Rocketry and Space Travel by Wernher von Braun and Frederick I. Ordway III, Thomas Y. Crowell Co., 1966.

Thirteen: The Flight That Failed by Henry Cooper, Dial Press, 1973.

Robotics

This demonstration robot at the Henry Ford Museum simulates an industrial painting operation.

Twentieth Century

ROBOTICS technology deals with the use of industrial robots, important machine tools used in modern manufacturing centers. So it may seem unusual that the word *robotics* came into the English language from a science fiction story. In the March 1942 issue of *Astounding Science Fiction*, one of author Isaac Asimov's characters said, "Now, let's start with the three fundamental Rules of Robotics." That was the first time the word "robotics" appeared in print. Other science fiction authors of the time wrote about human-like robots that were usually sinister. In those stories, robots and humans often engaged in unpleasant confrontations. Asimov took a different view. He characterized robots as helpful and trustworthy participants in society. In later stories, Asimov referred again to his Three Laws of Robotics. Though written in the 1940s, the laws Asimov established still have validity. They are as follows:

1. A robot may not injure a human being or, through inaction, allow harm to a human being.

2. A robot must obey orders given to it by a human being, except where such orders would conflict with the First Law.

3. A robot must protect its own existence as long as such protection does not conflict with the First or Second Laws.

Isaac Asimov (1920-1992) was an insightful author who wrote more than 460 books and articles. Many were nonfiction, and Asimov is often viewed as the founder of the field of popular science writing. His books for preteens received the 1985 Children's Book Guild Nonfiction Award. For advanced university students, Asimov also wrote about such subjects as nuclear physics, astronomy, and anatomy. His entertaining science fiction stories were well crafted and technically possible. Among the world's most prolific writers, Asimov worked with subjects as diverse as those of any writer who ever lived.

Born in Russia, Asimov came with his family to America when he was three. His parents owned a small candy store in Brooklyn and he often worked there. Asimov said he was attracted to science fiction by the magazines sold in his parents' store. He became an American citizen in 1928 and later graduated from Columbia University with three degrees in chemistry. He was a long-time faculty member in Boston

University's School of Medicine. Although Asimov wrote about robots and maintained an interest in them, his skills lay in scientific research and writing. He never directly participated in the design or construction of an industrial robot.

Early Robots

Inventors and tinkerers took some halting steps in the sixteenth century to make robot-like entertainment devices. These were intricate mechanical puppets that simulated human actions. Some early robots took the form of dancers or arm-waving court jesters. Others drew simple landscapes or functioned as banks for saving coins. They all imitated human movements and proved quite popular with the public.

Power for the stationary models came

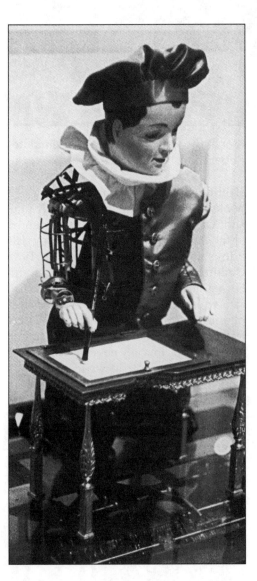

This writing automaton was an early example of a robot. It's on display at the Franklin Institute.

from weights unwinding on a drum. The few that rolled along the floor used spring-driven mechanisms. All had intricate arrangements of linkages, gears, and cams. They were called automatons. At that time, the word robot did not exist.

Like many words in the English language, *robot* comes from a foreign word. *Robota* means "compulsory service" in Czechoslovakian and the Czech playwright **Karel Capek** used it in one of his plays. *Rossum's Universal Robots* opened in London, England in 1921. The performance featured human-like robots with their own personalities. An Englishman named Rossum mass-produced the robots. Used as workers, they revolted against their makers and wiped out humanity. For the next two decades, fiction writers made their robots appear as menacing figures.

The popularity of Capek's play eliminated the word "automaton" from the language. In every language, the word "robot" replaced it. A robot is commonly seen as an artificial device that performs activities normally thought to be appropriate for human beings.

Use in Early Factories

Robots were not used in nineteenth-century factories. However, if they had been, they would have done their work in a standardized manner. That was not the case at the time for human workers, who decided on their own how to complete their tasks. Some worked safely and efficiently, others did not. **Frederick Taylor** (see pages 127-129), a Philadelphia steel mill supervisor in the 1880s, changed that practice. Taylor spent several years using a stopwatch to time individual operations and find the best way to do a job.

Taylor developed standardized methods, allowing workers to manufacture products more easily and more efficiently. His steel mill also provided bonus pay for above-standard performance. Other companies soon developed standard production techniques. Although Taylor did not know it at the time, his work in standardization of methods set the stage for industrial robots.

In 1921, the A. O. Smith Automatic Frame Plant in Milwaukee, Wisconsin, became the first factory to use machines that resemble industrial robots. The automobile industry provided the encouragement for **Lloyd Raymond Smith** (see pages 193-195) to have company engineers and technologists design a new manufacturing system. The son of **Arthur Oliver Smith**, Lloyd viewed the automobile industry as being on the verge of a great expansion. Over a period of six years, his company spent $8 million to retool for high production of automobile frames.

The A. O. Smith factory used uncut steel on huge rolls. Machines automatically unrolled the steel, cut it, bent it, assembled the sections, and riveted them together. Machines performed 552 separate operations. During peak production, the factory made a frame every eight seconds.

The most important tools in the process were the robot-like riveting machines. With strong clamping jaws that looked like the beak of a huge bird, the pneumatic machines set about 100 rivets per frame. A specially slotted floor allowed for repositioning them to build different frames. It took only 6 to 12 hours for the 200 employees to change dies and reset tooling. The relative ease of adjustment for new products was similar to that found in modern factories that use industrial robots.

Industrial Robots of the 1940s and 1950s

World War II required companies to increase production rates while maintaining high-quality. Aircraft engines, rifles, and electronic communication equipment were examples of critically needed products that had to be made in large quantities. Everyone's energy went toward high-volume production. Research in robotics declined until after the war ended, in 1945.

The rapid pace of computer development during the 1940s, led some people to consider using computers to control machine tools. Those who did so, worked on their own time, even after the war. Europe and Japan's manufacturing capacity had been devastated, and undamaged American factories were making much of the world's products. Companies still did not sponsor significant research into robotics because they did not have the time. All factories were still operating at their peak production rates.

Computers of the late 1940s were huge and expensive. Only the most visionary in-

dividuals could foresee the new technology of robotics. **George Devol** was one of those visionaries. A self-taught technologist who organized several companies, he developed a playback system in 1946 for teaching machine tools to remember their motions. It served as the basis for one of his 40 patents. Although briefly used by the Remington-Rand Corp., Devol's system was not practical. He investigated other possibilities and applied for a patent in 1954 for what he called "Program Controlled Article Transfer." The patent covered a programmable manipulator, the most important part of an industrial robot. It was the first patent of its kind.

Devol approached the International Business Machines Corp. (IBM). He wanted IBM to make an experimental industrial robot. IBM's president had an interest, but he thought IBM was busy enough with starting its computer business. Luckily, Devol attended a party in New York City in 1956 where he met Joseph Engelberger. The two found they had parallel interests in industrial robots.

Defining the Industrial Robot

The Robotic Industries Association defines a robot as a machine tool with "a reprogrammable multifunctional manipulator designed . . . for the performance of a variety of tasks." The key words are "reprogrammable" and "multifunctional." Using a digital keyboard, an industrial robot can be easily reprogrammed to complete new operations. This feature distinguishes robots from conventional machine tools that cannot easily adapt to new tasks. Robots are a key part of soft, or flexible, automation. Conventional machine tools can complete only one task and are part of hard automation.

If any one person can be singled out as establishing the field of robotics, it would be **Joseph Engelberger** (1925-). Born in Brooklyn, Engelberger enrolled at Columbia University and was one of 13 students in an accelerated technical instruction program. Among other subjects, he took Columbia's first course in servo theory. He eventually became the general manager of the aerospace division of the Manning, Maxwell, and Moore Co. in Stratford, Connecticut.

Both at work and at home, Engelberger pursued his interest in servo controls. When used in industrial robots, servos control the flow of hydraulic fluid to an actuator. Most robots are hydraulic and use several actuators, or cylinders, to provide motion and force. Servo controls allow a hydraulic actuator to move quickly or slowly, or to clamp firmly or loosely. Other types of controls are directional. That is, either ON or OFF. Direction control functions like an ordinary wall lamp switch that is flipped up for ON and down for OFF. Servo control is similar to a dimmer switch that can adjust light intensity in a variable way.

Engelberger and Devol became close friends and partners in a new venture. After obtaining a small amount of start-up money from investors, they visited 35 com-

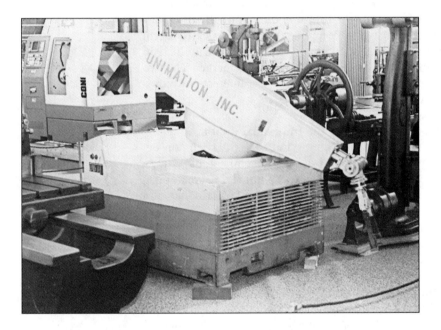

The world's first industrial robot is on public display at the Henry Ford Museum in Dearborn, Michigan.

panies to see what manufacturers might want in an industrial robot. The two men would have preferred to make a two-armed robot, but economics dictated the one-armed design. Devol was a bit older than Engelberger and had already established several companies. He agreed to let Engelberger organize the new company in Danbury, Connecticut, while Devol would provide his patents and advice. The two men named the company Unimation, for "universal automation."

The First Production Industrial Robot

Robotics is a combination of three existing technologies: computers, electricity, and hydraulics (or pneumatics). Electricity and hydraulics were fairly well established when Engelberger and Devol started their work together. However, tying them to a computer was a new step. One early decision Engelberger had to make was to choose between analog and digital computer systems. He decided in 1958 to go with the new digital techniques, hoping the price of expensive electronic components would drop dramatically. Other companies then making experimental robots decided to remain with the cheaper and better established analog systems.

Unimation's first 2,700-pound model was ready in 1961. Called the Unimate I, its manipulator ("arm") used hydraulic pressure to extend up to four feet. The end effector ("hand") operated from compressed air and could safely grasp objects from a fragile egg to a 25-pound metal casting. The robot resembled a small construction crane with a controllable arm. Its computer had a capacity of up to 200 sequential commands. General Motors Corp. (GM) bought it for use in its Trenton, New Jersey, plant. The world's first commercially used industrial robot, it transferred metal castings from one location to another.

Still, companies were not yet ready for the robotic revolution. Profitable factories were still running at high production rates in the early 1960s. Some viewed Engelberger as an outsider who wanted to tell them how to run their business. Others felt that robotics was a science fiction technology that would soon die out. Unimation sold only 30 Unimates through 1964.

The first major purchase of Unimation robots did not occur until 1966. At that time, GM placed a single order for 66 to use for spot welding at its Lordstown, Ohio, plant. Each one sold for about $15,000. Engelberger received the good news shortly before he appeared as a guest on the *Johnny Carson Show*. He proudly announced the order on national television.

Selling industrial robots was still an uphill battle, but Engelberger never lost his vision and continued to promote his robots. Although the pioneering Unimation did not make a profit until 1975, by the late 1960s the company was obviously on its way to success. By 1980, it had sold 3,000 of the expensive machines.

Engelberger helped establish the Robot Institute of America in 1975, later renamed the Robotic Industries Association (RIA). The RIA annually presents its Joseph F. Engelberger Award to an outstanding contributor to the practice of robotics.

References and Resources

Robotics in Practice by Joseph F. Engelberger, American Management Association, 1980.
Robots by Isaac Asimov and Karen A. Frenkel, Harmony Books, 1985.
Handbook of Industrial Robots edited by Shimon Y. Nof, John Wiley & Sons, 1985.
Introduction to Robots by James A. Rehg, Prentice-Hall, 1985.

Milacron introduced its T3 in 1975. The T3 was the first computer-controlled, all-hydraulic, commercially-available industrial robot.

Index